George Mavrotas (*editor*)
DOMESTIC RESOURCE MOBILIZATION AND FINANCIAL DEVELOPMENT

George Mavrotas and Anthony Shorrocks (*editors*)
ADVANCING DEVELOPMENT
Core Themes in Global Economics

Mark McGillivray (*editor*)
HUMAN WELL-BEING
Concept and Measurement

Mark McGillivray (*editor*)
INEQUALITY, POVERTY AND WELL-BEING

Robert J. McIntyre and Bruno Dallago (*editors*)
SMALL AND MEDIUM ENTERPRISES IN TRANSITIONAL ECONOMIES

Vladimir Mikhalev (*editor*)
INEQUALITY AND SOCIAL STRUCTURE DURING THE TRANSITION

E. Wayne Nafziger and Raimo Väyrynen (*editors*)
THE PREVENTION OF HUMANITARIAN EMERGENCIES

Machiko Nissanke and Erik Thorbecke (*editors*)
GLOBALIZATION AND THE POOR IN ASIA
Can Shared Growth Be Sustained?

Machiko Nissanke and Erik Thorbecke (*editors*)
THE IMPACT OF GLOBALIZATION ON THE WORLD'S POOR
Transmission Mechanisms

Matthew Odedokun (*editor*)
EXTERNAL FINANCE FOR PRIVATE SECTOR DEVELOPMENT
Appraisals and Issues

Laixiang Sun (*editor*)
OWNERSHIP AND GOVERNANCE OF ENTERPRISES
Recent Innovative Developments

Guanghua Wan (*editor*)
UNDERSTANDING INEQUALITY AND POVERTY IN CHINA
Methods and Applications

UNU-WIDER (*editors*)
WIDER PERSPECTIVES ON GLOBAL DEVELOPMENT

Studies in Development Economics and Policy
Series Standing Order ISBNs 978–0–333–96424–8 hardback; 978–0–230–20041–8 paperback
(*outside North America only*)

You can receive future titles in this series as they are published by placing a standing order. Please contact your bookseller or, in case of difficulty, write to us at the address below with your name and address, the title of the series and one of the ISBNs quoted above.

Customer Services Department, Macmillan Distribution Ltd, Houndmills, Basingstoke, Hampshire RG21 6XS, England

---

Globalization and the Poor in Asia

Can Shared Growth Be Sustained?

Edited by

Machiko Nissanke

and

Erik Thorbecke

in association with the United
Nations University – World Institute
for Development Economics Research

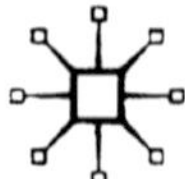

First published 2008 by
PALGRAVE MACMILLAN
Houndmills, Basingstoke, Hampshire RG21 6XS and
175 Fifth Avenue, New York, N.Y. 10010
Companies and representatives throughout the world.

PALGRAVE MACMILLAN is the global academic imprint of the Palgrave Macmillan division of St. Martin's Press, LLC and of Palgrave Macmillan Ltd. Macmillan® is a registered trademark in the United States, United Kingdom and other countries. Palgrave is a registered trademark in the European Union and other countries.

ISBN-13: 978–0–230–20188–0
ISBN-10: 0–230–20188–1

This book is printed on paper suitable for recycling and made from fully managed and sustained forest sources. Logging, pulping and manufacturing processes are expected to conform to the environmental regulations of the country of origin.

A catalogue record for this book is available from the British Library.

Library of Congress Cataloging-in-Publication Data
Globalization and the poor in Asia : can shared growth be sustained? / edited by Machiko Nissanke and Erik Thorbecke.
p. cm.—(Studies in development economics and policy)
Includes bibliographical references and index.
ISBN 0–230–20188–1 (alk. paper)
1. Poverty – Asia. 2. Asia – Economic policy. 3. Globalization – Economic aspects. I. Nissanke, Machiko. II. Thorbecke, Erik, 1929–
HC415.P6G56 2008
339.4′6095—dc22   2008000191

10 9 8 7 6 5 4 3 2 1
17 16 15 14 13 12 11 10 09 08

Transferred to Digital Printing in 2009

Contents

List of Figures

List of Tables

Acknowledgements

The editors are most grateful to all the staff of UNU-WIDER, who provided efficient logistic support to us in the management of this large research project, and who have worked expertly to see the study through to fruition.

UNU-WIDER extends special thanks to the Finnish Ministry for Foreign Affairs for its support to this project, and gratefully acknowledges the financial contributions to the research programme by the governments of Denmark (Royal Ministry of Foreign Affairs), Finland (Ministry for Foreign Affairs), Norway (Royal Ministry of Foreign Affairs), Sweden (Swedish International Development Cooperation Agency – Sida) and the United Kingdom (Department for International Development).

The use of particular designations of countries or territories does not imply any judgement by United Nations University (UNU) as to the legal status of such countries or territories, or their authorities and institutions or of the delimitation of their boundaries.

The designations 'developed' and 'developing' regions are intended for statistical and analytical convenience and do not necessarily express a judgement about the stage reached by a particular country or area in the development process.

Notes on the Contributors

Rimjhim M. Aggarwal is Assistant Professor at the School of Sustainability at Arizona State University. She completed her PhD in Economics from Cornell University, USA. She has conducted extensive theoretical and empirical research on the linkages between population, poverty and natural resource management (in particular, water resources) in South Asia and Africa. She has also worked as a consultant to the World Bank.

Jonna P. Estudillo is Faculty Fellow of the Foundation for Advanced Studies on International Development (FASID) and Associate Professor at the National Graduate Institute for Policy Studies (GRIPS) in Tokyo, Japan. She earned a PhD in Economics at the University of Hawaii, USA. Her research interests include gender and development, income and poverty dynamics, and the impacts of the Green Revolution.

Tomoki Fujii is Assistant Professor at the School of Economics, Singapore Management University. His primary areas of research interest are development, environment and applied econometrics.

Xavier Giné is an economist in the Development Research Group at the World Bank. Since joining the Bank as a Young Economist in 2002, his research has focused on access to credit and rural financial markets. Prior to joining the Bank he was a Postdoctoral Fellow and lecturer at the Economic Growth Center at Yale University, USA. He holds a BA in Economics from Pompeu Fabra University (Spain), and an MA and a PhD in Economics from the University of Chicago (USA).

Nanak Kakwani is a visiting scholar at the University of Sydney, Australia, having previously been Principal Researcher and Director/Chief Economist at the UNDP International Poverty Centre in Brasilia, Brazil. He was Professor for thirty years at the University of New South Wales in Sydney, Australia, was elected a Fellow of the Australian Research Committee of Social Science, awarded the Mahalanobis gold medal for outstanding contribution to quantitative economics, and has been Visiting Professor at numerous universities and a consultant to the World Bank, UNDP and the Asian Development Bank. His research and 100-plus publications are in the areas of poverty, inequality, pro-poor growth, taxation, public policies and human development (MDGs). Professor Kakwani is on the advisory board of the *Journal of Economic Inequality*.

Stefan Klonner earned a PhD in Economics at the Institute of South Asian Studies in Heidelberg, Germany, in 2001. He was a Postdoctoral Fellow at

Yale University. USA, before joining Cornell's Economics Department as an Assistant Professor in 2003. His research focuses on the microeconomics of contracts and credit in low-income countries. His regional expertise is Southern India, where he has conducted several field studies.

K. S. Kavi Kumar is a faculty member at Madras School of Economics, Chennai, India. His research interests are in the field of Environmental and Development Economics. He has a specific interest in the economics of global climate change. He teaches master's-level courses on Mathematical Economics, Environmental Economics and Cost–Benefit Analysis.

Zhicheng Liang is a PhD candidate at CERDI, University of Auvergne/ Université d'Auvergne, France. His major research fields include market-orientated reforms in transitional countries; sources of economic growth; income distribution; finance and monetary economics; decentralization and regional disparities.

Justin Yifu Lin is Professor and founding Director of the China Center for Economic Research, Peking University, China. He has published numerous books and journal articles in the areas of economic and agricultural development, transitional economics, new institutional economics and China's economic development, and has served as an adviser in many international organizations and Chinese governmental departments.

Peilin Liu is Associate Research Fellow of Department of Development Strategy and Regional Economy, the Development Research Center of the State Council, China. He has published journal articles on economic growth, poverty, regional economy and energy economics.

Machiko Nissanke is Professor of Economics at the School of Oriental and African Studies (SOAS), University of London. She worked previously at Birkbeck College, University College London, and the University of Oxford, and was a Research Fellow of Nuffield College and the Overseas Development Institute, UK. She has published numerous books and journal articles on financial and international economics, and has served many international organizations as adviser and co-ordinator of research programmes.

Mahvash Saeed Qureshi obtained a PhD in Economics from Trinity College, University of Cambridge, and is currently associated with the Overseas Development Institute, UK. Her research interests include international trade, investment and growth, globalization and institutions, international trade standards, and trade and the environment. She has conducted research for the Asian Development Bank, International Monetary Fund, Sustainable Development Policy Institute, UNU-WIDER, and HM Treasury, UK.

David Roland-Holst is Adjunct Professor of Agricultural and Resource Economics, University of California, Berkeley, USA. His research includes development, environment and energy economics.

Yasuyuki Sawada is Associate Professor in the Faculty of Economics, University of Tokyo. His research interests include econometric investigations of household and firm behaviour, using micro-data from Pakistan, the Philippines, Sri Lanka, India, Indonesia, Korea, Kenya and Japan. He completed his MA in Food Research and PhD in Economics at Stanford University, USA in 1996 and 1999, respectively.

Hyun H. Son is an economist at the Asian Development Bank. Before joining ADB, she was a poverty economist/specialist at the International Poverty Centre, United Nations Development Programme (UNDP). She also worked at the World Bank in Washington DC, and held an academic position at Macquarie University, Sydney, Australia. She has published and researched in the areas of economic development, poverty, inequality, public policies, and pro-poor growth and policies.

Erik Thorbecke is the H.E. Babcock Professor of Economics Emeritus, Graduate School Professor and former Director of the Program on Comparative Economic Development at Cornell University. He has published extensively in the areas of economic and agricultural development, the measurement and analysis of poverty and malnutrition, the Social Accounting Matrix and general equilibrium modelling, and international economics. The Foster–Greer–Thorbecke poverty measure has been adopted almost universally by international organizations and researchers doing empirical work on poverty.

Brinda Viswanathan is a faculty member at Madras School of Economics, Chennai, India. She works in the fields of applied econometrics and development economics. Her current research interests include gender and the labour market, and nutrition and poverty. She teaches graduate-level courses on statistics and econometrics.

List of Abbreviations

ADB	Asian Development Bank
AP	Andhra Pradesh (state), India
ARMM	Autonomous Region of Muslim Mindanao
ASEAN	Association of South East Asian Nations
BBD	beneficial brain drain
CACP	Commission on Agricultural Costs and Prices
CAD	Comparative advantage-defying strategy
CAF	Comparative advantage-following strategy
CAR	Cordillera Autonomous Region
CARP	Comprehensive Agrarian Reform Programme
CCI	Cotton Corporation of India
CGE	Computable General Equilibrium
CLT	certificate of land transfer
CMI	Census of Manufacturing Industries
COMTRADE	Commodity Trade Statistics Database, UN
CPI	consumer price index
DSDT	Doha Special and Differential Treatment
EEFS	embodied environmental factor services
EP	emancipation patent
EPA	Federal Environmental Protection Agency of Pakistan
EPZs	Export-processing zones
ESI	Environmental Sustainability Index
EXIM	export and import dependent ratio
FDI	foreign direct investment
FGT	Foster–Greer–Thorbecke poverty index
FIES	family income and expenditure surveys
FL	full liberalization
GDP	gross domestic product
GoP	Government of Pakistan
GoI	Government of India
GRDP	gross regional domestic product
GSO	General Statistical Office
GTAP	Global Trade Analysis Project
HOV	Heckscher–Ohlin–Vanek model of trade in factor services
HYV	high-yield variety
ICRISAT	International Crops Research Institute for the Semi-Arid Tropics

IIPS	Institute for Population Sciences
IPC	International Poverty Centre, UNDP
IPPS	Industrial Pollution Projection System, World Bank
ISIC	International Standard Industrial Classification system
LAHTI	Linear Acute Human Toxicity Index
LDCs	least developed countries
MDGs	Millennium Development Goals
MSPs	minimum support prices
NBS	National Bureau of Statistics
NCR	national capital region
NCS	National Conservation Strategy, Pakistan
NEP	National Environment Policy
NEQS	national environmental quality standards
NGO	non-governmental organization
NSB	National Statistical Bureau, China
NSCB	National Statistical Coordination Board, the Philippines
NSO	National Statistics Office
NSSO	National Sample Survey Organization, India
OECD	Organisation for Economic Co-operation and Development
OIC	Organization of the Islamic Conference
PBG	poverty bias of growth
PD	presidential decree
PEGR	poverty equivalent growth rate
PEPA	Pakistan Environmental Protection Act
PHH	pollution haven hypothesis
PPGI	pro-poor growth index
PPP	purchasing power parity
R&D	research and development
RFAS 2003	Rural Financial Access Survey, conducted in 2003
ROSCA	Rotating Savings and Credit Association
SAARC	South Asian Association for Regional Co-operation
SAE	Small Area Estimation
SAM	Social Accounting Matrix
SDBR	shortest distance by road
SES	socio-economic surveys
SEZs	special economic zones
Sida	Swedish International Development Co-operation Agency
SITC	Standard International Trade Classification system, UN
SOEs	state-owned enterprises
SPM	suspended particulate matter
SRA	Social Reform Agenda, Ramos Administration (1992–8)
SSHMI	small-scale and household manufacturing industries
TCI	technological choice index

UL	unilateral liberalization
URAA	Uruguay Round on Agreement on Agriculture
UNDP	United Nations Development Programme
UNU-WIDER	World Institute for Development Economics Research of the United Nations University
VLSS	Vietnam Living Standard Survey
WTO	World Trade Organization

1
Globalization and Poverty in Asia: Can Shared Growth Be Sustained?

Machiko Nissanke and Erik Thorbecke

Background debate in the globalization–poverty nexus

The opportunities offered for economic growth through globalization can be large, and the forces of globalization have the potential to provide a major reduction in poverty in the developing world. However, the question is often raised as to whether the actual distribution of gains is fair and, in particular, whether the poor benefit proportionately less from globalization and could under some circumstances in fact be hurt by it. The risks and costs incurred by globalization can be significant for fragile developing economies and the world's poor.[1] The fear that the poor have been bypassed or even hurt by globalization has been highlighted by the findings from a number of recent studies, which point towards a continuing high inequality in world income distribution, and limited (if not a lack of) convergence among participating national economies and across regions as the world economy has become more interdependent and more integrated.[2] There is much empirical evidence suggesting that openness contributes to more within-country inequality.

The regional trends in income inequality measured by the Gini coefficient show that inequality has increased markedly in all regions except in the group consisting of the advanced, high-income OECD countries since the early 1980s (Milanovic 2005a, 2005b; Birdsall 2006). Within high-income countries too, there are many that have experienced growing inequality. The progress on poverty reduction has also been uneven. The share of the population of the developing countries living below US$1 per day declined from 40 per cent to 21 per cent between 1981 and 2001, but this was achieved mainly by the substantial reduction of the number of poor in Asia, in particular in China (Chen and Ravallion 2004). Overall in Asia between 1990 and 2001, the number of people living on less than

US$1 a day declined from 931 million to 679 million, or from 31 per cent to 20 per cent of a growing population (UNESCAP/ADB/UNDP 2005). Furthermore, the total number of people living on less than US$2 per day actually increased worldwide. More specifically, poverty has increased significantly in Africa in terms of poverty incidence as well as the depth of poverty.[3]

Though any trend in poverty and income inequality observed so far cannot be attributed exclusively (or even mainly) to the 'globalization' effect, as such, these various estimates, even the most optimistic ones, cannot dismiss the concerns raised that as it has proceeded so far it may have had at least some adverse effects on poverty and income distribution. Indeed, globalization has created winners and losers at numerous levels throughout modern history.[4] The losers include many of those who have participated actively in the process of globalization. These concerns have generated a passionate debate worldwide as well as a powerful anti-globalization movement. The question of how globalization affects the world's poor is one of the most pressing issues in international political economy and international relations, as many current problems are related to how fair the international economic and political system is perceived *vis-à-vis* the poor in developing countries.

The globalization–poverty relationship is complex and heterogeneous, involving multifaceted channels. It is highly probable that these relationships may be non-linear in many aspects, involving several threshold effects. Indeed, each subset of links embedded in the globalization (openness)–growth–income distribution–poverty nexus can be contentious and controversial. As well as the 'growth' effects of globalization on poverty (that is, the effects of globalization on poverty filtered through economic growth), the process of increased integration within the world economy is known to create winners and losers directly through other channels, affecting both vertical and horizontal inequalities (Ravallion 2004a). Because these multifaceted channels interact dynamically over space and time, the net effects of globalization on the poor can only be judged on the basis of context-specific empirical studies. Cross-country studies requiring precise measurements and definition of the two key concepts – globalization and poverty – tend to fail to give a robust insight into this critical nexus. Both concepts are multidimensional, and not easily captured in a composite index to be used in a meaningful manner in cross-country comparative studies or regressions.

Building on earlier research projects, UNU-WIDER initiated a study on 'The Impact of Globalization on the World's Poor' in 2004. The main objectives of the project were to produce a set of rigorous theoretical and empirical economic analyses, which would: (i) deepen our understanding of how conditions facing the world's poor have been evolving under globalization; and (ii) provide a framework yielding the elements of a strategy for 'pro-poor globalization'. In addition to the methodological and conceptual conference held in Helsinki in October 2004, the project held three regional conferences, in Tokyo, Johannesburg and Rio de Janeiro during 2005–6.[5]

In Nissanke and Thorbecke (2006a, 2006b), various channels and transmission mechanisms were identified and explored through which the process of globalization affects different aspects and dimensions of poverty in the developing world. The first and most important of these mechanisms is the growth–inequality–poverty channel. Other channels in the globalization–poverty nexus operate, respectively, through changes in relative factor and goods prices, factor movements, the nature of technological change and technological diffusion, the impact of globalization on volatility and vulnerability, the worldwide flow of information, global disinflation, and institutions, respectively.

This volume contains nine further chapters originally presented at the regional conference for the project, 'The Impact of Globalization on the Poor in Asia', held in Tokyo in April 2005. The Asia perspective on this critical issue is interesting and important, since Asia is the region widely regarded as having benefited most from the dynamic *growth* effect of the recent wave of globalization. Poverty has been declining steadily since the 1970s in most Asian countries, notably in China and India. The growth pattern achieved through increased trade and foreign direct investment (FDI) in *East* Asia is particularly seen as being highly inclusive, and is often viewed as a model of 'shared growth' (World Bank 1993; Campos and Root 1996; Ahuja *et al.* 1997). Yet, there is growing evidence that inequality has been rising through the integration process in many parts of Asia. Hence, detailed examinations of mechanisms at work in the globalization–poverty nexus in Asia are both intellectually exciting for academics as well as highly relevant to policymakers. Before turning to the synthesis of the nine detailed case studies, in the next section, we shall present some key features characterizing the globalization–poverty relationship typical of Asia as a region.[6]

Globalization and poverty in Asia

In discussing the openness–growth link, several general observations appear to be relevant (Nissanke and Thorbecke 2006b, 2006c). First, openness through trade, foreign direct investment and financial markets can contribute significantly to economic growth through both static and dynamic efficiency gains. However, the direction of causality in this link is still being debated (the consensus view is that the causality is more likely to go from trade to growth rather than the reverse) as well as how trade and capital flows could be interlinked into a virtuous circle. Furthermore, the positive openness–growth link is neither automatically guaranteed nor universally observable. The growth-enhancing effect of trade openness depends critically on the way a country is integrated into the global economy.

Similarly, the transfer of technology, skills and management know-how that is assumed to accompany FDI is not necessarily automatic or guaranteed. Further, the postulated positive effects of portfolio and other capital flows (hot money) on growth have been questioned increasingly in recent years. Rather, it is widely recognized that short-term capital flows contribute to increased vulnerability to external shocks within the recipient developing countries. In turn, the poor in these countries are likely to suffer the most following financial crises without an adequate safety net in place.

In the case of most Asian countries, however, there is very little disagreement over the powerful growth-enhancing effects of openness through trade and FDI. In particular, following an aggressive 'outward-orientated development strategy', most East Asian economies not only accelerated the process of integration into the world economy but also upgraded their linkages in the years of their rapid economic growth. Furthermore, prior to the financial crisis of 1997–8, many of the East Asian economies registered not only 'admirable' growth rate but also accomplished a substantial poverty reduction process with dynamically evolving changes in their socio-economic structures. A number of earlier studies, such as *The East Asian Miracle, Everyone's Miracle,* and *Shared Growth* by the World Bank and the Brookings Institution (World Bank 1993; Campos and Root 1996; Ahuja *et al.* 1997) attributed their successful growth performance to an appropriate set of economic policies and institutions well suited to the conditions prevailing in East Asia during that period.[7] The relatively quick turnaround of many emerging economies in East Asia in the years following the severe crisis of 1997–8 is often attributed to their strong export performance and renewed adaptability and flexibility in responding swiftly to new opportunities offered by globalization.

Any discussion of the impact of growth on poverty reduction needs to define the meaning of pro-poor growth – a concept that is used widely in the literature. At one extreme it can mean that growth is only required to yield a positive reduction of poverty. In this sense, it would be enough for a major increase in GDP per capita to reduce poverty by a single person to satisfy the above definition. Hence any elasticity of poverty reduction with respect to growth algebraically larger than zero would be considered as pro-poor. This is a *weak* definition. Although used widely and part of the conventional wisdom, it has elicited a reaction within the development community leading to an alternative definition of pro-poor growth requiring the poor to benefit more than proportionally from growth than do the non-poor. A corollary of this relative definition of pro-poor growth is that it will bring about a more equal (or less unequal) distribution of income. Since different authors adopt, either explicitly or implicitly, the weak or the strong definition, above the discussion of pro-poorness can be confusing. Since income inequality has increased in most (if not all) Asian countries since the 1980s, as discussed below, the growth pattern can only be considered to be pro-poor under the weak definition above. At the same time it should be emphasized that the elasticity of poverty reduction with respect to growth under the weak definition can cover a very wide range, from 0 to −1. If it is close to the latter, a high growth rate can translate into a major, yet less than proportional, reduction in poverty.

Notwithstanding the ongoing urbanization process, the great majority of the poor in Asia continue to be in the rural areas – 63 per cent at a recent count (Cook 2006). The accelerating rural-to-urban migration has contributed to economic growth in urban areas and to the alleviation of poverty in rural areas by reducing surplus labour in agriculture and the remittances from migrant workers that at present account for a significant share of rural household income.

Ozawa (2006) explains the catch-up process and associated growth dynamism in Asia as a whole, in terms of the 'flying geese paradigm', wherein a sequence of staggered catch-up growth has taken place successively in the region since the end of the Second World War: the early growth success of Japan was followed first by the NIEs (Hong Kong, Singapore, Taiwan and South Korea), then by ASEAN-4 (Thailand, Malaysia, Indonesia and the Philippines) and more recently by China, India and Vietnam. Importantly, as Ozawa notes, throughout the growth process a very substantial reduction of abject poverty has been achieved in many economies: the headcount ratio of US$1 a day in China decreased from 53 per cent in 1984 to 13 per cent in 2003; in Indonesia from 38 per cent in 1984 to 7 per cent in 2003; in Thailand from 18 per cent in 1988 to 1 per cent in 2003; and in India from 46 per cent in 1987 to 31 per cent in 2003 (Asian Development Bank 2004, 2005). The most recent estimates by the Asian Development Bank predicts that the incidence of extreme poverty as measured in the headcount ratio below the 'US$1 a day' poverty line further declined to 7.1 per cent in 2005 in China, and it has practically disappeared in Thailand. In Vietnam, it is estimated to have declined from 51 per cent in 1990 to 7 per cent in 2005 (Ali and Zhuang 2007; Asian Development Bank 2007).

These figures illustrate that if the growth rate of GDP per capita is high a major reduction in poverty can be achieved even when the poor do not share the benefits of growth proportionally as much as the non-poor. Ozawa further observes that poverty alleviation has been occurring, in flying-geese style, among these rapidly-catching-up Asian economies. The incidence of extreme poverty is estimated to have declined dramatically from 33 per cent in 1990 to 7 per cent in 2005 in East Asia including China, and from 24 per cent to 7 per cent in South East Asia for the same period, whereas it declined less, from 42 per cent to 32 per cent in South Asia.[8]

In addition to other policy and institutional factors, Ozawa explains this particular pro-poor growth pattern (weak definition) in terms of the flying geese paradigm of *comparative advantage recycling* in production and export of labour-intensive goods. He argues that the region's economic development is pro-growth as well as pro-poor, because the economies in this region have successfully initiated a succession of growth in spurts based on a strong demand for unskilled labour, driven by exporting labour-intensive goods and pro-trade FDI through effective transfer of technology and knowledge skills. In flying geese style (or the hegemon-led growth model), growth clustering develops, in which a hegemon economy (the lead economy or 'goose') propagates growth stimuli to its closely aligned cohort of countries at various earlier stages of development and structural transformation. The stimuli include dissemination of technology, knowledge, information, skills and demand (via access to the hegemon's home market), and provision of development finance – and, above all, transplantation of growth-inducing institutional arrangements. Ozawa suggests that the region's synergistic interactions result in agglomeration economies, enabling the *entire* hierarchy of countries mutually to gain, grow and prosper.

Yet it is widely acknowledged that globalization and market-driven economic growth tend to increase inequality, as 'global markets are inherently disequalizing' (Birdsall 2006: 18).[9] With the current wave of globalization, 'within country' income inequality has been steadily rising (Milanovic 2005a).[10] Asia is no exception to this trend. In the early period, the prevailing initial conditions of lower levels of inequality in income and productive assets, as well as public policy and institutional arrangements in many high-performing East Asian economies, were known to be extremely favourable to the generation of a process of relatively *shared* growth (World Bank 1993). However, the growing inequality in East Asia, including China, Thailand and Indonesia, was already evident before the financial crisis of 1997–8, and the rising spatial disparity in growth performance was seen as a characteristic phenomenon (Ahuja *et al.* 1997). The financial crisis undoubtedly exacerbated this trend in the region.

As discussed below, while both China and India have accelerated the catching-up process, resulting in a very fast growth in their mean national incomes, income inequality among provinces and states, as well as interpersonal inequality, has been rising in both countries in recent decades, particularly after a decisive step was taken towards opening the respective economies. Cook (2006) notes that the Gini coefficient of income inequality increased in most Asian developing countries between 1980 and 2002; for example, from about 0.24 to 0.35 in China, and from 0.25 to 0.32 in Bangladesh. Disturbingly, there is growing evidence that 'within-country' inequality has been increasing at an accelerated pace across most developing economies in Asia over a roughly ten-year period from the early 1990s to the first half of 2000s. Among twenty-one developing countries, fifteen countries registered a rise in the Gini coefficient. The sharp increase of 5–10 per cent in the Gini coefficient is observed in five countries, including Nepal and

China (Asian Development Bank 2007; Ali 2007). Growing inequality is observed both in terms of income inequality and non-income inequality, such as in health and education. This rising inequality in most developing Asian countries is the result of 'the rich getting richer faster than the poor' rather than 'the rich getting richer and the poor getting poorer' (Asian Development Bank 2007).

As noted in Nissanke and Thorbecke (2006b), in contrast to the classical approach of viewing income inequality and wealth inequality as a necessary condition for faster capital accumulation and economic growth at the earlier stage of economic development (Kaldor 1956), the new political economic theories argue that growth patterns yielding more inequality in income distribution would, in turn, engender lower future growth paths.[11]

A number of UNU-WIDER studies (Addison and Cornia 2001; Cornia 2004; Shorrocks and van der Hoeven 2004), argue that the widespread rise in inequality has been detrimental to the objective of poverty reduction, because large rises in inequality have stifled growth, and because poverty, at any given growth rate of GDP, falls less rapidly in the case of a more unequal distribution than in the case of a more equitable one. The obvious policy implication following from these studies is that successful poverty alleviation depends not only on favourable changes in average GDP per capita growth but also on favourable changes in income inequality.

A critical question is whether or not inequality is an impediment to poverty-reducing growth or, in other words, whether high inequality attenuates the growth elasticity of poverty (Ravallion 2002). Ravallion's analysis confirms that the elasticity of poverty with respect to growth is found to decline with the extent of inequality. Taking this line of argument, we argue that while it is most likely that the poor will benefit from growth, the ultimate poverty reduction effects will depend on how the growth pattern affects income distribution. Inequality is the filter between growth and poverty reduction. If growth leads to an increase in income inequality, the poor may benefit only slightly or, in some instances, in fact be hurt by the globalization process.

We argue specifically that the *pattern* of economic growth and development, rather than the rate of growth per se, may have significant effects on a country's income distribution and poverty profile. Indeed, the recent debate on the meaning of pro-poor growth is related to the complex triangular relationships between poverty, growth and inequality. Clearly, significant poverty reduction would require some combination of higher growth and a more pro-poor distribution of the gains from growth. Hence, what is relevant for poverty reduction is a 'distribution corrected' rate of growth, as Ravallion notes (2004b), and in our view, growth is considered to be pro-poor if, in addition to reducing poverty, it also decreases inequality consistent with the strong definition of pro-poor growth discussed above. Economic growth can be considered to be genuinely pro-poor only if that growth is accompanied by a decline in inequality in such a manner that the poor benefit relatively more than the non-poor (Kakwani and Pernia 2000).

In Asia, it appears that economic growth has so far produced a marked reduction in poverty despite the adverse distributional changes with regard to the poor; that is, growth produced an adverse distribution effect, but the former was so vigorous that it more than compensated for the latter (Asian Development Bank 2004). A number of empirical studies have been carried out to examine the dynamic trajectory of the interrelationships between poverty, growth and inequality in Asia by decomposing the changes in poverty into two components: the growth component, and the distribution component. The results of the earlier decomposition study for five countries in East Asia (Malaysia, Thailand, Indonesia, rural China and the Philippines) generally confirm that growth was sufficiently buoyant to more than compensate for greater income inequality and keep poverty reduction on track (Ahuja *et al.* 1997).

The recent 'decomposition' study for India by Bhanumurphy and Mitra (2006) shows that the growth effect dominates the inequality (distribution) effects in poverty reduction in two periods: (i) 1983 to 1993–94; and (ii) 1993–94 to 1999–2000 (the two periods are taken broadly to represent the pre-reform and post-reform periods, respectively). This is the case for both rural and urban areas of the fifteen major states, as well as for the all-India level. Their analysis suggests that the growth/mean effect dominates the inequality effect in both periods. India's economic growth, increased markedly from the 'Hindu rate of growth' of 4 per cent to the 'Bharat rate of growth' of 6 per cent after the deliberate policy shift towards pro-growth and pro-globalization in the early 1990s. This growth acceleration succeeded in reducing overall poverty, despite the rise in inequality in the second period. As the growth accelerated, there was a marked shift in the composition of GDP, with a sharp decline in the share of agriculture and a corresponding increase in the share of services. However, since no such shift was observed in the employment structure, with the agricultural sector still absorbing a majority of the labour force, the debate continues as to whether the increase in output growth in India is a 'jobless growth' or not.

In this context, Bhanumurphy and Mitra (2006) also examine the net effect of population mobility on poverty, which depends on the rural and urban components of poverty. This effect is seen to capture the changes in the spatial composition of growth, reflected in terms of rural–urban development disparity, which tends to lead to the migration of population from rural to urban areas. The decline in the incidence of poverty (rural–urban combined) depends on whether urban employment opportunities are large enough to absorb the increasing supplies of labour migrating from the rural areas. It is thought that even when the incidence of urban poverty rises as a result of the rural–urban migration, the decline in the combined poverty ratio may occur as a result of a fall in the rural poverty incidence following out-migration, as rural poverty dominates the poverty profile for all areas combined in the Indian economy. In India, the incidence of poverty declined in both rural and urban areas: rural poverty fell from 46 per cent in 1983 to 37 per cent in 1993–4, and further to 27 per cent in 1999–2000, while urban poverty was cut from 42 per cent in 1983 to 34 per cent in 1993–4, and further to 24 per cent in 1999–2000.

According to their decomposition analysis, there is a small 'population shift effect' in poverty reduction in rural areas resulting from the rural–urban migration, in the first period, but that effect was marginal compared to the growth effect. They conclude that, despite some variations across states, overall, the economic growth realized through pro-globalization reforms has produced a large decline in the incidence of poverty in India by raising labour productivity and employment opportunities with the shift in value-added mix towards industry and tertiary activities such as information technology, business process outsourcing services, financial institutions and infrastructure services.

Hayami (2006) also emphasizes the employment-creating impact of globalization benefiting landless labourers as an important conduit for reducing rural poverty. Using the survey data collected over three decades in a rice-cultivating village in East Laguna in the Philippines, he examines the transformation of the village community under the forces of globalization manifested through: (i) population growth resulting from the importation of advanced medical and public health technology; (ii) the Green Revolution that brought the transfer of advanced agricultural technology and the introduction of irrigated double cropping; (iii) land reform programmes, shifting land tenure status from sharecropping tenancy towards leasehold tenancy and owner-farming; and (iv) the expansion of non-farm employment opportunities as well as the greater use of hired labourers who had been affected negatively by the land reforms. The first two channels are considered to be the outcomes of international knowledge transfer under the current wave of globalization. While the Green Revolution reduced real rice prices received by farmers, it also kept the cost of wage goods (and thus also the wage rates in labour-intensive manufactures) from rising. This process allowed this rural community, as elsewhere in East Asia, to gain a competitive edge in producing industrial goods at the lower end of skill requirements, as part of the region's recycling of comparative advantages under the process of globalization discussed above.

Hayami further suggests that the creation of non-farm employment opportunities associated with rural-based industrialization under globalization is seen as a most significant and direct factor in creating opportunities for rural communities to reduce poverty and inequality in East Asia. In this context, he places a special emphasis on the importance of public investment in transportation and communication infrastructure, industrial extension activities and school education as well as building market-supporting institutions to protect property rights and enforce contracts.

Indeed, as Ozawa (2006) remarks, the pro-poorness of growth (weak definition) in East Asia as a whole is not purely a manifestation of market-driven growth effects. In addition, pro-active policy interventions and institutional arrangements were in place to lessen the adverse distributional effect and produce shared, pro-poor growth. Ozawa further articulates that because poverty reduction is a public good, pro-poor policy interventions and institutional set-ups can always be justified and required to spawn growth-led poverty reduction. For example, the pro-poor pattern of public expenditure in favour of the rural poor, such as extensive public provision of education, and physical and social infrastructure was a decisive contributing factor sustaining the shared growth in many countries in East Asia.

Despite the impressive achievement in poverty reduction, the growing inequality under globalization has become a particularly pressing concern in China. As Zhang and Wan (2006) explain, since the late 1980s the engine of China's economic take-off has shifted from agricultural growth spurred by the de-collectivization of the rural areas to manufacturing exports fuelled by large FDI inflows. At the same time, progress in poverty reduction has stalled in urban China since the late 1980s (Ravallion and Chen 2004), or has even been reversed (Hussain 2003; Khan *et al.* 1999). This casts doubt on the claim made by Dollar and Kraay (2002) that the poor benefit from globalization as much as the rest of the population.

Through the estimation of the probability density functions for all the provinces, Zhang and Wan (2006) find the following characteristics of *urban* poverty in China: (i) the income of the poor has not grown as fast as average income, and the income shares of the poor have fallen accordingly; (ii) the income growth of the poor has been particularly slow since the mid-1990s and, in several provinces, real income growth of the poor has stagnated; and (iii) the further one moves away from the coast, the less favourable income distribution tends to become for the poor.

Further, they present the results of a number of regression analyses, based on provincial level data, of the impact of globalization measured in openness to foreign trade and foreign investment on *urban* poverty. Their findings indicate that when the globalization is accounted for separately in addition to the income growth measured by per capita income, globalization in general, and trade openness in particular, increases the income shares of the poor.[12] However, their results confirm that the inequality-reducing effect of trade was significantly weakened after 1992. Further, they find that the benefit from globalization accrues to the urban poor in the inland provinces just as much as it does to their counterparts in the coastal region. Hence, they conclude that globalization cannot simply be characterized as a process of pro-rich or pro-coastal provinces in China, as was popularly feared.

Overall, the preceding review suggests strongly that the process of integration of many Asian economies into the global economy has generated such a strong growth impact that the poor have not been omitted from its beneficiary effects. This is particularly so when economic growth was accompanied by increasing employment opportunities for the poor. At the same time, the Asian experience underscores the importance of policy and institutional measures to build up the productive assets of the poor through substantial investment in education, health, extension services and infrastructure as well as through the redistribution of assets in favour of the poor – for example, through land tenure reforms. However, there is also mounting evidence that the distribution-effect engendered by the globalization process generally does not favour the poor, and that growth has been increasingly disequalizing over time in the region. In this sense, the economic growth of the globalizing Asian economies is certainly not 'pro-poor' in the sense that the poor benefit proportionately more than the non-poor.

Indeed, despite the sharp reduction in the incidence of extreme poverty measured in the 'US$1-a-day' poverty headcount ratio, poverty remains high in much of developing Asia, if it is measured on the basis of the 'US$2-a day' poverty incidence. It is estimated that the latter declined from 86 per cent in 1990 to 77 per cent in 2005 in South Asia; from 66 per cent to 43 per cent in South East Asia; and from 72 per cent to 29 per cent in East Asia (dominated by China) over the same period. The reduction in this measure is appreciable, in particular in East Asia, but poverty is still widespread in Asia, and the challenge facing policy-makers in the region in attacking poverty of this magnitude is non-trivial. The 'inequality-increasing' effect of globalization should be attenuated by public policy measures to ensure that benefits from globalization-induced growth are shared more equally and equitably. In this context, it is worth remembering that the pattern of *shared* growth from wealth-sharing policy measures provided legitimacy for governments to pursue pro-growth and pro-business economic policy in the early drive for rapid industrialization in many countries in East Asia (see Campos and Root 1996). Sustaining the shared growth is therefore critical to ensure that economic growth continues under this era of globalization. Alternatively, growing inequalities can weaken social cohesion and risk reducing the momentum for economic growth and integration in the region.[13]

As discussed earlier, detailed and specific case studies are required to enhance our understanding of the critical relationships between globalization and poverty, since the globalization–poverty nexus is very complex and context-specific, involving numerous channels, counteracting forces and threshold effects. The following nine chapters examine different aspects of the globalization–poverty nexus from a context-specific perspective in several different Asian settings. Many of the case studies included in this volume use panel data based on a series of households surveys to scrutinize the globalization–inequality–poverty links.

Synopsis of the book

Chapter 2, by Kakwani and Son, examines the interrelationship between economic growth, inequality and poverty under globalization by defining and measuring the 'pro-poorness' of economic growth. After discussing different definitions of pro-poor growth, they advance the concept of 'poverty equivalent growth rate' (PEGR), which takes into account not only the magnitude of growth, but also how the benefits of growth are distributed to the poor and the non-poor through changes in inequality. They suggest that, since proportional reduction in poverty is a monotonically increasing function of the PEGR, the larger the PEGR, the greater the proportional reduction in poverty will be. Applying the PEGR to the household survey data, they present an evolution of the extent of the 'pro-poorness' in the growth pattern as observed in three Asian countries – Korea, Thailand and Vietnam – in the 1990s. According to their calculations, while Korea and Vietnam experienced a pro-poor growth pattern in the 1990s, the growth pattern in Thailand was on the whole not pro-poor. They argue that, as the Vietnam experience suggests, a 'growth with redistribution' strategy (such as land reforms) could be instrumental in ensuring that economic growth under globalization is pro-poor. Further, the episode of the deep financial crises experienced by both Korea and Thailand reaffirms the importance of enacting social safety nets promptly to protect the poor from their extreme vulnerability to economic shocks associated with globalization.

Indeed, Vietnam is often considered as one of low-income countries which has benefited most from integration into the global economy since the late 1980s. Its pro-globalization reform programmes produced impressive growth rates in output and exports, with some substantial poverty reduction. While its growth pattern is described as pro-poor by Kakwani and Son (Chapter 2), trade liberalization has generated winners and losers, and the growing spatial inequality has become an increasing concern. Applying an integrated micro simulation CGE (computable general equilibrium) model to household survey and census data, Fujii and Roland-Holst examine in Chapter 3 the changes in the spatial incidence of poverty in Vietnam in response to its accession to the WTO. They first calibrate a macroeconomic CGE model for Vietnam to the 2000 Vietnam Social Accounting Matrix for a baseline scenario, and then compare three counterfactual scenarios to the baseline: Unilateral Liberalization (UL); Full Liberalization (FL); and Doha Special and Differential Treatment (DSDT). Under each scenario, a poverty map is drawn. Their simulation results show that aggregate poverty falls when Vietnam removes all import tariffs and export subsidies under the UL scenario. The amount of improvement would be even larger if other countries also remove tariffs against Vietnamese products under the FL scenario. On the other hand, the DSDT scenario leads to a slight increase in poverty. Importantly, impacts of Vietnam's accession to the WTO are spatially heterogeneous. The heterogeneity is particularly large under the FL scenario. The poor provinces in the north-western region may benefit little from trade liberalization. Hence, they advocate the need to develop geographic targeting policies that complement trade liberalization policies, which could conserve public resources and prevent poor areas from lagging further behind.

Chapter 4, by Sawada and Estudillo, investigates how the two channels of globalization – that is, integration through international trade, and emigration – affected poverty reduction in the Philippines. The Philippines has increased its economic openness through trade and FDI substantially during the period 1985–2000, though this trend was interrupted by the Asian financial crisis of 1997–8. The process was facilitated by the creation of the Special Economic Zones for labour-intensive manufactures, which were relocated to four regional zones from the national capital region during this period. The Philippines is also known as a major supplier of international migrants to Saudi Arabia, Japan and other Asian NICs, as well as to the USA. The number of these immigrant workers increased markedly during the period under consideration.

Using Family Income and Expenditure Surveys (disaggregated by province) for selective years between 1985 and 2000, they found the following results:

(i) Openness per se, measured as the ratio of the value of regional exports to regional GDP, increases poverty. However, when the openness measure is included separately for each year of observation, the results reveal that trade openness reduced the poverty headcount in 1988 and 1994, but not in 2000 because of the debilitating effect of the financial crisis of 1997–8.

(ii) The growth elasticity of poverty reduction in the Philippines is −0.44, much smaller compared with other Asian economies as well as other developing countries, including countries in Sub-Saharan Africa. It would require an increase of the annual rate of income growth to 6. 5 per cent from the historical trend of 1.3 per cent to halve the poverty incidence by 2015 as targeted in the Millennium Development Goals.

(iii) Inequality, measured through the inter-provincial standard deviation of household income, increases poverty. The size of the inequality effect is large. Lowering the level of income inequality by one standard deviation can lead to a 30 per cent reduction in poverty.

(iv) Disaggregating income into non-transfer and transfer income, the study finds that at the provincial level of aggregation, the growth of non-transfer income is a significantly more important driving force behind poverty reduction than transfer income.

The regression analysis at the household level, on the other hand, reveals that both non-transfer and transfer incomes reduced the incidence and depth of poverty significantly, but transfer income had a greater impact on reducing the poverty of poor and non-poor households alike. In the Philippines, about 5 per cent of total household income comes from overseas transfers, and about 4 per cent from domestic transfers. Since overseas job placements require a significant sunk cost for job placement fees and pocket money, credit availability is a key deciding factor for a household to invest in overseas emigration. Their regression results show that the effect of land reform in inducing transfer income from abroad was significant only in the 1990s, when land pawning revenues had become important in paying job placement fees overseas. Yet, as the ultra poor are commonly landless households that were left out as beneficiaries of the land reform, they are also excluded from receiving overseas transfer income because of their disadvantages in obtaining credit. As discussed earlier in reference to the work by Hayami, non-farm employment opportunities are the most important mechanism for reducing the poverty of these landless households.

It was suggested in Nissanke and Thorbecke (2006b) that the globalization–poverty relationship might be non-linear, involving some threshold effect. Chapter 5 by Liang investigates the nonlinearity of the impact of globalization on the poor, applying recent endogenous threshold regression techniques to panel data from *rural* provinces of China over the period 1986–2002. Hence, Liang's chapter on the effect of globalization on the rural poor complements the paper by Zhang and Wan with its focus on the *urban* poor, reviewed above.

China has experienced a sharp reduction in rural poverty since the market-orientated reforms were initiated in 1978. According to China's official poverty line, more than 220 million people have been lifted out of absolute poverty in the rural regions over the period, from 250 million in 1978 to 28 million in 2002. Alternatively, using the World Bank's international standard poverty line of income measure of US$1 per day (in purchasing power parity), the number of China's rural poor decreased dramatically from 261 million in 1990 to 88 million in 2002. When estimated with the poverty line of consumption set at US$1 per day, the number of rural poor experienced an even greater drop, from 358 million in 1990 to 161 million in 2002. There is not much dispute over the fact that the evolving patterns of rural poverty reduction are highly influenced by the country's reform policies and development strategies. China experienced one of the most impressive rural poverty reductions in history during the period of 1978–85, mainly a result of de-collectivization, with the rural poverty incidence falling dramatically from 30.7 per cent in 1978 to 14.8 per cent in 1985, based on China's official estimates. While there was a marked slowdown in the rate of poverty reduction for the period of 1986–93, the subsequent concerted efforts in attacking rural poverty meant that the headcount ratio declined further to 3 per cent in 2002. However, the special concentration of rural poverty in the western inland region poses a serious challenge to the Chinese government.

Against this background, Liang's results with an endogenous threshold regression technique show that the globalization index, as measured by the ratio of the sum of exports and imports to GDP, has a non-linear relationship to rural poverty, as applied to panel data covering twenty-five provinces in China: poverty will increase at low levels of globalization, while high levels of globalization lead to a decline in poverty. While this threshold effect may be a reflection of the strong spatial concentration in both the globalization index and the rural poverty in China, the regression results also confirm the significant influence that both income growth and the specifically-targeted government funds for alleviating rural poverty have had on reducing poverty in rural China. Liang suggests that effective policy measures should be in place for the poor to be given more opportunities in the accelerated process of China's integration into the global economy.

China covers a large territory of heterogeneous regions with different comparative advantages. Chapter 6, by Lin and Liu, advances a framework of juxtaposing two 'mutually exclusive' development strategies as the key to understanding the relationship between openness, growth and poverty: (i) a comparative advantage-defying (CAD) strategy, which attempts to encourage firms to deviate from the economy's existing comparative advantages in their entry into an industry or choice of technology; and (ii) the comparative advantage following (CAF) strategy, which attempts to facilitate the firms' entry into an industry or choice of technology according to the economy's existing comparative advantages. They argue that the accumulation of per capita capital, which will be faster under a CAF strategy than under a CAD strategy, will provide a basis for upgrading the industrial/technological structure of the economy; and that by following CAF strategy, the speed of endowment structure (capital–labour ratio) upgrading and technological progress will be faster than under a CAD strategy. They also suggest that efficiency and equity can be achieved under a CAF strategy, where initial relative endowments would favour the creation of employment opportunities for unskilled workers.

Using this framework, they identify the beginning of economic reforms in 1978 in China as a distinctive switch from a CAD strategy to a CAF strategy. However, they argue that the degrees to which various regions deviated from their comparative advantage differed before reform, and their degrees of shifts to a CAF strategy also vary across regions. They observe that, after reform, all levels of government, especially local government, often use administrative measures to encourage firms to ignore the region's specific comparative advantages in their choice of industries or technologies. They conjecture that the regional divergence in the rate of rural poverty reduction is related to the differences in the development strategy followed across the regions, and test this hypothesis using provisional panel data. Their econometric results confirm that: (i) the greater the deviation from the CAF strategy in a province, the less open that province will be, and the higher the incidence of rural poverty in that province. Foreseeing a likely increase in the severity of urban poverty and poverty among migrants from rural areas as well as a continued adverse tend in income inequality, they strongly advocate an adoption of a CAF development strategy and a promotion of labour-intensive industries as a strategy for poverty reduction in both urban and rural areas across all regions in China.

The poor in low-income countries are much more vulnerable to large shocks emanating from a deeper integration into the global economy, as witnessed by the impact of the Asian financial crisis (see Chapter 2, by Kakwani and Son). Applying a framework of Fuzzy models to the Indian economy, Chapter 7, by Kumar and Viswanathan, develops regional level indices of vulnerability for two time points: one in 1990–1 and the other in 1999–2000, representing 'pre'- and 'post'-reform periods, to capture the impact of globalization – in particular, trade liberalization – on rural poverty. In their analysis, the vulnerability is conceptualized and measured as a multidimensional function of its exposure, sensitivity and adaptive capacity. Sixteen Indian states are then ranked accordingly in terms of their vulnerability to welfare loss.

Vulnerability (to external shock) of a system is hypothesized to increase with exposure and sensitivity, but decline with adaptive capacity. Exposure is captured through two indicators: instability in cereal production; and share of investment in the manufacturing sector. Sensitivity is assessed through three broad indices: agricultural, demographic and health. In turn, adaptive capacity is measured through three broad indices: economic, human and infrastructure. With a decline in exposure and sensitivity, along with improvement in adaptive capacity, all states reduced their vulnerability in the 'post'-reform period compared with that in the 'pre'-reform period. Further, the changing ranks of states is seen to reflect the dynamic characteristic of vulnerability, and hence the vulnerability index is regarded as more forward-looking compared with other welfare indicators such as HDI and the proportion of the population below the poverty line.

Measured by the vulnerability index developed by Kumar and Viswanathan in Chapter 7, Andhra Pradesh is ranked among the states that are less vulnerable throughout, in both the pre- and post-reform periods. A north-western region (Telangana) in Andhra Pradesh is chosen by Aggarwal in Chapter 8 as the context for her detailed case study examining how globalization affects resource-poor farmers – small and marginal farmers with no access to any assured source of irrigation. These farmers participated aggressively in the new market opportunities that opened up with trade reforms in India, but experienced a worsening in their welfare. Andhra Pradesh is an interesting case for studying the globalization–poverty nexus, as it was at the forefront of the World Bank-led reforms initiated in the areas of fiscal discipline, decentralized governance, and the encouragement of foreign direct investment, and received a great share of funding from multilateral organizations as well as private investors. Since the mid-1990s, Andhra Pradesh has witnessed higher growth rates than the average for the rest of the country, and has been widely hailed as the 'state that would reform India'. It has become known for a particularly impressive performance in the area of information technology. Yet it experienced an increase in rural poverty and agrarian distress, with a rising trend in the rate of farmers' suicides.

Aggarwal argues that these small and marginal farmers, far from being left behind, were at the frontier of the globalization wave: they increased their participation in export markets (in both absolute and relative terms) and have been highly receptive to international technology transfers in the form of hybrid seeds, fertilizers and pesticides. She illustrates how resource-poor farmers who shifted to cotton production have been led into a debt trap and chronic poverty. As cotton prices increased sharply following the reforms, a number of poor farmers shifted to cotton cultivation, involving higher risks because of rainfall variability and large price fluctuations. Cotton cultivation requires much greater technical expertise, working capital and a larger marketing network than those needed for traditional crops.

In addition to a sharp reduction in public investment in rural infrastructure and services, state support to farmers and agricultural production, including formal bank credits and extension services, declined drastically under the economic reform. At the same time, the network of private traders expanded rapidly to meet not only the marketing needs of the new crops but also to provide working capital, technical expertise and information. She shows how this expanded, and largely unregulated, operation of private traders in multiple markets also provided them with the opportunity to extract greater surplus from the farmers. She argues that while increased participation in external markets exposed farmers to greater price risks and fraudulent dealings by the private traders, the shrinking role of the state reduced the farmers' ability to cope with these risks. The result was a decline in average incomes of the resource-poor farmers and rising levels of indebtedness, as costs of production grew sharply. Thus, as several pro-poor public investments and social programmes were cut back, markets grew fast, but regulation and governance over market activities lagged far behind. The poor suffered disproportionately from these unregulated activities.

She shows, through a regression analysis of a household survey data set collected under the 'Situation Assessment Survey of Farmers' in 2002–3, how resource-poor cotton farmers are likely to suffer from rising indebtedness. She concludes that for the poor to take full advantage of new opportunities presented by their integration into the global economy, there should be complementary measures such as the provision of institutional credit, targeted safety nets, and technical and marketing support. In the absence of these measures, globalization could lead to higher input costs for poor farmers, rising indebtedness and chronic poverty, as well as environmental degradation.

Chapter 9, by Giné and Klonner, examines the effects of globalization on the livelihoods of fishing communities in Tamil Nadu, South India. Tamil Nadu is one of the least vulnerable states in India according to the vulnerability index developed by Kumar and Viswanathan (see Chapter 7). Giné and Klonner focus their analysis on one facet of globalization effects – the diffusion of a capital-intensive technology (beach-landing fibre-reinforced plastic boats – FRP), and the resulting income and inequality dynamics within a fishing village. Through a carefully conducted case study based on household survey fieldwork, they show that inequality and lack of asset wealth is responsible for a socially inefficient sequence of individual adoptions, whereby the rich and not the most able fishermen adopt first. They suggest that lack of wealth delays technology adoption, mainly through credit constraints and, to a lesser extent, higher risk aversion among poorer households.

During the diffusion process, inequality follows Kuznets' well-known inverted U-shaped curve. Initially, technological innovation widens the gap between rich and poor, but after the entire community has completed the technological shift, inequality drops to a lower level than before, which implies that, in the long run, the innovation studied benefits the poor more than proportionally. Applying simulation analysis, they conclude that redistributive policies favouring the poor result in accelerated economic growth and a shorter duration of sharpened inequality.

Today, the environmental impacts of globalization have increasingly become one of most pressing issues facing the global community. Chapter 10, by Mahvash Qureshi, examines the environmental consequences of trade liberalization in Pakistan. She first places her study in a general context, where the effect of trade liberalization on the environment is debated in terms of: (i) the *scale effect*, whereby trade-induced economic growth causes over-exploitation and misuse of environmental resources; and (ii) the *composition effect*, whereby low-income countries, as a result of lax environmental regulations, treat the environment as a relatively abundant factor of production and specialize in the production of pollution-intensive products as a result of trade liberalization. Environmentalists argue that the scale effect complements the composition effect, exacerbates natural resource degradation, and causes ecological poverty that accentuates economic poverty and gravely limits prospects for growth in these countries. In contrast, the proponents of free trade assert that the lowering of barriers to trade and investment facilitates the cross-border movement of environmentally friendly technologies, management techniques and information. Hence, they argue that trade gives rise to a positive *technique effect*, which has the potential to outweigh the negative scale effect of increased production. Moreover, they argue that liberalization leads to a *positive* and not *negative* composition effect via income growth: an increase in per capita income induced by greater openness enhances consumers' preference for environmentally friendly products, advances cleaner production techniques and reduces the share of pollution intensive products in the total output.

Specifically, Qureshi examines the pollution haven hypothesis resulting from asymmetries between the environment regulations of developed and developing countries through a systematic analysis of its trade and production patterns. Using bilateral trade statistics from 1975–2003, she tests the hypothesis that Pakistan's net exports of pollution-intensive products to the OECD countries have increased since trade liberalization. She also investigates whether the stringency of environmental governance in the importing countries plays a part in determining Pakistan's exports of pollution-intensive products. The results reveal that there has been a change in the composition of output and exports, towards pollution-intensive manufacturing, that parallels the opening of the economy. Overall, the findings affirm the pollution haven hypothesis and call for an effective environmental policy response for poverty alleviation and sustainable development. In this context, she emphasizes that the poor suffer disproportionately more from environmental degradation as a result of the absence of effective policies and concerted efforts on environmental protection. The poverty rate is very high in Pakistan, where more than 75 per cent of its total population lives or less than US$2 a day. The poor are particularly vulnerable to falling into 'ecological poverty', as they are subject to both environment-related health hazards as well as grave threats to their livelihood from severe depletion of natural resources, following the process of pollution-intensive pattern of development over recent decades.

A certain number of conclusions can be drawn from the case studies in this volume. First, the impact of globalization on growth, inequality and ultimately on poverty tends to be highly context-specific. The impact depends crucially on the prevailing initial conditions – particularly in terms of the resource endowment and its distribution among the population – and on the specific development strategy adopted and pursued.

Second, within the broad Asian context there is persuasive evidence that the forces of globalization contributed substantially to the observed decline in poverty. However, globalization also brought about a more unequal income distribution among households, regions and provinces – a process that could become potentially destabilizing and dampen growth prospects and related poverty alleviation. Third, the development strategy followed by most East and South East Asian countries, of integrating their production and export structures to conform to the flying geese paradigm within the region, ensured that they remained faithful to the concept of dynamic comparative advantage and moved up the product-cycle ladder one rung at a time. Finally, the Asian experience underscores the importance of policy and institutional measures to build up productive assets of the poor through substantial investment in education, health, extension services and infrastructure, as well as through the redistribution of assets in favour of the poor, as observed, for example, through land tenure reforms. Further, special measures, such as the provision of a social safety net, should be in place so that the poor are better protected against and less vulnerable to globalization-induced economic shocks.

Notes

1 Birdsall (2002, 2006), for example, argues that it is the poorer countries and the poor who tend to bear the risks and costs of the higher volatility brought about by globalization.
2 See Nissanke and Thorbecke (2006b) for a review of the literature and a more detailed discussion of the concepts used for analysing the trends in world inequality and the related empirical evidence. For historical trends towards income divergence, see Pritchett (1997). Quah (1996) also discusses the twin peaks in the world's distribution dynamics, characterized by the tendency for stratification and polarization.
3 See Deaton (2001, 2002) and Wade (2002) for critical discussions of the World Bank's estimates of global poverty and inequality used in these studies.
4 See Williamson (2002) for winners and losers from globalization in modern history.
5 See Nissanke and Thorbecke (2006d, 2006e) for main findings from the papers presented at the conceptual and methodological conferences in Helsinki. Nissanke and Thorbecke (2006c) present a preliminary policy framework for encouraging globalization to be more pro-poor.
6 Our discussion draws partly on four papers presented at the Tokyo conference which are to appear in a separate volume devoted to the comparative analysis of the three regions – Asia, Sub-Saharan Africa and Latin America, as part of our UNU-WIDER project publications.
7 The eight countries, referred to as the High Performing Asian Economies in the East Asian Miracle Study, are Japan, Hong Kong, the Republic of Korea, Singapore, Taiwan, Indonesia, Malaysia and Thailand. Perkins (1994) groups these eight economies into three quite distinct categories and models: (i) the manufactured-export-led state interventionist models of Japan, Korea and Taiwan; (ii) the free port service commerce dominated model of Singapore and Hong Kong; and (iii) the natural-resource-rich model of Indonesia, Malaysia and Thailand. The East Asian Miracle has subsequently been subjected to several critical evaluations. For a summary of these critical reviews in a comparative perspective, see Nissanke and Aryeetey (2003).
8 According to recent estimates (Asian Development Bank 2007), the incidence of extreme poverty is still very high in both Bangladesh and India, where this ratio was estimated at 36 per cent in 2005. The incidence of extreme poverty is still very prevalent in South Asia, where 476 million still live below the US$1-a-day poverty line at the time of writing. In India, the numbers of the poor increased from 374 million in 1990 to 397 million in 2005, even though the relative share of the poor declined overall.

9　Milanovic (2005b) notes that, while the disequalizing force inherent in economic growth is noted by many classical development writers such as Rosenstein-Rodan (1943), Myrdal (1957) and Hirschman (1958), the interesting question remains open whether there are countervailing forces to render growth spatially equalizing in the long-run.

10　Strictly speaking, the trends in world (global) income inequality depend on which concept of inequality is used for measurement (Milanovic 2005a; Nissanke and Thorbecke 2006b). Among different estimates, the 'between country' inequality weighted by population but ignoring 'within country' inequality shows a declining trend largely driven by the China factor, while all other estimates show clearly that world inequality has been increasing.

11　For a synthesis of this vast literature, see Thorbecke and Charumilind (2002).

12　However, they also conclude that the growth in China has not been pro-poor or distribution-neutral, as the negative signs on per capita income in their regression results are interpreted as an adverse effect of average income growth on the income shares of the poor.

13　See Asian Development Bank (2007) and Ahuja *et al.* for the concept of 'inclusive growth' and the associated policy strategy advocated for the region.

References

Addison, T. and Cornia, G. A. (2001) 'Income Distribution Policies for Faster Poverty Reduction', WIDER Discussion Paper 2001/93, UNU-WIDER, Helsinki.

Ahuja, V., Bidani, B., Ferreira, F. and Walton, M. (1997) *Everyone's Miracle? Revisiting Poverty and Inequality in East Asia* (Washington, DC: World Bank).

Ali, I. (2007) 'Pro-Poor to Inclusive Growth: Asian Prescription', ERD Policy Brief 48, May, Asian Development Bank, Manila.

Ali, I. and Zhuang, J. (2007) 'Inclusive Growth Toward a Prosperous Asia: Policy Implications', ERD Working Paper 97, July, Asian Development Bank, Manila.

Asian Development Bank (2004) *Key Indicators of Developing Asian and Pacific Countries* (Manila: ADB).

Asian Development Bank (2005) *An Initial Assessment of the Impact of the Earthquake and Tsunami of December 26, 2004 on South and Southeast Asia* (Manila: ADB).

Asian Development Bank (2007) *Key Indicators 2007: Inequality in Asia* (Manila: ADB).

Bhanumurthy, N. R. and Mitra, A. (2006) 'Globalization, Growth and Poverty in India', WIDER Research Paper 2006/41, UNU-WIDER, Helsinki.

Birdsall, N. (2002) 'A Stormy Day on an Open Field: Asymmetry and Convergence in the Global Economy', Paper presented at the conference on Globalization, Living Standards and Inequality, Sydney, 27–28 May.

Birdsall, N. (2006) 'The World Is Not Flat: Inequality and Injustice in our Global Economy', WIDER Annual Lecture 9, UNU-WIDER, Helsinki.

Campos, E. and Root, H. L. (eds) (1996) *The Key to the East Asian Miracle* (Washington, DC: Brookings Institution).

Chen, S. and Ravallion, M. (2004) 'How Have the World's Poorest Fared since the Early 1980s?', World Bank Policy Research Department Working Paper 3341, World Bank; Washington, DC.

Cook, S. (2006) 'Asian Paths to Poverty Reduction and Inclusive Development', Institute of Development Studies, University of Sussex, and the Overseas Development Institute, London.

Cornia, G. A. (ed.) (2004) *Inequality, Growth, and Poverty in an Era of Liberalization and Globalization* (Oxford: Oxford University Press for UNU-WIDER).

Deaton, A. (2001) 'Counting the World's Poor: Problems and Possible Solutions', *World Bank Research Observer*, 16(2): 125–47.

Deaton, A. (2002) 'Is World Poverty Falling?', *Finance and Development*, 39(2): 4–7.

Dollar, D. and Kraay, A. (2002) 'Growth Is Good for the Poor', *Journal of Economic Growth*, 7: 195–225. Republished in A. Shorrocks and R. van der Hoeven (eds) (2004), *Growth, Inequality and Poverty* (Oxford: Oxford University Press for UNU-WIDER).

Hayami, Y. (2006) 'Globalization and Rural Poverty: A Perspective from a Social Observatory in the Philippines', WIDER Research Paper 2006/44, UNU-WIDER, Helsinki.

Hirschman, A. (1958) *The Strategy of Economic Development* (New Haven, Conn.: Yale University Press).

Hussain, A. (2003) 'Urban Poverty in China: Measurement, Patterns, and Policies' (Geneva: ILO).

Kakwani, N. and Pernia, E. (2000) 'What Is Pro-poor Growth?', *Asian Development Review*, 16(1): 1–16.

Kaldor, N. (1956) 'Alternative Theories of Distribution', *Review of Economic Studies*, 23(2): 83–100.

Khan, A., Griffin, K. and Riskin, C. (1999) 'Income Distribution in Urban China during the Period of Economic Reform and Globalization', *American Economic Review*, 89(2): 296–300.

Milanovic, B. (2005a) *World Apart: Measuring International and Global Inequality* (Princeton, NJ and Oxford: Princeton University Press).

Milanovic, B. (2005b) 'Half a World: Regional Inequality in Five Great Federations', World Bank Policy Research Working Paper 3699, World Bank, Washington, DC.

Myrdal, G. (1957) *Economic Theory and Underdevelopment Regions* (London: Hutchinson).

Nissanke, M. and Aryeetey, E. (2003) *Comparative Development Experiences of Sub-Saharan Africa and East Asia: An Institutional Approach* (Aldershot: Ashgate).

Nissanke, M. and Thorbecke, E. (2006a) 'Overview', in M. Nissanke and E. Thorbecke (eds), *The Impact of Globalization on the World's Poor: Transmission Mechanisms* (Basingstoke: Palgrave Macmillan for UNU-WIDER).

Nissanke, M. and Thorbecke, E. (2006b) 'Channels and Policy Debate in the Globalization–Inequality–Poverty Nexus', in M. Nissanke and E. Thorbecke (eds), *The Impact of Globalization on the World's Poor: Transmission Mechanisms* (Basingstoke: Palgrave Macmillan for UNU-WIDER). Also published in *World Development*, 34(8), UNU-WIDER special issue.

Nissanke, M. and Thorbecke, E. (2006c) 'A Quest for Pro-Poor Globalisation', WIDER Research Paper 2006/46; also published in G. Mavrotas and A. Shorrocks (eds) (2007), *Advancing Development: Core Themes in Global Economics* (Basingstoke: Palgrave Macmillan for UNU-WIDER).

Nissanke, M. and Thorbecke, E. (eds) (2006d) 'The Impact of Globalization on the World's Poor', *World Development*, 34(8), UNU-WIDER special issue.

Nissanke, M. and Thorbecke, E. (eds) (2006e) *The Impact of Globalization on the World's Poor: Transmission Mechanisms* (Basingstoke: Palgrave Macmillan for UNU-WIDER).

Ozawa, T. (2006) 'Asia's Labour-driven Economic Development, Flying-Geese Style', WIDER Research Paper 2006/59, UNU-WIDER, Helsinki.

Perkins, D. H. (1994) 'There Are at Least Three Models of East Asian Development', *World Development*, 22(4): 655–61.

Pritchett, L. (1997) 'Divergence, Big Time', *Journal of Economic Perspectives*, 11(3): 3–17.

Quah, D. T. (1996) 'Twin Peaks: Growth and Convergence in Models of Distribution Dynamics', *The Economic Journal*, 106 (July): 1045–55.

Ravallion, M. (2002) 'Growth, Inequality and Poverty: Looking Beyond Averages', Paper presented at World Bank Annual Bank Conference of Development Economics Europe, June, Oslo.

Ravallion, M. (2004a) 'Competing Concepts of Inequality in the Globalization Debate', Paper presented at the Brookings Trade Forum on Globalization, Poverty and Inequality, 13–14 May, Washington, DC.

Ravallion, M. (2004b) 'Pro-poor Growth: A Primer', World Bank Policy Research Working Paper 3242, Washington, DC, World Bank.

Ravallion, M., and Chen, S. (2004) 'China's (Uneven) Progress Against Poverty', Policy Research Working Paper 3408, Washington, DC, World Bank.

Rosenstein-Rodan, P. (1943) 'Problems of Industrialisation of Eastern and Southern Europe', *Economic Journal*, 53: 202–11.

Shorrocks, A. and van der Hoeven, R. (eds) (2004) *Growth, Inequality and Poverty* (Oxford: Oxford University Press for UNU-WIDER).

Thorbecke, E. and Charumilind, C. (2002) 'Economic Inequality and Its Socio-economic Impact', *World Development*, 30(9): 1477–95.

UNESCAP/ABD/UNDP (2005) *A Future Within Reach* (New York: UNESCAP/ABD/UNDP).

Wade, R. H. (2002) 'Globalization, Poverty and Income Distribution: Does Liberal Argument Hold?', Paper presented at the conference on Globalization, Living Standards and Inequality, Sydney, 27–28 May.

Williamson, J. G. (2002) 'Winners and Losers over Two Centuries of Globalization', WIDER Annual Lecture 6, UNU-WIDER, Helsinki.

World Bank (1993) *The East Asian Miracle: Economic Growth and Public Policy* (New York: Oxford University Press).

Zhang, Y. and Wan, G. (2006) 'Globalization and the Urban Poor in China', WIDER Research Paper 2006/42, UNU-WIDER, Helsinki.

2
Pro-Poor Growth:
The Asian Experience

Nanak Kakwani and Hyun H. Son

Introduction

The basic idea of globalization is that it moves resources from less productive uses to more productive ones, thus enhancing economic growth by utilizing comparative advantage, which is endowed differently from one country to another. Similarly, some are in favour of globalization because many economies have achieved unprecedented material progress, contributing significantly to a reduction in global poverty. However, a recent study by Kakwani and Son (2007) has shown that the current process of globalization is generating unbalanced outcomes; many countries and people are left out of the benefits of globalization. Kakwani and Son's cross-country study of eighty countries during the period of 1984–2001 revealed that, out of 237 growth spells, 106 (44.7 per cent) had negative growth rates and 131 (55.3 per cent) positive growth ones.[1] Of 131 spells when growth rates were positive, growth was pro-poor in 55 (23.2 per cent) cases and anti-poor in 76 (32.1 per cent) cases. In 53 out of 106 spells of negative growth rates, the poor suffered a proportionally greater decline in their consumption compared to the non-poor. For a rapid reduction in poverty, a country needs to achieve positive growth rates that are pro-poor. According to these results, this does not seem to be happening globally.

The most important goal for the developmental effort has become poverty reduction, which can be achieved by economic growth and/or by the redistribution of income. Issues related to the benefits of growth accrued to the poor have been a priority of development policy in the 1990s. An emerging consensus is that growth alone is a rather blunt tool for poverty reduction.[2] To achieve a rapid reduction in poverty, policies of redistribution of income and assets, providing equal access to opportunities for work and employment, social services and benefits, need to be emphasized. A policy agenda that addresses both distributional concerns and poverty reduction could lead to the enhancement of both economic growth and equity. Indeed, the growth–poverty–inequality relationship is complex and interdependent between each element. Merely increasing the degree of globalization is unlikely to solve these complex issues.

A view widely held in the domain of development economics is that the benefits of economic growth diffuse automatically across all segments of society. This is indeed the well-known trickle-down hypothesis, which dominated thinking in the 1950s and 1960s. In a similar manner, the result derived from a number of recent studies suggests that economic growth overall reduces poverty. Among these studies, the paper by Dollar and Kraay (2000) has attracted much attention.[3] This study, based on cross-country regressions, has been criticized for depicting only an average picture of the relationship between growth and poverty. When large differences across countries are averaged out, the results are potentially deceptive, because country-specific experiences can differ widely. Under the surface of aggregate outcomes there are often individual countries that experience an increase in poverty during spells of positive economic growth, at least in the short run (Ravallion 2001).

The relationship between growth and inequality has also been debated extensively. In his well-known 1955 article, Simon Kuznets found an inverted-U pattern between per capita income and inequality, based on a cross-section of countries: as per capita income rises, inequality first worsens and then improves. The major driving force was presumed to be structural change that occurred because of labour shifts from a poor and less productive traditional sector to a more productive and differentiated modern sector. The hypothesis was supported by a number of studies – including those by Kravis (1960), Oshima (1962), Adelman and Morris (1971), Paukert (1973), Ahluwalia (1974, 1976), Robinson (1976) and Ram (1988). Yet, with better quality datasets and testing on individual countries, Kuznets' inverted-U has been challenged and seems to have evaporated (Anand and Kanbur 1984; Fields 1989; Oshima 1994; Deininger and Squire 1996). For example, Deininger and Squire (1996) attempted a comprehensive test of the hypothesis and confirmed that there was no evidence of an inverted-U curve for individual countries.

Overall, the relationship between growth and poverty is complex to explain, and is also determined by the level and changes in inequality. Pro-poor growth is concerned with the interrelation between the three elements of growth, poverty and inequality. While there remains no consensus on how to define or measure pro-poor growth, the issue has attracted a fair amount of attention within academia as well as among development practitioners. The pro-poor growth debate has its roots in the pro-distribution arguments by Chenery and Ahluwalia in the 1970s. Chenery and Ahluwalia's (1974) model of 'redistribution with growth' could be regarded as the inception of the whole debate on pro-poor growth, as well as a culmination of the critique of the trickle-down hypothesis. More recently, pro-poor growth was also implicit in the term 'broad-based growth' used in the 1990 *World Development Report*. While the concept was never defined at that time, it subsequently shifted to become referred to as pro-poor growth during the course of the 1990s.

This chapter analyses pro-poor growth using the 'poverty equivalent growth rate (PEGR)' proposed by Kakwani and Son (2007), which takes into account not only the magnitude of growth, but also how much benefit the poor receive from the growth. It is shown that proportional reduction in poverty is a monotonically increasing function of the PEGR: the larger the PEGR, the greater the proportional reduction in poverty will be. Thus maximizing the PEGR implies a maximum reduction in poverty. This study derives the PEGR for an entire class of additively decomposable Foster–Greer–Thorbecke (1984) poverty measures. The impact of globalization on the standard of living should be evaluated in terms of the PEGR, which, in conjunction with the actual growth rate, provides a clearer insight into pattern of growth that encompasses the three elements of growth, poverty and inequality.

Pro-poor growth classification

Pro-poor growth may be referred as growth that benefits the poor and provides them with opportunities to improve their economic situation, as often cited by international agencies (UN 2000; OECD 2001). This definition is vague and provides little guidance as to its measurement or its policy implications. Lately, a number of studies have attempted to define and measure a pro-poor growth. These studies include Kakwani and Pernia (2000), McCulloch *et al.* (2000), Ravallion and Chen (2003) and Son (2003).[4] Each of these studies has its own merits and limitations. A brief review of the different approaches is given below.

General versus strict approach

The World Bank's definition of pro-poor growth is *general* and less strict. It defines growth as pro-poor if it reduces poverty (by however small an amount) (Ravallion 2004). Under this general definition, the poor may receive only a small fraction of total benefits of growth, but still the growth process will be called pro-poor. In this chapter, we characterize this situation as trickle-down when the poor receive proportionally less benefit from growth than do the non-poor. Literally, 'pro-poor' implies that the poor should receive relatively more (at least not less than) benefits compared to the non-poor. The World Bank's definition is rather too general and will classify most growth processes as pro-poor.

The other broad definition of pro-poor growth is rather *strict* and emphasizes inequality reduction that occurs with poverty reduction during economic growth. Studies – including McCulloch and Baulch (2000), Kakwani and Pernia (2000) and Son (2003) – all suggest a measure of pro-poor growth that takes into account improvements in inequality.

While the definition of pro-poor growth used in this chapter is strict, our approach is further categorized in terms of *relative* or *absolute* pro-poor growth. The relative concept arises when economic growth benefits the poor proportionally more than the non-poor. The implication is that, while growth reduces poverty, it also improves relative inequality. This definition may be referred to as a relative approach, as it implies a reduction in relative inequality. Conversely, a measure of pro-poor growth is absolute if the poor receive the absolute benefits of growth equal to, or greater than, the absolute benefits received by the non-poor. Under this definition, absolute inequality would fall during the course of economic growth. In fact, this is the strongest requirement for achieving pro-poor growth, and may thus be referred to as 'super pro-poor'.

When growth is negative, poverty in general increases. However, there may be a situation where a negative growth results in poverty reduction. This situation can take place only if the effect of inequality reduction on poverty outweighs the adverse impact of negative growth on poverty. This growth scenario may be termed as 'strongly pro-poor'. Another classification of a growth scenario occurs when negative growth raises poverty. This may be termed as 'anti-poor' even if inequality improves during the course of growth. In this situation, the proportional reduction in income of the poor is less than the proportional reduction in income of the non-poor. Taking a step further from anti-poor, a situation may be called 'strongly anti-poor' if both poverty and inequality become worse during spells of negative growth.

Partial or full approach

The *partial approach* classifies under what conditions growth can be said to be pro-poor or anti-poor without specifying a poverty line and a poverty measure. A measure suggested by Ravallion and Chen (2003) falls into this classification in the sense that pro-poor growth is measured based on the first-order stochastic dominance condition. Similarly, a pro-poor growth measure proposed by Son (2003) can be also categorized as partial because a growth process is primarily determined to be pro-poor (or not pro-poor) by the second-order stochastic dominance condition. The greatest advantage of using this partial approach is that it is valid for all poverty lines and poverty measures. On the other hand, one limitation of the approach is that if the dominance conditions are not met, then one cannot infer whether a growth process is pro-poor or not pro-poor. On this ground, the approach derived from the dominance conditions may be referred to as 'partial'. Under this partial approach, there are certain circumstances where it is impossible to draw conclusive results from the pattern of growth. Another limitation of the partial approach is that it does not provide an answer as to the degree of pro-poor growth. In other words, the partial approach does not tell us by how much one growth process is more pro-poor than another.

The *full approach*, on the other hand, is always able to provide us with a conclusive result as to whether or not growth is pro-poor. Studies – including

McCulloch and Baulch (2000), Kakwani and Pernia (2000), and Ravallion and Chen (2003) – are based on the full approach.[5] This approach gives the complete rankings of growth processes because, unlike the partial approach, a growth process under the full approach is judged from a rate or an index of pro-poor growth, and not from a curve. To implement this full approach, though, a poverty line as well as a poverty measure needs to be specified. This demands an inevitable value judgement in choosing both poverty line and poverty measures. The PEGR suggested in this chapter can be regarded as the full approach.

Monotonicity criterion

The *monotonicity* axiom implies that the magnitude of poverty reduction should be a monotonically increasing function of the pro-poor growth rate. As poverty reduction depends on both growth and the distribution of its benefits among the poor and the non-poor, maximizing growth alone is a necessary – but not sufficient – condition for poverty reduction. This suggests that there is no monotonic relationship between growth and poverty reduction. This calls for a measure of pro-poor growth that captures a direct linkage (or monotonic relation) with poverty reduction, indicating that poverty reduction takes into account not only growth but also how benefits of growth are shared by individuals in society. On this account, a pro-poor growth measure that satisfies the monotonicity axiom provides a necessary *and* sufficient condition for the reduction of poverty.

McCulloch and Baulch (2000) propose a measure of pro-poor growth known as the poverty bias of growth (PBG). The PBG is derived from the negative of the inequality component obtained from the symmetric poverty decomposition methodology, suggested by Kakwani (2000).[6] The PBG does not always satisfy the monotonicity criterion. Higher values of the PBG may not imply a greater reduction in poverty, because poverty also depends on the growth effect.[7] Thus the PBG will only satisfy the monotonicity criterion if it is assumed that the growth effect is constant (which is highly unlikely).

Ravallion and Chen's pro-poor growth measure also violates the monotonicity axiom. This occurs because they estimate their pro-poor growth measure using numerical integration up to the headcount ratio in the initial period (see the Appendix on page 40). Their measure does not utilize the poverty rate in the terminal period.[8]

Kakwani and Pernia (2000) proposed an index to measure the degree of pro-poor growth. This index is known as the pro-poor growth index (PPGI), and is the ratio of total poverty reduction to poverty reduction that would occur if growth were distribution-neutral. A growth process is said to be pro-poor if the PPGI is greater than 1. The values of the PPGI are defined separately for the trickle-down and immiserizing growth scenarios.[9] Like the PBG, the PPGI is merely an index that does not address the monotonicity axiom.

While the PPGI captures the distribution of growth benefits among both the poor and non-poor, the index does not take into account the level of the growth rate itself. In response to this, we propose another pro-poor growth measure called a 'poverty equivalent growth rate' (PEGR), which takes into account the limitation underlying the PPGI measure. Moreover, the PEGR satisfies the monotonicity criterion (its formal derivation is shown later).

Additively decomposable poverty measures

Poverty can be conceptualized in terms of absolute deprivation suffered by the population. A person suffers from absolute deprivation if he or she cannot enjoy the society's minimum standard of living, to which everyone should be entitled. In practice, we cannot measure directly the deprivation suffered by any individual because of non-availability of income or consumption enjoyed by individuals, so we measure this deprivation using the per capita consumption (or income) of households, which is readily available from household surveys. Suppose we have a household survey consisting of n sample households, of which the ith household has per capita consumption of x_i. Then the deprivation suffered by the ith sample household can be measured by the variable I_i, given by:[10]

$$I_i = 1 \quad \text{if } x_i < z$$
$$ = 0 \quad \text{if } x_i \geq z$$

where z is the per capita household poverty line. Suppose w_i is the share of population that is represented by the ith sample household. Then the average deprivation suffered by the whole society is given by:

$$H = 100 \times \sum_{i=1}^{n} I_i w_i$$

H is the percentage of population that suffers the deprivation, because their income is below the society's minimum standard of living. H thus measures the incidence of poverty in the society and is called the 'headcount ratio'.

The headcount ratio is a crude measure of poverty. It assumes that everyone whose income is below the poverty line suffers the same degree of deprivation, therefore it does not take into account the intensity of deprivation suffered by the poor. To take this intensity into account, we define the degree of absolute deprivation suffered by individuals in the ith household as:

$$D(x) = \left[\frac{z - x_i}{z}\right]^{\alpha} \quad \text{if } x_i < z$$
$$ = 0 \qquad\qquad \text{if } x_i \geq z$$

which implies that the deprivation decreases monotonically with consumption (or income). The degree of poverty in the society may be measured by the average deprivation that is suffered by the society, given by:

$$P_\alpha = 100 \times \sum_{i=1}^{n} I_i \left[\frac{z - x_i}{z} \right]^\alpha w_i \tag{2.1}$$

which gives estimates of the class of Foster–Greer–Thorbecke (1984) poverty measures, where α is the inequality aversion parameter. When $\alpha = 0$, P_α gives the headcount ratio; when $\alpha = 1$, P_α gives the poverty gap ratio; and when $\alpha = 2$, P_α gives the severity of poverty index. The larger the value of α, the greater the weight given to the poor who are further below the poverty line. In this chapter, the pro-poorness of growth is analysed using these three poverty measures.[11]

Poverty equivalent growth rate

How does economic growth affect poverty reduction? To answer this question, we need to measure the factors that contribute to poverty reduction. Poverty reduction largely depends on two factors. The first is the magnitude of the economic growth rate: the larger the growth rate, the greater the reduction of poverty. Growth is generally accompanied by changes in inequality; an increase in inequality reduces the impact of growth on poverty reduction. The PEGR combines these two factors into one index, which has a monotonic relationship to the magnitude of poverty reduction.

Suppose η is the poverty elasticity with respect to growth, which is defined as the proportional change in poverty when there is a positive growth rate of 1 per cent. η can be decomposed into sum of two components, δ and ε, such that:[12]

$$\eta = \delta + \varepsilon \tag{2.2}$$

where δ is the pure growth effect and ε is the inequality effect. δ is the proportional change in poverty when the distribution of income does not change, whereas ε is the proportional change in poverty when inequality changes in the absence of growth. δ will always be negative, because when the growth rate is positive, poverty always reduces and when the growth rate is negative, poverty always increases, with distribution remaining constant. ε can be either negative or positive, depending on whether change in inequality accompanying growth reduces or increases poverty. Growth will obviously be pro-poor if ε is negative. Thus the degree of pro-poor growth can be measured by an index (Kakwani and Pernia 2000)

$$\phi = \frac{\eta}{\delta} \tag{2.3}$$

ϕ will be greater than 1 when $\varepsilon < 0$. Thus, growth will be pro-poor if $\phi > 1$, meaning that the poor benefit proportionally more than the non-poor: growth results in redistribution in favour of the poor. When $0 < \phi < 1$, growth is not strictly pro-poor (that is, growth results in a redistribution against the poor) even though it still reduces the incidence of poverty. This situation may be characterized generally as 'trickle-down' growth. If $\phi < 0$, then positive economic growth in fact leads to an increase in poverty. This situation may be characterized as 'immiserizing' growth (Bhagwati 1988).

The index ϕ measures how the benefits of growth are distributed across the population. Suppose g is the growth rate and P_α is a poverty measure, the proportional change in poverty may be written as:

$$\Delta\log(P)_\alpha = f(g,\phi) \tag{2.4}$$

which implies that there are two factors that determine a country's performance in poverty reduction. First is the growth rate g, which affects the mean income of society; and the second factor relates to the distribution of the benefits of economic growth, which is measured by the pro-poor index ϕ.

To determine $f(g,\phi)$, we introduce the idea of poverty-equivalent growth rate g^*, which is defined as the growth rate that will result in the same level of proportional poverty reduction as the present growth rate with no change in income inequality; that is, when everyone receives the same proportional benefits of growth.[13] It is obvious that g^* will be given by:

$$f(g^*, 1) = f(g, \phi) \tag{2.5}$$

Note that $\phi = 1$ when everyone receives the same proportional benefits. From Equation (2.4), we write:

$$\Delta\log(P_\alpha) = f(g,\phi) = g\eta \tag{2.6}$$

Which, when $\phi = 1$ and $\eta = \delta$, gives:

$$f(g^*,1) = \delta g^* \tag{2.7}$$

which, in view of Equations (2.3), (2.6) and (2.7), immediately gives the PEGR as:

$$g^* = g\phi \tag{2.8}$$

which can also be written as:

$$g^* = g + (\phi-1)g \tag{2.9}$$

The PEGR measured by g^* is the effective growth rate for poverty reduction. Substituting Equation (2.8) into Equation (2.6) gives:

$$\Delta \log(P_\alpha) = \delta g^* \qquad (2.10)$$

Since δ is always negative, the proportional reduction in poverty will be an increasing function of g^*: the larger is g^*, the greater will be the proportional reduction in poverty. Thus, maximizing g^* will be the equivalent of maximizing the total proportional reduction in poverty. This suggests that a country's performance should be judged on the basis of the poverty equivalent growth rate and not by growth rate alone.

The second term in the right-hand side of (2.9) gives a gain (loss) in growth rate when growth is pro-poor (anti-poor). To make our message clearer, suppose a country's total poverty elasticity is two-thirds of the growth elasticity of poverty, in which case $\phi = 2/3$. Then from Equation (2.9), we note that the country's actual growth rate of 9 per cent is equal to the poverty equivalent growth rate of only 6 per cent. Thus the effective growth rate for poverty reduction is 3 per cent lower than the actual growth rate, because the country is not following pro-poor policies. On the other hand, if the total poverty elasticity is supposedly 20 per cent higher than the growth elasticity of poverty, in which case $\phi = 1.2$, then the country's actual growth rate of 9 per cent will be equal to the poverty equivalent growth rate of 10.8 per cent. Thus there will be a gain in growth rate of 1.8 per cent points because growth is pro-poor.

Equation (2.9) implies that growth is pro-poor (anti-poor) if g^* is greater (less) than g. If g^* lies between 0 and g, the growth is accompanied by increasing inequality but still reduces poverty. This situation may be characterized as a trickle-down process when the poor receive proportionally less benefits from it than do the non-poor. However, it is possible that positive growth increases poverty, in which case g^* is negative. This can happen when inequality increases so much that the beneficial impact of growth is more than offset by the adverse impact of rising inequality. This is Bhagwati's (1988) 'immiserizing growth'. He outlines a scenario where the more affluent farmers adopt new seeds and raise grain production, resulting in lower prices. By contrast, the marginal farmers who cannot adopt the new technology find their stagnant output yielding even less income. Thus the green revolution may immiserize the poor. This situation may be rare, however, because in the long run the marginal farmers may also catch up with the new techniques. The more common situation is where the poor farmers also benefit from economic growth but to a much lesser extent than the better-off ones.

During the recession period, when $g < 0$, poverty generally increases but if inequality reduces so much that poverty decreases, in which case $g^* > 0$, then we call the recession strongly pro-poor. The recession will be pro-poor if $g < g^* < 0$, in which case, poverty increases but the poor are hurt proportionally less than the non-poor. The recession will be anti-poor if $g^* < g < 0$, in which case poverty increases and the poor are hurt proportionally more than the non-poor.

How to calculate the poverty equivalent growth rate

This section presents a methodology to estimate the PEGR by utilizing unit record data available for any two periods. Any poverty measure P can characterized fully by the poverty line z, mean income μ and the Lorenz curve $L(p)$, where p varies from 0 to 1:

$$P = P\,(z, \mu, L(p))$$

Since households differ in size, age composition and other characteristics, it is expected that they will have different needs. We assume that the household consumption (or income) that is the basis for computing μ and $L(p)$ has been adjusted for different household needs. Furthermore, if we are comparing poverty estimates over time, the mean consumption (or income) must also be adjusted for price changes. Thus, growth rates should be computed using the real consumption (or income).

We propose that the estimates of PEGR must satisfy the following intuitively natural axioms.

Axiom 1: The magnitude of poverty reduction must be monotonically an increasing function of the PEGR.

This is an essential axiom, because maximization of PEGR must imply the maximum reduction in poverty. This is possible only if there is a monotonic relationship between the magnitude of poverty reduction and the PEGR.

Suppose that g_{ij}^* is the PEGR when going from the base year i to the terminal year j, and similarly, g_{ji}^* is the PEGR when going from the terminal year j to the base year i. There should be symmetry between base and terminal years. This suggests the following axiom.

Axiom 2: $g_{ij}^* = -g_{ji}^*$ for all i and j.

This implies that if PEGR is 5 per cent when going from year i to year j, then intuitively PEGR must be -5 per cent when going from year j to year i.

Suppose the income distributions in the base year i and terminal year j have mean incomes μ_i and μ_j with the Lorenz curves $L_i(p)$ and $L_j(p)$, respectively. The total poverty elasticity in Equation (2.1) between years i and j can be estimated as:

$$\hat{\eta}_{ij} = (Ln\,[P\,(z, \mu_j, L_j(p)] - Ln[P\,(z, \mu_i, L_i(p)]) / \hat{g}_{ij} \qquad (2.11)$$

where $\hat{g}_{ij}$ given by:

$$\hat{g}_{ij} = Ln(\mu_j) - Ln(\mu_i)$$

is an estimate of the growth rate of mean income. It can easily be seen that $\hat{\eta}_{ij} = \hat{\eta}_{ji}$, which is an intuitive result because the total poverty elasticity must not change whether we estimate it by observing a change from i to j, or from j to i.

The estimate of PEGR is given by:

$$\hat{g}_{ij}^{*} = \left(\frac{\hat{\eta}_{ij}}{\hat{\delta}_{ij}}\right)\hat{g}_{ij} = \hat{\phi}_{ij}\,\hat{g}_{ij} \tag{2.12}$$

where $\hat{\delta}_{ij}$ is an estimate of the pure growth elasticity of poverty, which should satisfy Equation (2.2):

$$\hat{\eta}_{ij} = \hat{\delta}_{ij} + \hat{\varepsilon}_{ij} \tag{2.13}$$

where $\hat{\varepsilon}_{ij}$ is an estimate of the inequality effect of poverty reduction when going from year i to year j. Kakwani's (2000) poverty decomposition methodology can then be used to estimate $\hat{\delta}_{ij}$ and $\hat{\varepsilon}_{ij}$ by the following formulae:

$$\hat{\delta}_{ij} = \frac{1}{2}\left[\ln\left(P(z, \mu_j, L_i(p)\right) - \ln\left(P(z, \mu_i, L_i(p)\right) + \ln\left(\theta(z, \mu_j, L_j(p)\right)\right.$$

$$\left. - \ln\left(\theta(z, \mu_i, L_j(p)\right)\right] \tag{2.14}$$

and

$$\hat{\varepsilon}_{ij} = \frac{1}{2}\left[\ln\left(P(z, \mu_i, L_j(p)\right) - \ln\left(P(z, \mu_i, L_i(p)\right) + \ln\left(P(z, \mu_j, L_j(p)\right)\right.$$

$$\left. - \ln\left(P(z, \mu_j, L_i(p)\right)\right] \tag{2.15}$$

which will always satisfy Equation (2.13).[14] This methodology can be used to estimate the PEGR for the entire class of poverty measures given in Equation (2.1).

The proportional reduction in poverty from year i to year j (as shown in Equation (2.11)) is equal to $\hat{\eta}_{ij}\,\hat{g}_{ij}$, which is equal to $\hat{\delta}_{ij}\,\hat{g}_{ij}^{*}$. Since $\hat{\delta}_{ij}$ in Equation (2.14) is always negative (unless $\mu_1 = \mu_2$), the magniude of poverty reduction will be monotonically an increasing function of $\hat{g}_{ij}^{*}$; the larger is $\hat{g}_{ij}^{*}$, the greater the proportional reduction in poverty between the years from i to j. Thus Axiom 1 will be always satisfied by the proposed estimator of PEGR.[15]

Further, from Equation (2.14), it can be seen that $\hat{\delta}_{ij} = \hat{\delta}_{ji}$ for all i and j, which on substituting in Equation (2.12) gives $\hat{\phi}_{ij} = \hat{\phi}_{ji}$ and $\hat{g}^*_{ij} = -\hat{g}^*_{ji}$ for all i and j. Thus, Axiom 2 is always satisfied.

Data sources and concepts used

The data for Korea comes from the country's household survey, called the Family Income and Expenditure Survey and is conducted every year by the National Statistical Office in Korea. These household surveys are unit-recorded data; those used for this study cover the period 1990 to 1999. They include income and consumption components for more than 20,000 households in urban areas. We utilized the minimum cost-of-living basket developed in 1994 by the Korean Institute for Health and Social Affairs (KIHASA) as the poverty line. We modify this poverty line by taking into account different costs-of-living between Seoul and other cities. The poverty line has been updated for other years by using the separate consumer price indices for Seoul and other cities.

It must be emphasized that we have used a Korea-specific poverty line, which measures the minimum acceptable standard of living in Korea. Therefore, the incidence of poverty computed here cannot be compared with the incidence of poverty in other countries. Our main objective here is to analyse changes in poverty and how it has been affected by the economic growth in Korea.

The data source for Thailand comes from the socio-economic surveys (SES) covering the period 1988 to 1998. These SES data are unit-record household surveys conducted every two years by the National Statistical Office in Thailand. The surveys are nationwide and cover all private, non-institutional households residing permanently in municipalities and villages. However, it excludes the parts of the population living transiently in hotels or rooming houses, boarding schools, military barracks, temples, hospitals, prisons and other such institutions. The SES contains, on average, information on more than 17,000 households between 1988 and 1998.

In estimating poverty, this study uses the official poverty line developed for Thailand, which takes into account spatial price indices as well as individual needs that differ depending on household size and its composition.

For Vietnam, the Vietnamese Living Standard Surveys (VLSS) are utilized, covering the period 1992/3–1997/8. While the 1992/3 VLSS included 4,800 households, 5,999 households were interviewed for the 1997/8 VLSS. These comprise living standard measurement surveys, which provide information on total expenditure of each household included in the survey. The poverty lines used for this study are 1,160.842 and 1,793.903 thousand dong per capita (16,000 dong equates to c.US$1) per annum in 1992/3 and 1997/8, respectively.

We use per capita welfare consumption expenditure as a welfare measure in estimating poverty in Korea, Thailand and Vietnam. Per capita welfare consumption expenditure is expressed as the ratio of per capita total consumption expenditure to the per capita poverty line (expressed in percentages).

Empirical illustration: the Asian experience

As shown in Table 2.1, the poverty equivalent growth rates overall are higher than the actual growth rates in Korea during the 1990s. This is particularly so before the crisis. For example, the headcount ratio in Korea decreased from 39.6 per cent in 1990 to 8.6 per cent in 1997 (Kakwani and Son 2002). This rapid reduction in poverty during the 1990–7 period was achieved through two factors. One was a high economic growth rate of about 7–8 per cent per annum that prevailed in the economy; the other was a steady decline in inequality,[16] which facilitated a rapid reduction in poverty in addition to the positive growth rates. The largest reduction in poverty occured in 1996–7 when the PEGR was 9 per cent, whereas the annual growth rate was actually only 1.8 per cent in the same period. What does this imply? It suggests that, before the crisis, the poor benefited proportionally much more than the non-poor, as was reflected in a dramatic reduction in poverty.

After the onset of the financial crisis, actual growth rates became higher than the PEGRs between 1997 and 1999. This indicates that the crisis had a more adverse impact on the poor than on the non-poor. This result is to be

Table 2.1 Poverty equivalent growth rates for Korea

Years	Actual growth rate	Poverty equivalent growth rate		
		Percentage of poor	Poverty gap ratio	Severity of poverty
1990–1	9.6	10.7	10.4	10.0
1991–2	4.0	4.1	3.7	3.6
1992–3	4.8	5.8	6.6	6.8
1993–4	7.3	7.2	7.3	7.5
1994–5	8.2	9.7	9.5	8.9
1995–6	5.8	5.1	5.0	4.6
1996–7	1.8	9.0	8.3	9.6
1997–8	−7.6	−9.0	−10.0	−10.9
1998–9	9.8	9.6	10.5	11.5

expected, as poor people are more vulnerable to such unexpected economic shocks. This, in turn, calls for a permanent system of social safety nets, which can protect vulnerable groups of people in society from economic downturns.

Note that there was a sign of recovery in the economy in 1998–9; the headcount ratio declined from 19 per cent in 1998 to 13.4 per cent in 1999 (Kakwani 2000). Despite this positive sign, our result suggests that the growth process is not classifiable as pro-poor. The benefits generated from the positive growth during 1998–9 did flow proportionally more to the non-poor than to the poor. More interestingly, our result points out that, compared to the non-poor, the poor overall benefited less from the recovery process; among poor people, the ultra-poor received proportionally more benefits than not-so-poor ones (which is indicated by the higher values of PEGR for the severity of poverty). This could have happened because of the Korean government's prompt response to the crisis through social welfare programmes. In response to the financial crisis, the government introduced many of these social welfare programmes, including public works programmes and temporary livelihood protection. Public works programmes were particularly effective in helping the ultra-poor, who were largely unemployed and laid-off within the labour market during the economic downturn. Similarly, temporary livelihood protection (which was implemented based on an income means test) was also more helpful to the ultra-poor.

What has been Thailand's growth experience in the 1990s? During 1988–92, growth was not classified as pro-poor. In spite of more than an 8 per cent annual rate of economic growth for that period, the poverty reduction was small during the period. This occurred because the growth process benefited the non-poor proportionally more than the poor. Furthermore, the proportional benefit flowing to the ultra-poor in 1990–2 was even less than that flowing to the poor: as can be seen from Table 2.2, the magnitude of

Table 2.2   Poverty equivalent growth rates for Thailand

Years	Actual growth rate	Poverty equivalent growth rate		
		Headcount ratio	Poverty gap ratio	Severity of poverty
1988–90	9.06	5.5	5.9	6.1
1990–2	7.49	4.3	3.4	3.0
1992–4	7.65	8.8	8.7	8.8
1994–6	5.75	7.4	7.2	7.2
1996–8	−1.00	−2.7	−2.5	−2.5
1998–2000	−0.85	−2.3	−3.8	−4.4
1988–2000	4.68	3.6	3.3	3.1

PEGRs gets smaller as the poverty measure becomes more sensitive to the well-being of poorer individuals.

The trend was reversed during 1992–6, when the PEGRs were higher than the actual growth rates. Thus growth is found to be pro-poor between 1992 and 1996. The large amount of poverty reduction that happened during that period stemmed from the positive effects of both high growth rates and the decline in inequality.[17]

During 1996–2000, the Thai economy was influenced by the financial crisis. As expected, its economic and social impacts were extremely detrimental: while the growth in per capita welfare declined at an annual rate of almost 1 per cent, poverty increased sharply from 11.4 per cent in 1996 to 16.2 per cent in 2000 (Son 2003). As shown in Table 2.2, the adverse impacts of the crisis were prevalent throughout the period and were deepened among the ultra-poor in 1998–2000. Unlike Korea, there were no prompt responses to the crisis from the Thai government to protect the ultra-poor and the vulnerable from the economic shock.

Although the Thai government has provided little by way of programmes constituting social safety nets, the financial crisis has clearly enabled the government to learn how existing social systems function under duress. The crisis has revealed that considerable effort needs to be directed to the setting up, or further development, of social safety nets in the country. This is especially so because traditional family systems of support – though resilient during the early part of the crisis – are likely to weaken over time, given continuous socio-economic change and urbanization, and the further demands placed on them. Household coping mechanisms and the informal safety nets provided through traditional family systems have their limitations during such a crisis.

Table 2.3 presents the empirical results for Vietnam. The table shows that during the 1992–7 period, the PEGRs were consistently higher than the annual growth rates of per capita expenditure (5.02 per cent for Vietnam as a whole). This indicates that the growth process in the country was pro-poor in a way that benefited the poor proportionally more than the non-poor. The PEGR for the severity of poverty index is greater than those for the poverty gap ratio and the incidence of poverty. This implies that during 1992–7, growth in Vietnam had a more beneficial impact on the ultra-poor. Similarly, both urban and rural sectors have experienced pro-poor growth. This occurred because not only did both sectors enjoy high growth rates, but both also showed a decline in inequality, as estimated by the Gini index of per capita expenditure. The Gini index for urban areas fell from 35.07 per cent in 1992/3 to 34.17 per cent in 1997/8, whereas for rural areas it declined to 26.42 per cent in 1997/8 from 28.86 per cent in 1992/3 (Son 2003).

Vietnam has emerged as one of the fastest-growing economies in Asia since the mid-1980s. More importantly, our results have shown that its

Table 2.3   Poverty equivalent growth rates for Vietnam, 1992/3–1997/8

	Total	Urban	Rural
Actual growth rate	5.02	5.28	4.04
Poverty equivalent growth rates for			
Headcount ratio	5.08	6.28	4.61
Poverty gap ratio	5.33	6.46	5.04
Severity of poverty	5.43	6.59	5.19

growth process during 1992/3–1997/8 was pro-poor, thus benefiting the poor proportionally more than the non-poor. This has been attributed to a series of reforms, known as *Doi Moi* (Renovation), which were launched in the latter part of the 1980s. Reforms began primarily in the agricultural sector which, at the time, accounted for close to 40 per cent of gross domestic product (GDP) and 70 per cent of total employment. The country's reform effort focused initially on the dismantling of collective farms, the redistribution of land to peasant households through long-term leases, and an abolition of price controls on goods and services. It then eliminated production and consumption subsidies, and streamlined the public sector (Dollar and Litvack 1998; Weinns 1998). Furthermore, the reform effort included the stabilization of inflation and the liberalization of foreign trade and investment (Dollar 2002). This series of reforms paved the way for the country's spectacular growth in the 1990s, which in turn contributed to a remarkable poverty reduction.

Concluding remarks

This chapter has proposed a measure of pro-poor growth denominated 'poverty equivalent growth rate', which can be calculated for any poverty measures. This measure takes into account not only the magnitude of growth, but also how the benefits of growth are distributed to the poor and the non-poor. It has been argued in the chapter that this new measure satisfies the monotonicity axiom, which sets out a condition that the proportional reduction in poverty is a monotonically increasing function of the poverty equivalent growth rate. As the poverty equivalent growth rate meets the monotonicity criterion, it can be said that in order to achieve a rapid reduction in poverty, the poverty equivalent growth rate should be maximized rather than the actual growth rate.

The methodology developed in this chapter has been applied to a few Asian countries, including Korea, Thailand, and Vietnam. By and large, while Korea and Vietnam have experienced a pro-poor growth pattern in the 1990s, Thailand has on the whole not been pro-poor. Two other important policy implications emerge from the empirical analysis. First, the financial crisis experienced by both Korea and Thailand at the end of the 1990s has revealed that considerable effort needs to be directed to the setting up, or further development, of social safety nets in these countries. Although the Korean government's response to the crisis included the prompt expansion of various social welfare programmes, the crisis demonstrated a call for social safety nets to be enacted on a permanent basis. During the crisis it was realized that household coping mechanisms and traditional family systems of support cannot insulate people from such substantial economic shocks. Second, as the Vietnam experience shows, a 'growth with redistribution' strategy has played a significant part in achieving impressive growth and poverty outcomes. Redistribution policies, such as land reforms, may be necessary to set up the economic and political conditions necessary to ensure that subsequent economic growth is not highly unequalizing (Adelman 1975). This has also proved to be the case for some countries – including Korea and Taiwan – in the early stages of economic development.

The main message of this chapter has been that broad policies such as 'growth is good for the poor' or 'globalization will generate material progress for all' are very deceptive, because individual country-specific experiences can differ widely. This chapter has provided methodologies to analyse the pro-poorness of economic growth in individual countries. Future research should focus on determining why growth is pro-poor in some countries and not in others, or pro-poor in one period and not in another.

Appendix

In this Appendix, we demonstrate theoretically as well as empirically, with the help of a hypothetical example, that Ravallion and Chen's (2003) estimate of pro-poor growth will violate their basic Axiom 1:

Axiom 1: The measure should be consistent with the direction of change in poverty, in that a positive (negative) rate of pro-poor growth implies a reduction (increase) in poverty.

The violation of this axiom will imply that the magnitude of poverty reduction will not necessarily be a decreasing function of pro-poor growth. Thus our Axiom 1 is violated by their measure.

The estimate of Ravallion and Chen's (2003) is given by:

$$RC_t = \frac{\int_0^{H_{t-1}} \Delta \ln(x_{t-1}(p)) dp}{H_{t-1}} \tag{2.A1}$$

where H_{t-1} is the head-count ratio in period $t-1$. The motivation of this index comes from their equation:

$$dW = -\int_0^{H} d \ln(x(p)) dp \tag{2.A2}$$

where W is the Watts measure of poverty.

In order to satisfy Axiom 1, $RC_t > 0 \; (< 0)$ should always imply $\Delta W_t < 0 \; (> 0)$, where

$$\Delta W_t = \int_0^{H_t} \ln(z/x_t(p)) dp - \int_0^{H_{t-1}} \ln(z/x_{t-1}(p)) dp$$

which will not always hold, because Equation (2.A2) does not imply Equation (2.A3) given by:

$$\Delta W_t = -\int_0^{H_{t-1}} \Delta \ln(x(p)) dp \tag{2.A3}$$

Thus Ravallion and Chen's (2003) estimate of the pro-poor index will violate Axiom 1, which implies that the magnitude of poverty reduction will not necessarily be a decreasing function of the pro-poor index.

Acknowledgements

This study was presented at the UNU-WIDER conference on globalization held in Tokyo. We express our gratitude to Anthony Shorrocks and Eric Thorbecke for giving us very helpful comments, along with those from three referees in revising the chapter. Note that the STATA do-file is available upon request to compute the poverty equivalent growth rate proposed in this chapter. This is a revised version of the paper 'Pro-Poor Growth: Concepts and Measurement with Country Case Studies', Working Paper 1, International Poverty Centre, UNDP, Brasilia.

Notes

1   Growth spells refer to the periods of time spanning two successive household surveys for a given country. In our dataset, there are seven growth periods for each country, covering the time between 1981 and 2001 (1981–3, 1983–6, 1986–9, 1989–92, 1992–5, 1995–8, 1998–2001). The total number of growth periods for eighty countries should be 280, but for some countries, income distribution data were not available for all the seven periods. Therefore, we could have only 237 growth periods in total for eighty countries.

2   There is no one-to-one relationship between growth and poverty reduction. A recent study by Son (2007) shows that, in many Asian countries, positive growth has led to an increase in poverty, and negative growth has led to a reduction in poverty. In urban China, for example, a growth rate of 5.07 per cent in per capita income between 1996 and 1999 led to an increase in poverty as measured by all three poverty measures – namely, headcount ratio, poverty gap and severity of poverty. Similarly in the Philippines, positive growth increased poverty in the period 1987 to 1990. There are also examples of negative growth rates resulting in reduction in poverty – for example, Indonesia (1996–9), Malaysia (1984–7), Pakistan (1993–6) and Thailand (1996–9).

3   Other studies include Bruno *et al.* (1998), World Bank (2000), White and Anderson (2001), and Christiaensen *et al.* (2002).

4   This chapter provides a review of various approaches for defining and measuring pro-poor growth.

5   The pro-poor growth measure suggested by Ravallion and Chen (2003) is based on both partial and full approaches: it first derives the growth incidence curve (partial approach) and, at the second stage, the pro-poor growth rate as the area under the growth incidence curve (full approach).

6   To evaluate whether growth is pro-poor (or anti-poor), the PBG measures the extent to which the observed pattern of growth deviates from a distributionally neutral benchmark. McCulloch and Baulch capture the measure of pro-poor growth by comparing the actual distribution of income with the one that would have occurred under the distribution-neutral scenario. In this respect, their measure reflects a relative approach to defining pro-poor growth.

7   Growth effect measures the change in poverty caused by a change in mean income when the distribution of income does not change.

8   See the Appendix, which shows that Ravallion and Chen's pro-poor growth measure violates monotonicity using a numerical example. Similarly, Klasen (2004) has pointed out that, as Ravallion and Chen's measure deals with the growth rates of

quantiles of income distribution, individuals in the initial period may be excluded from the terminal period or vice versa in the process of calculating the pro-poor growth rate suggested by Ravallion and Chen.

9   PPGI lies between zero and one in the case of trickle-down, whereas the index is negative for immiserizing growth scenarios. Immiserizing growth refers to a situation where positive growth increases poverty (Bhagwati 1988).

10   A person suffers deprivation when his or her consumption is less than the poverty line, in which case I_i takes the value 1, and if their income is greater than the poverty line, they do not suffer any deprivation, in which case I_i takes value 0. If a household is identified as suffering deprivation, then all its members are also assumed to be suffering deprivation.

11   The methodology presented here is general and can be applied to all poverty measures, including non-additively-decomposable poverty measures such as that of Sen (1976) and Kakwani (1980a, 1980b).

12   See Kakwani *et al.* (2004).

13   For a more detailed discussion of the poverty equivalent growth rate, see Kakwani and Son (2007b). This paper also develops an idea of absolute poverty equivalent growth rate.

14   Kakwani (2000) justifies this decomposition using an axiomatic approach. Kraay (2004) estimates the growth and inequality effects using Datt and Ravallion's (1992) poverty decomposition, consisting of three components – namely, growth component, inequality component and a residual term. Kakwani calls this decomposition the discrete-time analog of Equation (2.2). Equation (2.2) consists of only growth and inequality components. So estimating Equation (2.2) using a discrete-time analog with three components will give inconsistent estimates of growth and inequality components.

15   Our estimator of PEGR satisfies the monotonicity requirement, but in the Appendix we show that the pro-poor growth rate proposed by Ravallion and Chen (2003) violates the monotonicity axiom.

16   The Gini index declined steadily from 29 per cent in 1990 to 27.9 per cent in 1997.

17   The Gini index declined from 41 per cent and 39.2 per cent in 1992 and 1996, respectively (Kakwani and Son 2002).

References

Adelman, I. (1975) 'Development Economics: A Reassessment of Goals', *American Economic Review*, 65 (May): 302.

Adelman, I. and Morris, C. T. (1971) *Economic Growth and Social Equity in Developing Countries*, Stanford, Calif.: Stanford University Press.

Ahluwalia, M. S. (1974) 'Income Inequality: Some Dimensions of the Problem', in H. Chenery *et al.* (eds), *Redistribution with Growth* (Oxford: Oxford University Press).

Ahluwalia, M. S. (1976) 'Inequality, Poverty and Development', *Journal of Development Economics*, 3(4): 307–42.

Anand, S. and Kanbur, S. M. R. (1984) 'The Kuznets Process and the Inequality Development Relationship', *Journal of Development Economics*, 40(1): 25–52.

Bhagwati, J. N. (1988) 'Poverty and Public Policy', *World Development Report*, 16(5): 539–54.

Bruno, M., Ravallion, M. and Squire, L. (1998) 'Equity and Growth in Developing Countries: Old and New Perspectives of the Policy Issues', in V. Tanzi and K.-Y. Chu (eds), *Income Distribution and High-Quality Growth* (Cambridge, Mass.: MIT Press).

Chenery, H. and Ahluwhalia, M. (1974) *Redistribution with Growth* (Oxford: Oxford University Press).

Christiaensen, L., Demery, L. and Paternostro, S. (2002) 'Economic Growth and Poverty in Africa: Message from the 1990s', Mimeo, World Bank, Washington, DC.

Datt, G. and Ravallion, M. (1992) 'Growth and Redistribution Component of Changes in Poverty Measures: A Decomposition with Applications to Brazil and India in the 1980s', *Journal of Development Economics*, 38: 275–95.

Deininger, K., and Squire, L. (1996) 'Measuring Income Inequality: A New Data-Base', *World Bank Economic Review*, 10(3): 565–91.

Dollar, D. (2002) 'Reform, Growth, and Poverty Reduction in Vietnam', Policy Research Working Paper 2837, World Bank, Washington, DC.

Dollar, D. and Kraay, A. (2000) 'Growth is Good for the Poor', Working paper, Development Research Group, World Bank, Washington, DC.

Dollar, D. and Litvack, J. (1998) 'Macroeconomic Reform and Poverty Reduction in Vietnam', in D. Dollar, P. Glewwe and J. Litvack (eds), *Household Welfare and Vietnam's Transition* (Washington, DC: World Bank).

Fields, G. S. (1989) 'Changes in Poverty and Inequality in the Developing Countries', Mimeo, Cornell University, Ithaca, NY.

Foster, J., Greer, J. and Thorbecke, E. (1984) 'A Class of Decomposable Poverty Measures', *Econometrica*, 52(3): 761–66.

Kakwani, N. (1980a) 'On a Class of Poverty Measures', *Econometrica*, 48(2): 437–46.

Kakwani, N. (1980b) *Income Inequality and Poverty: Methods of Estimation and Policy Applications* (New York: Oxford University Press).

Kakwani, N. (2000) 'On Measuring Growth and Inequality Components of Poverty with Application to Thailand', *Journal of Quantitative Economics*, 16: 67–80.

Kakwani, N. and Pernia, E. (2000) 'What Is Pro-poor Growth?', *Asian Development Review*, 16(1): 1–22.

Kakwani, N. and Son, H. (2002) 'Economic Growth, Inequality and Poverty: Korea and Thailand', in D. Newman, G. Asher and T. Snyder (eds), *Public Sector Policy in Asia: Implications for Business and Government* (Westport, Conn.: Green Publishing Group).

Kakwani, N. and Son, H. (2002) *Pro-poor Growth and Poverty Reduction: The Asian Experience* (Bangkok: Poverty Center, Office of Executive Secretary, ESCAP).

Kakwani, N. and Son, H. (2007a) 'Global Estimates of Pro-Poor Growth', *World Development* (forthcoming).

Kakwani, N. and Son, H. (2007b) 'Poverty Equivalent Growth Rate'. *Review of Income and Wealth* (forthcoming).

Kakwani, N., Khandker, S. and Son, H. (2004) 'Pro-Poor Growth: Concepts and Measurement with Country Case Studies', Working Paper 1, UNDP-International Poverty Centre, Brasilia.

Klasen, S. (2004) 'In Search of The Holy Grail: How to Achieve Pro-Poor Growth?', in B. Tungodden, N. Stern and I. Kolstad (eds), *Annual World Bank Conference on Develoment Economics – Europe 2003: Towards Pro-Poor Policies: Aid, Institutions, and Globalization* (Washington, DC: World Bank).

Korean Institute for Health and Social Affairs (1994) *The Estimation of the Minimum Cost of Living* (Seoul: KIHASA).

Kraay, A. (2004) 'When Is Growth Pro-poor? Cross-Country Evidence', IMF Working Paper 04/47, Washington, DC.

Kravis, I. B. (1960) 'International Differences in the Distribution of Income', *Review of Economics and Statistics*, 42: 408–16.

Kuznets, S. (1955) 'Economic Growth and Income Inequality', *American Economic Review*, 45: 1–28.

McCulloch, N. and Baulch, B. (2000) 'Tracking Pro-Poor Growth', *ID21 Insights*, 31, (Sussex: Institute of Development Studies).

McCulloch, N., Robson, M. and Baulch, B. (2000) 'Growth, Inequality and Poverty in Mauritania: 1987–1996', IDS Working Paper (Sussex: Institute of Development Studies).

Organisation for Economic Co-operation and Development (OECD) (2001) 'Rising to the Global Challenge: Partnership for Reducing World Poverty', Statement by the DAC High Level Meeting, 25–26 April, OECD, Paris.

Oshima, H. (1962) 'International Comparison of Size Distribution of Family Incomes with Special Reference to Asia', *Review of Economics and Statistics*, 44 (November): 439–45.

Oshima, H. (1994) 'Kuznets Curve and Asian Income Distribution', in T. Mizoguchi (ed.), *Making Economies More Efficient and More Equitable: Factors Determining Income Distribution*, Economic Research Series 29, The Institute of Economic Research, Hitotsubashi University (Tokyo: Oxford University Press).

Paukert, F. (1973) 'Income Distribution at Different Levels of Development: A Survey of Evidence', *International Labour Review*, 108(2): 97–125.

Ram, R. (1988) 'Economic Development and Income Inequality: Further Evidence on the U-curve Hypothesis', *World Development*, 16(11): 1371–6.

Ravallion, M. (2001) 'Growth, Inequality and Poverty: Looking Beyond Averages', *World Development*, 29(11): 1803–15. Reprinted in A. Shorrocks and R. van der Hoeven (eds) (2004), *Growth, Inequality and Poverty: Prospects for Pro-poor Economic Development* (Oxford: Oxford University Press for UNU-WIDER).

Ravallion, M. (2004) 'Pro-poor Growth: A Primer', Policy Research Working Paper 3242, World Bank, Washington, DC.

Ravallion, M. and Chen, S. (2003) 'Measuring Pro-poor Growth', *Economic Letters*, 78(1): 93–9.

Robinson, S. (1976) 'Sources of Growth in Less Developed Countries', *Quarterly Journal of Economics*, 85(3): 391–408.

Sen, A. (1976) 'Poverty: An Ordinal Approach to Measurement', *Econometrica*, 44: 219–31.

Son, H. H. (2003) *Pro-Poor Growth: Definitions and Measurements* (Washington, DC: World Bank).

Son, H. H. (2004) 'A Note on Pro-Poor Growth', *Economics Letters*, 82(3): 307–14.

Son, H. H. (2007) 'Interrelationship between Growth, Inequality and Poverty', The Asian Development Bank, Manila, unpublished paper.

United Nations (2000) *A Better World for All* (New York: United Nations).

Watts, H. (1968) 'An Economic Definition of Poverty', in D. P. Moynihan (ed.), *On Understanding Poverty* (New York: Basic Books).

Weinns, T. B. (1998) 'Agriculture and Rural Poverty in Vietnam', in D. Dollar, P. Glewwe and J. Litvack (eds), *Household Welfare and Vietnam's Transition* (Washington, DC: World Bank Regional and Sectoral Studies).

White, H. and E. Anderson (2001) 'Growth versus Distribution: Does the Pattern of Growth Matter?', Mimeo, IDS, Brighton.

World Bank (2000) *World Development Report 1990* (New York: Oxford University Press).

World Bank (2001) *Vietnam Living Standards Survey (VLSS), 1997–98: Basic Information* (Washington, DC: World Bank, Poverty and Human Resources Division).

3

How Does Vietnam's Accession to the World Trade Organization Change the Spatial Incidence of Poverty?

Tomoki Fujii and David Roland-Holst

Introduction

Trade liberalization is good for growth, and growth is good for the poor. This argument is simple but powerful. It has served as the departure point for a discussion of the link between trade and poverty among economists and policy-makers, regardless of whether and to what extent they buy this argument. Krueger (1998) considers the inefficiencies that import substitution strategy creates, and argues that trade liberalization undertaken at a period of low or negative growth rates can normally lead to a period of higher growth. Bhagwati and Srinivasan (2002) emphasize the empirical evidence of China and India. That is, these two giant economies achieved faster growth and poverty reduction through greater integration into the world economy. Dollar and Kraay (2002, 2004) use cross-country regression to support this argument.

However, there are also many researchers who have strong reservations about this argument, for at least two reasons. The first is methodological. Rodríguez and Rodrik (2001), for example, severely criticized earlier studies supporting this argument because either the measurement or the method was flawed. Ravallion (2001) points out that working with aggregate numbers can be misleading.

The second reason is the possibility of an adverse impact of trade liberalization on the poor. As pointed out by Winters (2002), there are a number of reasons why the poor may be affected adversely by trade liberalization. Important links include the change in prices of goods and services that poor households transact in relatively large amounts. Trade liberalization and poverty are also connected though government revenue and vulnerability of the economy to negative external shocks. Winters *et al.* (2004) provide an extensive survey of the relationship between trade liberalization and poverty. While they find no simple connection, the empirical evidence broadly supports the notion that trade liberalization alleviates poverty in the long run and on an average basis. Yet trade liberalization almost always creates winners and losers, and the losers may well include poor people.

Trade liberalization would be difficult to justify from the standpoint of poverty reduction if it affected this group adversely. This point is particularly important in a country where a substantial portion of the population lives below or close to the poverty line. Aggregate growth alone is not enough to justify trade liberalization policies, particularly if poverty might worsen. Governments may not want to forgo liberalization, but must choose carefully the right mixture of policies, and be ready to implement mitigating policies when necessary.

Some argue that it is indeed possible to do so. Using a computable general equilibrium (CGE) model with a detailed panel of households, Harrison *et al.* (2003) argue that trade liberalization in Turkey can be designed to ensure that the poor will not lose by using direct compensation to the losers, or by using limited policy reform. Their research is an improvement on previous work with very limited treatment of heterogeneity among households. However, making side payments for particular segments of households is not straightforward. As Harrison *et al.* (2003) noted, limited policy reform may induce rent-seeking.

In this study we consider geographical targeting as a way of directing progressively more resources to areas that are affected least favourably by trade liberalization. Geographical targeting has several advantages. It is easy to understand and straightforward to implement. The distortion caused by geographic targeting is usually considered to be small, because the cost of changing locations, especially for the poor, is often prohibitively high. Further, many countries already have some programmes targeted at poor areas. We only need to modify the set of areas to make a programme more efficient for poverty reduction, instead of implementing a new programme. Hence, given the pre-existence of such a programme, the political cost would also be relatively small.

Of course, the formulation of an effective policy of geographic targeting requires the knowledge of the changes in spatial distribution of the poor after market liberalization. Economic research has provided only limited guidance in this area, because socio-economic survey data with the high temporal and spatial resolution needed for poverty monitoring are usually unavailable. While policy-makers need information on the detailed incidence of trade liberalization, prior studies on these impacts were able to provide estimates only for a few representative household categories, very limited spatial decomposition or none at all.

To overcome the limitations of previous studies and elucidate more detailed incidence, we synthesize microsimulation, economy-wide CGE modelling, and small-area estimation in an application to Vietnam's World Trade Organization (WTO) accession. This new generation of analytical tools reveals the incidence of trade liberalization at an unprecedented level of microeconomic and spatial detail. The basic idea is straightforward: economy-wide CGE modelling allows us to find the impacts of trade liberalization on aggregate sectors, which in turn is translated by microsimulation into the impacts for households and individuals in the survey. We then use small-area estimation to find the impacts for small geographical areas.

We present our results in the form of maps, which help policy-makers to visualize the spatial impact of trade liberalization on the poor, facilitating the design and implementation of geographically-targeted assistance. The approach set out in this paper is readily applicable to other countries and can help to enlarge the scope of the benefits of trade liberalization across a wider variety of countries and populations. Our study sheds new light on the geographical properties of poverty. It also helps to resolve the conflicts between 'Finance Ministry' and 'Civil Society' orientations, as described by Kanbur (2001), by offering a solution in which all the relevant parties, including the poor, can enjoy the benefits of trade liberalization.

Trade liberalization and poverty in Vietnam

Since the introduction of *Doi Moi* (Renovation) in 1986 and further market-orientated reforms in 1989, most of the elements of Vietnam's centrally-planned trade regime had been removed by the early 1990s. These reform policies were extremely successful and resulted in very high growth rates of both output and exports. The reform continued generally through the late 1990s, and tariff measures associated with membership in the ASEAN Free Trade Area (AFTA) were implemented. Since then, the bilateral trade agreement between Vietnam and the USA in 2000 has given additional momentum to the reform process.

As standard economic theory would predict, trade liberalization has generally been beneficial to the overall Vietnamese economy and to its trading partners. Fukase and Martin (2000) estimate that aggregate Vietnamese welfare gains from the USA granting most-favoured-nation status would be about US$118 million annually, or about 1 per cent higher average real income per capita. Using a multisector CGE model, Heng and Gayathri (2004) predict that participation in the ASEAN–China Free Trade and the ASEAN–Japan Free Trade agreements will bring about positive and significant welfare gains to Vietnam. The CGE simulation of various trade liberalization policies by Fukase and Martin (2001) also suggests that a higher level of welfare can be achieved from more comprehensive liberalization. It is beyond dispute that market-orientated reforms have contributed to poverty reduction in Vietnam. Jenkins (2004) argues that improved employment brought about by the growth of exports is one potential way in which globalization has had a positive impact on poverty.

As part of its accession agreement, Vietnam has made substantial commitments to trade policy reforms. These include lowered import tariffs, reduced coverage of tariff rate quotas, removal of export subsidies and non-tariff barriers, the opening of some service sectors, compliance with the agreements of trade-related investment measures (TRIMs) and trade-related intellectual property rights (TRIPs). Further, the state-owned enterprises also need to be reformed.[1] Anderson (1999) argues that after the successful accession to the WTO, and given that some appropriate measures are taken, a number of broad-brush effects can be anticipated, including economic growth, expansion of agriculture and export-orientated light manufacturing, enhanced food security, more equitable income distribution, and increased government revenue.

However, the higher economic growth induced by further liberalization does not automatically imply reductions in poverty or inequality. Jensen and Tarp (2005), for example, predict that poverty will rise following a revenue-neutral lowering of trade taxes. Niimi *et al.* (2004) show that employment in the garment and textiles industries was affected adversely in the 1990s by trade policies. Liu (2001) analyses poverty and inequality in Vietnam by using the Vietnam Living Standards Surveys (VLSS) for 1992–3 and 1997–8. While Vietnam achieved a very rapid poverty reduction before the US bilateral trade agreement or WTO accessions, rural areas have lagged behind urban areas and inequality has increased slightly overall. Decomposition of inequality measures shows that urban–rural and regional differences have been the major source of rising national inequality over time.

Indeed, not everyone in Vietnam has benefited from the broad improvement in living standards, as indicated by results such as Litchfield and Justino (2004). Using the VLSS datasets, their regression model of the change in consumption suggests that there are large differences in household performance in different regions. Glewwe *et al.* (2002) also reported similar findings using the VLSS datasets.

One of the factors that had a significant effect on the probability of escaping poverty during the 1990s was location. Urban households, as well as households in the Red River Delta and the South-east, had a higher probability of escaping poverty.

Tarp *et al.* (2002) appraise the consequences of Vietnam's shifting import and export patterns, and argue that trade and other reforms will not realize their full potential for all Vietnamese households in the absence of deliberately corrective fiscal measures. Further, Le and Winters (2001) argue that there is an imbalance between aid that promotes economic growth and aid that directly targets the poor. They also argue that aid is not regionally directed in a manner conducive to poverty alleviation, and is urban-biased.

The above observations motivate us to examine the spatial dimension of trade policy incidence and its implications for poverty. Changes in the spatial distribution of poverty have some practical importance as well, because such changes alter the efficient geographical targeting scheme. However, previous studies gave little guidance about how to shift resources in response to a changing macroeconomic environment. In this study, we show which part of the country is least likely to benefit from trade liberalization. In addition to contributing Vietnamese evidence to the more general debate on globalization and poverty, these results provide guidance for those policy-makers who want to formulate geographical targeting policies for poverty reduction.

Data and measurement

We combine four different datasets in this study. First, the information required is a socio-economic dataset. We use the VLSS 1997–8 dataset, which contains a wide array of microeconomic data, such as information on housing, employment, household enterprises, income and asset holdings. The survey was conducted by Vietnam's General Statistical Office (GSO). The United Nations Development Programme (UNDP) and the Swedish International Development Cooperation Agency (Sida) provided financial assistance, whereas the World Bank provided technical assistance. The sample of VLSS 1997–8 is nationally representative and stratified into two groups, representing urban and rural areas. The number of households in the sample is 4,270 in rural areas and 1,730 in urban areas (World Bank, 2001).

Second, we used the 1999 Population and Housing Census. The census was carried out by the GSO, with financial and technical support from the United Nations Population Fund and UNDP. The census dataset contains individual-level information such as age, sex, education and occupation as well as household-level information such as housing characteristics and asset holdings. It also contains the employment status of each individual. We used a 33 per cent sample of the census, which contains records for every third household, organized by an administrative unit. The sample selection was made by GSO. The sample includes 5,553,811 households and 25,447,457 individuals.

Third, we use a compilation of geographical variables. These include elevation, precipitation, soil quality, sunshine duration and access to cities. Some of the variables are based on remotely sensed data, while others are mean values from community-level data. The geographical variables can be merged into the census and the survey via the administrative codes.

Finally, we use the 2000 Social Accounting Matrix (SAM) for Vietnam as a core building block of the CGE model, representing 97 production activities and commodities, 13 factors of production (labour and capital), 5 household types, and 94 international trading partners. The aggregated version of SAM includes aggregate wage incomes for 8 labour segments defined by male/female, skilled/unskilled and urban/rural. It also includes the non-wage household incomes for urban and rural areas.

Let us now briefly discuss the measurement of poverty. In the standard analysis of socio-economic survey data such as the VLSS, poor people are defined as those living in households whose per capita consumption is below the poverty line. Consumption has some advantages over other income measures and proxies. First, it is a money-metric measure and easy to interpret. Second, it does not vary in the short run, unlike income. Despite these advantages of consumption, however, we use the per capita income measure for the household. This is because we need to aggregate the information in the VLSS dataset in a way that is consistent with the SAM, and to allow the individuals in the microsimulation to switch their employment status. We shall come back to the details of this point in the next section.

To calculate the income measures, we first identified the employment status of all the individuals in the potential labour force. We regarded individuals aged between 15 and 64 who are not students or invalid as being part of the potential labour force. We then classified those in the potential labour force into the following three categories: (i) wage earners; (ii) self-employed; and (iii) not working. Wage earners are those who earn any wage income and do not engage in the household enterprise. Self-employed people are those who engage in at least one of their household enterprises. All the other people are defined as not working. Employment status data is available in both the census and survey datasets.

We calculated wage incomes for wage-earners, and non-wage household incomes for all the households, on an annual basis using the VLSS dataset. To find the non-wage household income, we calculated the sum of incomes from each household enterprise, asset incomes and transfers. We summed all the wage incomes in the household and non-wage household income, and divided by the household size to arrive at the per capita income measure. To remove seasonal and regional price variations, we apply the same price deflator as the one used to calculate consumption poverty.

It is useful to look at how income and consumption measures differ. Table 3.1 provides some summary statistics for the per capita consumption and income measures. The national-level mean of the per capita consumption is about 13 per cent lower than the corresponding figure for the per capita income, while the standard deviation for consumption is about half of that for income.

The comparison of columns 1 and 5 gives the differences in mean per capita income and consumption at the regional level, at which the VLSS is representative. The number of households and the population share of each region are reported in columns 9 and 10, respectively. At the regional level, income and consumption exhibit a very similar pattern and their

Table 3.1   Summary statistics of income and consumption measures

Column Region	1 Con.	2 (SE)	3 P_0^C	4 (SE)	5 Inc.	6 (SE)	7 P_0^I	8 (SE)	9 Obs	10 Share
Red River Delta	2938	(99)	28.7	(2.2)	3094	(188)	36.9	(2.3)	1175	19.6
North-east	1987	(94)	55.8	(4.9)	1860	(208)	57.4	(4.2)	731	15.0
North-west	1567	(85)	73.4	(4.9)	1599	(287)	54.2	(8.1)	128	2.8
North	2197	(89)	48.1	(4.2)	2122	(175)	47.5	(4.1)	708	13.8
South Central Coast	2648	(114)	34.5	(4.3)	3075	(322)	36.8	(4.7)	628	8.5
Central Highlands	1850	(241)	57.9	(9.4)	2191	(622)	52.4	(8.2)	276	2.8
South-east	4523	(189)	13.5	(3.2)	5860	(395)	15.2	(3.0)	1241	15.9
Mekong River Delta	2536	(87)	36.9	(2.4)	3218	(147)	29.7	(2.3)	1112	21.5
Vietnam	2764	(43)	37.4	(1.3)	3171	(85)	37.4	(1.4)	5999	100.0

Note: The standard errors are calculated by bootstrapping accounting for the strata, clustering and weights. Poverty rates, their associated standard errors and population share are expressed in percentages.

Source: Authors' calculations based on VLSS 1997–8.

correlation is higher than 0.98. Even at the individual level, the correlation is as high as 0.64.

We can also compare consumption-based poverty (P_0^C) and income-based poverty (P_0^I) measures. To make the consumption-based and income-based poverty measures comparable, we set the poverty line so that they have the same poverty rates of 37.4 per cent (see World Bank 2001). We set the poverty line at VND 3,452.06 per day per capita.[2]

The poverty rates are identical in construction, but there may be regional differences. This can be checked by looking at columns 3 and 7. It appears that the spatial distribution of income and consumption poverty are reasonably close, though there are two notable differences. First, in the Red River Delta, income poverty is much higher than consumption poverty, but on the other hand, in the Mekong River Delta region consumption poverty is much higher than income poverty. Overall, income and consumption measures show a similar pattern of spatial distribution, though income measure is on average a much noisier measure than consumption.

Methodology

Estimation of poverty and other economic indicators at the level of small geographical areas is generally constrained by the availability of representative data. In Vietnam, the VLSS data do not support reliable poverty measures even at the provincial level, because the sampling strata are more aggregated than provinces. However, the small area estimation (SAE) developed by Elbers *et al.* (2002, 2003) has enabled us to estimate measures of poverty and inequality reliably at a spatially disaggregated level.

The SAE approach typically combines survey and census data source. Consumption or income regression models are estimated with the survey data set. The regressors contain only the variables in the geographical dataset or the variables that also appear in the census dataset. The left-hand-side variable is then imputed to each census record and aggregated to obtain poverty and inequality measures of interest. Using a Monte Carlo simulation technique provided by Elbers *et al.* (2002, 2003), imputation and aggregation are done repeatedly to develop point estimates of poverty and inequality measures as well as their associated standard errors.

The SAE estimates of poverty rates are often plotted on a map, conventionally named a 'poverty map'. The poverty map is visually immediate and popular among policy-makers and other stakeholders. The SAE estimates can support geographical targeting policies to focus assistance on the neediest people. Such estimates can also be used to analyse the spatial relationship between poverty and geographical variables. In Vietnam, Minot (2000) created a poverty map using the 1992–3 VLSS and the Agricultural Census for 1994 with the probit model. Minot *et al.* (2003) have produced consumption-based small-area estimates of poverty and inequality using the 1997–8 VLSS and the Population Census for 1999.

Although the SAE estimates are useful, limitations remain. Since existing SAE techniques can only generate static maps, they do not reveal how the poverty map will change as a result of the changing macroeconomic environment. Hence, the geographical targeting policy based on the static SAE estimates may be inappropriate after Vietnam's accession to the WTO. To overcome the static nature of poverty mapping, this study combines the SAE method with an integrated microsimulation-CGE model.

This chapter uses a CGE approach to elucidating linkages between trade and poverty, and joins a large and growing literature on this subject. Beginning with Adelman and Robinson's (1978) work on Korean growth in the 1970s, CGEs have found application to trade, growth and poverty issues in scores of developing countries. A complete survey of these contributions is outside the scope of this paper, but readers can find an extensive set of applications as well as literature synthesis in a recent volume by Hertel and Winters (2006).

The present approach represents a recent line of CGE techniques that integrate traditional economy-wide models with microeconomic simulation methods calibrated to household survey and census data. This increases the resolution of economic analysis significantly and captures essential structural heterogeneity. Integrated microsimulation-CGE methods were first proposed by Bourguignon *et al.* (2005). They apply their method to analyse the impact of a change in the foreign trade balance before the Asian financial crisis in

Indonesia. Unlike standard CGE models, an integrated microsimulation-CGE model explicitly takes into account detailed heterogeneity among households and linkages between different sectors of the economy. It can be used to analyse a range of national–level policies, such as trade and taxation, as well as macroeconomic shocks.

While the integrated microsimulation-CGE model allows us to identify heterogeneous impacts of trade liberalization, it provides policy-makers with little useful information to support geographical targeting after, or in co-ordination with, trade policy. This is because the spatial disaggregation of the SAM is usually very limited, and thus the CGE model allows for very limited spatial disaggregation. It is only by embedding the SAE method in an integrated microsimulation-CGE model that we can adequately represent the spatial distribution of poverty after trade liberalization and in response to complementary policies.[3]

As noted earlier, for the present discussion we use per capita household income as a measure of welfare. We find a scaling factor for each segment of the economy so that non-wage household income, individual wages and labour supply in the survey sum to the corresponding macroeconomic figures in the CGE. Formally, this is equivalent to solving for scaling factors SC in the following equations:

$$WGI_l = SC_l^{WGI} \sum_{\{(h,i):f(h,i)=l\}} \mathbf{w}_{hi} \tag{3.1}$$

$$NWI_m = SC_m^{NWI} \sum_{\{h:g(h)=m\}} \mathbf{y}_h \tag{3.2}$$

$$TNW_l = SC_l^{TNW} \sum_{\{(h,i):f(h,i)=l\}} \mathbf{IW}_{hi} \tag{3.3}$$

$$TNS_l = SC_l^{TNS} \sum_{\{(h,i):f(h,i)=l\}} \mathbf{IS}_{hi} \tag{3.4}$$

In Equations (3.1)–(3.4), the subscript l is the labour segment, a combination of skilled/unskilled, male/female and urban/rural. The subscript m represents the household segment, which is urban/rural. The left-hand-side variables WGI, NWI, TNW and TNS are aggregate wage income, non-wage income, the total number of wage earners and total number of self-employed individuals in the SAM. $\mathbf{w}$, $\mathbf{y}$, $\mathbf{IW}$ and $\mathbf{IS}$ are, respectively, the individual wage income, non-wage household income, indicator variable for being a wage-earner, and indicator variable for being a self-employed individual. The function $f(h,i)$ maps the individual i in household h to the labour segment to which the individual belongs. The function $g(\cdot)$ maps household h to an urban or rural area.[4]

To elucidate the spatial incidence of trade liberalization, we first estimate poverty measures for small areas before trade liberalization. This step is conceptually similar to the standard SAE approach. The difference is that we use multiple equations for this estimation. We assume that **w**, **y**, **IW** and **IS** are related to individual or household characteristics through the following equations:

$$\log \mathbf{w}_{hi} = \alpha_{g(h,i)} + \mathbf{x}_{hi}\,\beta_{g(h,i)} + \mu_{hi} \tag{3.5}$$

$$\log \mathbf{y}_h = \gamma_{f(h)} + \mathbf{z}_h \delta_{f(h)} + \mathbf{S}_h \lambda_{f(h)} + \eta_h \tag{3.6}$$

$$\mathbf{IW}_{hi} = \mathrm{Ind}\!\left(a^w_{g(h,i)} + \mathbf{v}_{hi} b^w_{g(h,i)} + u^w_{hi} > \sup\!\left(u^n_{hi},\, a^s_{g(h,i)} + \mathbf{v}_{hi} b^s_{g(h,i)} + u^s_{hi} \right)\right) \tag{3.7}$$

$$\mathbf{IS}_{hi} = \mathrm{Ind}\!\left(a^s_{g(h,i)} + \mathbf{v}_{hi} b^s_{g(h,i)} + u^s_{hi} > \sup\!\left(u^n_{hi},\, a^w_{g(h,i)} + \mathbf{v}_{hi} b^w_{g(h,i)} + u^w_{hi} \right)\right) \tag{3.8}$$

$$\mathbf{S}_h \equiv \sum_{i \in \mathcal{I}_h} \mathbf{IS}_{hi} \tag{3.9}$$

$$\mathbf{H}_h \equiv \frac{1}{\mathbf{N}_h}\left(\mathbf{y}_h + \sum_{i:i\in\mathcal{I}_h,\,\mathbf{IW}_{hi}=1} \mathbf{w}_{hi} \right) \tag{3.10}$$

In Equation (3.5), individual logarithmic wage is related to individual characteristics $\mathbf{x}_{hi}$.[5] In Equation (3.6), logarithmic household non-wage income is related to household characteristics $\mathbf{z}_h$ and the number of self-employed individuals in the household $\mathbf{S}_h$.

Labour supply is modelled by Equations (3.7) and (3.8), where individual characteristics $\mathbf{v}_{hi}$ are related to the 'utility' from being a wage-earner and self-employed. u^n_{hi} can be considered as the random reservation utility for working. We assume that the error terms μ_{hi}, η_h, u^w_{hi}, u^s_{hi} and u^n_{hi} are independent. Furthermore, we assume that μ_{hi} follows a normal distribution with mean zero and variance σ^2_μ, and η_h a normal distribution with mean zero and variance σ^2_η. We also assume that u^w_{hi}, u^s_{hi} and u^n_{hi} follow an identical Gumbel distribution.

Equation (3.9) simply states that the number of self-employed is the sum of $\mathbf{IS}_{hi}$ over the set of individuals $\mathcal{I}_h$ within household h. The per capita household income $\mathbf{H}_h$ is, of course, the sum of wage and non-wage income earned by the household members divided by the household size $\mathbf{N}_h$, as it is defined in Equation (3.10).

As with the standard SAE, we consider the above equations as a predictive model, using a rich set of regressors to explain the variation of left-hand-side variables in Equations (3.5), (3.6), (3.7) and (3.8). However, regressors can only include the variables shared by the census and the survey.

We first estimate the parameters of the equations above. Only the survey data set is used at this stage. We run OLS to estimate Equations (3.5) and (3.6), whereas we use a multinomial logit model to jointly estimate Equations (3.7) and (3.8). Therefore, we estimate the regression coefficients α, β, γ, δ, λ, a^w, a^s, b^w and b^s and their associated variance–covariance matrix adjusted for the clustering of the survey sample. We also estimate the distribution parameters σ_μ^2 and σ_η^2. We shall denote the estimates with a hat (for example, $\hat{\alpha}$).

As with Elbers *et al.* (2003), we estimate left-hand-side variables in Equations (3.5)–(3.10) for each census record repeated by a Monte Carlo simulation. To allow for the error in the estimated regression coefficients, we draw regression coefficients from a multinomial normal distribution in each round of the simulation. We shall denote the drawn coefficients by superscript (r) to specify the rth round of the simulation. In addition, we draw error terms for each census record. For example, the estimate of wage income $\hat{\mathbf{w}}_{hi}^{(r)}$ for (census) household h and individual i in the rth round is calculated as follows:

$$
\hat{\mathbf{w}}_{hi}^{(r)} = \exp\left(\hat{\alpha}_{g(h,i)}^{(r)} + \mathbf{x}_{hi}\hat{\beta}_{g(h,i)}^{(r)} + \hat{\mu}_{hi}^{(r)} \right) \tag{3.11}
$$

where $\mathbf{x}_{hi}$ comes from the census data set and $\hat{\mu}_{hi}^{(r)}$ is drawn from the normal distribution with mean zero and variance $\hat{\sigma}_\mu^2$. Note that we know the employment status of each individual in the census and thus we observe IW_{hi} and IS_{hi}. However, we still need to draw $\hat{u}_{hi}^{w,(r)}$, $\hat{u}_{hi}^{s,(r)}$ and $\hat{u}_{hi}^{n,(r)}$ for the later simulation. We can draw $\hat{u}_{hi}^{n,(r)}$ from the Gumbel distribution. $\hat{u}_{hi}^{w,(r)}$ and $\hat{u}_{hi}^{s,(r)}$ must be drawn conditionally on the observed dummy variables for the employment status IW_{hi}, IS_{hi} as well as the drawn error term $\hat{u}_{hi}^{n,(r)}$ in order to be consistent with the observed employment status.

It is straightforward to impute household non-wage income using Equation (3.6). By Equation (3.10), we get an estimate of the per capita household income $\hat{\mathbf{H}}_h^{(r)}$. We can then obtain aggregate welfare measures such as the FGT measure of poverty; see Foster *et al.* (1984). Letting $\mathscr{H}_p$ be the set of households in province p, and z be the poverty line, the head count poverty rate $P_p^{(r)}$ in province p for the rth simulation can be written as follows:

$$
P_p^{(r)} = \frac{\sum_{h\in\mathscr{H}_p} \text{Ind}\left(\hat{\mathbf{H}}_h^{(r)} < z \right)\cdot \mathbf{N}_h}{\sum_{h\in\mathscr{H}_p} \mathbf{N}_h} \tag{3.12}
$$

Taking the average and standard deviation across simulations, we arrive at the point estimate of poverty rate for province p and its associated standard error. The aggregate welfare estimates derived in this manner serve as the baseline information for each province or any geographical units. We shall refer to the poverty estimates before the trade liberalization created in this way as the *ex ante* poverty estimates.

The next step is to simulate how much change would occur across different sectors of the economy. As with Bourguignon *et al.* (2005), we need to find error terms for each survey record. It is straightforward to find μ_{hi} and η_h, because they are just the observed value minus the predicted value. When the wage data is missing, μ is drawn from the normal distribution. We also draw $\hat{u}_{hi}^w$, $\hat{u}_{hi}^s$ and $\hat{u}_{hi}^n$ from a Gumbel distribution in a way that is consistent with the observed employment status. Therefore, combining Equations (3.1)–(3.4) and Equations (3.5)–(3.8), we have the following relationship:

$$WGI_l = SC_l^{WGI} \sum_{\{(h,i):g(h,i)=l\}} \exp\left(\hat{\alpha}_l + \mathbf{x}_{hi}\hat{\beta}_l + \hat{\mu}_{hi} \right)$$

$$NWI_m = SC_m^{NWI} \sum_{\{h:f(h)=m\}} \exp\left(\hat{\gamma}_m + \mathbf{z}_h\hat{\delta}_m + \mathbf{S}_h\hat{\lambda}_m + \hat{\eta}_h \right)$$

$$TNW_l = SC_l^{TNW} \sum_{\{(h,i):g(h,i)=l\}} \mathrm{Ind}\left(\hat{a}_l^w + \mathbf{v}_{hi}\hat{b}_l^w + \hat{u}_{hi}^w > \sup\left(\hat{u}_{hi}^n, \hat{a}_l^s + \mathbf{v}_{hi}\hat{b}_l^s + \hat{u}_{hi}^s \right) \right)$$

$$TNS_l = SC_l^{TNS} \sum_{\{(h,i):g(h,i)=l\}} \mathrm{Ind}\left(\hat{a}_l^s + \mathbf{v}_{hi}\hat{b}_l^s + \hat{u}_{hi}^s > \sup\left(\hat{u}_{hi}^n, \hat{a}_l^w + \mathbf{v}_{hi}\hat{b}_l^w + \hat{u}_{hi}^w \right) \right)$$

The macroeconomic CGE provides us with aggregate wage and non-wage household incomes in each segment of the economy, as well as the aggregate labour supply from wage-earners and self-employed individuals. In other words, we obtain the aggregate macroeconomic account after the trade liberalization, which we shall denote with tilde (for example $\widetilde{WGI}_l$). To maintain the consistency between the left-hand side and the right-hand side of the system of equations shown above, we need to change at least one of the parameters in each equation. Following the method outlined by Bourguignon *et al.* (2005), we assume that the macroeconomic changes are channelled through the intercepts in the above equations. Bourguignon *et al.* (2005) show that this assumption implies a neutrality of the change with regard to individual or household characteristics. For example, the ratio of wages in the same labour segment will not be altered before and after the trade liberalization. Similarly, the relative change in the probability that an individual has a certain occupation depends only on the initial *ex ante* probability of the various occupational choices, and not on individual characteristics. The problem we face is therefore equivalent to solving for the adjustment coefficients $\Delta\alpha$, $\Delta\gamma$, Δa^w and Δa^s which are the difference in the *ex ante* and *ex post* intercepts in the following equations:

$$WGI_l = SC_l^{WGI} \sum_{\{(h,i):g(h,i)=l\}} \exp\left(\Delta\alpha_l + \hat{\alpha}_l + \mathbf{x}_{hi}\hat{\beta}_l + \hat{\mu}_{hi} \right) \tag{3.13}$$

$$NWI_m = SC_m^{NWI} \sum_{\{h:f(h)=m\}} \exp\left(\Delta\gamma_m + \hat{\gamma}_m + \mathbf{z}_h\hat{\delta}_m + \mathbf{S}_h\hat{\lambda}_m + \hat{\eta}_h \right) \tag{3.14}$$

$$TNW_l = SC_l^{TNW} \sum_{\{(h,i):g(h,i)=l\}} \mathrm{Ind}\Big(\Delta a_l^w + \hat{a}_l^w + \mathbf{v}_{hi}\hat{b}_l^w + \hat{u}_{hi}^w$$

$$> \sup\Big(\hat{u}_{hi}^n, \Delta a_l^s + \hat{a}_l^s + \mathbf{v}_{hi}\hat{b}_l^s + \hat{u}_{hi}^s \Big)\Big) \tag{3.15}$$

$$TNS_l = SC_l^{TNS} \sum_{\{(h,i):g(h,i)=l\}} \mathrm{Ind}\Big(\Delta a_l^s + \hat{a}_l^s + \mathbf{v}_{hi}\hat{b}_l^s + \hat{u}_{hi}^s$$

$$> \sup\Big(\hat{u}_{hi}^n, \Delta a_l^w + \hat{a}_l^w + \mathbf{v}_{hi}\hat{b}_l^w + \hat{u}_{hi}^w \Big)\Big) \tag{3.16}$$

After finding the adjustment coefficients, we can again impute individual wage income, the 'utility' of each individual, and the non-wage household income. This time, however, we include the adjustment coefficients. For example, we replace $\hat{\alpha}_l^{(r)}$ by $\Delta\alpha_l + \hat{\alpha}_l^{(r)}$ in Equation (3.11). It should be noted by that the *ex post* employment status may be different from the observed *ex ante* employment status, which in turn affects the non-wage household income. Once we have the individual wage income and non-wage household income, we can calculate the per capita income for each census household as well as the poverty status in each round of the simulation. By aggregating geographically, we can obtain the poverty estimates after trade liberalization, or the *ex post* poverty estimates.

Results

Macroeconomic CGE

For economy-wide analysis, a macroeconomic CGE for Vietnam was calibrated to the new 2000 Vietnam SAM for a 'business as usual' baseline. This reference scenario was then used to evaluate comparative static experiments provided by GTAP global liberalization results. To implement the latter, we obtained data from GTAP on induced price and external demand changes for the purpose of re-calibrating Vietnamese exports against downward-sloping external demand functions. Finally, we assume the so-called Hertel–Keeney medium-run closure. That is, all factors are fully employed before and after experiments, and labour and capital are mobile across sectors, but we maintain a specific factor (land) in agriculture. There is no imperfect competition, and no economies of scale or dynamic gains from trade (Hertel 1997).

In this chapter, we compare three counterfactual scenarios to the baseline, which we call Unilateral Liberalization (UL), Full Liberalization (FL) and Doha Special and Differential Treatment (DSDT).[6] The baseline scenario corresponds to the *ex ante* case. In the UL scenario, we assume that Vietnam's last offer to the WTO is accepted, and the country joins the organization. We assume that Vietnam removes all import tariffs and export subsidies. However, Vietnam's trading partners maintain baseline protection levels with respect to this country, and all others. In this case, the benefits of fuller participation in the international economy are severely limited by Vietnam's inability to penetrate new markets, and the gains of domestic price reform have more limited impact on the growth of income.

The FL scenario includes the same external policy, but embeds this into a larger agenda. This scenario is calibrated to protection rates from the Vietnamese WTO offer, but further assumes that Vietnamese export prices and demand patterns shift according to consensus estimates for a FL scenario obtained using the GTAP database and model. This scenario would greatly expand export opportunities for Vietnam, allowing it to take fuller advantage of efficiency gains arising from border price reforms. In the DSDT scenario, we also assume that Vietnam removes all exports subsidies, but it preserves the Special and Differential Treatment of developing countries. As such, domestic support and tariffs are reduced but not eliminated.

Aggregate comparative static results for these counterfactuals are presented in Table 3.2. In terms of aggregate growth, these scenarios are generally consistent with intuition. In particular, FL is the biggest stimulus to Vietnam, followed by UL and DSDT. Real GDP rises moderately under the UL and FL scenarios, but declines slightly under the DSDT scenario. FL also brings about a higher level of real consumption than do UL and DSDT. This is not only a result of greater trade stimulus but also of improved terms of trade. At the other extreme, removing export support in the DSDT scenario induces an adverse terms of trade effect, making Vietnam exporters less competitive, and more than offsetting efficiency gains from tariff removal. Given existing distortions elsewhere in the trading system, a piecemeal approach such as DSDT would be inferior to even the status quo.

Our CGE results show that textiles, technology and machinery sectors expand significantly, accompanied by construction, and trade and transport services, while the agricultural sector remains prominent, as shown in Table 3.3. More fundamentally, these results begin to reveal the mechanisms

Table 3.2 Changes in aggregate indices from the macroeconomic CGE under various scenarios

Scenario	UL	FL	DSDT
Real GDP	3.97	5.31	−0.27
GDP at factor cost	3.69	12.90	−1.23
GDP at market prices	−2.81	5.81	−1.25
Real consumption	7.02	10.71	−0.47
Imports	16.46	27.54	−1.28
Exports	14.02	20.53	−0.82
Consumer price index	−5.62	−1.33	−0.61
Terms of trade	−2.89	2.18	−0.74

Note: The numbers are expressed in percentages.

by which external liberalization can affect poverty and inequality in Vietnam. Like many developing countries, Vietnam's poor majority are farmers living at or near subsistence level. Their assets are generally limited to labour, small land holdings of uncertain quality, and livestock. In the Asian context, external liberalization has generally provided the most direct growth impetus to urban populations through expansion of light, intermediate and heavy industrial activities. The majority of the rural poor have two channels through which they can participate in urban-based growth – migration, and the marketing of food products. The comparative static model used here does not model the former, so we confine our attention to changing income opportunities.

The sectoral results of Table 3.3 presage our subsequent poverty analysis. The most important difference between the scenarios in this context has to do with food prices and domestic output responses. Under the UL scenario, food prices are suppressed by import liberalization, and farmers suffer both directly and indirectly. In the case of FL, all primary food prices rise, and farm output and income respond accordingly. Clearly, a low-income, agrarian country such as Vietnam needs to see significant agricultural returns from any multilateral trade agreement if its poor rural majority are to benefit in the short or medium term.

Changes in poverty rates after trade liberalization

As noted in the previous section, our analysis starts by looking at the spatial distribution of poverty under the baseline (*ex ante*) scenario. We estimated relevant parameters in Equations (3.5)–(3.8) using the VLSS data set.

For Equation (3.5), we simply ran OLS for each wage-earner of the 8 labour segments to find coefficients. The R^2 statistic varied between 0.24 and 0.42,

Table 3.3 Baseline sectoral output US$ millions for the year 2000, and changes in sectoral output and prices (percentages)

Sector scenario	Baseline output	Change in output			Change in price		
		UL	FL	DSDT	UL	FL	DSDT
Rice	105,145	1.11	4.50	0.05	−0.80	8.54	−0.76
Raw rubber	2,442	−1.44	9.42	0.37	0.19	15.23	−0.54
Coffee beans	7,262	1.96	−5.02	−0.64	−0.55	1.32	−1.18
Sugar cane	2,911	0.45	6.86	−0.69	−1.74	12.96	−1.61
Other crops	35,761	0.43	−0.58	−0.18	−0.09	5.54	−1.09
Pigs	13,687	3.55	5.75	−0.33	−1.08	5.19	−0.94
Cattle	1,107	4.18	6.80	−0.25	−1.11	5.19	−0.88
Poultry	6,116	1.01	1.57	−0.10	0.70	8.10	−1.07
Other livestock	5,242	4.84	10.43	−0.09	−2.11	3.72	−0.81
Irrigation services	1,277	1.35	3.24	−0.13	−1.61	3.72	−0.78
Other agr. services	4,839	1.24	4.00	−0.04	−2.23	2.73	−0.71
Forestry	7,717	1.68	0.11	0.20	−0.07	5.34	−0.83
Fisheries	26,000	6.57	2.94	−1.77	−2.81	1.59	−0.82
Energy	57,461	−3.29	−7.80	0.91	−3.27	0.21	−0.57
Mining	3,529	0.25	−4.72	0.54	−1.20	3.22	−0.66
Meat	2,883	1.45	−1.09	0.26	−1.45	5.31	−1.11
Dairy products	4,815	−1.59	24.47	3.78	−5.76	−4.10	−1.01
Fruits and vegetables	1,739	−2.46	−0.77	−0.28	−1.65	3.34	−0.83
Refined sugar	6,794	0.26	7.93	−0.80	−0.90	8.30	−1.09
Coffee and tea beverages	1,538	1.80	1.79	−0.95	−1.15	3.39	−0.90
Other bev. and tobacco	21,428	−12.24	−12.32	−0.38	−4.11	0.83	−0.79
Seafood	20,412	6.79	−6.94	−3.11	−4.96	−0.61	−0.68
Animal feed	4,219	−9.29	−11.39	0.10	−2.89	2.31	−0.76
Other processed foods	19,521	−4.80	−6.18	−0.56	−3.10	1.88	−0.72
Building materials	36,658	2.27	1.72	−0.04	−1.77	3.08	−0.74
Industrial chemicals	24,785	0.23	10.42	0.48	−2.84	−1.06	−0.46
Agro chemicals	5,909	−5.35	−10.80	1.08	−2.55	0.36	−0.47
Tech manufacturing	6,184	29.04	14.74	4.52	−8.19	−5.59	−0.65
Vehicles	29,836	−32.79	−32.02	0.37	−15.52	−13.69	−0.43
Machinery	14,014	8.71	9.91	1.60	−6.74	−5.32	−0.39
Metals	18,976	3.41	1.20	0.66	−5.10	−3.09	−0.31
Textiles and apparel	58,078	38.19	67.32	−4.25	−17.09	−16.17	0.01
Other industry	20,574	−2.29	−5.76	0.82	−8.61	−6.13	−0.42
Utilities	19,061	2.46	3.21	−0.14	−0.26	5.63	−0.84
Construction	84,600	4.62	10.31	−0.83	−3.08	0.64	−0.56
Trade and transport	94,185	6.75	10.02	−0.53	−3.38	1.80	−0.77
Private service	101,236	3.16	2.52	−0.21	−0.97	4.03	−0.70
Public service	56,309	1.63	0.27	0.18	−2.54	2.13	−0.68

depending on the labour segment. For Equation (3.6), we ran OLS of logarithmic non-wage income for both urban and rural areas, capturing about 35 per cent and 38 per cent of variations, respectively. There are about 1.2 per cent of households with no non-wage income, and these were excluded from the estimation. Multinomial logit regressions were run to estimate Equations (3.7) and (3.8) for each labour segment. We were able to predict 73 per cent of the individuals correctly after applying the relevant weights. Detailed estimation results are reported in the Appendix on page 71.

The macroeconomic CGE results also gives us the aggregate wage income for each combination of skilled/unskilled, male/female and urban/rural as well as the non-wage income for rural and urban households. This allows us to calculate the adjustment coefficients by solving Equations (3.13)–(3.16). The adjustment coefficients for each scenario are also reported in the Appendix.

We first imputed the household income for each census record for each round of the Monte Carlo simulation without applying the adjustment coefficients. We then calculated poverty rates for each province using Equation (3.12) and plotted them on a map, as shown in Figure 3.1, which we shall call the baseline map. The maximum, minimum and average standard error for the provincial-level estimates of poverty rate were 11.6 per cent, 0.4 per cent and 2.1 per cent, respectively. Thus, while there are a few provinces with quite high levels of standard errors, provincial-level estimates are on average accurate enough to justify this presentation.

To see how our estimates correspond to others in the literature, we first calculated the poverty rate for Vietnam. The point estimate and its associated standard error were 34.6 per cent and 0.7 per cent, respectively. The difference between this estimate and the survey-only estimate is not significant. However, the gap is not as small as one would usually find in the standard small-area estimation. This is possibly because we need to estimate many more equations than does the standard method. We also plotted, in Figure 3.2, the provincial-level estimates of our income poverty rates against the provincial-level consumption poverty rates calculated by Minot *et al.* (2003). There is a moderately strong correlation between the two measures with the correlation coefficient of 0.4. Overall, our baseline estimates of poverty seem reasonable.

In order to see how income poverty changes after Vietnam's accession to the WTO under various scenarios, we applied the adjustment coefficients and recalculated the household income for each census household and for each scenario. Then, we recalculated the poverty rates for each province. This yields *ex post* estimates of poverty. The *ex post* estimates of poverty in Vietnam have decreased by 0.8 per cent and 6.8 per cent under the UL and FL scenarios, respectively. However, under the DSDT scenarios, the national poverty rate increased by 0.6 per cent. Again, we see that the FL helps the most in reducing poverty.

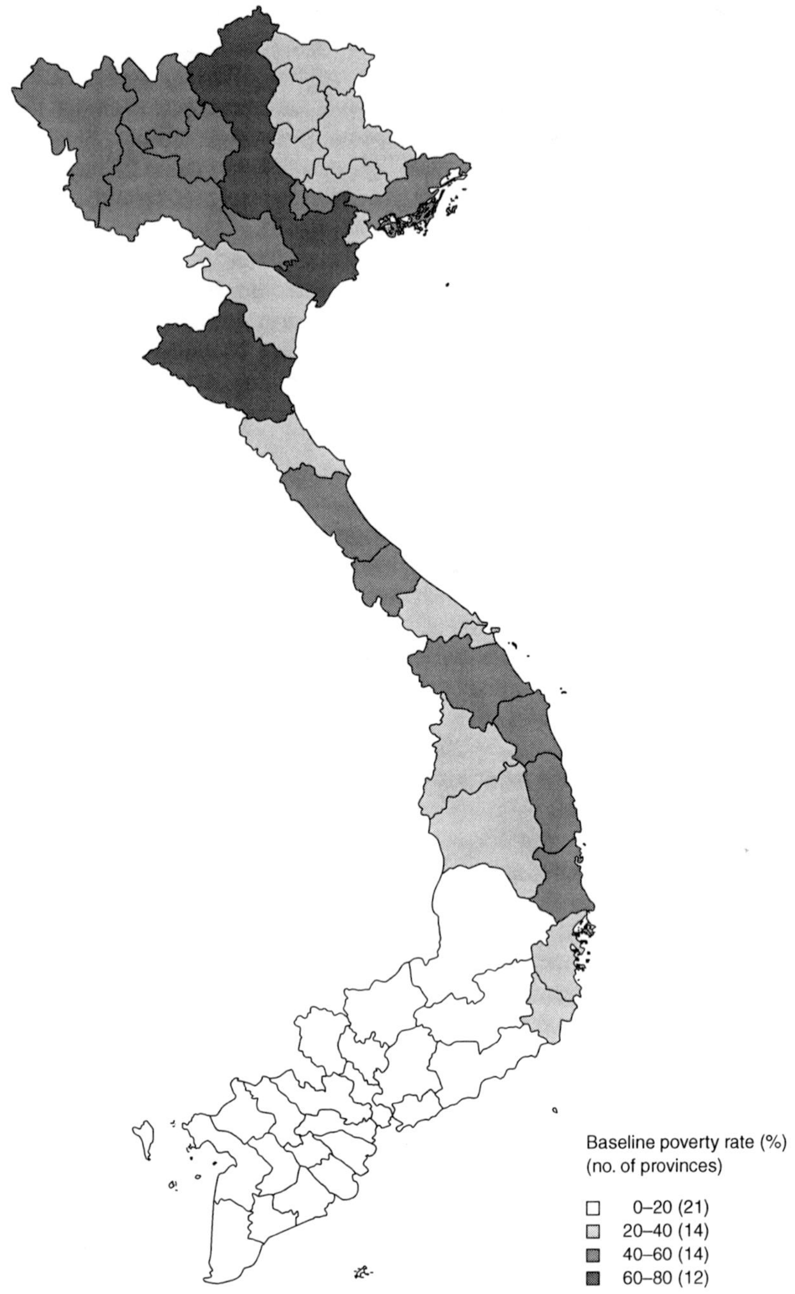

Figure 3.1   Baseline income poverty map, Vietnam

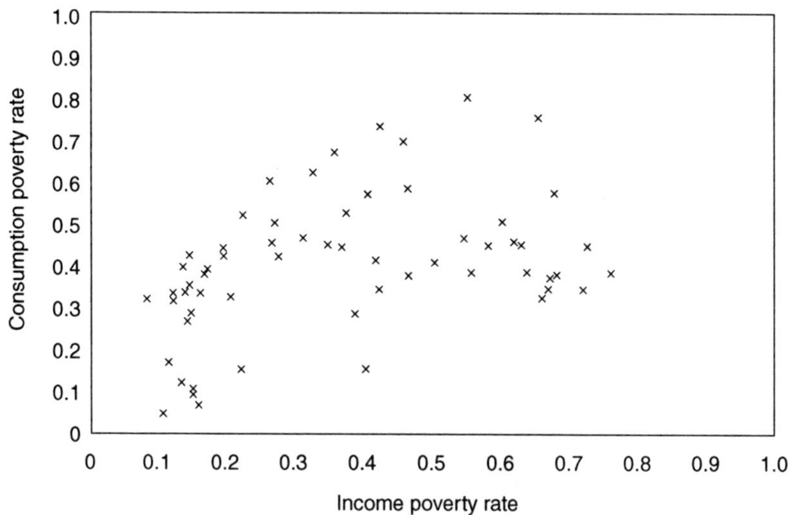

Figure 3.2 Scatter plot for provincial-level income poverty versus consumption poverty

Source: Authors' calculations and Minot *et al.* (2003).

We also looked at changes in poverty rates at the provincial level. Figure 3.3 shows the spatial incidence of trade policy under the UL scenario. Figures 3.4 and 3.5 are for the FL and DSDT scenarios, respectively. In each map, the lighter colours represent higher levels of improvement or lower levels of aggravation in terms of the provincial-level poverty rate. In other words, the lighter colours gain relatively more beneficial impacts from trade liberalization.

Three salient points deserve emphasis here. First, the magnitude of the impact of trade policy on poverty can vary quite substantially across the country. Under the FL scenario, one province achieves a 14.3 per cent reduction in headcount poverty, while another only achieves a 2.4 per cent reduction. This difference is adducible to differences in the initial distribution of income, as well as heterogeneity in the composition of households and individuals. Under the UL and DSDT scenarios, spatial differences in absolute terms are much smaller, because the changes in aggregates are also smaller.

Second, the trade liberalization appears to be consistent with poverty reduction overall. The correlations between the *ex ante* poverty rates and the changes in poverty after trade liberalization at the provincial level are –0.26, –0.71 and –0.60 for the UL, FL and DSDT scenarios. This suggests that

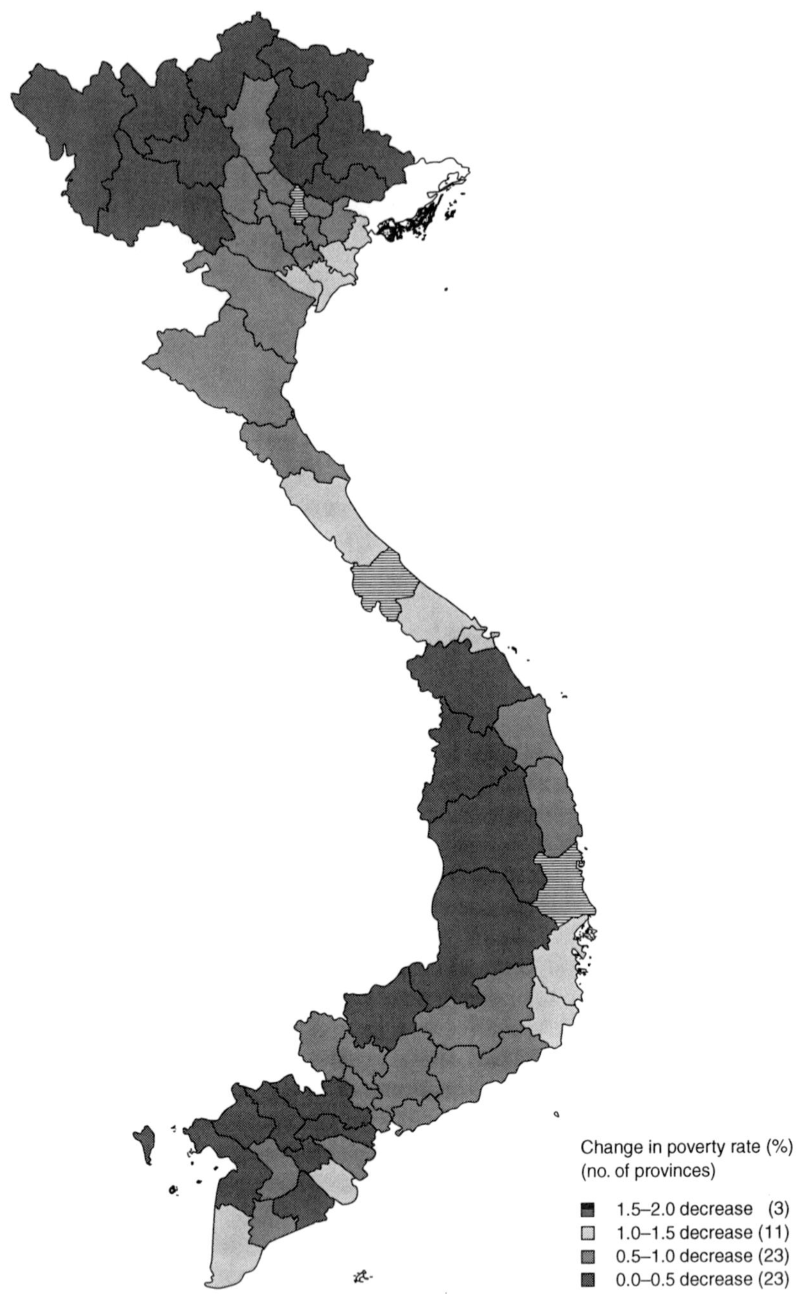

Figure 3.3   The change in provincial-level poverty rates under the UL scenario, Vietnam

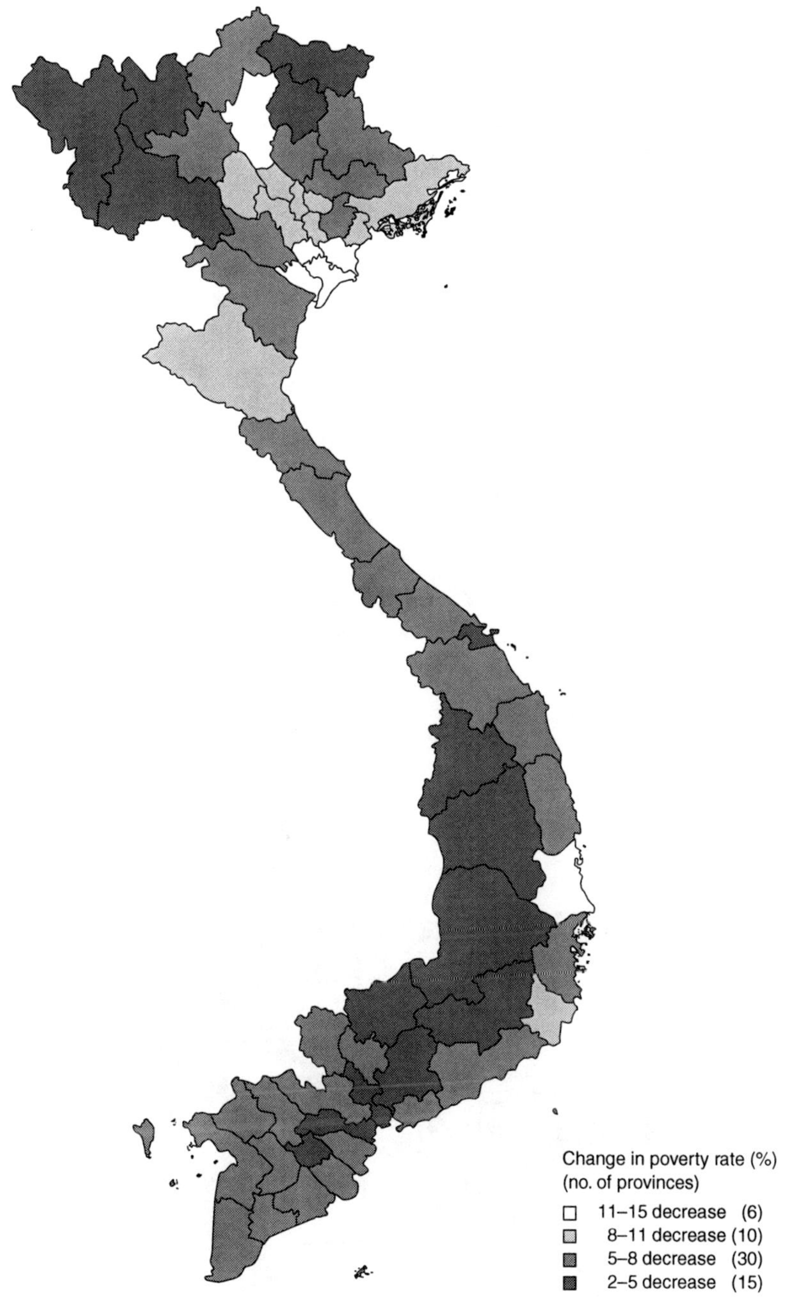

Figure 3.4   The change in provincial-level poverty rates under the FL scenario, Vietnam

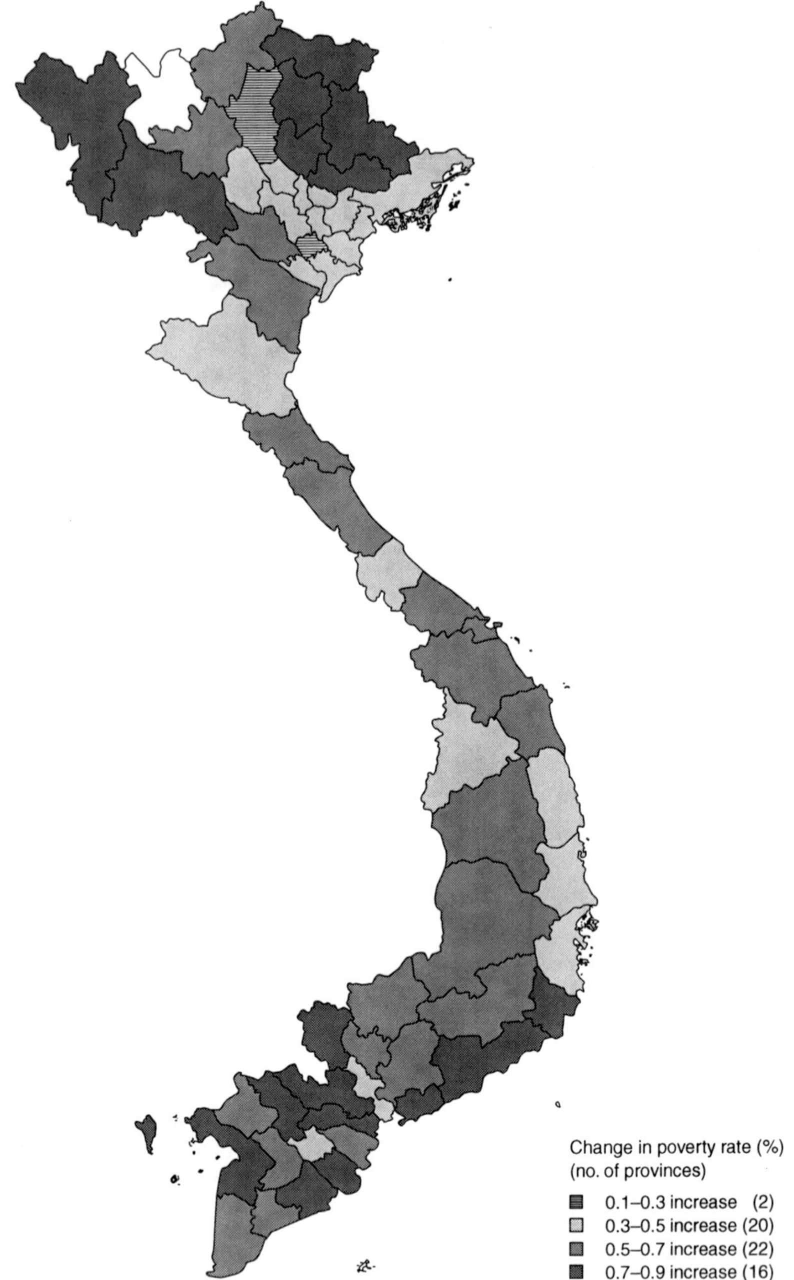

Figure 3.5   The change in provincial-level poverty rates under the DSDT scenario, Vietnam

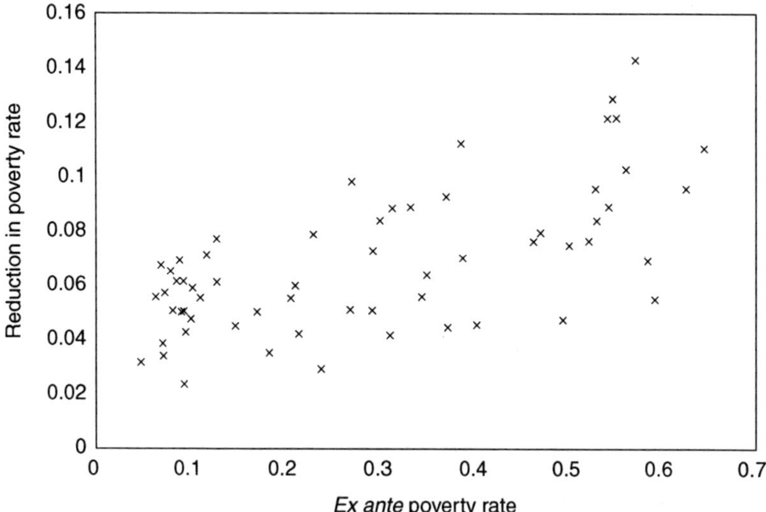

Figure 3.6   *Ex ante* poverty rate versus reduction in poverty rate at the provincial level (N = 61)

the FL scenario not only achieves the largest poverty reduction among all the scenarios, but also helps the most impoverished areas. This point may be seen more clearly from Figure 3.6. This plots the *ex ante* poverty rate against the change in poverty rate under the FL scenario. It shows that the reductions in poverty rate are generally higher for the areas that are poor *ex ante*. On the other hand, the change in poverty rates varies substantially among the provinces with similar *ex ante* poverty rates.

The third point to note is that the spatial pattern is similar across all the scenarios considered. We generally see a greater improvement (or less adversity in the case of the DSDT scenario) in poverty along the coastal areas, whereas the north-west of Vietnam and the areas along the border between Laos and Vietnam will not see much improvement. On the other hand, the lagging north-western provinces are of particular concern, because the poverty rates there are already high. It might therefore be desirable to target this region for further assistance.

So far, we have ignored changes in consumer prices. To account for this, we divided the poverty line by the *ex post* consumer price index. This treatment is rudimentary because we cannot capture potential differences in the changes in consumer prices across the country. However, we can estimate the magnitude of price effects in aggregate terms. If we account for the changes in the consumer prices, there will be additional real benefits of 1.4 per cent and 0.3 per cent, respectively, for the UL and FL scenarios in poverty reduction. Under the DSDT scenario, the increase in poverty rate will be reduced to just 0.4 per cent.

Conclusion

This study explored the spatial dimension of poverty associated with Vietnam's accession to the WTO. While Vietnam as a whole is likely to benefit from the accession, the degree and spatial composition of poverty reduction across the country is more ambiguous. The main constraint in this context is estimating the spatial incidence of structural adjustments arising from trade liberalization. By combining the integrated microsimulation-CGE model with the small-area estimation technique, we were able to overcome this constraint.

Our simulation results show that aggregate poverty will decrease when Vietnam removes all import tariffs and export subsidies. The amount of improvement will be even larger when other countries also remove tariffs against Vietnamese products. On the other hand, the DSDT scenario leads to a slight increase in poverty.

As Figures 3.3–3.5 show, the impacts of Vietnam's accession to the WTO are spatially heterogeneous, and this heterogeneity is particularly large under the FL scenario. Our study suggests that poor provinces in the north-western regions may benefit little from trade liberalization. This is of concern from the viewpoint of spatial equity within the country. Further, spatial heterogeneity in poverty reduction affects the efficiency of the targeting policies. Thus, our estimates provide guidance for policy-makers to develop efficient targeting policies that complement trade liberalization policies. Such policies would conserve public resources and prevents poor areas from lagging further behind national growth.

Of course, policy application of the modelling exercise must be done with great caution, as modelling necessariliy involves abstraction and simplification. For example, the SAE method requires the stability of parameter values in the sense that the relationship between the left-hand-side and right-hand-side variables holds both before and after the trade liberalization. The CGE model requires a number of simplifying assumptions about the interaction of various economic sectors. Further, our estimates do not take into account impacts other than trade liberalization policies. Given these, our estimates should not be the sole basis for choosing the target areas. Instead, policy-makers could use our estimates as initial search points to determine the target areas.

The method we developed in this study has relevance to many other economic policy issues. For example, we can simulate the spatial incidence of exogenous price shocks or hypothetical taxes and other fiscal instruments. While the amount of computation and data requirements (survey, census and social accounting matrix) may be significant, there are many countries that already possess such resources. Geographical targeting is already used widely in developing countries, but it is often formulated independently of their macroeconomic policies. Our method of combining the integrated microsimulation-CGE model with small-area estimation provides an opportunity to link the two to achieve a more complete set of microeconomic and macroeconomic objectives.

Appendix

There are three subsections in this Appendix. Section A1 provides the regression results for the wage equation – Equation (3.5), and the adjustment coefficients for Equation (3.13). Section A2 provides the non-wage household income equation – Equation (3.6) and the adjustment coefficient for Equation (3.14). Section A3 provides the regression results for the employment status equations – Equations (3.7)–(3.8), and the adjustment coefficients for Equations (3.15) and (3.16). SDBR stands for 'shortest distance by road'. In each table, we present the estimated coefficients and their associated standard errors in the top part of the table. In the middle part of the table we present some diagnostic statistics for the regression, and in the lower part, we present the adjustment coefficients.

A1 Wage equation

Table 3.4   Wage equation for rural/male/unskilled

Description	Est.	SE
Arable land in district (thousand km^2)	0.018***	(0.005)
Head is married	0.902*	(0.472)
Max. education, at least secondary completed	−2.801***	(0.981)
Average annual humidity duration	−0.024***	(0.005)
Head's child	−0.962***	(0.272)
Not immediately related to head	−1.227***	(0.321)
Age squared/1,000	−0.554***	(0.141)
Female head	−0.366**	(0.147)
Head has at least secondary education	3.820***	(1.093)
Total length of road in district	−1.870***	(0.364)
Number of elderly people in household	−1.381***	(0.329)
Maximum monthly precipitation in a year	2.294***	(0.594)
Age of head	0.036***	(0.008)
Ratio of elderly in household	3.825***	(1.347)
Spouse has at least 8 years of schooling	0.729***	(0.230)
An Giang province	−0.363*	(0.213)
Bac Lieu province	0.998**	(0.390)
Can Tho province	−0.847***	(0.280)
Constant	29.972***	(4.794)

Continued

Table 3.4   Continued

Description	Est.	SE
Obs	255	
$F(18, 236)$	6.14	
p-value	0.000	
R^2	0.319	
σ_μ	0.839	
$\Delta\alpha_{UL}$	−0.002	
$\Delta\alpha_{FL}$	0.082	
$\Delta\alpha_{DSDT}$	−0.010	

Notes: * significant at a 10% level; ** significant at a 5% level; *** significant at a 1% level.

Table 3.5   Wage equation for rural/male/skilled

Description	Est.	SE
Head's ethnicity is Kinh	0.397***	(0.109)
Max. education, at least college	0.339**	(0.140)
Spouse	0.354***	(0.136)
Distance from district town to a city[a]	0.001***	(0.000)
Age	−0.001	(0.003)
Number of dependants	0.065**	(0.027)
Ratio of children in household	−0.551***	(0.183)
Dong Nai province	0.373**	(0.156)
Tien Giang province	−0.444***	(0.138)
Quang Tri province	−1.405***	(0.282)
Nghe An province	−0.714***	(0.139)
Thua Thien-Hue province	−1.004***	(0.219)
Ho Chi Minh City	0.845***	(0.165)
Binh Duong province	0.885**	(0.429)
Ha Noi province	0.503**	(0.220)
Bac Giang province	−0.720**	(0.283)
Nam Dinh province	−0.474**	(0.182)
Hai Duong province	−0.796***	(0.146)
Can Tho province	−0.899***	(0.291)
Constant	7.580***	(0.150)
Obs	750	
$F(19, 730)$	12.06	
p-value	0.000	
R^2	0.239	
σ_μ	0.790	
$\Delta\alpha_{UL}$	−0.027	
$\Delta\alpha_{FL}$	0.030	
$\Delta\alpha_{DSDT}$	−0.008	

Notes: * significant at a 10% level; ** significant at a 5% level; *** significant at a 1% level.
[a] city with population greater than 1,000,000.

Table 3.6 Wage equation for rural/female/unskilled

Description	Est.	SE
Distance from district town to a city[a]	0.029	(0.017)
Length of navigable river in district (km)	−0.020***	(0.005)
Max. education, at least 8 years	−0.879***	(0.220)
Arable land in district (km^2)	0.000	(0.001)
Parent of the head	−1.515*	(0.868)
Household owns house	1.162*	(0.668)
Distance from district town to a city[b]	−0.007***	(0.005)
Percentage of area covered by plant/ forest in district	−0.112***	(0.030)
Distance from district town to a city[c]	0.005	(0.001)
Ratio of dependents in household	3.387***	(0.926)
House is at least 10 years old	1.278***	(0.380)
Head's religion is Catholic	−0.584*	(0.332)
Length of main road (km)	5.740*	(2.870)
Head has at least 5 years of education	0.328*	(0.188)
Average elevation of district (km)	−1.328*	(0.726)
Water is not from running water/rain/well	0.441**	(0.173)
Household size	0.235***	(0.069)
Number of dependants	−0.655***	(0.179)
Semi-permanent house	1.062***	(0.375)
Thua Thien-Hue province	2.085***	(0.741)
Ho Chi Minh City	1.259**	(0.539)
Constant	3.748***	(0.879)
Obs	169	
F(21, 147)	3.82	
p-value	0.000	
R^2	0.353	
σ_μ	0.884	
$\Delta\alpha_{UL}$	−0.013	
$\Delta\alpha_{FL}$	0.061	
$\Delta\alpha_{DSDT}$	−0.008	

Notes: * significant at a 10% level; ** significant at a 5% level; *** significant at a 1% level.
[a] city with population greater than 10,000; [b] city with a population greater than 100,000; [c] city with a population greater than 250,000.

Table 3.7 Wage equation for rural/female/skilled

Description	Est.	SE
Head at least some education	0.376**	(0.173)
At least secondary completed	0.411***	(0.090)
Head's child	0.235**	(0.108)
Water from well	0.324***	(0.092)

Continued

Table 3.7 Continued

Description	Est.	SE
Age	0.012**	(0.005)
Minimum monthly precipitation in a year	−0.014***	(0.004)
Household has radio	0.292***	(0.078)
Tien Giang province	−0.802***	(0.232)
Quang Tri province	−2.115***	(0.420)
Kien Giang province	−0.911***	(0.329)
Hai Duong province	−1.587***	(0.238)
Quang Binh province	−1.146**	(0.503)
Ho Chi Minh City	0.497***	(0.188)
Ha Tay province	−0.593***	(0.218)
Constant	6.880***	(0.262)
Obs	405	
$F(14, 390)$	17.26	
p-value	0.000	
R^2	0.383	
σ_μ	0.770	
$\Delta\alpha_{UL}$	−0.013	
$\Delta\alpha_{FL}$	0.032	
$\Delta\alpha_{DSDT}$	−0.006	

Notes: * significant at a 10% level; ** significant at a 5% level; *** significant at a 1% level.

Table 3.8 Wage equation for urban/male/unskilled

Description	Est.	SE
Head is married	−1.421***	(0.531)
North-central coast region	−1.171**	(0.525)
Water from well	−0.459***	(0.170)
Age of head	−0.018***	(0.006)
House is shared with other household (s)	0.580**	(0.245)
Water from rain	−1.735***	(0.417)
Constant	9.602***	(0.337)
Obs	84	
$F(6, 77)$	9.23	
p-value	0.000	
R^2	0.418	
σ_μ	0.679	
$\Delta\alpha_{UL}$	0.023	
$\Delta\alpha_{FL}$	0.100	
$\Delta\alpha_{DSDT}$	−0.002	

Notes: * significant at a 10% level; ** significant at a 5% level; *** significant at a 1% level.

Table 3.9 Wage equation for urban/male/skilled

Description	Est.	SE
Logarithmic population of district	0.162***	(0.033)
Never married	−0.356***	(0.062)
Logarithmic living area	0.411***	(0.062)
Temporary house	1.522***	(0.262)
Length of navigable river in district (km)	−0.024***	(0.004)
Percentage of bare rock surface in district	−0.027**	(0.007)
Household size	−0.049**	(0.014)
Head's religion is Catholic	−0.279***	(0.127)
Binh Thuan province	−0.488**	(0.246)
Thua Thien-Hue province	−0.699***	(0.222)
Ha Noi province	−0.195**	(0.090)
Hai Phong province	−0.353***	(0.135)
Nam Dinh province	−0.740***	(0.209)
Dong Thap province	−0.484***	(0.152)
Yen Bai province	−0.505***	(0.188)
Son La province	−1.171	(0.955)
Constant	6.073***	(0.452)
Obs	819	
$F(16, 802)$	17.90	
p-value	0.000	
R^2	0.263	
σ_μ	0.814	
$\Delta\alpha_{UL}$	0.021	
$\Delta\alpha_{FL}$	0.097	
$\Delta\alpha_{DSDT}$	−0.010	

Notes: * significant at a 10% level; ** significant at a 5% level; *** significant at a 1% level.

Table 3.10 Wage equation for urban/female/unskilled

Description	Est.	SE
Number of dependants	−0.744***	(0.229)
Head has at least 8 years of education	−0.828***	(0.267)
Head's religion is Catholic	−0.919**	(0.343)
Household size	0.312***	(0.092)
Head is married	2.093***	(0.668)
Age	0.008	(0.008)
Head's ethnicity is Kinh	−0.541**	(0.253)

Continued

Table 3.10 Continued

Description	Est.	SE
Ratio of dependants in household	4.621***	(1.258)
House is 3–9 years old	0.865***	(0.251)
Constant	6.503***	(0.653)
Obs	67	
$F(9, 57)$	4.47	
p-value	0.000	
R^2	0.414	
σ_μ	0.791	
$\Delta\alpha_{UL}$	−0.016	
$\Delta\alpha_{FL}$	0.095	
$\Delta\alpha_{DSDT}$	−0.010	

Notes: * significant at a 10% level; ** significant at a 5% level; *** significant at a 1% level.

Table 3.11 Wage equation for urban/female/skilled

Description	Est.	SE
Maximum education, at least 10 years	0.300***	(0.081)
Distance from district town to a city[a]	−0.002***	(0.000)
House is at least 10 years old	−0.210***	(0.066)
Head has no religion	0.229***	(0.078)
Average annual humidity duration	−0.010***	(0.002)
At least 8 years of education	0.327***	(0.091)
Distance to provincial town	−0.012***	(0.004)
Age	0.010***	(0.003)
Hai Phong province	−0.531***	(0.157)
Nam Dinh province	−0.931***	(0.256)
Tien Giang province	−0.487***	(0.180)
Constant	18.180***	(1.988)
Obs	618	
$F(11, 606)$	21.22	
p-value	0.000	
R^2	0.278	
σ_μ	0.766	
$\Delta\alpha_{UL}$	0.012	
$\Delta\alpha_{FL}$	0.120	
$\Delta\alpha_{DSDT}$	−0.010	

Notes: * significant at a 10% level; ** significant at a 5% level; *** significant at a 1% level.

[a] city with population greater than 250,000.

A2 Non-wage income equation

Table 3.12 Non-wage equation for rural areas

Description	Est.	SE
Number of self-employed	0.507***	(0.037)
Number of self-employed squared	−0.053***	(0.006)
Household has TV	0.409***	(0.037)
Head's ethnicity is Kinh	0.360***	(0.060)
Ratio of students in household	0.659***	(0.085)
Max. educ., at least 10 yrs	0.231***	(0.039)
Max. educ., at least some education	0.296***	(0.098)
Household has a radio	0.119***	(0.034)
House is 3–9 years old	−0.670***	(0.098)
Non-flushing toilet	−0.463***	(0.092)
Electricity available	0.317***	(0.049)
Ratio of elderly in household	0.500***	(0.101)
Max. education at least 5 yrs	0.218***	(0.053)
Semi-permanent house	−0.361***	(0.056)
Log of the living area	0.143***	(0.017)
Head's marital status is divorced/separated/widowed	−0.200***	(0.049)
Head's age	0.003**	(0.002)
Arable land in district (thousand km^2)	0.014***	(0.002)
Thua Thien-Hue province	1.552***	(0.166)
Monthly minimum precipitation in a year	−0.030***	(0.003)
Bac Ninh province	0.426***	(0.100)
Bac Giang province	−0.404***	(0.109)
Ha Tinh province	1.169***	(0.222)
Hai Duong province	−0.477***	(0.089)
Quang Tri province	0.835***	(0.188)
Vinh Phuc province	−0.683***	(0.173)
Phu Tho province	−0.436***	(0.101)
Lam Dong province	0.750***	(0.181)
Elevation of district town	−0.425***	(0.124)
Quang Ninh province	0.552***	(0.165)
Long An province	−0.527***	(0.133)
Thai Binh province	−0.372***	(0.105)
Percentage of area covered by plant or forest in district	−0.023***	(0.008)
Tra Vinh province	−0.430***	(0.131)
Total length of road in district (1,000 km)	−0.346***	(0.103)
Tien Giang province	−0.282***	(0.109)

Continued

Table 3.12 Continued

Description	Est.	SE
Dong Thap province	−0.403***	(0.126)
Thai Nguyen province	−0.457***	(0.173)
Ha Nam province	−0.283***	(0.105)
Tuyen Quang province	0.536***	(0.187)
Binh Duong province	−0.400**	(0.168)
Proportion of steep slope (8–15%)	0.012***	(0.003)
Ninh Thuan province	−0.721***	(0.204)
Yen Bai province	−0.368**	(0.171)
Quang Nam province	−0.236*	(0.130)
Hoa Binh province	−0.283**	(0.134)
Constant	6.813***	(0.175)
Obs	4248	
$F(46, 4201)$	56.58	
p-value	0.000	
R^2	0.383	
σ_γ	1.032	
$\Delta\gamma_{UL}$	0.013	
$\Delta\gamma_{FL}$	0.100	
$\Delta\gamma_{DSDT}$	−0.012	

Notes: * significant at a 10% level; ** significant at a 5% level; *** significant at a 1% level.

Table 3.13 Non-wage equation for urban areas

Description	Est.	SE
Number of self-employed	0.903***	(0.063)
Number of self-employed squared	−0.106***	(0.016)
Household has TV	0.394***	(0.082)
Non-flushing toilet	−0.194**	(0.076)
Max. education at least 10 years	0.332***	(0.066)
Ratio of dependants in household	0.768***	(0.129)
Logarithmic living area	0.346***	(0.066)
Semi-permanent house	−0.347***	(0.072)
House is 3–9 years old	0.754***	(0.278)
House is shared with other household(s)	−0.427***	(0.109)
Logarithmic population in district	0.214***	(0.029)
Minimum monthly precipitation in a year	−0.034***	(0.005)
Proportion of very deep slope (30%+)	0.033***	(0.008)
Hai Phong province	0.743***	(0.144)

Continued

Table 3.13 Continued

Description	Est.	SE
Maximum monthly precipitation in a year	1.425***	(0.491)
Bac Ninh province	0.716***	(0.234)
Dong Nai province	−0.333**	(0.168)
Max. education at least college	0.195**	(0.090)
Constant	3.915***	(0.458)
Obs	1676	
$F(18, 1657)$	49.82	
p-value	0.000	
R^2	0.351	
σ_γ	1.193	
$\Delta\gamma_{UL}$	0.013	
$\Delta\gamma_{FL}$	0.100	
$\Delta\gamma_{DSDT}$	−0.013	

Notes: * significant at a 10% level; ** significant at a 5% level; *** significant at a 1% level.

A3 Employment status equations

Table 3.14 Employment status equations for rural/male/unskilled

Description	Wage-earner		Self-employed	
	Est.	SE	Est.	SE
Spouse	−1.772***	(0.517)	−0.513	(0.580)
Head's child	−0.491	(0.369)	−0.548	(0.391)
Literate	1.070***	(0.234)	0.710***	(0.262)
Head's religion is Catholic	−0.653	(0.458)	−0.830	(0.534)
Head has no religion	−0.390	(0.253)	−0.560**	(0.283)
Semi-permanent house	0.840***	(0.283)	0.511	(0.324)
House is 6+years old	−0.210	(0.322)	−1.226***	(0.401)
House is 3–9 years old	2.358***	(0.735)	1.564*	(0.833)
Water from well	1.553***	(0.575)	1.626***	(0.617)
Water not from running water/rain water/well	1.613***	(0.568)	1.509**	(0.607)
Quang Ngai province	1.759*	(0.937)	0.824	(1.146)
Dac Lac province	−2.325	(1.538)	−2.110	(1.797)
Lam Dong province	−4.036***	(1.268)	−2.248	(1.438)
Tay Ninh province	1.064	(0.659)	1.292*	(0.758)
Long An province	0.696	(0.848)	1.660*	(0.915)
An Giang province	1.032*	(0.591)	1.930***	(0.624)
Tien Giang province	−0.362	(0.426)	1.137**	(0.480)
Ben Tre province	1.416**	(0.672)	0.446	(0.830)
Kien Giang province	0.643	(0.549)	0.954	(0.599)

Continued

Table 3.14 Continued

Description	Wage-earner		Self-employed	
	Est.	SE	Est.	SE
Tra Vinh province	1.888*	(1.017)	1.342	(1.084)
Soc Trang province	0.659	(0.502)	1.861***	(0.537)
Bac Lieu province	1.314	(0.809)	2.270**	(0.879)
Age	0.147***	(0.051)	0.179***	(0.059)
Age of spouse	0.011**	(0.005)	0.007	(0.006)
Ratio of dependants in household	−1.330**	(0.649)	−1.841**	(0.745)
Ratio of students in household	3.539***	(0.807)	2.972***	(0.905)
Age squared/1,000	−2.356***	(0.608)	−3.412***	(0.753)
Distance from district town to a city[a]	−0.023	(0.007)	−0.026***	(0.008)
Average elevation of district	0.006***	(0.001)	0.004***	(0.001)
Length of navigable river in district (km)	−0.012*	(0.006)	−0.024***	(0.008)
Total area over 1,500m elevation in district	−0.289***	(0.082)	−0.267**	(0.114)
Constant	−2.230*	(1.220)	−1.831	(1.331)
Obs	1382			
χ^2_{66}	400.55			
$\Delta\alpha_{UL}$	0.011		0.040	
$\Delta\alpha_{FL}$	0.432		0.430	
$\Delta\alpha_{DSDT}$	−0.058		−0.058	

Notes: * significant at a 10% level; ** significant at a 5% level; *** significant at a 1% level.
[a] city with population greater than 50,000.

Table 3.15 Employment status equations for rural/male/skilled

Description	Wage-earner		Self-employed	
	Est.	SE	Est.	SE
Age of spouse squared/1,000	0.567**	(0.241)	0.712***	(0.264)
Spouse	−1.026***	(0.264)	−0.546*	(0.312)
Never married	−0.826***	(0.286)	−0.375	(0.310)
Moved within 5 years from rural area	−0.387	(0.343)	−0.520	(0.387)
House is 6+years old	0.383**	(0.152)	0.328*	(0.170)
Electricity available	−0.490**	(0.202)	−0.472**	(0.227)
Water from rain	0.499*	(0.273)	1.078***	(0.307)
House is 3–9 years old	0.774***	(0.225)	1.014***	(0.257)
Household has radio	0.384***	(0.138)	0.333**	(0.157)
Head has at least some education	0.656**	(0.333)	0.671*	(0.372)
Head has at least college education	0.915	(0.798)	3.090***	(0.927)

Continued

Table 3.15 Continued

Spouse has at least 10 years of education	0.774	(0.544)	1.028*	(0.575)
Spouse has at least completed secondary	−0.868	(0.616)	−0.657	(0.651)
Spouse has at least college education	0.701	(0.827)	2.115**	(0.961)
Max. educ., at least college education	−0.857	(0.558)	−1.828**	(0.732)
Hai Phong province	−0.646	(0.478)	−0.893	(0.563)
Thai Binh province	−0.415	(0.376)	−0.982**	(0.466)
Ninh Binh province	−0.780	(0.731)	−1.275	(0.872)
Thai Nguyen province	−0.703	(0.533)	−2.488**	(1.041)
Thua Thien-Hue province	−3.096**	(1.543)	−3.368**	(1.608)
Da Nang province	−4.240*	(2.189)	−3.749*	(2.256)
Quang Nam province	−3.056*	(1.607)	−4.252**	(1.699)
Quang Ngai province	−2.761**	(1.356)	−2.034	(1.400)
Binh Dinh province	−1.406	(0.869)	−1.125	(0.917)
Ho Chi Minh City	−1.363***	(0.518)	−1.019*	(0.548)
Tay Ninh province	−1.083**	(0.530)	−1.209**	(0.578)
Binh Duong province	−1.525**	(0.597)	−2.539***	(0.791)
Dong Nai province	−0.698	(0.496)	−0.576	(0.530)
Ban Ria-Vung Tau province	−1.488**	(0.575)	−2.916***	(0.822)
Dong Thap province	−0.683	(0.429)	−1.441***	(0.521)
Tra Vinh province	−1.166**	(0.483)	−1.360**	(0.569)
Soc Trang province	−1.580**	(0.657)	−1.434*	(0.775)
Age	0.074*	(0.040)	0.225***	(0.047)
Age of spouse	−0.033**	(0.015)	−0.048***	(0.017)
Ratio of females in household	1.310***	(0.433)	1.305***	(0.487)
Ratio of students in household	1.193 ***	(0.395)	1.252***	(0.446)
Age squared/1,000	−1.444***	(0.473)	−3.729***	(0.583)
Percentage of bare rock surface in district	0.020	(0.015)	0.023	(0.017)
Distance from district town to a city[a]	−0.027**	(0.011)	−0.034***	(0.012)
Distance from district town to a city[b]	0.021*	(0.011)	0.035***	(0.012)
Total length of road in district (km)	−0.676**	(0.338)	−1.850***	(0.396)
Average annual sunshine duration	0.480*	(0.274)	1.428***	(0.302)
SDBR from district town to a city[a]	0.015**	(0.008)	0.019**	(0.008)
SDBR from district town to a city[b]	−0.011	(0.008)	−0.020**	(0.009)
Constant	−0.204	(1.099)	−5.401***	(1.251)
Obs	3764			
χ^2_{88}	483.70			
$\Delta\alpha_{UL}$	0.012		0.038	
$\Delta\alpha_{FL}$	1.777		1.766	
$\Delta\alpha_{DSDT}$	−0.108		−0.109	

Notes: * significant at a 10% level; ** significant at a 5% level; *** significant at a 1% level.
[a] city with population greater than 250,000; [b] city with population greater than 1,000,000.

Table 3.16 Employment status equations for rural/female/unskilled

Description	Wage-earner		Self-employed	
	Est.	SE	Est.	SE
Age of spouse squared/1,000	1.483***	(0.237)	1.594***	(0.370)
Head's child	−1.306***	(0.385)	−1.076*	(0.553)
Not immediately related to head	−1.572***	(0.288)	−1.645***	(0.492)
Never married	0.941***	(0.306)	1.381***	(0.432)
Literate	0.404***	(0.149)	0.212	(0.248)
Head's religion is Catholic	0.598**	(0.278)	0.645	(0.469)
Head has no religion	0.470***	(0.144)	0.375*	(0.227)
House is 3–9 years old	−0.272*	(0.139)	0.433*	(0.258)
Water from rain	0.379	(0.252)	0.447	(0.431)
Flushing toilet	0.967**	(0.382)	1.926**	(0.810)
Non-flushing toilet	0.922**	(0.364)	0.883	(0.800)
Head has at least some education	0.354*	(0.182)	−0.215	(0.282)
Head has at least 8 years of education	0.613**	(0.236)	0.830*	(0.457)
Max. education at least 5 years	0.159	(0.168)	−0.455*	(0.260)
Max. education at least 8 years	−0.282	(0.181)	−0.261	(0.351)
Age	0.184***	(0.036)	0.178***	(0.057)
Age of spouse	−0.082***	(0.014)	−0.092***	(0.022)
Age squared/1,000	−2.974***	(0.412)	−3.393***	(0.709)
Distance from district town to city[a]	0.012*	(0.007)	−0.070***	(0.018)
Distance from district town to a city[b]	−0.003***	(0.001)	−0.005***	(0.002)
Elevation of district town	0.600*	(0.357)	−2.718**	(1.156)
Average annual humidity duration	0.009**	(0.005)	−0.032***	(0.010)
SDBR from district town to a city[c]	0.001**	(0.000)	0.002**	(0.001)
Total area over 1,500m elevation in district	0.066	(0.053)	−0.195	(0.196)
Constant	−10.581**	(4.782)	28.744***	(9.695)
Obs	2302			
χ^2_{48}	539.72			
$\Delta\alpha_{UL}$	0.012		0.034	
$\Delta\alpha_{FL}$	0.219		0.226	
$\Delta\alpha_{DSDT}$	−0.059		−0.058	

Notes: * significant at a 10% level; ** significant at a 5% level; *** significant at a 1% level.
[a] city with population greater than 10,000; [b] city with population greater than 250,000; [c] city with population greater than 1,000,000.

Table 3.17 Employment status equation for rural/female/skilled

Description	Wage-earner		Self-employed	
	Est.	SE	Est.	SE
Head's child	−1.552***	(0.413)	−1.087**	(0.542)
Not immediately related to head	−1.053***	(0.386)	−0.556	(0.483)
Never married	0.943***	(0.306)	1.882***	(0.399)
Moved within 5 years from rural area	−0.885***	(0.334)	−0.373	(0.465)
Head's religion is Catholic	−0.447*	(0.252)	−1.599***	(0.376)
Head's religion is other than none/Buddhist/Catholic	0.433	(0.410)	1.015**	(0.473)
Electricity available	0.301*	(0.175)	0.418*	(0.229)
House is 3–9 years old	−0.115	(0.141)	−0.278	(0.175)
At least 10 years of education	−0.289	(0.218)	0.964***	(0.241)
Head is married	−1.397***	(0.532)	−2.117**	(0.745)
Nghe An province	0.408	(0.362)	1.360***	(0.440)
Ha Tinh province	1.323	(1.027)	1.144	(1.122)
Da Nang province	−1.698**	(0.730)	−1.493	(1.055)
Ho Chi Minh City	−1.856***	(0.371)	−0.346	(0.422)
Dong Nai province	−0.726*	(0.395)	0.739	(0.491)
Ban Ria-Vung Tau province	−1.030*	(0.562)	−0.862	(0.870)
Age	0.184***	(0.041)	0.327***	(0.054)
Household size	0.308**	(0.156)	0.311	(0.210)
Head's age	0.014	(0.010)	0.011	(0.012)
Ratio of dependants in household	−1.015*	(0.544)	−1.477**	(0.677)
Ratio of females in household	1.043**	(0.432)	0.700	(0.535)
Ratio of children in household	−1.382**	(0.614)	−1.921**	(0.747)
Ratio of students in household	2.710***	(0.504)	2.711***	(0.637)
Age squared/1,000	−2.794***	(0.501)	−4.604***	(0.698)
Household size squared/1,000	−0.026**	(0.012)	−0.027	(0.016)
Distance from district town to a city[a]	−0.110***	(0.029)	−0.103***	(0.034)
Elevation of district town	1.987***	(0.782)	1.089	(0.921)
Proportion of somewhat steep slope (8–15%)	0.025***	(0.010)	0.013	(0.012)
SDBR from district town to a city[a]	0.079***	(0.020)	0.053**	(0.024)
Mean distance to main road in district	−0.200***	(0.038)	−0.081*	(0.048)
Length of navigable river in district (km)	−0.004	(0.004)	−0.011**	(0.005)
Constant	−1.563*	(0.909)	−6.095***	(1.187)
Obs	3476			
χ^2_{62}	538.73			
$\Delta\alpha_{UL}$	0.015		0.029	
$\Delta\alpha_{FL}$	1.976		1.969	
$\Delta\alpha_{DSDT}$	−0.084		−0.075	

Notes: * significant at a 10% level; ** significant at a 5% level; *** significant at a 1% level.
[a] city with population greater than 10,000; SDBR = shortest distance by road.

Table 3.18 Employment status equation for urban/male/unskilled

Description	Wage-earner		Self-employed	
	Est.	SE	Est.	SE
Literacy	2.573***	(0.821)	2.552***	(0.790)
Head's ethnicity is Kinh	−2.395***	(0.901)	−2.271***	(0.849)
Semi-permanent house	1.773***	(0.621)	1.889***	(0.663)
Water from rain	2.529	(1.649)	2.349	(1.834)
Water from well	1.124	(0.886)	1.318	(0.895)
Non-flushing toilet	3.397***	(1.008)	3.130***	(1.021)
Head has at least some education	−1.791**	(0.848)	−2.230***	(0.842)
House is 3–9 years old	1.102	(0.703)	1.394*	(0.743)
Spouse has at least 5 years of education	−1.486*	(0.793)	−1.143	(0.815)
Max. educ. in household, at least 8 years	−0.979	(0.602)	−0.696	(0.619)
Age	0.392***	(0.119)	0.469***	(0.131)
Household owns house	−2.960**	(1.454)	−4.033***	(1.316)
Age squared/1,000	−5.153***	(1.540)	−7.475***	(1.828)
Area (km^2)	0.098***	(0.026)	0.090***	(0.027)
Percentage of natural forest	0.187***	(0.071)	0.221***	(0.070)
Distance from district town to a city[a]	−2.494***	(0.665)	−2.479***	(0.666)
Distance from district town to a city[b]	0.525***	(0.190)	0.562***	(0.191)
Distance from district town to a city[c]	−0.403**	(0.160)	−0.434***	(0.159)
Total length of roads in district	−0.060***	(0.017)	−0.061***	(0.017)
Average elevation of district	−0.101***	(0.029)	−0.071**	(0.030)
Elevation of district town	0.193***	(0.053)	0.165***	(0.054)
Percentage of moderate slope in district (4–8%)	−2.367***	(0.734)	−2.205***	(0.755)
Average annual precipitation	6.330	(5.433)	9.233*	(5.451)
Average annual temperature	−0.391**	(0.168)	−0.242	(0.180)
Average annual humidity duration	−0.555**	(0.225)	−0.353	(0.243)
SDBR from district town to a city[a]	−0.888***	(0.244)	−0.786***	(0.253)
SDBR from district town to a city[b]	2.003***	(0.538)	1.949***	(0.538)
SDBR from district town to a city[c]	−0.340***	(0.126)	−0.368***	(0.126)
SDBR from district town to a city[d]	0.314**	(0.122)	0.329***	(0.122)
Constant	650.9***	(267.3)	403.0	(288.7)
Obs	225			
χ^2_{58}	213.54			
$\Delta\alpha_{UL}$	0.085		0.112	
$\Delta\alpha_{FL}$	0.644		0.638	
$\Delta\alpha_{DSDT}$	−0.023		−0.029	

Notes: * significant at a 10% level; ** significant at a 5% level; *** significant at a 1% level.
[a] city with population greater than 50,000; [b] city with population greater than 100,000; [c] city with population greater than 250,000; [d] city with population greater than 1,000,000. SDBR = shortest distance by road.

Table 3.19 Employment status equation for urban/male/skilled

Description	Wage-earner		Self-employed	
	Est.	SE	Est.	SE
Never married	−1.206***	(0.274)	−0.530**	(0.267)
Divorced/separated/widowed	−1.597***	(0.398)	−1.469***	(0.435)
Moved within 5 years from urban area	−0.769**	(0.318)	−0.661**	(0.299)
Moved within 5 years from rural area	−0.655*	(0.392)	−0.879**	(0.397)
Head's ethnicity is Kinh	−0.354	(0.319)	−0.403	(0.318)
Electricity available	0.606	(0.580)	1.091	(0.670)
Household has TV	0.616***	(0.213)	0.570***	(0.213)
House is 3–9 years old	−0.556**	(0.241)	−0.400*	(0.242)
At least college education	0.498	(0.344)	1.649***	(0.329)
Head at least 10 years of education	−0.427**	(0.203)	−0.237	(0.204)
Spouse at least 10 years of education	0.551	(0.413)	0.486	(0.417)
Spouse at least completed secondary	−0.837*	(0.456)	−0.801*	(0.459)
Max. educ., at least secondary	0.430*	(0.223)	0.445*	(0.230)
Thai Nguyen province	−1.089**	(0.480)	−0.497	(0.447)
Thanh Hoa province	1.778**	(0.842)	2.062**	(0.851)
Age	0.124***	(0.042)	0.255***	(0.043)
Household owns house	0.688***	(0.235)	0.192	(0.225)
Ratio of students in household	1.382***	(0.426)	1.129***	(0.432)
Age squared/1,000	−2.036***	(0.490)	−3.920***	(0.511)
Constant	−1.330	(1.106)	−3.663***	(1.158)
Obs	1830			
χ^2_{38}	338.24			
$\Delta\alpha_{UL}$	0.059		0.071	
$\Delta\alpha_{FL}$	0.264		0.261	
$\Delta\alpha_{DSDT}$	−0.050		−0.050	

Notes: * significant at a 10% level; ** significant at a 5% level; *** significant at a 1% level.

Table 3.20 Employment status regression for urban/female/unskilled

Description	Wage-earner		Self-employed	
	Est.	SE	Est.	SE
Never married	0.404	(0.442)	1.153**	(0.509)
Divorced/separated/widowed	−0.516*	(0.309)	0.397	(0.480)
Literate	0.415	(0.296)	0.874*	(0.472)
Head has no religion	−0.281	(0.243)	−0.431	(0.334)
Head's ethnicity is Kinh	1.247***	(0.314)	0.407	(0.392)
House is 6+ years old	−0.322	(0.266)	−0.366	(0.387)
Electricity available	0.655	(0.524)	1.637*	(0.945)
House is 3–9 years old	1.269***	(0.286)	0.541	(0.439)
Head, at least some education	0.916**	(0.371)	0.910*	(0.517)

Continued

Table 3.20 Continued

Description	Wage-earner		Self-employed	
	Est.	SE	Est.	SE
Max educ., at least 10 years	−0.745***	(0.262)	−0.884**	(0.403)
Age	0.199***	(0.061)	0.293***	(0.084)
Ratio of dependants in household	−1.806**	(0.792)	−1.633	(1.134)
Ratio of students in household	2.696***	(0.923)	1.440	(1.230)
Age squared/1,000	−2.223***	(0.711)	−4.171***	(1.069)
Constant	−5.979***	(1.471)	−8.046***	(1.983)
Obs	458			
χ^2_{28}	143.46			
$\Delta\alpha_{UL}$	0.040		0.046	
$\Delta\alpha_{FL}$	0.162		0.150	
$\Delta\alpha_{DSDT}$	−0.071		−0.069	

Notes: * significant at a 10% level; ** significant at a 5% level; *** significant at a 1% level.

Table 3.21 Employment status equations for urban/female/skilled

Description	Wage-earner		Self-employed	
	Est.	SE	Est.	SE
Age of spouse squared/1,000	−0.332	(0.279)	−0.455	(0.292)
Spouse	−0.598***	(0.190)	−0.693***	(0.216)
Not immediately related to head	−0.542**	(0.218)	−0.289	(0.227)
Never married	0.226	(0.220)	0.838***	(0.231)
Head's religion is Catholic	0.222	(0.291)	0.406	(0.305)
Head's religion is other than none/Buddhist/Catholic	−0.556	(0.457)	−1.076*	(0.583)
Temporary house	−1.163**	(0.576)	−0.888	(0.625)
House is 3–9 years old	−0.299**	(0.140)	−0.327**	(0.154)
At least 8 years of education	0.217	(0.147)	0.465***	(0.171)
Head has at least college education	−0.524	(0.385)	1.254***	(0.348)
Spouse has at least some education	−0.524	(0.456)	−0.843*	(0.466)
Max. educ., at least college education	−0.225	(0.215)	0.429*	(0.233)
Age	0.234***	(0.038)	0.312***	(0.044)
Household size	−0.050	(0.034)	−0.047	(0.037)
Log of the living area	−0.151	(0.138)	−0.281*	(0.151)
Age of spouse	0.035	(0.022)	0.042*	(0.023)
Ratio of children in household	−0.449	(0.484)	−1.324**	(0.539)
Ratio of students in household	1.187***	(0.429)	1.319***	(0.472)
Age squared/1,000	−0.003***	(0.000)	−0.005***	(0.001)
Arable land in district (km^2)	−0.002	(0.002)	−0.003*	(0.002)
Logarithmic population of district	−0.558***	(0.086)	−0.294***	(0.096)
Distance from district town to a city[a]	0.075	(0.049)	0.084	(0.055)

Continued

Table 3.21 Continued

Description	Wage-earner		Self-employed	
	Est.	SE	Est.	SE
Distance from district town to a city[c]	0.008**	(0.003)	0.017***	(0.004)
Length of main road (km)	0.006	(0.004)	0.014***	(0.004)
SDBR from district town to a city[b]	0.004***	(0.001)	0.002***	(0.001)
SDBR from district town to a city[c]	−0.006**	(0.003)	−0.012*	(0.003)
Mean distance to main road in district	−0.423**	(0.189)	−0.309	(0.209)
Constant	3.975	(1.295)	−0.127	(1.450)
Obs	1899			
χ^2_{54}	556.96			
$\Delta\alpha_{UL}$	0.041		0.069	
$\Delta\alpha_{FL}$	0.187		0.180	
$\Delta\alpha_{DSDT}$	−0.029		−0.031	

Notes: * significant at a 10% level; ** significant at a 5% level; *** significant at a 1% level.
[a] city with population greater than 10,000; [b] city with population greater than 250,000; [c] city with population greater than 1,000,000. SDBR = shortest distance by road.

Acknowledgements

The authors thank Alain de Janvry, Michael Epprecht, Peter Lanjouw and Elisabeth Sadoulet. An earlier version of this paper was presented at the UNU-WIDER Project Conference on the Impact of Globalization on the Poor in Asia. Fujii thanks the Government of Japan under the Millennium PHRD Grant for financial support for the initial stage of this study. The usual caveats apply.

Notes

1 See Thanh (2005) for further discussion on the process and progress of Vietnam's efforts to become a WTO member.
2 According to the *World Development Indicators*, the Purchasing Power Parity conversion factor (for 1998) was US$1 = VND 2,673.
3 If we are interested in the impacts of price changes in a particular sector on the spatial distribution of poverty, we could use a partial equilibrium model. We could, for example, predict nominal consumption using the SAE method and then estimate the changes in real consumption by exploiting the heterogeneity in consumption pattern across the country.
4 An alternative approach is to calibrate the sum so that these equations hold without the scaling factor. Either way, we have to make somewhat arbitrary adjustments. This is unavoidable, because the sum of the survey observations is not necessarily consistent with the SAM. Note that we are only concerned about the ratios of these macroeconomic indicators before and after Vietnam's accession to the WTO.
5 **x**, **z** and **v** are expressed in a row vector format.
6 The policy context for the DSDT scenario is discussed extensively in Hertel and Winters (2006).

References

Adelman, I. and Robinson, S. (1978) *Income Distribution Policies in Developing Countries* (Stanford: Stanford University Press).

Anderson, K. (1999) *Vietnam's Transforming Economy and WTO Accession* (Singapore: Institute of Southeast Asian Studies).

Bhagwati, J. and Srinivasan, T. N. (2002) 'Trade and Poverty in Poor Countries', *American Economic Review*, 92(2): 180–83.

Bourguignon, F., Robilliard, A. and Robinson, S. (2005) 'Representative Versus Real Households in the Macroeconomic Modeling of Inequality', in T. J. Kehoe, T. N. Srinivasan and J. Whalley (eds), *Frontiers in Applied General Equilibrium Modelling* (Cambridge: Cambridge University Press).

Dollar, D. and Kraay, A. (2002) 'Growth is Good for the Poor', *Journal of Economic Growth*, 7(3): 195–225.

Dollar, D. and Kraay, A. (2004) 'Trade, Growth, and Poverty', *Economic Journal*, 114: F22–F49.

Elbers, C., Lanjouw, J. O. and Lanjouw, P. (2002) 'Welfare in Villages and Towns: Micro-level Estimation of Poverty and Inequality', Working Paper 2911, World Bank, Washington, DC.

Elbers, C., Lanjouw, J. O. and Lanjouw, P. (2003) 'Micro-level Estimation of Poverty and Inequality', *Econometrica*, 71(1): 355–64.

Foster, J., Greer, J. and Thorbecke, E. (1984) 'A Class of Decomposable Poverty Measures', *Econometrica*, 52(3): 761–65.

Fukase, E. and Martin, W. (2000) 'The Effects of the United States Granting MFN Status to Vietnam', *Weltwirtschaftliches Archiv*, 136(2): 539–59.

Fukase, E. and Martin, W. (2001) 'A Quantitative Evaluation of Vietnam's Accession to the ASEAN Free Trade Area', *Journal of Economic Integration*, 16(4): 545–67.

Glewwe, P., Gragnolati, M. and Zaman, H. (2002) 'Who Gained from Vietnam's Boom in the 1990s?', *Economic Development and Cultural Change*, 50(4): 773–92.

Harrison, G. W., Rutherford, T. F. and Tarr, D. G. (2003) 'Trade Liberalization, Poverty and Efficient Equity', *Journal of Development Economics*, 71: 97–128.

Heng, M. T. and Gayathri, V. (2004) 'Impact of Regional Trade Liberalization on Emerging Economies: The Case of Vietnam', *ASEAN Economic Bulletin*, 21(2): 167–82.

Hertel, T. W. (1997) (ed.) *Global Trade Analysis: Modeling and Applications* (Cambridge: Cambridge University Press).

Hertel, T. W. and Winters, L. A. (eds) (2006) *Poverty and the WTO: Impacts of the Doha Development Agenda* (Washington, DC: World Bank).

Jenkins, R. (2004) 'Vietnam in the Global Economy: Trade, Employment and Poverty', *Journal of International Development*, 16: 13–28.

Jensen, H. T. and Tarp, F. (2005) 'Trade Liberalization and Spatial Inequality: A Methodological Innovation in a Vietnamese Perspective', *Review of Development Economics*, 9(1): 69–86.

Kanbur, R. (2001) 'Economic Policy, Distribution and Poverty: The Nature of Disagreements', *World Development*, 29(6): 1083–94.

Krueger, A. O. (1998) 'Why Trade Liberalisation is Good for Growth', *Economic Journal*, 108(450): 1513–22.

Le, T. H. and Winters, P. (2001) 'Aid Policies and Poverty Alleviation: The Case of Vietnam', *Asia-Pacific Development Journal*, 8(2): 27–44.

Litchfield, J. and Justino, P. (2004) 'Welfare in Vietnam during the 1990s: Poverty, Inequality and Poverty Dynamics', *Journal of the Asia Pacific Economy*, 9(2): 145–69.

Liu, A. Y. C. (2001) 'Markets, Inequality and Poverty in Vietnam', *Asian Economic Journal*, 15(2): 217–35.

Minot, N. (2000) 'Generating Disaggregated Poverty Maps: An Application to Vietnam', *World Development*, 28(2): 319–31.

Minot, N., Baulch, B. and Epprecht, M. (2003) 'Poverty and Inequality in Vietnam: Spatial Patterns and Geographic Determinants', Research Report 48, International Food Policy Research, Washington, DC.

Niimi, Y., Vasudeva-Dutta, P. and Winters, L. A. (2004) 'Storm in a Rice Bowl: Rice Reform and Poverty in Vietnam in the 1990s', *Journal of the Asia Pacific Economy*, 9(2): 170–90.

Ravallion, M. (2001) 'Growth, Inequality and Poverty: Looking Beyond Averages', *World Development*, 29(11): 1803–15.

Rodríguez, F. and Rodrik, D. (2001) 'Trade Policy and Economic Growth: A Sceptic's Guide to the Cross-national Evidence', in B. S. Bernanke and K. Rogo (eds), *NBER Macroeconomics Annual 2000*, vol. 15 (Cambridge, Mass.: MIT Press).

Tarp, F., Roland-Holst, D. and Rand, J. (2002) 'Trade and Income Growth in Vietnam: Estimates from a New Social Accounting Matrix', *Economic Systems Research*, 14(2): 157–84.

Thanh, V. T. (2005) 'Vietnam's Trade Liberalization and International Economic Integration: Evolution, Problems, and Challenges', *ASEAN Economic Bulletin*, 22(1): 75–91.

Winters, L. A. (2002) 'Trade Liberalisation and Poverty: What Are the Links?', *World Economy*, 25(9): 1339–67.

Winters, L. A., McCulloch, N. and McKay, A. (2004) 'Trade Liberalization and Poverty: The Evidence So Far', *Journal of Economic Literature*, 42(1): 72–115.

World Bank (2001) *Vietnam Living Standards Survey (VLSS), 1997–98. Basic Information* (Washington, DC: World Bank, Poverty and Human Resources Division).

4
Trade, Migration and Poverty Reduction in the Globalizing Economy: The Case of the Philippines

Yasuyuki Sawada and Jonna P. Estudillo

Introduction

In September 2000, the 189 member countries of the United Nations (UN) made poverty reduction a global objective by setting Millennium Development Goals (MDGs). The most important of the MDGs was Goal 1: to eradicate extreme poverty and hunger, and Target 1: to halve the proportion of people living on less than a (US) dollar a day, and those who suffer from hunger. The UN aims to achieve both Goal 1 and Target 1 between 1990 and 2015.

In the Philippines, poverty eradication has been a top priority of its government since 1986. The centrepiece of the Aquino Administration (1986–92) was economic and social development through the comprehensive agrarian reform programme (CARP), initiated in the second half of the 1980s. The Ramos Administration (1992–98) had the social reform agenda (SRA), the first effort towards human development in the Philippines (Balisacan 2003). The Estrada Administration (1998–2001) initiated the *Lingap Para sa Mahihirap* (literally meaning 'looking after the poor') programme to alleviate poverty. The Arroyo Government (2001–) has adopted the *Kapit-Bisig Laban sa Kahirapan* (KALAHI) (that is, 'linking arms against poverty') programme, focusing on a comprehensive development of agricultural communities, some of them covered by land reform implementation.

While these targeted poverty reduction programmes may be effective, the costs of such programmes may be too prohibitive to cover a large enough number of poorer communities and households. Many authors believe that another effective alternative approach towards more comprehensive poverty reduction is to enhance economic growth (Ravallion 2001; Dollar and Kraay 2002). It has been shown that an important driving force to enhance economic growth is globalization, defined as the cross-national integration of

"

goods, labour and financial markets (World Bank 2002). Since economic growth has been found to be an effective instrument in reducing poverty (Dollar and Kraay 2002), globalization has been hypothesized to be an important force that can lead to poverty reduction (Nissanke and Thorbecke 2007). Yet there remains an empirical question as to whether such a hypothesis holds in the context of the Philippines.

There are different channels of the so-called globalization–growth–poverty-reduction nexus. First, there is a direct positive relationship between the trade openness of a country and its economic growth (Harrison 1996; Dollar and Kraay 2004).[1] Second, foreign direct investment (FDI) is considered to be an important venue to the transfer of technology. FDIs contribute relatively more to economic growth than do domestic investments. This positive nexus between FDI and growth is observed especially when sufficient absorptive capability of advanced technologies is available in the host economy (Borensztein *et al.* 1998). Third, in addition to the FDI, the indirect capital flows might also affect economic growth positively. Harrison (1996) and the World Bank (1991) found that a higher black-market premium was negatively associated with growth, suggesting that capital account openness positively enhances macro level economic growth. And, finally, international labour migration might affect economic growth through two channels. On the one hand, there is an *ex ante* 'brain effect', because migration induces domestic investments in education, given the higher returns to education abroad. On the other, an *ex post* 'drain effect' arises when the more educated labour force migrate out. The so-called beneficial brain drain (BBD) emerges when the brain effect outweighs the drain effect. Indeed, Beine *et al.* (2001) find supportive evidence for the possibility of a BBD. Moreover, international emigration reduces poverty through the remittances sent by the migrants. Indeed, Adams and Page (2003) found that international emigration exerts a strong, statistically significant and positive effect on reducing poverty in a broad cross-section of developing countries.

Despite the compelling evidence using cross-country macro data, there is relatively little empirical evidence on the role of the two types of globalization – that is, integration of international trade and emigration – in reducing poverty at the household level. This chapter tries to fill in this gap in the literature by using household-level data from the Philippines, and we employ Target 1 of the MDGs as the benchmark in evaluating the effects of globalization on poverty reduction.

The provincial poverty lines

The poverty line can be the domestic poverty line, set by the National Statistical Co-ordination Board (NSCB) of the Philippine government or the international poverty line, which is pegged at US$1.08 per capita per day purchasing power parity (PPP) equivalent (Chen and Ravallion 2004). The use of the PPP may indeed be appropriate in assessing the poverty situation of the country as a whole (World Bank 2005). The PPP, however, may not measure accurately the spatial variations of poverty within the country, because it fails to incorporate inter-provincial price differences. Price variations across provinces may be considerable in large and poorly integrated economies such as the Philippines (Baulch 1997). In this chapter, we estimate better and internationally comparable provincial poverty lines by carefully assessing and incorporating the inter-provincial price differences.

Provincial PPP and the provincial one-dollar-a-day poverty line

The PPP for province j in the Philippines in year t is defined as:

$$\frac{P_{j,t}^{Ph}}{P_{1993}^{US}} \tag{4.1}$$

where $P_{j,t}^{Ph}$ is the overall price level in province j in the Philippines and P_{1993}^{US} is the aggregate price level of the USA in the benchmark year of 1993. The provincial PPP in Equation (4.1) can be represented as a product of the country-level PPP and the ratio of the provincial-specific price level to the national price level:

$$\underbrace{\frac{P_{j,t}^{Ph}}{P_{1993}^{US}}}_{\substack{Provincial \\ PPP}} = \underbrace{\frac{P_{j,t}^{Ph}}{P_{t}^{Ph}}}_{\substack{(A) \\ Relative \\ price \\ (Term\ A)}} \times \underbrace{\frac{P_{t}^{Ph}}{P_{1993}^{Ph}}}_{\substack{(B) \\ CPI\ in \\ the\ Philippines \\ (Term\ B)}} \times \underbrace{\frac{P_{1993}^{Ph}}{P_{1993}^{US}}}_{\substack{(C) \\ Benchmark \\ PPP \\ (Term\ C)}} \tag{4.2}$$

where P_{t}^{Ph} is the overall price level in the Philippines.

The provincial relative price (Term A) in Equation (4.2) can be computed through a two-step procedure. In the first stage, we used the detailed provincial-level individual commodity price information collected by the National Statistics Office (NSO) to obtain the benchmark-relative prices in 2003 for all provinces. For example, the overall price level in province j at year 2003, $P_{j,2003}^{Ph}$, can be calculated from the commodity-wise price data in the province:

$$P_{j,2003}^{Ph} = \sum_{k=1}^{N} w_k P_{j,2003}^{k,Ph}, \quad \sum_{k=1}^{N} w_k = 1 \tag{4.3}$$

where k is an identifier of consumption items and w_k is the share of the commodity in the household budget. We take the price information in 2003 on rice as a major staple, poultry meat as source of protein, and electricity as a non-food expenditure item to construct this benchmark price. We also calculate the aggregate price level, P_{2003}^{Ph}, by applying Equation (4.3) to the national-level data. In the second stage, we use the provincial- and national-level consumer price index (CPI) to compute the relative price for year t using the formula:

$$\underbrace{\frac{P_{j,t}^{Ph}}{P_t^{Ph}}}_{\substack{Relative \\ price}} = \underbrace{\frac{P_{j,2003}^{Ph}}{P_{2003}^{Ph}}}_{\substack{Benchmark \\ relative\ price}} \times \underbrace{\frac{\overbrace{P_{j,t}^{Ph} / P_{j,2003}^{Ph}}^{\substack{Provincial \\ CPI}}}{P_t^{Ph} / P_{2003}^{Ph}}}_{\substack{National \\ CPI}} \tag{4.4}$$

Equation (4.4) constitutes the entire Term A of Equation (4.2). Term B of Equation (4.2) is simply the ratio of the aggregate CPI in the Philippines at time t and the CPI in 1993, with the CPI being taken from the NSO database. Finally, following World Bank (2005), the benchmark PPP in Term C of Equation (4.2) is simply the consumption PPP in 1993 drawn directly from the Penn World Tables 5.7.[2] By using the province-specific PPP of Equation (4.2), it is straightforward to compute the poverty line for each province in the local currency equivalent of US$1.08 per capita per day.

The NSCB is the agency responsible for setting domestic poverty lines. The NSCB poverty line, however, is considerably higher than the US$1.08 per capita per day PPP equivalent. For example, the NSCB annual poverty line in the year 2000 was Php 13,966, whereas the US$1.08 per capita per day is only Php 6,614. We thus expect that the proportion of households and individuals that are classified as poor is significantly higher when using the NSCB poverty line.[3]

Poverty trends in the Philippines, 1985–2000

We assessed the provincial poverty situation by applying the province-specific US$1.08 per capita per day to the per capita expenditure (see Table 4.1). We use household size as weights in our calculations of poverty incidence and poverty gap ratio, to correct for possible sampling bias associated with household size – that is, the poverty contribution of smaller households is magnified if there is no correction for household size in the calculations.

For each province, we construct two poverty measures: the incidence of poverty or the headcount ratio, $P(0)$, and the poverty gap measure, $P(1)$, where $P(\alpha)$ is the Foster–Greer–Thorbecke (FGT) (1984) poverty index, defined as:

$$P(\alpha) = \int_0^Z \left(\frac{Z - C}{Z}\right)^\alpha f(C)dC, \ \alpha \geq 0 \tag{4.5}$$

where C is the individual consumption level, $f(C)$ is its consumption density function, and Z is the poverty line. We do all our calculations using the rounds of family income and expenditure surveys (FIES) from 1985, 1988, 1991, 1994, 1997 and 2000. The FIES in the Philippines is a large-scale, repeated cross-section and multipurpose household survey collected and compiled by the NSO.

Table 4.1 shows the poverty measures at the level of individual members of the household for the Philippines as a whole, using the US$1.08 per capita per day poverty line. The proportion of poor individuals remained fairly similar at about 25 per cent from 1985 to 1991, decreased to 16.6 per cent in 1997 but increased to 18.1 per cent in 2000.[4] The increase in 2000 is possibly a result of the negative impacts generated by the Asian financial crisis and the severe drought caused by *El Niño*. Datt and Hoogeveen (2003) found that the *El Niño* shock accounted for the largest share of the overall impact, mainly because a substantial number of poor Filipino households make their living from agriculture.

The Appendix (see page 110) shows the provincial-level poverty incidence for 1985–2000. The incidence of poverty in 1985 was generally higher in provinces located in the Bicol region – namely Catanduanes, Masbate and Sorsogon – but the decline in poverty in these provinces was remarkable in the 1990s. The Central Luzon region – more notably the provinces of Bulacan, Nueva Ecija and Pampanga – had the lowest poverty incidence in all the years surveyed.

Cebu experienced the most remarkable decline in poverty in the Central Visayas, and Camiguin in Northern Mindanao. Davao and Davao del Sur had the lowest poverty in Southern Mindanao, comparable with the provinces in Central Luzon. Provinces located in Southern Tagalog, Central Luzon and Ilocos are less poor compared with provinces in other regions because of their

Table 4.1 Poverty lines and poverty indicators at the individual level in the Philippines, 1985–2000

	1985	1988	1991	1994	1997	2000
Poverty lines in Php annual values						
NSCB	3,856	5,008	7,292	8,878	10,998	13,966
US$1.08 [1]	2,003	2,497	3,452	4,343	5,413	6,614
Poverty incidence at the individual level (%) [2]						
US$1.08 [1]	23.5	24.9	24.6	17.5	16.6	18.1
Poverty gap at the individual level (%) [2]						
US$1.08 [1]	6.04	6.34	6.53	4.18	3.89	4.38

Notes:
[1] Per capita per day adjusted for interprovincial price differences.
[2] Based on per capita expenditure data.

Source: National Statistical Coordination Board (NSCB), *Statistical Yearbook*, various years.

proximity to the national capital region (NCR). Provinces in the Southern Tagalog region that belong to the CALABARZON group (Cavite, Laguna, Batangas and Quezon) are expected to be less poor because of their proximity to the NCR and the government's efforts to build infrastructure to induce industries and residential areas to relocate to CALABARZON in an attempt to decongest the NCR. On the other hand, the poorest provinces in the year 2000, where the incidence of poverty is more than 50 per cent are Masbate in Bicol, Eastern Samar in Eastern Visayas, Ifugao, Kalinga, and Mount Province in CAR. Overall, we can observe wide variations in poverty across provinces and different years, which can be explained partly by the wide variations in provincial household income and price levels.

Poverty, international trade and emigration

The Philippines can be characterized by an increasing external openness, which we define as a ratio of the total value of exports to GDP, from 1986 to 1998, except for 1997, during the Asian currency crisis, when the degree of openness in the Philippines declined sharply (see Figure 4.1). Using household data from the Philippines, Pernia and Quising (2003) find that trade openness appears to be beneficial to regional economic growth because it induces a movement of the production base away from the NCR, which had

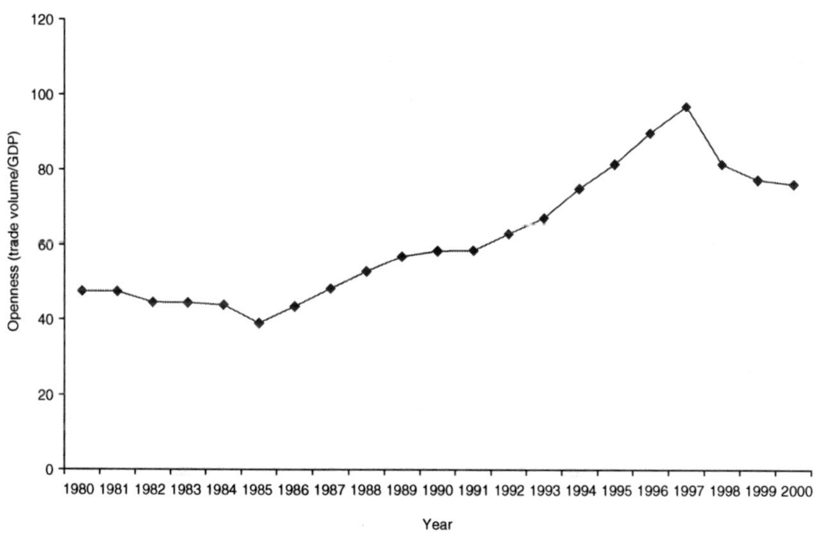

Figure 4.1 Openness in the Philippines, 1980–2000

Note: The openness index is defined as the ratio of export value to GDP.

Source: Penn World Tables.

been the hub of major economic growth in the country. Pernia and Quising (2003) find that most of the special economic zones (SEZs) (which are largely export processing zones – EPZs), have started to move out of NCR to relocate to Southern Tagalog, Central Luzon and Central Visayas. The movement of industries away from NCR has been facilitated by the Bases Conversion and Development Act, enacted in 1995, mandating the conversion of the former US bases into SEZs. The Special Economic Zone Act, on the other hand, facilitates the flow of exports overseas from these four regions. The NCR had a 24 per cent share of the total value of exports in 2000, Southern Tagalog had 52 per cent, Central Luzon 7 per cent, and Central Visayas 6 per cent. Machines and transport equipment, which are largely labour-intensive products, were the major exports of the Philippines, consisting of 22 per cent in 1994 and 37 per cent in 2000 of the total value of exports.

The Philippines is also known as a major supplier of international migrants. Contract workers in Saudi Arabia and permanent emigrants to the USA are major groups of Filipino migrants. Figure 4.2 presents the number of registered Filipino emigrants in the professional, technical and related categories. It is evident that the numbers of these workers increased remarkably from the late 1990s. It is noteworthy that overseas workers were made up of 51 per cent males and 49 per cent females in 2002. Common country destinations are Saudi Arabia, Japan and Taiwan for males, and Hong Kong, Singapore, Japan and Saudi Arabia for females.

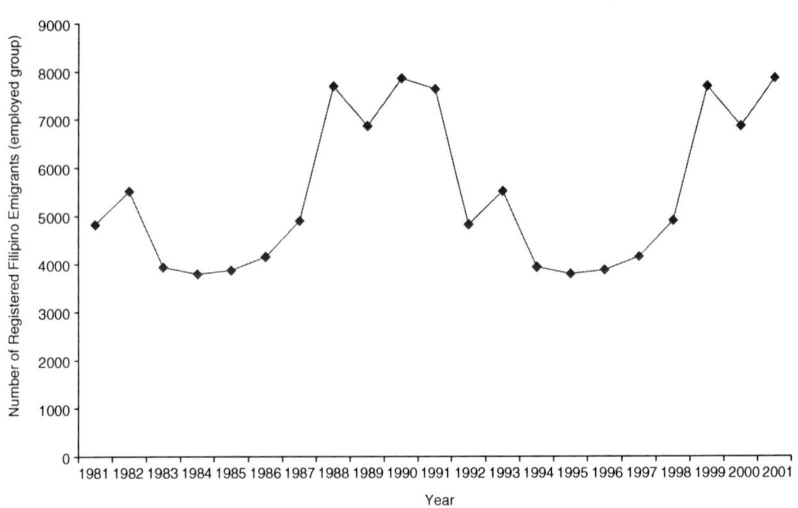

Figure 4.2   Number of registered Filipino emigrants, 1981–2001*

Note: * Refers to employed professional, technical and related workers only.

Source: National Statistical Coordintion Board, *Philippine Statistical Yearbook*, various issues.

Using household-level data, Rodríguez (1998) shows that an expansion in international emigration increased the per capita income growth in the Philippines, even though the amount of remittances (in US$) does not necessarily comply with this pattern of labour emigration (see Figure 4.3). This is possibly because the level of remittances sent to the Philippines is explained mainly by the level of income of the host countries and not merely by the number of Filipino workers overseas in the respective host countries. Specifically, workers going to East Asian countries such as Japan, Korea and China tend to send more remittances home because these are higher-income countries, where wages are higher.

Impacts of external openness and emigration on poverty reduction: provincial-level estimates

To investigate the role of international trade and emigration in poverty reduction, we apply a reduced-form cross-country regression approach, suggested by Besley and Burgess (2003), to the provincial-level data in the Philippines. The Besley and Burgess (2003) model is

$$\log P_{it} = \eta \log y_{it} + \theta_i + \varepsilon_{it} \tag{4.6}$$

where P_{it} and y_{it} are the incidence of poverty and average per capita household income, respectively, in the ith province at time t. The second and the last terms on the right-hand side are the provincial fixed effects, and a

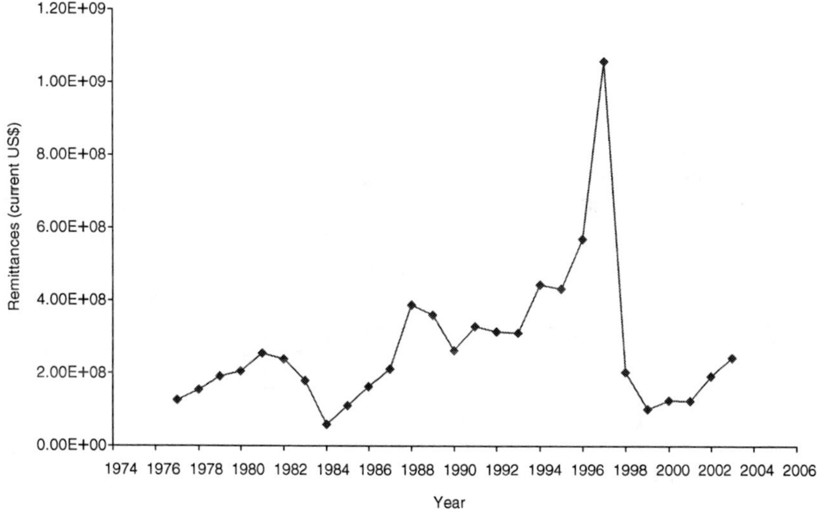

Figure 4.3   Remittances to the Philippines, 1977–2003
Source: World Bank, *World Developement Indicators*, various years.

well-behaved error term, respectively. With the estimated elasticity, η, we can compute the annual per capita household income growth rate necessary to achieve target 1 of the MDGs. We extend the Besley and Burgess (2003) model in Equation (4.6), by adding a variable for external openness, *OPEN*, and by decomposing total household income into non-transfer income, y^{NT}, and transfer income, y^T, both of which are extracted from the FIES:

$$\log P_{it} = \eta_{1(t)} \log OPEN_{it} + \eta_2 \log y_{it}^{NT} + \eta_3 \log y_{it}^T + \theta_i + \varepsilon_{it} \qquad (4.7)$$

Since the left-hand side variable is at the provincial level, y^{NT} and y^T refer to the average values for each province. *OPEN* is defined as the ratio of regional exports to the gross regional domestic products (GRDP) and we allow its coefficient to vary by year by interacting *OPEN* with the year dummies. The export data are extracted from the foreign trade statistics, while the GRDP is extracted from various issues of the *Philippine Statistical Yearbook*. *OPEN* is constructed for fourteen regions in 1988, 1994 and 2000, with the exclusion of only 1985, 1991 and 1997. While the sample size reduces to about half when we exclude these three years, Pernia and Quising (2003) argue that significant liberalization measures were introduced in the Philippine economy in 1988, 1994 and 2000, thus making these years particularly suitable for our analysis. Also, these three years cover the wake of the Asian currency crisis, when the national economic growth rate fell back significantly.

We further extend Equation (4.7) by adding an income inequality variable on the right-hand side, measured by the interprovincial standard deviation of household income, σ_{it}. And to examine the effects of the changing degree of globalization, we estimate Equation (4.7) by allowing *OPEN* to vary by year. The revised equation is:

$$\log P_{it} = \eta_{1(t)} \log OPEN_{it} + \eta_2 \log y_{it}^{NT} + \eta_3 \log y_{it}^T + \beta\sigma_{it} + \theta_i + \varepsilon_{it} \qquad (4.8)$$

Table 4.2 summarizes the descriptive statistics for the variables used in our estimations, while Table 4.3 shows the results of Equations (4.6), (4.7) and (4.8). We calculate an elasticity, η, of -0.44 with a standard error of 0.04; the coefficient was statistically significant at the 1 per cent level of significance (see Table 4.3: Specification (1)).[5] This implies that it would require a 6.5 per cent annual per capita income growth over 25 years to cut the poverty incidence by a half in the Philippines. Specifications (3) and (4) in Table 4.3 show that the coefficients on y^{NT} were negative and statistically significant, suggesting that y^{NT} had the effect of decreasing poverty, whereas the coefficients of y^T were not statistically different from zero. These results suggest that, at the provincial level of aggregation, the growth of y^{NT} was a significantly more important driving force behind poverty reduction. Unexpectedly, the sign of the coefficients of *OPEN* turned out to be positive, pointing to the possibility that trade openness created more poverty (see Table 4.3: Specifications (5) and (6)). We thus include the openness index for each year separately to identify during which specific year trade openness led to more poverty. Specification (7) in Table 4.3 shows that the coefficient of *OPEN* was negative and significant in 1988 and 1994, and positive and significant in 2000. The sharp change in the impact of trade openness on poverty incidence may be a reflection of the Asian currency crises that decreased living standards in the Philippines through the international transmission of negative international macroshocks to the Philippine economy. This finding is consistent with

Table 4.2 Descriptive statistics for the variables used in the estimations

Variable name		No. of valid observations	Mean	Standard deviation
		Province-level data		
Headcount ratio (in log)	lpoor	461	−2.094	1.228
Average income per adult equivalent in log	lpi	468	9.458	0.675
Average non-transfer income per adult scale equivalent in log	lpneti	468	9.384	0.659
Average transfer income per adult equivalent in log	ltr	466	6.442	1.376
Openness index (regional-level data)	open	223	0.264	0.441
Intra-province standard deviation of income per adult equivalent scale	di	468	0.721	0.102
Rate of implementation of land reform by province	carp	419	36.271	36.706
		Household-level data		
Dummy = 1 if a household's income per adult equivalent scale is below US$1 per day poverty line	wbpoor1	161,014	0.149	0.356
Poverty gap $(Z–C)/Z$ if a household income is below poverty line	adwb1	161,014	0.036	0.106
Non-transfer income per adult scale equivalent	netapci	161,645	19996.140	49331.78
Transfer income per adult equivalent	aptr	161,645	1845.789	10044.16
Openness index (regional-level data)	open	79,029	0.329	0.504

Table 4.3 Determinants of provincial poverty headcount ratio in the Philippines, 1985–2000, results of Equations (4.6), (4.7) and (4.8)

Variable	Specification						
	(1)	(2)	(3)	(4)	(5)	(6)	(7)
	Coef. (Std err.)	Coef. (Std err.)	Coef. (Std err.)	Coef. (Std err.)	Coef. (Std err.)	Coef. (Std err.)	Coef. (Std err.)
Total income[1]	−0.440 (0.040)	−0.540 (0.045)					
Non-transfer income[1]			−0.475 (0.064)	−0.522 (0.063)	−0.546 (0.132)	−0.608 (0.122)	−0.670 (0.138)
Transfer income[1]			0.028 (0.040)	−0.012 (0.040)	0.036 (0.080)	−0.056 (0.076)	−0.050 (0.076)
$OPEN^2$					0.207 (0.105)	0.215 (0.097)	
$OPEN$ in 1988							−0.387 (0.622)
$OPEN$ in 1994							−0.774 (0.397)
$OPEN$ in 2000							0.212 (0.100)
Std dev. of total income		1.730 (0.374)		1.714 (0.383)		2.964 (0.595)	2.779 (0.634)
Constant	2.072 (0.380)	1.762 (0.376)	2.186 (0.431)	1.648 (0.437)	2.740 (0.852)	1.788 (0.809)	2.552 (1.015)
No. of observations	461	461	459	459	220	220	220
No. of provinces	81	81	81	81	81	81	81

Notes:
[1] In logarithm and adult equivalent using the following weights: members 1–7 years old = 0.2; 8–15 years old = 0.4; 16–24 years old = 0.8; 25 years old and above = 1.0.
[2] Regional-level openness index defined as the ratio of the value of regional exports to the regional GDP in 1988, 1994 and 2000.

those of Datt and Hoogeveen (2003), who found a 5 per cent reduction in average living standards in the Philippines because of the Asian crises.

Our results are consistent with the hypothesis that inequality tends to increase poverty; the coefficients of the income inequality measure were all positive and highly significant in Specifications (2), (4), (6) and (7) in Table 4.3. More specifically, the estimated coefficient was 2.96, with a standard error of 0.595 and the variable's standard deviation of 0.102 (see Table 4.3: Specification (6)). This means that if we lower the level of inequality by one standard deviation, poverty declines by as much as 30 per cent – that is, 2.96 × 0.102.[6] This simple, back-of-the-envelope calculation suggests that a redistribution policy can lead to a considerable reduction of poverty in the Philippines. Indeed, Balisacan and Fuwa (2003) point out that the implementation of the CARP has had an important impact on both economic growth and asset and income redistribution in the Philippines.

The absolute magnitude of the elasticity in the Philippines is much smaller compared with that of the Asia and Pacific region and other regions in the world, as reported by Besley and Burgess (2003) (see Table 4.4). Hence it is reasonable to conclude that economic growth in the Philippines has had the lowest impact on poverty reduction in East Asia. The historical per capita real GDP growth rate from 1960 to 1990 was only 1.3 per cent per annum, which means that the Philippines needs to increase its speed of economic growth by about five times in order to achieve Target 1 of the MDGs. Since the speed of necessary growth necessary to achieve Target 1 is higher than the historical average, there is clearly a need to identify policy instruments to enhance economic growth and implement redistribution and institutional reforms that can reduce poverty even in a regime of slow growth. Land reform has been considered to be an effective redistributive

Table 4.4   Growth and poverty reduction in different regions, 1990–2015

	Philippines	World	Asia & the Pacific	Eastern Europe & Central Asia	Latin America	Middle East & North Africa	South Asia	Sub-Saharan Africa
Elasticity	−0.44	−0.71	−1.00	−1.14	−0.73	−0.72	−0.59	−0.49
Required growth (%)[1]	6.51	3.80	2.70	2.40	3.80	3.80	4.70	5.60
Average annual growth, 1960–90 (%)	1.30	1.70	3.30	2.00	1.30	4.30	1.90	0.20

Note: [1] Required growth rate to achieve Goal 1 and Target 1 of the Millennium Development Goals (MDGs).
Sources: Besley and Burgess (2003); Penn World Tables online.

programme targeted to benefit the poor and, in addition, we believe that macroeconomic and political stability, and revitalized public infrastructure, are equally important to enhance private investment and private sector development.

Impacts of external openness and emigrants on poverty reduction: household-level estimates

We investigate the determinants of poverty at the household level using $P(0)$ and $P(1)$ of the FGT index and the same regression equations that we apply at the provincial level. The econometric model for $P(0)$ is:

$$P_{it}^{*} = \beta_0 + \beta_1\, y_{it}^{NT} + \beta_2\, y_{it}^{T} + \varepsilon_{it} \tag{4.9}$$

$$HC_{it} = 1 \quad \text{if } P_{it}^{*} > 0$$

where P_{it}^{*} is a continuous latent variable, which indicates the degree of poverty. HC is a discrete variable, which takes the value of unity, if the household per capita income falls below the poverty threshold, and zero otherwise. We estimate the system of Equation (4.9) using a probit model under normality assumptions.

The econometric model for $P(1)$ is:

$$P_{it}^{*} = \beta_0 + \beta_1\, y_{it}^{NT} + \beta_2\, y_{it}^{T} + \varepsilon_{it} \tag{4.10}$$

$$GAP_{it} = P_{it}^{*} \quad \text{if } P_{it}^{*} > 0$$

$$= 0 \text{ otherwise}$$

where GAP is defined as $(Z-C)/Z$.

Table 4.5 shows the results of Equations (4.9) and (4.10). In all the specifications, the coefficients of y^{NT} and y^{T} were negative, suggesting that both types of income decreased the incidence and depth of poverty significantly. The magnitude of the coefficients of y^{T} was significantly larger than that of y^{NT} based on the Wald tests for the quality of coefficients, which means that at the household level, y^{T} is significantly more important than y^{NT} in decreasing poverty. Recall that in the provincial-level of analysis, we find the opposite, that is, y^{NT} was significantly more important than y^{T} in reducing the provincial headcount index. We believe that these contrasting results are simply an artefact of the aggregate data, which are provincial averages that do not capture the individual household effects of y^{T} in reducing poverty.

Our finding that y^{T} was more important than y^{NT} is consistent with the findings of Cox and Jimenez (1995), who found that the income shortfall of the poor induces a large increase in private transfers from the rich to the

Table 4.5 Determinants of the probability of being poor, and poverty gap ratio of poor households in the Philippines, 1985–2000; results of Equations (4.9), (4.10) and (4.11)

Dependent variable	Probability of being poor			Poverty gap ratio(for poor households only)		
Specification	(1)	(2)	(3)	(4)	(5)	(6)
Independent variable	Coef. (Std err.)	Coef. (Std err.)	Coef. (Std err.)	Coef. (Std err.)	Coef. (Std err.)	Coef. (Std err.)
Non-transfer income in adult equivalent scale (in 1,000 Php)	−0.184 (0.000142)	−0.188 (0.000204)	−0.228 (0.000238)	−0.060 (0.000473)	−0.059 (0.000646)	−0.067 (0.000697)
Transfer income in adult equivalent scale (in 1,000 Php)	−0.230 (0.000635)	−0.218 (0.00083)	−0.228 (0.000840)	−0.074 (0.000196)	−0.067 (0.00245)	−0.065 (0.00233)
OPEN in 1988, 1994 and 2000		0.512 (0.017)	−0.906 (0.08)		0.157 (0.00475)	−0.230 (0.021)
Additional coefficient of OPEN in 1988			−2.530 (0.104)			−0.723 (0.027)
Additional coefficient of OPEN in 2000			1.520 (0.080)			0.404 (0.021)
Constant	0.562 (0.010)	0.579 (0.015)	0.579 (0.015)	0.197 (0.0028)	0.196 (0.0040)	0.333 (0.0047)
Wald test statistics [p-value] on equality of non-transfer income and transfer income coefficients	51.42 [0.0000]	12.60 [0.0004]	0.11 [0.736]	49.76 [0.0000]	10.54 [0.0012]	0.84 [0.359]
No. of observations	161,014	161,014	78,714	161,014	161,014	78,714

poor, leading to a decline in poverty and an improved distribution of household income. Figure 4.3 also shows a marked increase in remittances in 1997 during *El Niño*, giving further support to Cox and Jimenez (1995). Private transfers in the Philippines commonly circulate among altruistically linked extended families.

To examine the direct impacts of trade openness on household-level poverty, we include *OPEN* in Equation (4.10), so that our latent equation for poverty becomes:

$$P_{it}^{*} = \beta_0 + \alpha_t\, OPEN_{it} + \beta_1\, y_{it}^{NT} + \beta_2\, y_{it}^{T} + \varepsilon_{it} \tag{4.11}$$

The coefficients of the openness index were positive and statistically significant, supporting the provincial-level evidence of a significant and positive relationship between trade openness and degree of poverty (see Table 4.5). Year-specific slope dummies for the openness index showed a negative and significant coefficient in 1988 and 1994, but a positive and significant coefficient in 2000, once again supporting our provincial-level results and suggesting that trade openness reduced poverty significantly before the Asian crises, while its impacts were reversed after the crises. The massive depreciation of the local currency caused large changes in relative prices that reduced the real income of the poor (World Bank 2000). Accordingly, trade openness generated a negative impact on the welfare of the poor during the crisis. In fact, more than 90 per cent of families reported being adversely affected by higher prices for food and other commodities (World Bank 2000: 114).

We augment the Tobit model of Equation (4.11) by adding observations on the poverty gap variable of the non-poor households along with the poor households. The resulting estimation model is the so-called treatment effect model, or the model with the endogenous dummy variable (Greene 2003: 787–9):

$$GAP_{it} = \beta_0 + \alpha OPEN_{it} + \beta_1\, y_{it}^{NT} + \beta_2\, y_{it}^{T} + \delta HC_{it} + \varepsilon_{it} \tag{4.12}$$

$$POV_{it}^{*} = Z_{it}\, \gamma + v_{it}$$

where *POV* represents the latent continuous variable of being in poverty. We estimate the system of Equation (4.12) by assuming that ε and v follow a bivariate normal distribution. We employ the Heckman two-step procedure to estimate the model with corrected standard errors. The first stage is a probit model of the probability of being poor, while the second stage is the regression of the determinants of the poverty gap ratio. The poverty gap ratio of the poor households was positive, while it was negative for the non-poor households. Accordingly, we include the sample selection correction term in the second stage, so that our second-stage equation becomes:

$$GAP_{it} = \beta_0 + \alpha OPEN_{it} + \beta_1 y_{it}^{NT} + \beta_2 y_{it}^{T} + \delta HC_{it} \tag{4.13}$$

$$+ \delta_{it}\alpha_1 \frac{\phi(Z_{it}\hat{\gamma})}{\Phi(Z_{it}\hat{\gamma})} - (1 - \delta_{it})\alpha_1 \frac{\phi(Z_{it}\hat{\gamma})}{1 - \Phi(Z_{it}\hat{\gamma})} + u_{it}$$

where $\phi(\cdot)$ and $\Phi(\cdot)$ are the density and cumulative density functions of a standard normal distribution, respectively. Table 4.6 shows that, in the pooled sample, consisting of both poor and non-poor households, the effect of y^T became larger than that of y^{NT}, which suggests that transfer income is

Table 4.6 Determinants of the poverty gap ratio of poor and non-poor households in the Philippines, 1988–2000; results of the Heckman two-stage procedure in Equation (4.13) with provincial fixed effects

Dependent variable	Probability of being poor (1st stage)	Poverty gap ratio (poor & non-poor households) (2nd stage)
Specification	(1)	(2)
Independent variable	Coef. (Std err.)	Coef. (Std err.)
Non-transfer income in adult equivalent scale (1,000 Php)	−0.188 (0.0020)***	−0.0832 (0.00021)***
Transfer income in adult equivalent scale (1,000 Php)	−0.218 (0.0083)***	−0.0714 (0.00098)***
OPEN in 1988, 1994 and 2000[1]	0.512 (0.017)***	0.372 (0.021)***
Headcount ratio (in log)		1.353 (0.056)***
Constant	0.579 (0.0150)***	−0.498 (0.017)***
$\alpha_1[\sigma(\varepsilon) \times \text{corr}(\varepsilon, v)]$		−0.262 (0.038)***
No. of observations		78,714

Note: [1] Regional-level openness index.

an especially important instrument in reducing the poverty of poor and non-poor households alike. The coefficients on the sample-selection correction terms were significantly different from zero, indicating that the exclusion of the non-poor households in the regression of the determinants of poverty gap ratio leads to a significant sample selection bias.

The determinants of transfer income from abroad

Overseas migration is a direct way by which households can participate in globalization. Overseas migration tends to reduce poverty through transfer income from overseas, even though transfer income from abroad causes an increase in household income inequality (Estudillo *et al.* 2001). In the Philippines, about 5 per cent of the total household income comes from overseas transfers, and about 4 per cent from domestic transfers.[7] Since overseas job placements require a significant amount of money for job placement fees and pocket money, credit availability is a key deciding factor for a household to invest in emigration. Credit availability increases with land ownership and access to usufruct, so that the implementation of the land reform programme may affect the household decision to invest in emigration, and therefore, the amount of transfer income received by the households.

The land reform programme in the Philippines was promulgated by Presidential Decree (PD) 27 during the Marcos Administration. PD 27 applies to rice and corn farms only. The programme converts share tenancy to leasehold tenancy, if the landlord owns less than 7 hectares of land, or to a certificate of land transfer (CLT) if the landlord owns more than 7 hectares. CLT holders receive an emancipation patent (EP) on completion of amortization payments to the Land Bank of the Philippines. The CARP under the Aquino Administration continued to implement the programmes under PD 27, and in addition transferred the ownership rights of public and alienable lands to cultivating tenants, increased the scope to include plantation crops as well as rice and corn, and decreased the maximum allowable landholdings from 7 ha. under the PD 27 to 3 ha.

Since the implementation of the land reform programme coincided with the green revolution, which had a significant impact on land productivity, the pawn values of land ownership and usufruct escalated, thus making land-pawning revenues an important source of funds for emigration. According to Otsuka (1991), the land reform programme has been implemented successfully in favourable rice-growing areas in the Philippines. Indeed, the areas that are characterized by favourable production environments and have undergone a successful land reform programme are those with a higher rate of emigration. Given the increase in de facto land ownership in the Philippines, and increased access to usufruct of land through the conversion of share tenancy to leasehold tenancy and CLT rights, land-pawning has become a dominant form of obtaining loans in the Philippines (Nagarajan *et al.* 1992).

Owned lands are commonly used as collateral to formal credit sources such as banks and co-operatives. Usufruct rights on land, such as leasehold rights and CLT rights, are pawned out to well-trusted informal credit sources such friends, relatives, fertilizer dealers and village money-lenders, because the pawning-out of usufruct rights is deemed to be illegal by the land reform laws. Revenues from pawning, on the other hand, are used to finance overseas job placement fees, the secondary and tertiary education of children, to cover sickness and death among family members, and to start a non-farm business endeavour such as the operation of village transport or a general store (Estudillo *et al.* 2007).

In any case, progress in land reform is likely to induce emigration and increase transfer income from abroad. In order to investigate this linkage, we regress transfer income from abroad at the provincial and household levels on the proportion of land under the land reform programme for each province. The estimation model is:

$$y_{it}^{TA} = \alpha_0 + \alpha_{(t)}\, CARP_{it} + \theta_i + \varepsilon_{it} \tag{4.14}$$

where *CARP* is the provincial-level proportion of land area under the implementation of the comprehensive agrarian reform programme, and θ_i is provincial fixed effects.

It is clear to see from Table 4.7 that the coefficient of *CARP* was positive and statistically significant at both the provincial and household levels, supporting our argument on the existence of the land reform–credit–emigration–transfer nexus. We also relax the constant coefficients on the implementation rate of land reform (see Table 4.7: Specifications 2 and 4). Interestingly, the net impact of the land reform coefficient was negative and statistically significant in 1985 and 1988, but the coefficient increased sharply after 1991. This implies that the effect of land reform was not positive in inducing transfer income from abroad in the 1980s, but the inducement effect had been enhanced significantly in the 1990s, possibly because pawning revenues had become an important source of funds to finance overseas migration.

While we believe that the implementation of land reform induced the rise in transfer income from abroad, we need to examine whether the implementation of land reform improved the poverty situation of the ultra poor. The ultra poor are commonly landless households that were not identified as beneficiaries of the land reform, thus we can expect that such households were not able to invest in emigration. Indeed, we find that the transfer income of the poorest of the poor, who belonged to

Table 4.7 Determinants of transfer income, the Philippines, 1985–2000: results of Equation (4.13) with provincial fixed effects

Specification	(1)	(2)	(3)	(4)
		Data at the:		
Independent variable	Province level Coef. (Std err.)	Province level Coef. (Std err.)	Household level Coef. (Std err.)	Household level Coef. (Std err.)
Percentage area in the province covered by land reform	0.018 (0.001)	−0.053 (0.029)	22.234 (0.792)	−113.062 (19.819)
Additional coefficient of land reform for:				
1988		0.040 (0.030)		77.130 (20.197)
1991		0.074 (0.028)		118.255 (19.128)
1994		0.067 (0.029)		120.365 (19.436)
1997		0.070 (0.029)		126.615 (19.532)
2000		0.071 (0.029)		135.514 (19.565)
Constant	5.719 (0.053)	5.796 (0.067)	639.293 (40.965)	976.863 (54.934)
No. of observations	408	408	133,168	133,168
No. of provinces	69	69	69	69

Table 4.8 Share of transfer income in total household income in the Philippines, by income decile, 2000

	I Poorest	II	III	IV	V	VI	VII	VIII	IX	X Richest
Share (%)	0.62	1.04	1.77	2.59	3.46	5.29	6.72	9.18	11.85	13.70
Standard deviation	4.73	5.97	8.17	10.00	11.82	15.43	17.11	20.51	23.18	25.04

the lowest income decile, was less than 1 per cent of the total income, whereas the transfer income of the highest income decile was about 14 per cent of the total income in 2000 (see Table 4.8). This implies that the ultra poor were excluded from the land reform–credit–emigration– transfer nexus.

Concluding remarks

The aim of this chapter was to assess how the two types of globalization – that is, integration of international trade and emigration – affected poverty reduction in the Philippines, using provincial panel data and repeated cross-sectional household data from 1985 to 2000. We have three important findings. First, both non-transfer and transfer incomes decreased poverty. At the provincial level of aggregation, the growth of non-transfer income was the more important driving force behind poverty reduction, while at household level, transfer income was more important. This implies that transfer income exerted a wide variation of household-specific effects in reducing poverty.

Second, external openness reduced poverty significantly in 1988 and 1994, whereas its impact was reversed in 2000. This sharp change may be a reflection of the Asian currency crisis, which decreased living standards through an international transmission of a negative macroshock to the Philippine economy. Third, and finally, progress in land reform implementation was likely to induce international emigration and increase transfer income from abroad. The effects of land reform in inducing transfers from abroad were not positive in the 1980s, but the inducement effect had been enhanced significantly by the 1990s perhaps because land-pawning arrangements had become popular in the 1990s. Pawning revenues were commonly used to pay job placement fees to ensure employment overseas. Unfortunately, we find that the ultra poor were left out of the land reform–credit–emigration–transfer nexus.

We believe that it is particularly important in future works to look closely at the households to identify other important transmission mechanisms by which emigration affected poverty reduction. For households that have benefited from previous emigration, we hypothesize that such emigration fosters further investments in the secondary and tertiary schooling of the younger generation, given that returns to higher levels of schooling are bound to be higher in overseas work (Estudillo and Otsuka 1999). But the ultra poor never ventured into emigration because they could afford to do so. An important question is how the benefits of emigration are transmitted to the ultra poor through interfamilial and intracommunity sharing mechanisms.

Appendix

Table 4.A1 Provincial poverty incidence at the individual level, 1985–2000[1] (US$1.08 per capita per day poverty line)

Region	Province	1985	1988	1991	1994	1997	2000
Philippines	Philippines	0.235	0.249	0.246	0.175	0.166	0.181
NCR	Metro Manila	0.035	0.133	0.021	0.003	0.021	0.033
Ilocos							
	Ilocos Norte	0.133	0.181	0.265	0.159	0.111	0.073
	Ilocos Sur	0.346	0.303	0.246	0.211	0.111	0.152
	La Union	0.167	0.222	0.231	0.229	0.246	0.194
	Pangasinan	0.355	0.322	0.346	0.228	0.256	0.251
Cagayan							
	Batanes	0.367	0.359	0.179	0.244	0.050	0.030
	Cagayan	0.459	0.575	0.479	0.373	0.317	0.360
	Isabela	0.386	0.398	0.420	0.336	0.386	0.342
	Nueva Vizcaya	0.382	0.361	0.361	0.161	0.180	0.211
	Quirino	0.334	0.671	0.670	0.692	0.445	0.448
Central Luzon							
	Bataan	0.063	0.350	0.155	0.149	0.036	0.022
	Bulacan	0.028	0.008	0.027	0.030	0.015	0.013
	Nueva Ecija	0.187	0.137	0.162	0.101	0.106	0.075
	Pampanga	0.093	0.146	0.117	0.063	0.019	0.047
	Tarlac	0.460	0.548	0.481	0.417	0.329	0.446
	Zambales	0.208	0.336	0.338	0.371	0.246	0.382
Southern Tagalog							
	Aurora	0.103	0.071	0.171	0.056	0.034	0.112
	Batangas	0.133	0.136	0.087	0.046	0.029	0.022
	Cavite	0.000	0.003	0.030	0.007	0.005	0.008
	Laguna	0.022	0.031	0.020	0.009	0.008	0.014
	Occidental Mindoro	0.088	0.294	0.348	0.160	0.373	0.416
	Oriental Mindoro	0.543	0.753	0.622	0.422	0.365	0.447
	Palawan	0.505	0.408	0.513	0.396	0.251	0.199
	Quezon	0.186	0.254	0.148	0.087	0.134	0.174
	Rizal	0.074	n.a.	0.035	0.006	0.003	0.018
	Romblon	0.535	0.826	0.730	0.650	0.556	0.671
Bicol							
	Albay	0.381	0.484	0.491	0.256	0.354	0.306
	Camarines Norte	0.348	0.219	0.392	0.250	0.299	0.362
	Camarines Sur	0.330	0.364	0.433	0.332	0.255	0.353
	Catanduanes	0.439	0.451	0.264	0.205	0.204	0.310
	Masbate	0.555	0.622	0.667	0.685	0.630	0.647
	Sorsogon	0.590	0.677	0.576	0.342	0.379	0.378
	Albay	0.381	0.484	0.491	0.256	0.354	0.306

Continued

Table 4.A1 Continued

Region	Province	1985	1988	1991	1994	1997	2000
Western Visayas							
	Aklan	0.326	0.364	0.410	0.333	0.284	0.344
	Antique	0.690	0.581	0.652	0.537	0.375	0.377
	Capiz	0.564	0.632	0.673	0.532	0.332	0.484
	Guimaras	n.a.	n.a.	n.a.	n.a.	0.067	0.057
	Iloilo	0.208	0.215	0.244	0.107	0.092	0.085
	Negros Occidental	0.403	0.284	0.208	0.166	0.155	0.244
Central Visayas							
	Bohol	0.476	0.522	0.565	0.488	0.333	0.393
	Cebu	0.325	0.228	0.264	0.152	0.140	0.152
	Negros Oriental	0.408	0.472	0.381	0.311	0.424	0.405
	Siquijor	0.506	0.629	0.516	0.107	0.541	0.427
Eastern Visayas							
	Eastern Samar	0.566	0.346	0.499	0.375	0.650	0.587
	Leyte	0.435	0.431	0.429	0.292	0.338	0.346
	Northern Samar	0.634	0.697	0.392	0.428	0.544	0.491
	Southern Leyte	0.437	0.358	0.476	0.318	0.359	0.313
	Western Samar	0.265	0.326	0.201	0.207	0.291	0.203
Western Mindanao							
	Basilan	0.244	0.228	0.244	0.072	0.007	0.098
	Zamboanga del Norte	0.279	0.327	0.434	0.244	0.111	0.310
	Zamboanga del Sur	0.244	0.223	0.200	0.168	0.115	0.211
Northern Mindanao							
	Bukidnon	0.214	0.193	0.369	0.347	0.229	0.270
	Camiguin	0.664	0.452	0.548	0.636	0.265	0.289
	Misamis Occidental	0.304	0.147	0.291	0.098	0.128	0.152
	Misamis Oriental	0.192	0.127	0.121	0.072	0.060	0.059
Southern Mindanao							
	Davao	0.000	0.026	0.012	0.015	0.015	0.021
	Davao del Sur	0.042	0.093	0.066	0.029	0.009	0.013
	Davao Oriental	0.245	0.254	0.297	0.145	0.299	0.191
	Sarangani	n.a.	n.a.	n.a.	n.a.	0.157	0.221
	Southern Cotabato	0.096	0.140	0.153	0.044	0.107	0.053

Continued

Table 4.A1   Continued

Region	Province	1985	1988	1991	1994	1997	2000
Central Mindanao							
	Cotabato	0.187	0.189	0.247	0.223	0.241	0.143
	Lanao del Norte	0.059	0.081	0.130	0.102	0.113	0.174
	Sultan Kudarat	0.039	0.038	0.085	0.061	0.017	0.051
Cordillera Autonomous Region							
	Abra	0.192	0.269	0.438	0.240	0.159	0.117
	Apayao	n.a.	n.a.	n.a.	n.a.	0.401	0.478
	Benguet	0.059	0.015	0.037	0.000	0.031	0.012
	Ifugao	0.623	0.673	0.831	0.681	0.657	0.697
	Kalinga	0.250	0.388	0.613	0.435	0.450	0.516
	Mt. Province	0.376	0.606	0.391	0.503	0.617	0.509
Autonomous Region of Muslim Mindanao							
	Lanao del Sur	0.022	0.039	0.191	0.080	0.199	0.087
	Maguindanao	0.065	0.175	0.270	0.108	0.158	0.273
	Sulu	0.000	0.058	0.245	0.147	0.088	0.093
	Tawi-Tawi	0.055	0.136	0.000	0.055	0.074	0.177
Caraga							
	Agusan del Norte	0.205	0.081	0.268	0.249	0.220	0.212
	Agusan del Sur	0.502	0.460	0.589	0.462	0.408	0.381
	Surigao del Norte	0.102	0.140	0.090	0.076	0.084	0.056
	Surigao del Sur	0.395	0.329	0.409	0.289	0.349	0.244

Notes: [1] Based on the unadjusted per capita expenditure.
n.a. = not available.
Source: Authors' calculations from the Family Income and Expenditure Surveys, 1985–2000.

Acknowledgements

We thank Anne Booth, Machiko Nissanke, Erik Thorbecke, Masahisa Fujita, Yujiro Hayami, Takashi Kurosaki, Keijiro Otsuka, Anthony Shorrocks and other participants in the JICA/UNU-WIDER meeting on the Impact of Globalization on the Poor in Asia, held in Tokyo, for their constructive comments and suggestions. We also express our gratitude to Jeff Ducanes, Jessaine Soraya Sugui and Laila Soliven for their excellent assistance in the preparation of this study, and the National Statistics Office for providing the data set. The usual caveat applies.

Notes

1 Krueger and Berg (2002) find that openness enhances economic growth while it does not affect poverty systematically.

2 The 1993 benchmark PPP is used by the World Bank (2005) as the benchmark PPP for assessing the poverty situation in the Philippines.
3 We compare our provincial poverty lines with the domestic provincial poverty lines calculated by the NSCB, and with the poverty line based on real expenditure calculated by Balisacan (2003). The NSCB domestic poverty lines are calculated using the prevailing domestic prices of a basket of commodities typically consumed by an average poor household. Balisacan's (2003) poverty line is calculated by deflating the nominal expenditure by the true cost of living index, which is defined for fixed reference prices and reference household characteristics. A simple OLS regression of our poverty line with that of the NSCB shows a slope of 0.56 and, in the case of Balisacan (2003), a slope of 0.17.
4 Estudillo *et al.* (2007), on the contrary, find a remarkable movement out of poverty in their study villages in Central Luzon and Panay Island.
5 The null hypothesis of zero fixed effects is rejected overwhelmingly.
6 Sawada (2004) shows that the major land reform in postwar Japan decreased the standard deviation of income from around 0.9 in 1940 to 0.6 in the late 1950s.
7 Overseas remittances are used to finance overseas placement fees and the educational expenditure of younger siblings; to build a house; purchase assets such as land; finance agricultural expenditure on current inputs such as fertilizer and pesticides; and invest in new agricultural equipment, such as water pumps and threshers (Estudillo *et al.* 2007).

References

Adams, R. and Page, J. (2003) 'International Migration, Remittances, and Poverty in Developing Countries', Policy Research Working Paper 3179, World Bank, Washington, DC.

Balisacan, A. M. (2003) 'Poverty and Inequality', in A. Balisacan and H. Hill (eds), *The Philippine Economy: Development, Policies, and Challenges* (Manila: Ateneo de Manila University Press).

Balisacan, A. M. and Fuwa, N. (2003) 'Growth, Inequality and Politics Revisited: A Developing-country Case', *Economics Letters*, 79(1): 53–8.

Baulch, B. (1997) 'Transfer Costs, Spatial Arbitrage, and Testing for Food Market Integration', *American Journal of Agricultural Economics*, 79(2): 477–87.

Beine, M., Docquier, F. and Rapoport, H. (2001) 'Brain Drain and Economic Growth: Theory and Evidence', *Journal of Development Economics*, 64(1): 275–89.

Besley, T. and Burgess, R. (2003) 'Halving Global Poverty', *Journal of Economic Perspectives*, 17(3): 3–22.

Borensztein, E., de Gregorio, J. and Lee, J. W. (1998) 'How Does Foreign Direct Investment Affect Economic Growth?', *Journal of International Economics*, 45(1): 115–35.

Chen, S. and Ravallion, M. (2004) 'How Have the World's Poorest Fared Since the Early 1980s?', *World Bank Research Observer*, 19(2): 141–69.

Cox, D. and Jimenez, E. (1995) 'Private Transfers and the Effectiveness of Public Income Redistribution in the Philippines', in D. van de Walle and K. Nead (eds), *Public Spending and the Poor: Theory and Evidence* (New York: Johns Hopkins University Press).

Datt, G. and Hoogeveen, H. (2003) 'El Niño or El Peso? Crisis, Poverty and Income Distribution in the Philippines', *World Development*, 31(7): 1103–24.

Dollar, D. and Kraay, A. (2002) 'Growth *Is* Good for the Poor', *Journal of Economic Growth*, 7(3): 195–225. Reprinted in A. Shorrocks and R. van der Hoeven (eds)

(2004), *Growth, Inequality and Poverty: Prospects for Pro-poor Economic Development* (Oxford: Oxford University Press for UNU-WIDER).

Dollar, D. and Kraay, A. (2004) 'Trade, Growth and Poverty', *Economic Journal*, 114: F22–F49.

Estudillo, J. P. and Otsuka, K. (1999) 'Green Revolution, Human Capital and Off-farm Employment: Changing Sources of Income among Farm Households in Central Luzon, 1966–94', *Economic Development and Cultural Change*, 47(3): 497–523.

Estudillo, J. P., Quisumbing, A. R. and Otsuka, K. (2001) 'Income Distribution in Rice-growing Villages during the Post-Green Revolution Periods: The Philippine Case, 1985 and 1998', *Agricultural Economics*, 25(1): 71–84.

Estudillo, J. P., Sawada, Y. and Otsuka, K. (2007) 'The Changing Determinants of Schooling Investments: Evidence from Villages in the Philippines 1985–89 and 2002–04', *Journal of Development Studies* (forthcoming).

Foster, J., Greer, J. and Thorbecke, E. (1984) 'A Class of Decomposable Poverty Measures', *Econometrica*, 52(3): 761–65.

Greene, W. H. (2003) *Econometric Analysis*, 5th edn (Upper Saddle River, NJ: Prentice-Hall).

Harrison, A. (1996) 'Openness and Growth: A Time-Series, Cross-Country Analysis for Developing Countries', *Journal of International Economics*, 48(2): 419–47.

Krueger, A. O. and Berg, A. (2002) 'Trade, Growth and Poverty: A Selective Survey', Paper presented at the World Bank's Annual Conference on Development Economics, 29–30 April, Washington, DC.

Nagarajan, G., David, C. C. and Meyer, R. (1992) 'Informal Finance through Land Pawning Contracts: Evidence from the Philippines', *Journal of Development Studies*, 29(1): 93–107.

National Statistical Co-ordination Board (NSCB) (various years) *Philippine Statistical Yearbook* (Makati City: NSCB).

Nissanke, M. and Thorbecke, E. (eds) (2007) 'Channels and Policy Debate in the Globalization–Inequality–Poverty Nexus', in *The Impact of Globalization on the World's Poor: Transmission Mechanisms* (Basingstoke: Palgrave Macmillan for UNU-WIDER).

Otsuka, K. (1991) 'Determinants and Consequences of Land Reform Implementation in the Philippines', *Journal of Development Economics*, 35(2): 339–55.

Penn World Tables. Available at: http://pwt.econ.upenn.edu/php_site/ pwt_index.php

Pernia, E. M. and Quising, P. F. (2003) 'Trade Openness and Regional Development in a Developing Country', *Annals of Regional Science*, 37(3): 391–406.

Ravallion, M. (2001) 'Growth, Inequality, and Poverty: Looking Beyond Averages', *World Development*, 29(11): 1815–2001. Reprinted in A. Shorrocks and R. van der Hoeven (eds) (2004), *Growth, Inequality and Poverty: Prospects for Pro-poor Economic Development* (Oxford: Oxford University Press for UNU-WIDER).

Rodríguez, E. R. (1998) 'International Migration and Income Distribution in the Philippines', *Economic Development and Cultural Change*, 46(2): 329–50.

Sawada, Y. (2004) 'The MDGs and Applied Econometrics', Paper presented at the Japanese Economic Association Annual Meeting, Meiji Gakuin University, 13 June, Tokyo.

World Bank (various years) *World Development Indicators* (Washington, DC: World Bank).

World Bank (2000) *East Asia: Recovery and Beyond* (Washington, DC: World Bank).

World Bank (2001) *World Development Report* 2001 (Washington, DC: World Bank).

World Bank (2001) *Philippines Poverty Assessment*, Vols I and II (Washington, DC: World Bank).

World Bank (2002) *Globalization, Growth, and Poverty: Building an Inclusive World Economy* (New York: Oxford University Press).

World Bank (2005) PovcalNet Available at: http://iresearch.worldbank.org/ PovcalNet/ jsp/index.jsp.

5
Threshold Estimation on the Globalization–Poverty Nexus: Evidence from China

Zhicheng Liang

Introduction

Since the start of the 1990s, there has been a growing interest among both academics and policy-makers in exploring the relationship between globalization and poverty (for example, Ravallion 2001, 2005; World Bank 2002; Dollar and Kraay 2002, 2004; Winters *et al.* 2004; Nissanke and Thorbecke 2007). Are the distributional effects of globalization neutral? More specifically, to what extent and under what conditions will globalization benefit the poor? These critical issues have been at the centre of many studies and the subject of passionate debate worldwide.

Globalization can affect poverty through multifaceted channels, creating both winners and losers. In their more recent, excellent, work, Nissanke and Thorbecke (2007) conclude that globalization could affect poverty both indirectly through 'growth effects' and directly through other channels, such as changes in relative prices of factors and products, differential cross-border factor mobility, the nature of technological progress and the technological diffusion process, volatility and vulnerability, the nature of the worldwide flow of information, and global disinflation. Meanwhile, a large number of empirical studies have been conducted to investigate the various channels and linkages through which globalization may affect the poor (for example, Hertel *et al.* 2001; Dollar and Kraay 2002, 2004; Levinsohn *et al.* 2003; Agénor 2004).

However, the existence of threshold effects and the possible non-linearity in the transmission of impacts of greater global integration on the poor may result in a more complex and heterogeneous globalization–poverty relationship. While earlier studies shed great light on this globalization–poverty linkage, there appears to have been comparatively little reported empirical evidence on the possible non-linear relationship between globalization and poverty.

In this chapter, using panel data from Chinese provinces over the period 1986–2001, and applying recent endogenous threshold regression techniques, we attempt to investigate empirically the globalization–poverty nexus in China, paying particular attention to the non-linearity of the impact of globalization on the poor.

Since the implementation of the 'open door' policy in the late 1970s, China has experienced increasingly intensive integration into the world economy, and achieved remarkable success in promoting economic growth. China's successful global integration and impressive economic growth were accompanied by great achievements in poverty reduction. Based on China's official poverty line, rural population in poverty dropped from 250 million in 1978 to 28 million in 2002, and the incidence of rural poverty, measured by the proportion of the poor in the rural population, declined dramatically from 30.7 per cent in 1978 to 3 per cent in 2002. Similar trends can also be noted using various poverty lines or different estimated standards (see, for example, World Bank 2000; Park and Wang 2001; Ravallion and Chen 2004).

China is a vast country with diverse regional development levels and contrasting economic structures, and as such both the development paths and the impacts of globalization on poverty reduction may vary across the regions of the country. Therefore, provincial level analyses of this variation allow us to better understand the causal links between globalization and poverty, and to obtain deeper insights into this critical nexus.

In the present study, because of the limits of the data, we focus primarily on rural poverty in China. More recently, urban poverty problems have also attracted considerable attention. However, China's urban poor have been relatively few in number; the size and severity of urban poverty remain much less than in rural areas, and therefore poverty in China is still mainly a rural phenomenon (Fan *et al.* 2004). In our study, by focusing on China's rural poverty, and using endogenous threshold estimation, we offer new insights into China's successful approach to reducing poverty during the globalization era, and thus contribute to the literature.

Threshold effects and non-linearities in the globalization–poverty nexus: a review

In the literature, the non-linearity and threshold phenomena have been recognized increasingly as one of critical issues in the ongoing process of globalization. Indeed, the globalization–poverty relationship is complex and heterogeneous, and it is highly probable that this relationship may be non-linear in many aspects, involving several threshold effects (Nissanke and Thorbecke 2007). In this section, we focus primarily on some critical literature concerning the existence of threshold effects, and the non-linear relationship between globalization and poverty.[1]

The possibility of a non-linear relationship between globalization and poverty has been acknowledged and well documented in a number of recent studies (for example, Agénor 2004; Nissanke and Thorbecke 2007; Sindzingre 2007). Agénor (2004) suggests that the globalization–poverty linkage may be non-monotonic, since possible discontinuities or threshold effects may come into play and lead to a non-linear relationship between globalization and poverty. The first is an *output effect*, which suggests that globalization may have an inverted J-curve effect on poverty: at the initial stage, globalization with greater trade liberalization may lead to a decline in the output of import-competing sectors, resulting in a decline in both aggregate output and per capita income that might affect the poor adversely, and then at the following stage, with the expansion of the exportable sector, aggregate output will gradually increase and contribute to poverty reduction.[2] The second effect is the *relative wage effect* through the impact of globalization on the skilled–unskilled wage differential. If we suppose that the relationship between the imported capital goods and unskilled labour is highly substitutable, then, at the initial stage of trade liberalization, greater openness may increase the wage differential between skilled and unskilled labour, which tends to worsen the living conditions of the latter and increase poverty; this initial widening of wage differentials may lead to an increase in investment in human capital and thus an increase in the supply of skilled labour over time, which tends to narrow the wage differential across skill categories and reduce poverty in the later stages, indicating an inverted U-shape relationship between globalization and poverty.

Sindzingre (2007) considers institutions to be an essential factor in creating the non-linear relationship between globalization and poverty, since institutions may generate threshold effects in the sense that they introduce processes of cumulative causation, and create discontinuities and multiple equilibria. Therefore, the ultimate net effects of globalization on poverty in a given setting will depend on the characteristics of certain institutions – for example, their levels of development; historical depth and stability (or 'quality'); the extent of their regulation of economic activity; the coherence between them and the associated linkage effects; their credibility; and the ways they organize and support particular market structures.

Meanwhile, a number of empirical studies have suggested that thresholds exist in the impacts of openness on growth, through which openness may affect the poor. For example, using cross-country data, Edwards (2001) investigates the effects of capital market openness on economic growth, and his empirical results suggest the existence of a threshold in development levels – that is, an open capital account can positively affect growth only after a country has achieved a certain degree of economic development. Moreover, in a more recent study, with the help of a dataset covering eighty-three countries over the period 1970–89, Girma *et al.* (2003) explore empirically the heterogeneity in the 'openness–productivity growth' relationship, and find evidence that thresholds exist in the effects of openness on growth that depend on the level of natural barriers.

However, few empirical studies have been conducted to test the non-linear relationship between globalization and poverty. A representative exception is the recent work of Agénor (2004). Using panel data for a group of developing countries covering the period from the late 1980s to the late 1990s, Agénor (2004) investigates empirically the non-linear globalization–poverty linkage. Estimation results suggest that a non-linear, Laffer-type relationship exists between poverty and globalization: at low degrees of globalization, it does hurt the poor, while at higher levels, it leads to a decline in poverty. Therefore, Agénor (2004) concludes that globalization may have hurt the poor, not because it went too far but rather because it did not go far enough.

However, Agénor's research suffers from several limitations. First, to capture the non-linear relationship between globalization and poverty, Agénor includes a squared term of globalization index in his regression model. This approach has obvious disadvantages, since it assumes that the non-linearity in the globalization–poverty linkage is of a particular form. Meanwhile, the inclusion of a squared term implies that the number of thresholds is chosen arbitrarily as being one, completely ignoring the possibility of multiple thresholds. Second, as Agénor has recognized, his research also suffers from problems concerning the quality of data and a lack of sufficient numbers of observations. Therefore, further studies with broader and more reliable datasets and more advanced regression techniques are required to draw more convincing and robust conclusions.

With the help of more recent and systemic data from Chinese provinces, this chapter attempts to add to the literature by exploring empirically the non-linear globalization–poverty nexus in China. In order to test the existence of threshold effects and avoid potential biases, we employ the endogenous threshold regression techniques proposed by Hansen (1996, 1999) with which the number and location of thresholds are determined endogenously in a given sample dataset, and therefore regression models can be tested with unknown threshold points rather than some specific values that are chosen exogenously and arbitrarily. To the best of our knowledge, this is the first study investigating the possible non-linear relationship between globalization and poverty in the case of China.

China's global integration and poverty reduction

Economic openness in China

The implementation of the open door policy since the late 1970s, and the choice of regional development strategy in accordance with its comparative advantage, have accelerated China's integration into the global economy, resulting in huge inflows of foreign direct investment (FDI) and a remarkable increase in foreign trade.

Local experimentation with the open door policy was first pursued in Guangdong and Fujian provinces, with the establishment of four special economic zones (SEZs) in 1979–80 (namely, Shenzhen, Zhuhai and Shantou in Guangdong province, and Xiamen in Fujian province), being followed by the opening-up process along the coast (that is, the successive establishment of fourteen open coastal cities, a number of open coastal development zones, an open coastal belt, the Hainan special economic zones, and Pudong new area in Shanghai) and then to inland regions.

Prioritization of the development of the coastal regions was stipulated clearly and definitely in the government's sixth five-year plan (1981–5) and the seventh five-year plan (1986–90), because the coastal regions are not only closer to international markets, and hence more advantageously located in geographical terms to engage in international trade, but are also more advanced regarding the level of human capital and social development. As such, they are better able to benefit from the favourable circumstances and make use of new opportunities to improve their productive efficiency, exploit their comparative advantage, expand their production and attain sustainable growth. Meanwhile, preferential policies were formulated for the coastal provinces for the purpose of promoting international trade, attracting FDI and accelerating economic development in these regions.

Preferential policies and the geographical advantages of these regions have promoted economic growth significantly in the coastal areas. Consistent with the regions' comparative advantages, a new pattern of regional specialization has emerged. Coastal regions have become highly specialized in industries with high value-added and up-graded technologies, while the inland regions, originally less industrialized, concentrated on energy production, raw materials and transformation industries, and energy-consuming industries. Hence, one notable objective of China's regional development strategy in the reform era was to exploit the comparative advantage of the regions and speed up regional development in the ongoing process of globalization.

More recently, China's accession to the World Trade Organization (WTO) further accelerated the expansion of its foreign trade. Between 1978 and 2002, China's total exports and imports grew at an average annual rate of 15.7 per cent and 14.7 per cent, respectively (see Figure 5.1); in 2002, China's share of total world exports and total world imports amounted to 4.3 per cent and 3.8 per cent, respectively, making China the fifth-largest international exporter and sixth-largest importer in the world. A similar trend can also be seen with regard to foreign capital utilization. The annual inflow of FDI in China grew from US$1.23 billion in 1984 to US$52.7 billion in 2002 (see Figure 5.2), making the country the largest recipient of FDI among developing countries. Through greater liberalization in trade and foreign investment, the opening-up policy has stimulated China's economic growth significantly.[3]

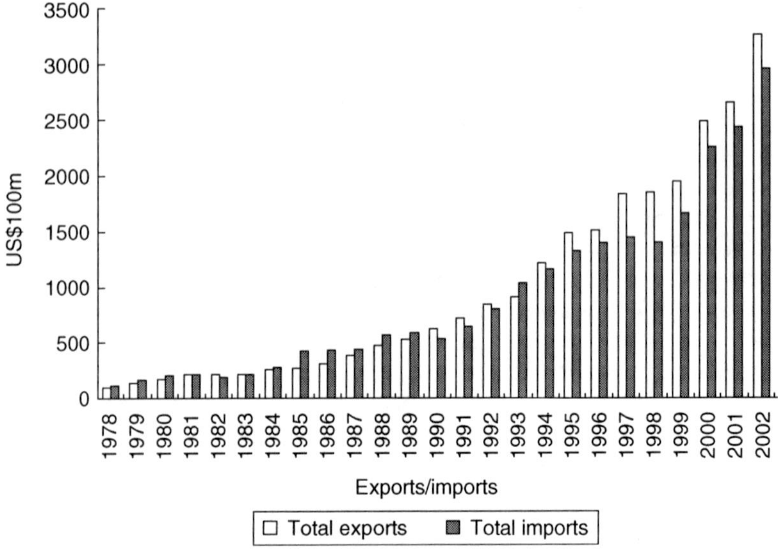

Figure 5.1 Foreign trade in China, 1978–2002 (US$100 millions)
Source: National Statistical Bureau of China, *China Statistical Yearbook*, various years.

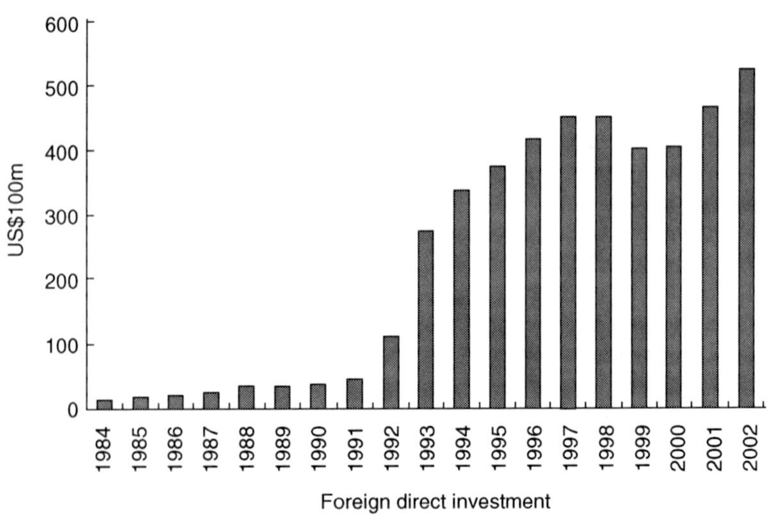

Figure 5.2 Foreign direct investment in China, 1984–2002 (US$100 millions)
Source: National Statistical Bureau of China, *China Statistical Yearbook*, various years.

Poverty reduction in rural China

After more than two decades of market-orientated reforms, China's rapid developments, especially its considerable achievements in stimulating economic growth and reducing poverty, have been widely highlighted in the literature. Based on China's official poverty line, the rural poverty incidence decreased dramatically from 30.7 per cent in 1978 to 3 per cent in 2002 – that is, more than 220 million people have been lifted out of absolute poverty in the country's rural regions during the period (see Table 5.1).[4]

Rural poverty estimates for China based on several alternative standards are presented in Table 5.1. For example, using the World Bank's international standard poverty line of income measure of US$1 per day (in purchasing power parity), the number of China's rural poor decreased dramatically, from 261 million in 1990 to 88 million in 2002. When estimated with the poverty line of consumption measure set at US$1 per day, the rural poverty population in China also indicated a substantial drop, from 358 million in 1990 to 161 million in 2002 (see Table 5.1). Therefore, although the virtual magnitude of China's absolutely poor population and of poverty incidence has still been the subject of much debate, there is no doubt that the country's rural poverty has decreased sharply in recent years.

Figure 5.3 presents the geographical distribution of the rural poor over the period of 1990–2002. We find that the rural poor population has become further concentrated in China's western regions since 1990. The ratio of western rural poor to the total number of China's rural poor rose from 38.6 per cent in 1990 to 51.8 per cent in 2002, whereas this ratio declined from 51.7 per cent to 35.4 per cent for the central regions, and from 15.9 per cent to 11.7 per cent for the coastal regions during the same period. Meanwhile, the incidence of rural poverty based on official estimates was also much higher in the western regions than in the other two regions, for all these years (see Figure 5.4).

Threshold estimations on the globalization–poverty nexus

In this section, we follow Hansen (1996, 1999) to apply the threshold regression techniques to investigate the non-linear relationship between globalization and poverty in China.

Modelling threshold effects

It has long been recognized in the literature that threshold effects and non-linearities exist in different economic relationships. Traditional threshold analyses are usually based on the exogenous sample-splitting approach, with which the splitting of sample depends simply on some value of threshold variable that is given ad hoc or chosen arbitrarily. However, disadvantages of the traditional approach in dealing with non-linearity and threshold effects

Table 5.1 Poverty line and incidence of poverty in rural China, 1978–2002

Year	China's official estimates			World Bank international standard			
				Income measure (US$1/day)		Expenditure measure (US$1/day)	
	Poverty line (current RMB)	Poor population (millions)	Rural poverty incidence	Poor population (millions)	Rural poverty incidence	Poor population (millions)	Rural poverty incidence
1978	100	250	30.7				
1986	213	131	15.5				
1987	227	122	14.3				
1988	236	96	11.1				
1989	259	102	11.6				
1990	300	85	9.5	261	29.1	358	40
1991	304	94	10.4	255	28.2	344	38
1992	317	80	8.8	253	27.7	344	37.7
1993	350	75	8.2	247	27.1	346	37.9
1994	440	70	7.6	220	24	296	32.3
1995	530	65	7.1	186	20.3	264	28.8
1996	580	58	6.3	129	14	208	22.6
1997	640	49	5.4	116	12.7	208	22.7
1998	635	42	4.6	99	10.8	210	22.8
1999	625	34	3.7	97	10.5	217	23.5
2000	625	32	3.4	111	12	195	21
2001	630	29	3.2	99	10.6	182	19.5
2002	627	28	3	88	9.4	161	17.2

Sources: National Statistical Bureau of China (various years) and World Bank (2000, 2002).

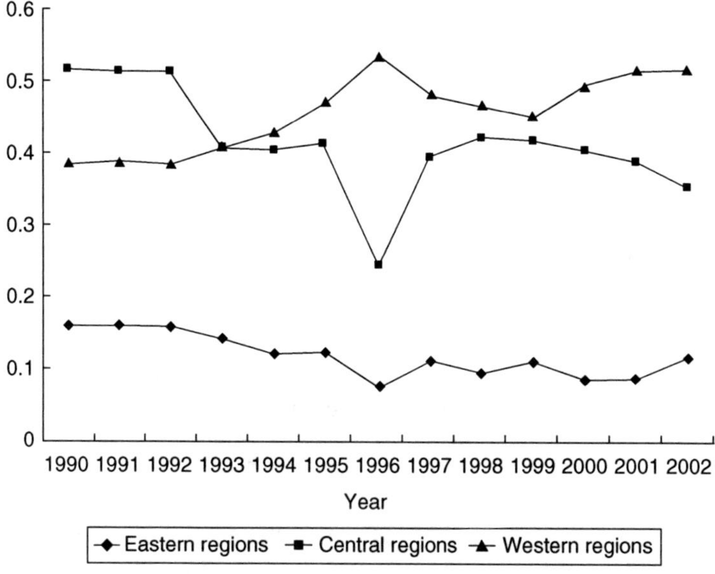

Figure 5.3   Geographical distribution of rural poor in China, 1990–2002

Note: The *y*-axis is the ratio of regional rural poor to the total number of China's rural poor.
Sources: National Statistical Bureau of China, *China Statistical Yearbook*, various years and author's calculations.

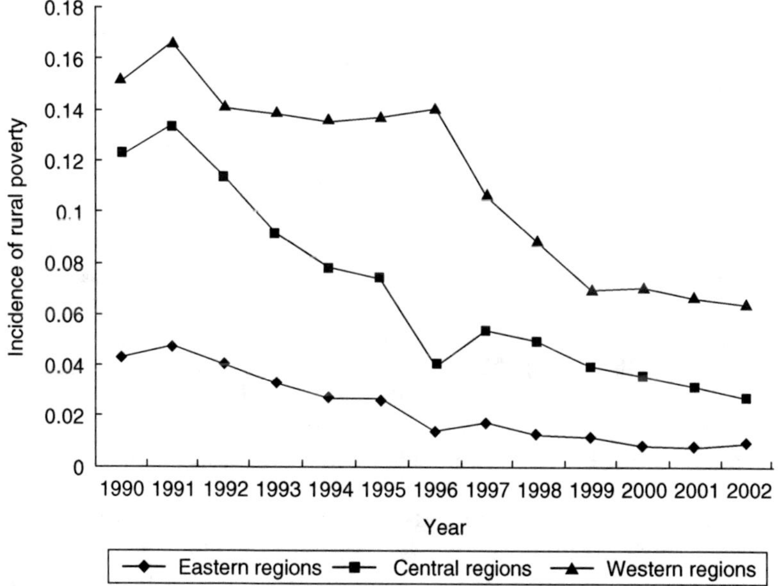

Figures 5.4   The incidence of rural poverty in China, 1990–2002

Sources: National Statistical Bureau of China, *China Statistical Yearbook*, various years and author's calculations.

are obvious: first, as Gomanee *et al.* (2003) argue, under this approach, both the number of regimes and location of sample splits are selected arbitrarily and not based on prior economic guidance. Furthermore, as the threshold is not determined within the model, it is not possible to derive confidence intervals for it. Second, the robustness of estimated results based on this approach is also questionable, since they are more likely to be highly sensitive to the choice of the value of the threshold point. Therefore, the use of ad hoc and arbitrary sample-splitting in empirical estimations has been highly disputed, and econometric estimators generated on the basis of such procedures may pose serious inference problems (Hansen 2000).

Another approach used in threshold analysis is the regression-tree methodology, with which the number and location of thresholds can be determined endogenously through the method of data sorting. However, this approach suffers greatly from the limitation that it fails to provide any distribution theory to test the statistical significance of thresholds.

In a series of original research studies, Hansen (1996, 1999 and 2000) develops new econometric techniques for threshold regression analysis; that is, endogenous threshold regression techniques.[5] Hansen's endogenous approach has critical advantages. First, it does not require any specified functional form of non-linearity, and the number and location of thresholds are determined completely endogenously by the data. Second, it provides an asymptotic distribution theory to construct confidence intervals for the parameters. In addition, a bootstrap method is also applied to assess the statistical significance of the threshold effects.

In the following discussion, we examine the impacts of globalization on China's poverty reduction by applying Hansen's endogenous threshold techniques. We begin by estimating the regression model as follows:

$$
\begin{aligned}
POV_{it} = {} & \alpha_1 G_{it} + \alpha_2 FUND_{it} + \alpha_3 TVED_{it} + \alpha_4 URGINI_{it} + \beta_1 GLOB_{it} \\
& \cdot I(GLOB_{it} \le \gamma) + \beta_2 GLOB_{it} \cdot I(GLOB_{it} > \gamma) + \mu_i + \varepsilon_{it}
\end{aligned} \tag{5.1}
$$

where the subscript *i* indexes the individual province, and the subscript *t* indexes time. In this model, *POV* is the rural poverty incidence (expressed in natural logarithm); *G* denotes the growth rate of real per capita net income of rural households; *FUND* is the per capita government expenditure for rural poverty alleviation; *TVED* is the variable of the development level of township and village enterprises (TVE), defined as the ratio of TVE output to total rural output; and *URGINI* is the income distribution variable. In the present study, we use the indicator of urban–rural income disparity as the income distribution variable,[6] which is defined as the ratio of per capita disposable income of urban households to per capita net income of rural households.[7] *GLOB* is the globalization index, measured by the ratio of total trade volume (that is, the sum of exports and imports) to GDP, which is used as a proxy to measure the level of globalization, and is chosen as the threshold variable in our estimations; $I(.)$ is the indicator function used to sort the data; and γ is the threshold value. Therefore, the observations are divided into two regimes depending on whether the threshold variable *GLOB* is smaller or larger than the threshold γ, and the two regimes are distinguished by different regression slopes β_1 and β_2. In our estimations, the threshold value and the slope parameters are jointly determined.

To estimate the threshold value, we first follow Hansen (1999) to eliminate the individual effects in our model. After these transformations, the threshold value can be obtained by least squares estimations by minimization of the concentrated sum of square errors, as recommended by Chan (1993) and Hansen (1999, 2000). Having obtained a threshold value, the slope parameters can easily be achieved through estimating Equation (5.1).

After we have found a threshold, the next step is to test the statistical significance of this threshold. More specifically, we attempt to test the null hypothesis of a no-threshold effect: H_0: $\beta_1 = \beta_2$, against the alternative hypothesis of having at least one threshold: H_1: $\beta_1 \neq \beta_2$. The null hypothesis of a no-threshold effect will be rejected if the bootstrap estimate of the asymptotic P value for this likelihood ratio test is smaller than the desired critical value.

When a threshold is found to be significant, the last step is to construct confidence intervals for this. We test the null hypothesis: H_0: $\gamma = \gamma_0$ (with γ_0 being the true value of the threshold), against the alternative hypothesis: H_1: $\gamma \neq \gamma_0$. The null hypothesis will be rejected if the likelihood ratio test statistic exceeds the desired critical value. After the confidence interval for the threshold value is obtained, the corresponding confidence interval for the slope coefficient can also easily be determined because the slope coefficient and the threshold value are jointly determined. Moreover, similar procedures can be conducted to deal with the case of double or multiple thresholds.

Data

Using panel data covering twenty-five Chinese provinces and regions over the period 1986–2001, we investigate the non-linear relationship between globalization and poverty.[8] Data used in our study are from the National Statistical Bureau (NSB) of China (various years) *China Statistical Yearbook*, the *China Rural Statistical Yearbook* and *Comprehensive Statistical Data and Materials on 50 Years of New China*.

Estimation results

Following Hansen (1999, 2000), we first estimate the number and location of the threshold effects. Table 5.2 presents the results of the likelihood ratio test for the statistical significance of threshold value. We find that the test for a single threshold is significant with a 1000 bootstrap P-value of 0.056, while the test for a second threshold is statistically insignificant with a

Table 5.2   Test results for threshold effects

Threshold estimate	0.1956
Test for single threshold	
The likelihood ratio statistic:	27.01
P-value	0.056
(10%, 5%, 1% critical value)	(22.70, 27.26, 39.73)
Test for double threshold	
The likelihood ratio statistic:	16.57
P-value	0.174
(10%, 5%, 1% critical value)	(19.30, 24.11, 30.93)

1000 bootstrap *P*-value of 0.174. These results provide strong evidence to suggest that one threshold exists in the regression relationship. The estimated threshold point is 0.1956, with which our sample can be split into two regimes – that is, the 'less globalized' and the 'more globalized' economies.

In the analysis, our threshold estimations are based on this single threshold model. Figure 5.5 presents the plots of the concentrated likelihood ratio test statistics. The estimated threshold is the value at which the likelihood ratio hits the zero axis.

The regression results are reported in Table 5.3. We find that the growth of per capita rural income (*G*) and the increase in per capita government expenditure for poverty alleviation (*FUND*) contribute significantly to China's poverty reduction. The coefficient of *G* is negative and significant at the 5 per cent level, and the coefficient of *FUND* is negative and significant at the 10 per cent level. Therefore, empirical results show that economic growth and government investments towards alleviating poverty are two critical driving forces behind China's successful achievements in poverty reduction. In addition, it is found that regions with a better TVE development level (*TVED*) will have a lower incidence of poverty. However, there is also evidence that the increase in urban–rural income disparity (*URGINI*) tends to raise poverty levels.

More interesting results are found for the role of globalization in the reduction of China's poverty. Our estimation results strongly suggest the existence of the threshold effects and the non-linearity in the relationship between globalization and poverty: globalization is good for the poor only after the economy has reached a certain threshold level of globalization.

Based on our estimations, for the 'less globalized' regions with a globalization level lower than the threshold value (that is, 0.1956 in our case), the globalization index (*GLOB*) is positively and significantly correlated with poverty, which implies that globalization will increase poverty at low levels of globalization. However, in sharp contrast, the coefficient of *GLOB* becomes negative and statistically significant for the 'more globalized'

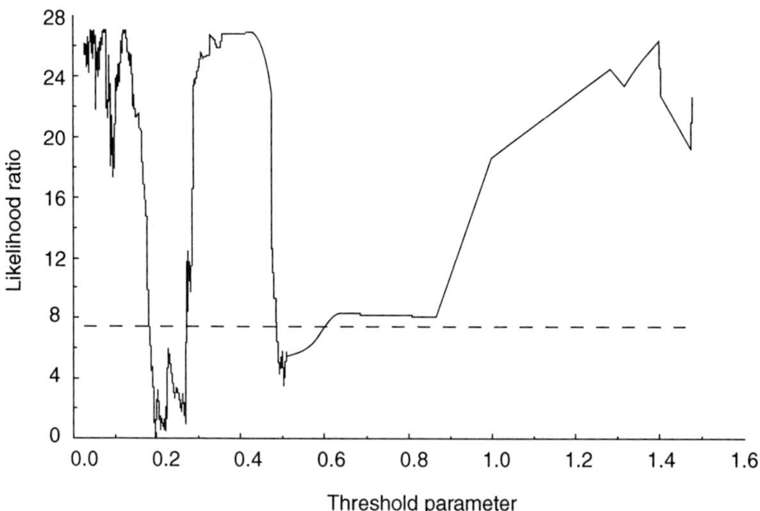

Figure 5.5   Confidence interval construction in a single threshold model

Table 5.3   Regression estimate on globalization and poverty in China: single threshold model (dependent variable: POV)

	Coefficient	OLS std error	White heteroskedasticity-corrected std error[a]	Robust *t*-statistics
G	−1.153	0.482	0.450	−2.566**
FUND[1]	−0.4691	0.2915	0.2677	−1.752*
URGINI	0.425	0.132	0.138	3.088***
TVED	−2.238	0.353	0.374	−5.990***
GLOB $I(GLOB \leq 0.1956)$	3.354	1.160	1.189	2.820***
GLOB $I(GLOB > 0.1956)$	−1.601	0.451	0.634	−2.526**
Observations	420			
Provinces	25			

Notes: [1] The variable *FUND* is expressed in 100 yuan.
[a] The calculation of the robust t-statistics is based on the white heteroskedasticity-corrected standard error.

*** significant at the 1% level; ** significant at the 5% level; * significant at the 10% level.

regions with a globalization level beyond this threshold value, indicating that globalization leads to a decline in poverty at high levels of globalization.

However, it is worth noting that an important part of the impact of globalization on poverty goes through the growth process. Therefore, controlling for growth (that is, the inclusion of the growth variable (G) in Equation (5.1)) would result in a failure to capture the poverty impacts of globalization through the growth process.[9] For a better comparison, we also report in Tables 5.4 and 5.5 the estimated results of the test for non-linearity after dropping the growth variable (G) from Equation (5.1). We find consistent results, as that reported before in Tables 5.2 and 5.3.

In sum, for the case of China, we find strong evidence that globalization does hurt the poor at low levels; but at higher levels, it helps to reduce poverty. These results are consistent with the findings of Agénor (2004).

Conclusion

Recent literature has highlighted the heterogeneity and non-linearity of the globalization–poverty relationship (for example, Agénor 2004; Nissanke and Thorbecke 2007; Sindzingre 2007). In this chapter, with the help of Chinese provincial data over the period 1986–2001, we apply endogenous threshold regression techniques to investigate the impacts of globalization on China's poverty reduction. The estimation results provide strong evidence to suggest that, for the case of China, there exists a threshold in the relationship between globalization and poverty – that is, the poverty-reducing effect of globalization becomes positive only after it has reached a certain threshold level. Our results confirm the findings in Agénor (2004) that globalization may hurt the poor, not because it has gone too far, but rather because it did not go far enough.

Moreover, we also find evidence that China's rapid economic growth and the government's sustained efforts and investments in the fight against

Table 5.4 Test results for threshold effects after dropping the growth variable

Threshold estimate	0.1956
Test for single threshold	
The likelihood ratio statistic:	24.61
P-value	0.075
(10%, 5%, 1% critical value)	(22.99, 27.16, 38.57)
Test for double threshold	
The likelihood ratio statistic:	17.94
P-value	0.114
(10%, 5%, 1% critical value)	(18.70, 23.41, 31.98)

Table 5.5 Regression estimate on globalization and poverty in China: single threshold model after dropping the growth variable (dependent variable: POV)

	Coefficient	OLS std error	White heteroscedasticity-corrected std error[a]	Robust *t*-statistics
FUND[1]	−0.376	0.291	0.259	−1.455
URGINI	0.479	0.131	0.136	3.524***
TVED	−2.471	0.341	0.353	−6.991***
GLOB I(GLOB ≤ 0.1956)	3.053	1.160	1.176	2.596**
GLOB I(GLOB > 0.1956)	−1.696	0.452	0.664	−2.555**
Observations	420			
Provinces	25			

Notes: [1] The variable *FUND* is expressed in 100 yuan.
[a] The calculation of the robust t-statistics is based on the White heteroscedasticity-corrected standard error.

*** significant at the 1% level; ** significant at the 5% level.

poverty are two critical driving forces behind its successful achievements in poverty reduction since the 1980s.

These findings have important policy implications for China's future efforts regarding poverty alleviation. Effective policy measures have to be put forward to accelerate China's integration into the global economy in order to stimulate economic growth, and to provide more opportunities for the poor to increase their income and escape poverty.

Appendix

Threshold regression techniques

Following Hansen (1996, 1999 and 2000), empirical estimations using threshold regression techniques with application to panel analyses may include four main steps: that is, eliminating the individual effects; estimating the threshold value and regression coefficients; testing for the statistical significance of the threshold; and forming a confidence interval for the threshold. In the following discussion, we take the single threshold model as an example to explain threshold regression techniques.[10] We begin by estimating the regression model as follows:

$$POV_{it} = \alpha X_{it} + \beta_1 GLOB_{it} . I(GLOB_{it} \leq \gamma) + \beta_2 GLOB_{it} . I(GLOB_{it} > \gamma) + \mu_i + \varepsilon_{it} \qquad (5.A1)$$

where *POV* is the rural poverty incidence; X is the vector of controlled variables; *GLOB* is the globalization index, which is also chosen as the threshold variable in our estimations; $I(.)$ is the indicator function used to sort the data; γ is the threshold value. Moreover, the subscript i indexes the individual province, and the subscript t indexes time, with $1 \leq i \leq n$ and $1 \leq t \leq T$. In our estimations, the threshold value and the slope parameters will be jointly determined.

An alternative representation of Equation (5.A1) is as follows:

$$POV_{it} = \alpha X_{it} + \beta GLOB_{it}(\gamma) + \mu_i + \varepsilon_{it} \qquad (5.A2)$$

with $\beta = (\beta_1 \beta_2)$ and $GLOB_{it}(\gamma) = \begin{pmatrix} GLOB_{it} \; I(GLOB_{it} \leq \gamma) \\ GLOB_{it} \; I(GLOB_{it} > \gamma) \end{pmatrix}$

Eliminating the individual effects
First, we follow Hansen (1999) to eliminate the individual effects in our model. By taking an average of Equation (5.A2) over the time index t yields:

$$\overline{POV}_i = \alpha \overline{X}_i + \beta \overline{GLOB}_i(\gamma) + \mu_i + \overline{\varepsilon}_i \qquad (5.A3)$$

with $\overline{POV}_i = T^{-1}\sum_{t=1}^{T} POV_{it};$

$\overline{X}_i = T^{-1}\sum_{t=1}^{T} X_{it};$

$$\overline{GLOB}_i(\gamma) = T^{-1}\sum_{t=1}^{T}GLOB_{it}(\gamma) \text{ and}$$

$$\overline{\varepsilon}_i = T^{-1}\sum_{t=1}^{T}\varepsilon_{it}$$

Then we take the difference between Equations (5.A2) and (5.A3), and we have:

$$(POV_{it} - \overline{POV}_i) = \alpha(X_{it} - \overline{X}_i) + \beta(GLOB_{it}(\gamma) - \overline{GLOB}_i(\gamma)) + (\varepsilon_{it} - \overline{\varepsilon}_i) \qquad (5.A4)$$

Estimating the threshold value and regression coefficients

As Chan (1993) and Hansen (1999) recommended, after eliminating the individual effect, the threshold value can be estimated by applying least squares. The estimated threshold value (denoted as $\hat{\gamma}$) is the value that minimizes the concentrated sum of squared errors. Let $S_1(.)$ denote the sum of squared errors in the presence of a threshold, then the least squared estimators of γ can be expressed by:

$$\hat{\gamma} = \arg\min_{\gamma} S_1(\gamma) \qquad (5.A5)$$

Having obtained a threshold value, the slope parameters β can also easily be achieved through estimating Equation (5.A4).

Testing for the significance of the estimated threshold

After we have found a threshold, the next step is to test the statistical significance of this. More specifically, we attempt to test the null hypothesis of no threshold effect: H_0: $\beta_1 = \beta_2$, against the alternative hypothesis of having at least one threshold: H_1: $\beta_1 \neq \beta_2$. Let S_0 denote the sum of squared errors under the null hypothesis, and S_1 denotes the sum of squared errors under the alternative. Then the likelihood ratio statistic for testing H_0: $\beta_1 = \beta_2$ can be given by:

$$F_1 = \frac{(S_0 - S_1(\hat{\gamma}))}{\hat{\sigma}^2} \text{ with } \hat{\sigma}^2 = \frac{1}{n(T-1)}S_1(\hat{\gamma}) \qquad (5.A6)$$

However, given that the threshold γ is not identified under the null hypothesis, the distribution of F_1 is non-standard. Hansen (1996) suggested a bootstrap procedure to stimulate the asymptotic distribution for F_1 under the null hypothesis, which enables us to compute the P value for the likelihood ratio test. The null hypothesis of linearity (that is, no threshold effect) will be rejected if the P value for this likelihood ratio test is smaller than the desired critical value.

Forming confidence intervals for the estimated threshold

When a threshold is found to be significant, the last step is to construct confidence intervals for this. We test the null hypothesis: H_0: $\gamma = \gamma_0$ (with γ_0 being the true value of the threshold), against the alternative hypothesis: H_1: $\gamma \neq \gamma_0$. However, in the presence of a threshold, the distribution of γ is highly non-standard. Hansen (1999) suggested using the likelihood ratio statistic for testing and forming the confidence interval for γ. The likelihood ratio statistic for testing the null hypothesis H_0: $\gamma = \gamma_0$ can be given by:

$$LR_1(\gamma) = \frac{S_1(\gamma) - S_1(\hat{\gamma})}{\hat{\sigma}^2} \text{ with } \hat{\sigma}^2 = \frac{1}{n(T-1)}S_1(\hat{\gamma}) \tag{5.A7}$$

The null hypothesis will be rejected if the likelihood ratio test statistic exceeds the desired critical value. According to Hansen (2000), the critical value can be calculated from $c(\alpha) = -2 \log(1 - \sqrt{1-\alpha})$, and thus the 10 per cent critical value is 6.53, while the 5 per cent and 1 per cent critical values are 7.35 and 10.59, respectively. In the present study, we use the 5 per cent critical value (that is, 7.35) for our estimation.

Acknowledgements

The author is grateful to the project directors, Machiko Nissanke and Erik Thorbecke, for their great support. Any remaining errors are the responsibility of the author.

Notes

1 For a more extensive survey on the globalization–poverty nexus, please refer to Winters (2000), Reimer (2002), and the more recent excellent overview papers of Hertel and Reimer (2004); Winters *et al.* (2004); Nissanke and Thorbecke (2007).
2 However, the output effect discussed above should be treated with caution. As our referee pointed out, in reality (especially when the expenditure-switching policies are taken into account), the output effects of trade liberalization may become much more complex than that described in Agénor (2004).
3 However, foreign trade and FDI were more concentrated in the coastal regions. The unbalanced spatial distribution of foreign trade and foreign investment has led to increasing regional income disparity in China. The coast–interior dichotomy has also posed serious challenges for China's further development.
4 China's official poverty lines currently adopted by the National Bureau of Statistics (NBS) are based on a minimum nutritional standard of a daily calorie intake of 2,100 per person and a standard food bundle recommended by the Chinese Nutrition Association.
5 See Appendix of this chapter for more details on Hansen's threshold regression model.
6 In the literature, it is the Gini coefficients that are more widely employed for capturing the characteristics of income distribution. However, data on Gini coefficients are not available at the provincial level for China. Because of this data limitation, we use here the indicator of urban–rural income disparity to serve as a proxy for income distribution variable.
7 Meanwhile, a number of recent studies show that urban–rural income disparity has become the most significant component of overall income inequality in post-reform China (for example, World Bank 1997; Yao and Zhu 1998; Chang 2002).
8 China comprises thirty-one provinces, autonomous municipalities and autonomous regions. In this paper, we focus primary on rural poverty in China, and thus three autonomous municipalities – that is, Beijing, Tianjin and Shanghai – are excluded from our sample because these three cities are mainly urban economies. In addition, Tibet

and Hainan are also excluded from our sample because of the problems of omitted data and missing value. Moreover, the Chongqing municipality area, which was established quite recently and separated from Sichuan province in 1997, is still included in the calculations for Sichuan province.

9 We thank the referee for reminding us of this important point.
10 The method can be extended to the double threshold model and higher-order threshold models as well. See Hansen (1996, 1999 and 2000) for more detailed discussions.

References

Agénor, P. R. (2004) 'Does Globalization Hurt the Poor?', *International Economics and Economic Policy*, 1(1): 21–51.

Chan, K. S. (1993) 'Consistency and Limiting Distribution of the Least Squares Estimator of a Threshold Autoregressive Model', *The Annals of Statistics*, 21: 520–33.

Chang, G. H. (2002) 'The Cause and Cure of China's Widening Income Disparity', *China Economic Review*, 13: 335–40.

Dollar, D. and Kraay, A. (2002) 'Growth Is Good for the Poor', *Journal of Economic Growth*, 7(3): 195–225. Reprinted in A. Shorrocks and R. van der Hoeven (eds) (2004), *Growth, Inequality and Poverty: Prospects for Pro-poor Economic Development* (Oxford: Oxford University Press for UNU-WIDER).

Dollar, D. and Kraay, A. (2004) 'Trade, Growth, and Poverty', *The Economic Journal*, 114: 22–49.

Edwards, S. (2001) 'Capital Mobility and Economic Performance: Are Emerging Economies Different?', NBER Working Paper 8076, National Bureau of Economic Research, Cambridge, Mass.

Fan, S., Zhang, L. and Zhang, X. (2004) 'Reforms, Investment, and Poverty in Rural China', *Economic Development and Cultural Change*, 52(2): 395–421.

Girma, S., Henry, M., Kneller, R. and Milner, C. (2003) 'Threshold and Interaction Effects in the Openness–Productivity Growth Relationship: The Role of Institutions and Natural Barriers', GEP Research Paper 2003/32, Leverhulme Centre, Nottingham.

Gomanee, K., Girma, S. and Morrissey, O. (2003) 'Searching for Aid Threshold Effects'. Paper presented at the WIDER Development Conference, Sharing Global Prosperity, 6–7 September, UNU-WIDER, Helsinki.

Hansen, B. E. (1996) 'Inference when a Nuisance Parameter is not Identified under the Null Hypothesis', *Econometrica*, 64(2): 413–30.

Hansen, B. E. (1999) 'Threshold Effects in Non-Dynamic Panels: Estimation, Testing, and Inference', *Journal of Econometrics*, 93(2): 345–68.

Hansen, B. E. (2000) 'Sample Splitting and Threshold Estimation', *Econometrica* 68(3): 575–603.

Hertel, T. W. and Reimer, J. J. (2004) 'Predicting the Poverty Impacts of Trade Reform', Policy Research Working Paper 3444, World Bank, Washington, DC.

Hertel, T. W., Preckel, P. V. and Reimer, J. J. (2001) 'Trade Policy, Food Price Variability, and the Vulnerability of Low-Income Households', Paper prepared for the Meeting of the American Agricultural Economics Association, 6–8 August, Chicago.

Levinsohn, J., Berry, S. and Friedman, J. (2003) 'Impacts of the Indonesian Economic Crisis: Price Changes and the Poor', in M. Dooley and J. Frankel (eds), *Managing Currency Crises in Emerging Markets* (Chicago: University of Chicago Press).

National Statistical Bureau (NSB) of China (various years) *China Statistical Yearbook*, the *China Rural Statistical Yearbook* and *Comprehensive Statistical Data and Materials on 50 Years of New China* (Beijing: NSB).

Nissanke, M. and Thorbecke, E. (eds) (2007) 'Channels and Policy Debate in the Globalization–Inequality–Poverty Nexus', in *The Impact of Globalization on the World's Poor: Transmission Mechanisms* (Basingstoke: Palgrave Macmillan for UNU-WIDER).

Park, A. and Wang, S. (2001) 'China's Poverty Statistics', *China Economic Review*, 12(4): 384–98.

Ravallion, M. (2001) 'Growth, Inequality and Poverty: Looking Beyond Averages', *World Development*, 29(11): 1803–15. Reprinted in A. Shorrocks and R. van der Hoeven (eds) (2004), *Growth, Inequality and Poverty: Prospects for Pro-poor Economic Development* (Oxford: Oxford University Press for UNU-WIDER).

Ravallion, M. (2005) 'Looking Beyond Averages in the Trade and Poverty Debate', WIDER Research Paper 2005/29, UNU-WIDER, Helsinki. See also (2006) *World Development*, 34(8): 1374–92.

Ravallion, M. and Chen, S. (2004) 'China's (Uneven) Progress Against Poverty', Policy Research Working Paper 3408, World Bank, Washington, DC.

Reimer, J. J. (2002) 'Estimating the Poverty Impacts of Trade Liberalization', GTAP (Global Trade Analysis Project) Working Paper 20, Purdue University, West Lafayette, Inc.

Sindzingre, A. (2007) 'Explaining Threshold Effects of Globalization on Poverty: An Institutional Perspective', in M. Nissanke and E. Thorbecke (eds), *The Impact of Globalization on the World's Poor: Transmission Mechanisms* (Basingstoke: Palgrave Macmillan for UNU-WIDER).

Winters, L. A. (2000) 'Trade, Trade Policy, and Poverty: What are the Links?', *World Economy*, 25(9): 1339–67.

Winters, L. A., McCulloch, N. and McKay, A. (2004) 'Trade Liberalization and Poverty: The Evidence so Far', *Journal of Economic Literature*, XVII: 72–115.

World Bank (1997) *Sharing Rising Incomes: Disparities in China* (Washington, DC: World Bank).

World Bank (2000) *China: Overcoming Rural Poverty* (Washington, DC: World Bank).

World Bank (2002) *Globalization, Growth and Poverty* (Washington, DC: World Bank).

Yao, S. and Zhu, L. (1998) 'Understanding Income Inequality in China: A Multi-Angle Perspective', *Economics of Planning*, 31: 133–150.

6
Economic Development Strategy, Openness and Rural Poverty: A Framework and China's Experiences

Justin Yifu Lin and Peilin Liu

Introduction

Since the disintegration of the colonial system in the 1950s, many newly independent countries have been striving to develop their economies and alleviate poverty. However, thus far, except for a few countries in East Asia, most have not realized these goals. Living standards in most of these countries have not improved substantially, and for those in areas such as Sub-Saharan Africa there has been almost no change.

The trend towards globalization in the last decades of the twentieth century provided many opportunities and challenges for countries in the developing world. Though there is much interest in the relationship between globalization and poverty, a satisfactory analytical framework is lacking. Also, there is no consensus on the impact of globalization on poverty from the perspective of cross-country empirical studies. As Nissanke and Thorbecke (2007: 23) point out:

> Cross-country studies requiring precise measurements and definition of the two key concepts – globalization and poverty – tend to fail to provide a deeper insight into this critical nexus. While in some cases cross-country studies can provide hypotheses relating to the physiology of the growth process in our view, only detailed case studies are able to delineate the role of path dependence of multiple factors such as resource endowments, trade and production structures, policies and institutions. Such research, if carefully conducted, should yield high dividends in identifying appropriate policy responses to globalization in relation to the over-riding policy objective of poverty reduction.

China's experience[1] after implementing reform and its open-door policy in 1978 is an interesting case in the study of globalization and poverty. The average annual growth rate of GDP and trade in 1979–2003 reached 9.4 per cent and 16.0 per cent, respectively (NSB 2004).[2] According to current prices, the proportions of primary industry, secondary industry and tertiary industry as part of GDP, respectively, changed from 28.1 per cent, 48.2 per cent and 23.7 per cent in 1978 to 14.6 per cent, 52.2 per cent and 33.2 per cent in 2003. Similarly, the make-up of the employment structure in the same industries changed from 70.5 per cent, 17.3 per cent and 12.2 per cent in 1978 to 49.1 per cent, 21.6 per cent and 29.3 per cent in 2003 (NSB 2004).[3] The life expectancy of Chinese people also increased, from 66.8 years in 1980 to 70.7 years in 2002 (World Bank 2004),[4] while the rate of illiteracy decreased from 22.81 per cent in 1982 to 6.72 per cent in 2000. In addition, the proportion of people with education above high school level grew from 7.39 per cent in 1982 to 14.76 per cent in 2000 (NSB 2004).

In the study of globalization and poverty, the Chinese experience deserves special attention: with an average annual growth rate of 16.0 per cent, China's foreign trade dependency ratio has increased dramatically since 1978; and China has also attracted a large amount of foreign direct investment (See Tables 6.1 and 6.2). Poverty has been decreasing significantly. According to Ravallion and Chen (2004), in terms of both the official Chinese poverty line[5] and the new poverty line established by the National Statistical Bureau (NSB),[6] there has been a significant reduction in the headcount index; the poverty gap index; and the squared poverty gap index of rural areas, urban areas and the country as a whole (See Table 6.3). The world development index (See Table 6.4) also indicates that China has achieved great success in poverty reduction. However, despite these achievements,

Table 6.1   China's foreign trade dependence ratio

	Commodities exports		Commodities imports		Trade dependent ratio (%)
	US$ billions	to GDP (%)	US$ billions	to GDP (%)	
	(1)	(2)	(3)	(4)	(5) = (2) + (4)
1978	9.75	4.62	10.89	5.17	9.79
1980	18.12	6.00	20.02	6.61	12.61
1985	27.35	9.02	42.25	14.03	23.05
1990	62.09	16.10	53.35	13.88	29.98
1995	148.78	21.29	132.08	18.89	40.18
2000	249.20	23.06	225.09	20.83	43.89
2003	438.228	30.95	412.76	29.16	60.11

Source: National Statistical Bureau of China, *China Statistical Yearbook*, various years.

Table 6.2 FDI and China's investment

	FDI (US$ trillions)	FDI/total investment in fixed assets* (%)	Exchange rate (RMB/100$)
1985	1.658	1.91	293.66
1990	3.487	3.69	478.32
1995	37.521	15.65	835.10
2000	40.715	10.24	827.84
2003	53.505	7.97	827.70

Note: *Gross capital formation, which includes changes in inventories, is derived from Expenditure-Approach National Accounting.
Source: National Statistical Bureau of China, *China Statistical Yearbook*, various years.

Table 6.3 Poverty in China, 1981–2001 (per cent)

	Earlier poverty line					New poverty line				
	1981	1986	1991	1996	2001	1981	1986	1991	1996	2001
Rural										
Headcount index	28.62	9.85	11.66	4.20	4.75	64.67	23.50	29.72	13.82	12.49
Poverty gap index	6.84	1.92	2.84	1.13	0.81	19.99	5.99	8.52	3.55	3.32
Squared poverty gap index	2.35	0.52	1.17	0.58	0.19	8.44	2.16	3.43	1.50	1.21
Urban										
Headcount index	0.82	0.22	0.00	0.18	0.00	6.01	3.23	1.66	0.61	0.50
Poverty gap index	0.22	0.00	0.00	0.07	0.00	1.01	0.46	0.53	0.16	0.16
Squared poverty gap index	0.14	0.00	0.00	0.06	0.00	0.35	0.09	0.38	0.09	0.11
National										
Headcount index	23.02	7.49	8.52	2.97	2.96	52.84	18.53	22.16	9.79	7.97
Poverty gap index	5.51	1.45	2.08	0.81	0.51	16.17	4.63	6.37	2.52	2.13
Squared poverty gap index	1.90	0.40	0.85	0.42	0.12	6.81	1.65	2.61	1.07	0.80

Source: Ravallion and Chen (2004).

Table 6.4   Headcount index of Chinese poverty, 1996–2001

Index	1996	1998	2001
Poverty gap index at US$1 per day (%)	–	–	3.94
Poverty gap index at US$2 per day (%)	–	–	18.44
Headcount index, national (% of population)	6.00	4.60	–
Headcount index, rural (% of population)	7.90	4.60	–
Headcount index, urban (% of population)	2.00	2.00	–

Source: World Bank (2004).

China has begun to face increasing income disparity and new kinds of poverty in recent years. It is important that a systematic analysis of China's experiences in opening-up and poverty reduction be carried out, as well as lessons drawn from its achievements and shortfalls.

On the basis of previous studies (Lin *et al.* 1996; Lin 2003), this chapter develops a general framework to analyse openness and poverty in developing countries,[7] followed by an empirical analysis of China's experience.

Our main arguments are as follows. The volume and structure of international trade, income distribution and poverty of a country are all determined endogenously by its economic development strategy. Countries adopting a comparative-advantage-following (CAF) strategy will be more open, achieve rapid economic growth, and create more jobs for low-income groups, who rely mainly on physical labour for their livelihood. As a consequence, income distribution in these countries will remain relatively even and poverty can be alleviated gradually. In contrast, countries adopting a comparative-advantage-defying (CAD) strategy to promote capital-intensive industries will inevitably see the opposite happen. This is because investment in the priority sectors of a CAD strategy creates limited job opportunities, excluding most poor labourers from formal labour markets. Moreover, firms in the priority sectors are non-viable in open, competitive markets. The survival of such firms depends on government subsidies and protection from international competition and, as a result, the economy becomes closed. As investment in priority sectors requires large amounts of capital, only the rich or those with good government connections have the ability to make the investments. The burden of providing subsidies to non-viable firms will ultimately be carried by those with less wealth and power. It will inevitably further distort income distribution and make it difficult to alleviate poverty.

Literature review

Globalization and poverty: theoretical and cross-country empirical studies

The history of studies on globalization, economic development, income distribution and poverty is as long as that of economics itself. There is a huge amount of literature on these topics. Nissanke and Thorbecke (2007) have conducted an extensive literature review. According to their study, economists have yet to reach a consensus on the relationship between openness, globalization and poverty. Economic growth and improving income distribution are essential steps towards alleviating poverty. At present, there are two opposing views on the impact of openness and trade on economic development and income distribution. Some economists believe that market opening and participation in globalization will contribute to economic development and improve income distribution, while others take the opposite position.

The most recent empirical works fail to reach a conclusion on this issue. Milanovic (2002) and Easterly (2003) argue that the relationship between globalization and income distribution (then poverty) can be expressed as an inverted U-curve. These conclusions may be useful in describing past phenomena, but have no implications for applicable policy on poverty reduction in the future. Milanovic (2002) concluded that 'It seems that openness makes income distribution worse before making it better – or differently that the effect of openness on country's income distribution depends on the country's initial income level.' However, we cannot derive a policy implication from his argument that the developing countries at a very low-income level should not adopt an openness policy for the sake of income equity. Easterly (2003) found that in the current wave of globalization there is an inverted U-curve between inequality and openness, measured as (Exports + Imports)/GDP, and inequality. Easterly speculated that trade at low levels of openness involves natural resources, which are usually distributed unequally, raises inequality. At higher levels of openness, trade may involve more labour-intensive manufactures and traded goods, and will raise the returns to a factor that is largely held by the poorest part of the population. However, Easterly (2003) did not convey any special policy suggestion to developing countries to cope with the income distribution issue. Should developing countries first redistribute nature resources evenly or transfer the control rights of resources from private to state to maintain equity when they are involved in globalization? According to our observations, many developing countries pursuing the priority of the development of capital-intensive industries failed to improve their income distribution even when their governments controlled the natural resources.

Obviously, openness and trade are treated as exogenous variables in these analyses. But, in our opinion, openness, income distribution and poverty are endogenous to a country's development strategy, which will be discussed later.

The effects of openness and globalization on poverty are determined by the following factors: (i) the intrinsic characteristics of an economic structure before openness; and (ii) a country's approach to openness and globalization. For example, should a country invest a large amount in the newest technologies, or just purchase technologies that are suitable for its current economic needs? Will it develop the necessary basic infrastructure or engage in risky R&D that requires a large number of foreign loans? Will it export products made using relatively abundant domestic resources, or those using far scarcer resources that can only be obtained with the help of government subsidies?

Literature on poverty in China

There have been many studies concerning China's openness and poverty, both individually and jointly. Anderson *et al.* (2004) analysed China's rural economy and rural poverty after its accession to the WTO with a GTAP model, and found that cutting down agricultural import protections and removing agricultural subsidies worsened the situation of rural residents who rely on an agriculture-based income, compared with that of urban residents. But if the Chinese government were to reduce the negative nominal protection rate of rice, meat, vegetables and fruit to zero after accession to the WTO, the decrease in wages for rural residents would be less. Anderson *et al.*'s analysis, on the other hand, emphasizes that the reduction of agricultural protection in developed countries would contribute to the reduction of rural poverty in China. The analysis divides rural households into three categories: category A includes households whose proportion of non-farm income was 0 per cent; and categories B and C include households for whom the proportions were 30 per cent and 60 per cent, respectively. After accession to the WTO, the income of households in categories A and B decreased, while for those in category C it increased. Of course, the elimination of negative agricultural protection would improve the situation of households in categories A and B.

Chen and Ravallion (2004) found that accession to the WTO would have little impact on average household income, household income inequity and poverty in China, but the impact varied greatly among households with different characteristics. Generally speaking, the study found that rural households would be harmed in the process, while urban households could benefit from it. The most vulnerable households are those who relied heavily on income from agriculture. Hertel *et al.* (2004) prove that, after accession to the WTO, if labour could move freely between the agricultural and non-agricultural sectors, both rural households and urban households would benefit in the long run, though rural households would benefit less. However, in the short run, rural households would experience a small loss because of the restriction of labour mobility.

Xue and Wei (2004) and Li (2004) analysed recent urban poverty problems in China, and found that increasing numbers of laid-off and unemployed individuals, a result of enterprise reform, have increased urban poverty; the influx of migrants from rural areas is an important element of urban poverty;

and poverty is also related to level of education and the health of residents. They suggest that increasing employment is a way to solve the problem of urban poverty.

Li and Knight (2004) developed a new classification of poverty, based on the permanent income hypothesis. According to an individual's current levels of income and consumption, poverty can be divided into three categories: permanent poverty; selective poverty; and temporary poverty. Permanent poverty includes individuals whose current income and consumption are both below the poverty line. Temporary poverty refers to those whose current income is below the poverty line, but whose consumption level is above the poverty line because their permanent income is higher than their current income; current consumption is financed either by past savings or by new loans. Selective poverty refers to those people whose current income is above the poverty line but consumption level is below the poverty line. Their choice to lower consumption is either because they are making up for past overconsumption or have expectations of making large expenditures in the future. According to their 1999 survey, Li and Knight (2004) discovered that the overall urban poverty rate was 9.4 per cent in China, 29 per cent of which could be categorized as permanent poverty, 20 per cent as temporary poverty, and the remaining 50 per cent as selective poverty.[8] The propensity for high savings rates and low rates of expenditure among families categorized within the selective poverty category was because most of these families did not have members who were ill or children who were still at school, so their current expenditure was very low.

Studies conducted by Ravallion and Chen (2004) can be taken as an authoritative analysis of Chinese poverty. They not only evaluated the change in the rate and extent of poverty since 1978, but also provided a theoretical explanation for it. According to the poverty line defined in their analysis, in the twenty years since 1981, the proportion of the Chinese population in a state of poverty decreased from 53 per cent to 8 per cent, but the speed of this decrease has slowed since the end of the 1990s. At the same time, the degree of inequity in China was found to be increasing, which, the analysis pointed out, has become a common focus in the study of economic development and poverty reduction.

What is more, another important finding of the study was that 'the approach to economic development can affect poverty reduction'. Although we agree with this finding, we have reservations about Ravallion and Chen's explanation of it, which is based on the idea that if the overall growth rate of each industry[9] remained constant since 1981, it would take 10 years rather than 20 years for incidences of poverty to decrease to 8 per cent.[10] The reason for our objection is simple: if the growth rate of secondary industry and tertiary industry remained at 1981 levels since then (the growth of per capita income), the demand for agricultural products would not have been as high as the actual levels we have seen. In the extreme situation of a closed economy, since the demand elasticity of agricultural products with regard to both income and price is very low, an increase in agricultural production may result in a decrease, rather than an increase, in farmers' incomes. Although Ravallion and Chen (2004) correctly conclude that past reductions in China's rural poverty was mainly a result of agricultural growth, it can hardly be useful to suggest this as a future policy for the reduction of rural poverty. Given the current endowment structure of population and land, depending on growth in agricultural output alone is hardly a sustainable method for reducing poverty.

Although the views of the above literature may be different, they are all based on detailed econometric analysis and simulation. This chapter does not intend to judge where a reasonable poverty line should be set, or which measurement of poverty is more precise. What concerns us most is the construction of a general framework for analysing the relationship between poverty and openness. The literature on Chinese poverty mentioned above has thus far failed to do so.

Economic development strategy, openness and poverty: a framework[11]

Not including the instances of poverty that result from a loss of ability to work because of illness, or natural or man-made disasters, the majority of instances of low income in developing countries are the result of the interaction of economic growth and income distribution. Obviously, if the increase in per capita income of an economy is so slow that it remains under the poverty line, most people will live in poverty no matter how equally income is distributed. The analysis by Dollar and Kraay (2000) using data from eighty countries over about fourty years shows that 'the income of the poor rises one-for-one with overall growth'. Similarly, if income disparity in an economy is increasing along with its per capita income, the problem of poverty will also worsen. Thus the combination of economic growth and improved income distribution is a basic and sustainable way for solving the problem of poverty. Therefore, it is imperative to find a mode of development that can promote economic growth and improve income distribution simultaneously.

Economists have long striven for such an approach to development. Many suggestions have been put forward in different periods of history and different contexts. However, economists have become less confident in making new suggestions. In a paper entitled 'Growth Strategies' prepared for the *Handbook of Economic Growth*, Rodrik (2004) cites two paragraphs by Harberger, one in 1985 and another in 2003. The first highly praised the power of economic principles in influencing development policies, but the second one lost almost all confidence in the economic principles it had previously praised. Rodrik ends his article as follows, 'rule-of-thumb economics, which has long dominated thinking on growth policies, can be safely discarded'. This remark reflects the frustration of economists in facing the many problems of development in today's world.

We believe that the key to understanding the relationship between openness, growth and poverty is the government's economic development strategy. According to Lin (2003), a country's development strategy can be divided broadly into two mutually exclusive groups, introduced earlier in the chapter: (i) a comparative advantage-defying (CAD) strategy, which attempts to encourage firms to deviate from the economy's existing comparative advantages in their entry into an industry or choice of technology; and (ii) the comparative advantage-following (CAF) strategy, which attempts to facilitate the entry of firms into an industry or choice of technology according to the economy's existing comparative advantages.[12]

When development economics began to take shape in the mid-twentieth century, the dominant view among development economists was to advise governments in the least developed countries (LDCs) to ignore their own comparative advantages and to adopt an inward-looking variant of the CAD strategy, telling them to focus on developing heavy industry or import substitution. The endowment structure of most LDCs is characterized by a relative abundance of labour and a lack of capital, whereas the projects supported by a CAD strategy are capital-intensive and are not consistent with the comparative advantage of most LDCs. As a result, firms in government-selected priority sectors are not viable in an open and competitive market. Therefore, governments must support these firms by intervening in the natural function of the market. Specific measures used include (but are not limited to) the following variants: interest-rate suppression in order to lower investment and operational costs for heavy-industry projects, an overvalued domestic currency that makes importing equipment for heavy industry projects cheaper, and the creation of legal monopolies that allow firms to charge high prices in order to ensure high enough profits (Lin *et al.* 1996).

Unlike many other developing economies, Japan, Korea, Singapore, Hong Kong and Taiwan followed a development approach that was closer to a CAF rather than a CAD strategy. After the Second World War, these countries upgraded their industries in accordance with the changes in their comparative advantages at each stage of development, and they have achieved much better performance than their counterparts who adopted a CAD strategy. Lin (2003) argues that a country's economic development strategy matters; and an economy's growth, trade structure, income distribution and poverty are endogenous to its choice of development strategy.

Development strategy and growth

The most important sources of per capita income growth are per capita capital accumulation and technological progress. Capital accumulation depends on the size of economic surpluses and the rate of savings in the economy. When firms enter the industries in which an economy has comparative advantages and adopt cost-minimizing technology in their production, the firms will be competitive, the economy's products will maximize their share in domestic and international markets, and the economy will maximize its possible surplus. Meanwhile, capital will have the highest possible rate of return when it is invested in industries in which the economy has comparative advantages. The incentive to save will also be maximized. Moreover, the government will not need to distort the prices of inputs and outputs, nor will it need to use administrative methods to create legal monopolies and provide subsidies in order to protect firms. Therefore, there will be no space for wasteful rent-seeking activities. The firms will have hard budget constraints and will need to earn profits by improving management practices and their competitiveness in the market. A CAD strategy will result in just the opposite effect with regard to competitiveness, the rate of return to capital, rent-seeking activities, and the softness of budget constraints for firms in priority industries. Therefore, the accumulation of capital under a CAF strategy will be faster than under a CAD strategy.

The accumulation of per capita capital will provide a basis for upgrading the industrial/technological structure of the economy (Basu and Weil 1998). Despite possibly being borrowed from developed countries (DCs), these upgraded industries/technologies will be new to the firms of an LDC. The learning costs will be lower under a CAF strategy because the distance between the new industry/technology and existing industry/technology is smaller (Barro and Sala-i-Martin 1997). Moreover, the patent protections of many targeted technologies under a CAF strategy are likely to have expired; and even if they are still under patent protection, the licensing fee will be lower for technologies needed under the CAF strategy because, *ceteris paribus*, most of the targeted technologies will be older than those needed under a CAD strategy. In some cases, firms under a CAD strategy will not be able to obtain necessary technology from DCs and will need to 'reinvent the wheel' on their own through investment in costly and risky R&D. Therefore, the acquisition cost of technology will be lower under a CAF strategy than under a CAD one.

So, by following a CAF strategy, the speed of endowment structure (capital–labour ratio) upgrading and technological progress will be faster than under a CAD strategy. We have tested these hypotheses, using cross-country data and provincial data within China, and the results are consistent with the above predictions (Lin 2003; Lin and Liu 2003a).

Development strategy and openness

A country adopting a CAF strategy will import products for which it does not have comparative advantages, and export products for which it has comparative advantages. For such a country, the degree of openness (the value of imports and exports as a percentage of GDP) is endogenous to the country's comparative advantages.

If the government of an LDC adopts a CAD strategy and attempts to substitute the importation of capital-intensive goods with domestic production, not only will the country's import volume be reduced, but its exports will also fall. The latter is the result of resources being redirected to priority industries from the industries in which the economy has a comparative advantage, in addition to the exchange rate possibly being overvalued to facilitate the import of technology/equipment for the development of priority industries. Both will hamper the development of exports. The economies that followed the model include the socialist countries, India, Latin-American countries and many other developing countries. The performance of these countries had been miserable compared with the East Asian economies that adopted a CAF strategy. The government of an LDC may adopt a CAD strategy while at the same time encouraging firms in its priority-sector capital-intensive industries to export. In this case, even though a large proportion of the firms' products may be sent to foreign markets and may see fast technological improvement, the products exported will not be profitable. The survival of these firms depends on government protection via preferential loans and other policy support. As a result of these policies, the country will have poor external accounts, accumulate massive foreign debt, and be sensitive to external shock.

It may be better for an LDC to adopt a CAD strategy that encourages exports rather than one that encourages import substitution. However, the overall economic performance of a country that adopts a strategy encouraging exports will still be worse than that of a country that adopts a CAF strategy. Since the optimal level of openness of an economy is determined endogenously by its comparative advantages, it is not true that emphasis on external trade is a better policy for promoting economic growth in an LDC.[13]

Development strategy, income distribution and poverty[14]

To reduce poverty and distribute income more equally, the economic situation of low-income groups must be improved. Low-income individuals, unlike the wealthy, have little in the way of land, capital, higher education, personal relations or social networks that might help them generate income. The major source of income for the poor is the physical labour they can provide. Therefore, to increase the income of these individuals continuously, both absolutely and relatively, it is essential to create employment opportunities and to increase wages for them as much as possible. This is the only feasible and sustainable way to improve the economic situation of low-income individuals in LDCs. If a CAF strategy is adopted and labour-intensive industries developed, these people will have sufficient job opportunities. Moreover, this strategy will accelerate the accumulation of capital, which will in turn initially cause relatively abundant labour to become scarcer. In this process, industry and technology become increasingly capital-intensive and the marginal productivity of labour increases, as do wages. With sufficient employment and an increase in wages, poverty can be eliminated. Meanwhile, as capital becomes increasingly abundant, the return to capital declines. The relative gap in income of people originally with an advantage in capital and those who can only depend on physical labour will be narrowed. Therefore, income will become distributed more equally. It is by adopting a CAF strategy that efficiency and equity can be achieved simultaneously in LDCs.

In contrast, if an LDC adopts a CAD strategy, and gives priorities to capital-intensive industries, it will fail to create a large number of jobs. Most labourers will remain in the agricultural sector, where both marginal productivity and their wages remain low (Lin *et al.* 1996). Meanwhile, only the rich and the powerful that have easy access to subsidized loans from banks will have the financial resources to invest in prioritized capital-intensive industries. However, firms in the priority industries will not be viable. Their investment and survival rely on government protection and subsidies, which must ultimately come from the pockets of the poor and powerless. Therefore, inequality in income distribution will be exacerbated.

The CAD strategy will also reduce social transfers to groups in relatively weak positions such as the poor, jobless, disabled and elderly. These groups are universally acknowledged as the ones in need of social protection, either through social security networks or relief funds, or through assistance from other family members. However, the resources that could be allocated to support these groups depend on overall economic growth. Under a CAD strategy, low economic performance reduces the total amount of resources that can be used to help these people. Sometimes, the government may even divert resources that would have been allocated to the social security system, to subsidize prioritized sectors. This will lead to a deterioration in the standard of living for disadvantaged people.

Openness and poverty in China after reform

Before reform began in 1978, China adopted a typical CAD strategy, resulting in poor economic performance, but since the reform started, China's economic development has moved gradually toward a CAF strategy.

The reform started with the replacement of collective farming by the household responsibility system in rural areas at the end of 1978. This institutional change greatly increased agricultural productivity (Lin 1992). Along with agricultural reform, the government also increased the autonomy of state-owned enterprises (SOEs) and allowed them to share in profits through a profit retention system, later on a contract system and recently the modern corporation system. Meanwhile, township and village enterprises and other private enterprises had begun to emerge and grow. These new enterprises were faced with a hard budget constraint, as they were not entitled to government protection and subsidies, leaving them to fight for survival among fierce competition.

The entry of new enterprises also increased the pressure on SOEs to face competition and forced them to improve performance. Since the mid-1990s, most small- and medium-sized SOEs and collectively-owned enterprises have been privatized. With the progress of reform, the government reduced its direct interference on resource allocation and prices. Apart from the financial markets, most other markets have been liberalized. The reduction of the government's interventions has shifted China's development away from CAD to CAF strategy.

With the progress of reform and the change in development strategy, China has turned from being an inward-orientated economy to integrating increasingly with the world economy. By establishing special economic zones, attracting foreign direct investment (FDI) and liberalizing trade, the link between the Chinese economy and the global economy has become closer, especially after China's accession to the WTO in 2001. China's trade-dependent ratio (the percentage of total imports and exports as a percentage of GDP) increased from 9.79 per cent in 1978 to 60.11 per cent in 2003 (see Table 6.1). Among the largest economies in the world, China has become the most open economy, as measured by the trade dependent ratio. At the same time, FDI in China increased from almost nothing in the early 1980s to US$53.5 billion in 2003, the largest recipient of FDI in the world that year. The share of FDI in China's fixed asset investment increased from 1.9 per cent in 1985 to 17 per cent in 1994 and remained at around 10 per cent from the late 1990s into the early 2000s (see Table 6.2 on page 137). The composition of China's trade also experienced a big change, with a significant increase in the proportion of manufactured products in imports and exports (see Figures 6.1 and 6.2).

However, integration with the world economy is not even throughout all the provinces and regions in China. As shown in Figures 6.3–6.5, the coastal provinces, especially Guangdong, received significantly more FDI, and their imports and exports comprise a much higher proportion of their total value-added than is the case with provinces in the central and western regions.

Foreign enterprises in China have provided many jobs and account for a large portion of China's imports and exports. At the same time, foreign enterprises have also contributed to China's change in development strategy. Foreign enterprises face a hard budget constraint, and to minimize costs they must follow the comparative advantage in their chosen industry and technology. Moreover, by listing in the equity markets abroad or forming joint ventures, some large SOEs are able to gain access to foreign capital and remove the constraint of China's relative capital scarcity on their viability (Lin and Tan 1999).

However, China's transition to an economy totally observing the CAF strategy is far from complete. First, reform in some key areas is not finished. For example, interest rates have not been liberalized; and the banking system still bears the burden of subsidizing large SOEs. Second, the degree to which

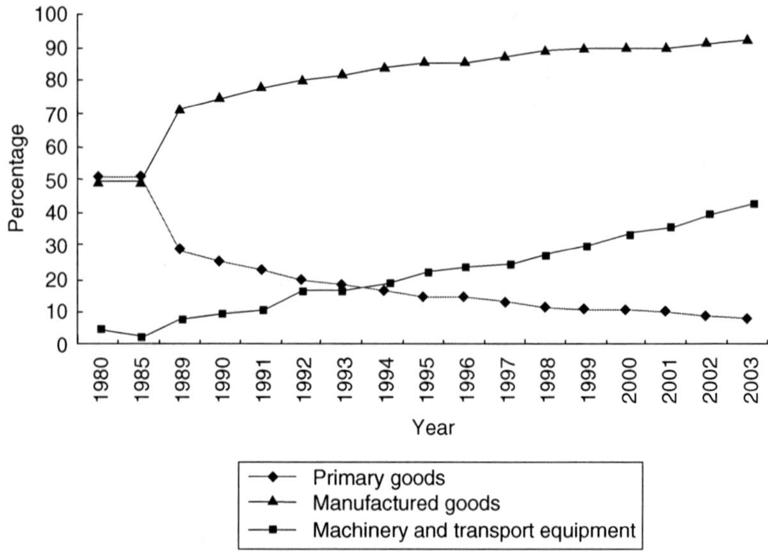

Figure 6.1   China's export structure, 1980–2003
Source: National Statistical Bureau of China, *China Statistical Yearbook*, various years.

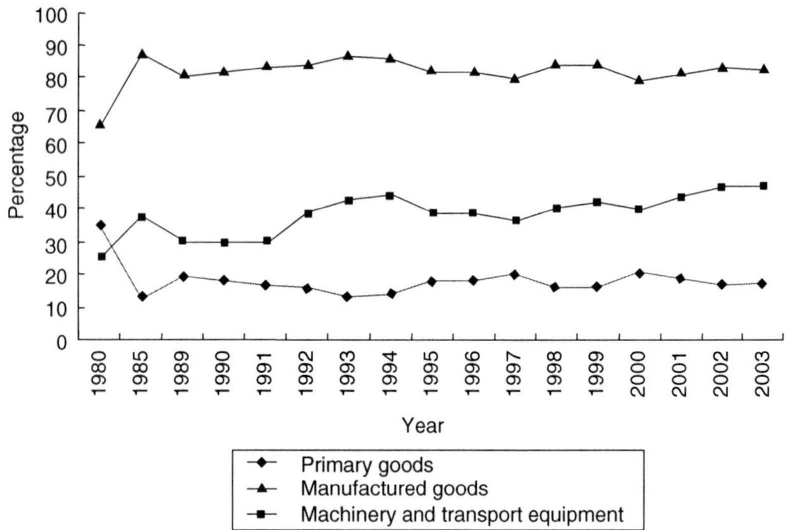

Figure 6.2   China's import structure, 1980–2003
Source: National Statistical Bureau of China, *China Statistical Yearbook*, various years.

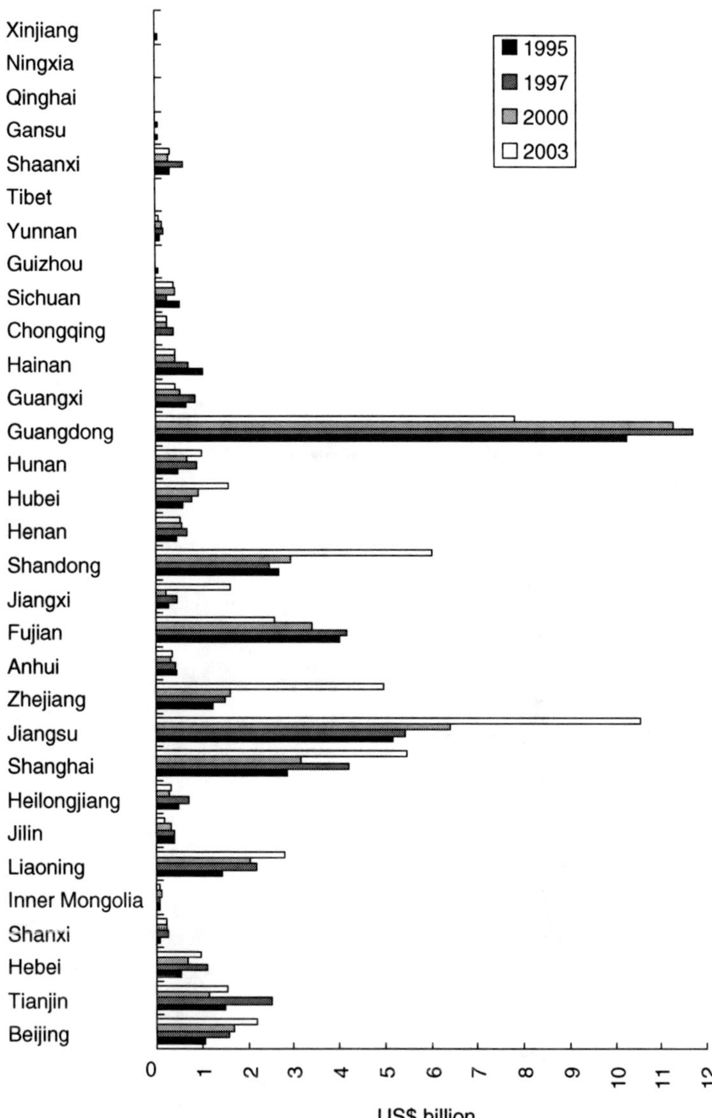

Figure 6.3 The regional distribution of FDI (US$ billion)

Source: National Statistical Bureau of China, *China Statistical Yearbook*, various years.

150

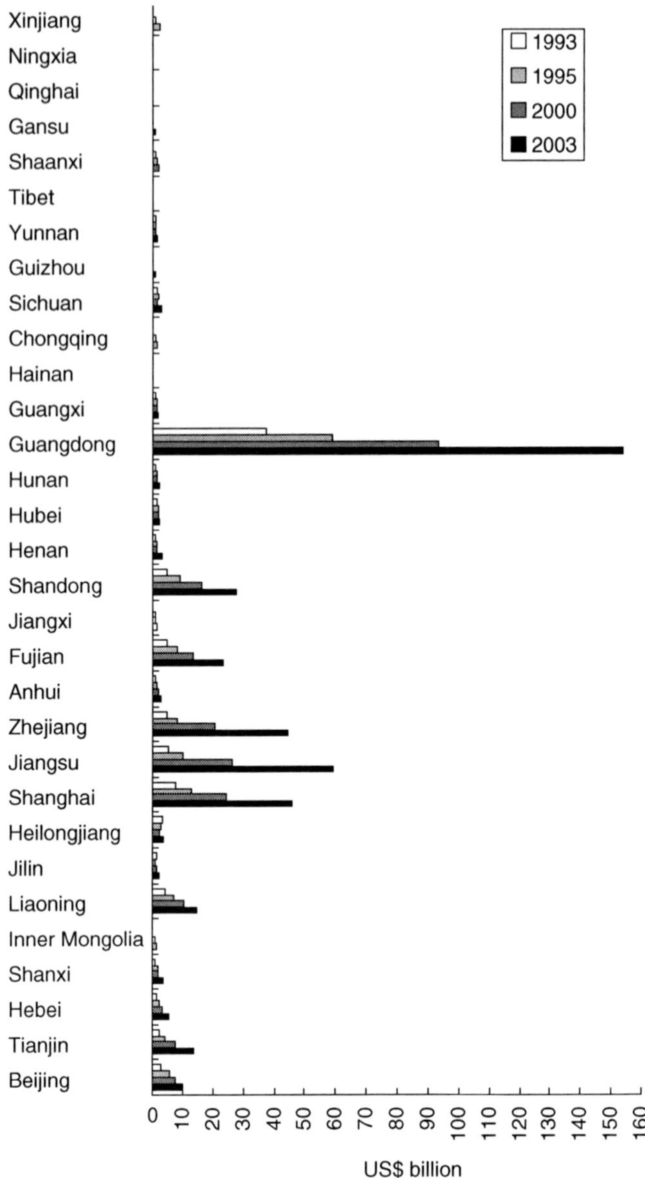

Figure 6.4 Commodity exports according to location of origin in China (US$ billion)
Source: National Statistical Bureau of China, *China Statistical Yearbook*, various years.

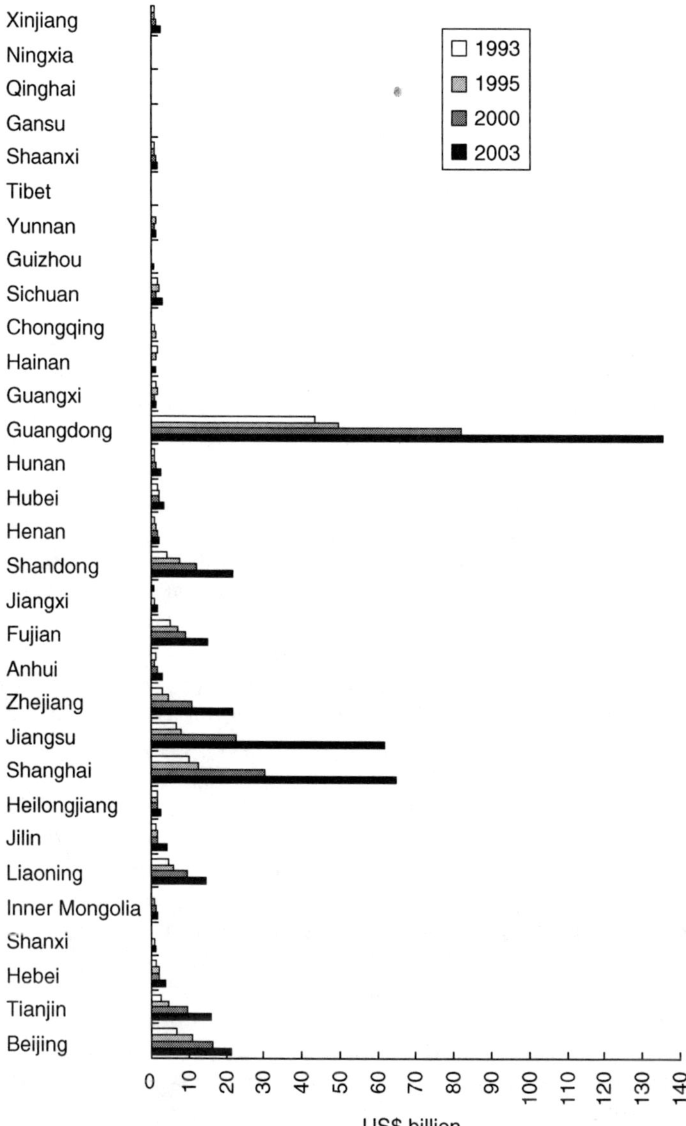

Figure 6.5 Commodity imports according to destination in China (US$ billion)

Source: National Statistical Bureau of China, *China Statistical Yearbook*, various years.

various regions deviated from their comparative advantage differed before reform, and their degree of shift to a CAF strategy also varies across regions. Third, after reform, all levels of government, especially local government, often use administrative measures (such as deliberately keeping land prices low, reducing local taxes, lowering environmental protection standards, creating entry barriers for products produced in other provinces and so on) to encourage firms to ignore the region's specific comparative advantages in their choice of industries or technologies. Evidence from productivity differences between agricultural and non-agricultural sectors clearly indicates that the change in China's development strategy is still incomplete.

In an open, competitive market, the marginal return of a factor of production in various sectors will be equalized. Figure 6.6 shows that the agricultural sector's labour productivity is increasing. If the differences between the agricultural sector's labour productivity and those of manufacturing and other industries are narrowing, we can conclude that the marginal productivity gaps between agriculture and other industries are diminishing. Otherwise, we can reach the opposite conclusion.[15] Figure 6.7 shows the relative labour productivity of non-agricultural sectors compared to that of agriculture. We see that, before the 1990s, differences in productivity between agriculture and other sectors were decreasing; however, from the first half of the 1990s, the differences have grown and for several sectors have exceeded those at the beginning of reform.[16]

Another proxy is the incremental labour–output ratio, the results of which are shown in Table 6.5.[17] We see that, after reform, the incremental labour–output ratios in the national economy, primary, secondary and tertiary industries all show an upward trend, especially in the first half of the 1990s and after 1999, a fact that indicates an increase in marginal labour productivity in all sectors. But, compared with other industrial sectors and the national economy as a whole, the increase in the incremental labour–output ratio of primary industries is much slower. That is to say, the increase in marginal labour productivity in agricultural sectors is much lower than in non-agricultural sectors.

Of course, even in ideal conditions, labour productivity in different sectors cannot be exactly the same because of differences in technologies, transaction costs and for other reasons. However, if the productivity gap between agriculture and other industries continues to increase, the difference in income distribution between the rural agricultural population and those in the urban sectors will become greater. As long as most of the poor rely on agriculture for their livelihood, poverty will not be eliminated.

The evidence discussed above has two implications for poverty reduction: first, there is a large potential for success in China's future poverty reduction, especially in reducing poverty in rural areas. Contrary to Ravallion and Chen's (2004) recommendation of reducing rural poverty by developing agriculture, we advocate a new approach to rural poverty reduction. We

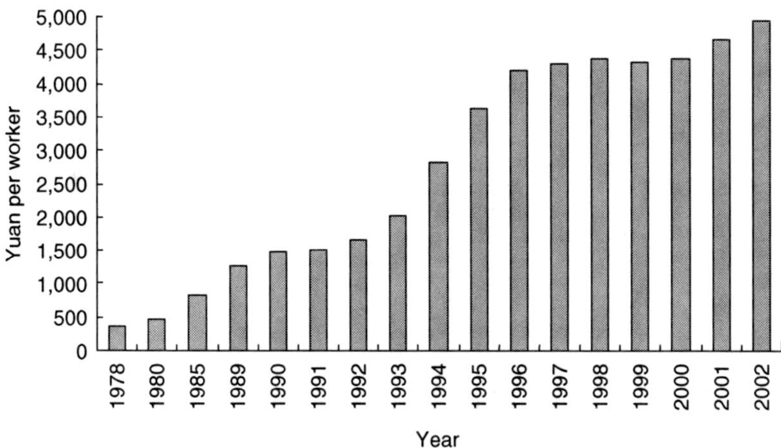

Figure 6.6   Labour productivity of the agricultural sector (yuan per worker)

Source: National Statistical Bureau of China, *China Statistical Yearbook*, various years.

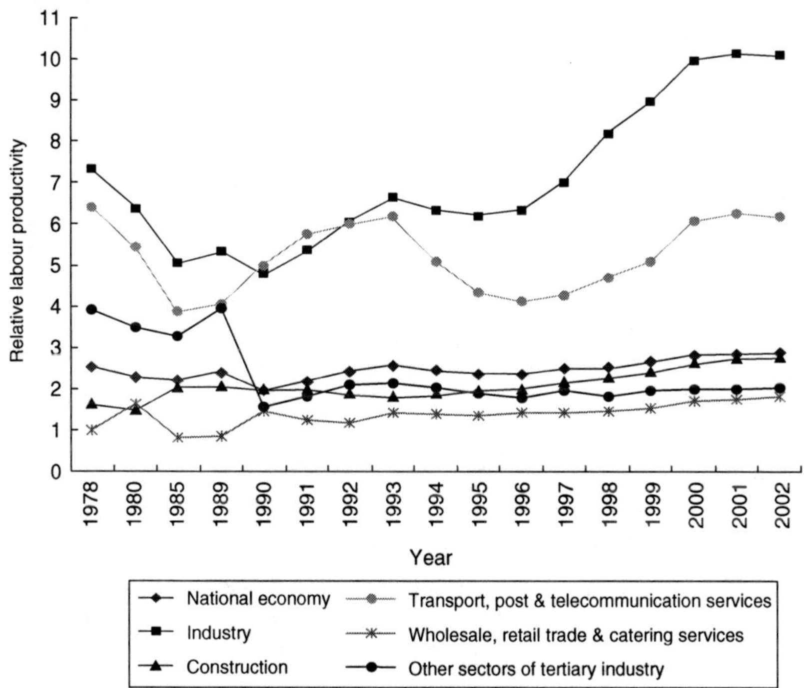

Figure 6.7   Relative labour productivity of non-agricultural to agricultural sectors

Source: National Statistical Bureau of China, *China Statistical Yearbook*, various years.

Table 6.5 Incremental output–labour ratio, 1978–2003

	National economy	Primary industry	Secondary industry	Manufacturing	Construction	Tertiary	Transport, post & telecommunication	Retail trade, & catering services
1978–9	0.47	0.76	0.63	0.79	0.09	0.02	0.34	−0.49
1979–80	0.36	0.21	0.56	0.55	0.67	0.29	0.99	−0.05
1980–1	0.25	0.28	0.21	0.20	0.33	0.23	0.16	0.33
1981–2	0.28	0.20	0.37	0.50	0.12	0.61	0.75	−0.67
1982–3	0.56	0.68	0.79	1.11	0.36	0.34	0.49	0.21
1983–4	0.70	*−1.18*	0.50	0.78	0.12	0.39	0.33	0.69
1984–5	1.07	0.94	0.96	1.57	0.27	1.27	0.51	1.49
1985–6	0.88	1.79	0.75	0.82	0.54	0.86	0.71	0.61
1986–7	1.17	1.08	1.49	1.71	0.95	0.96	0.90	1.33
1987–8	1.91	1.07	3.14	3.73	1.35	1.85	1.71	2.75
1988–9	1.99	0.41	*−3.93*	*−7.68*	0.19	4.63	125.0	2.56
1989–90	0.17	0.14	0.23	0.25	0.18	0.22	1.37	−0.57
1990–1	4.14	1.48	8.71	9.38	5.57	3.54	7.03	4.68
1991–2	7.60	*−1.28*	7.64	12.64	2.41	2.66	6.65	3.35
1992–3	12.19	*−1.06*	7.75	19.48	2.11	2.05	36.57	1.31
1993–4	18.74	*−2.45*	17.13	22.93	6.09	2.67	3.29	2.08
1994–5	19.21	*−2.31*	17.98	25.98	5.90	2.21	2.84	1.75
1995–6	10.63	*−2.61*	9.26	13.15	3.29	2.37	3.18	1.67
1996–7	7.56	18.35	10.49	18.76	1.68	5.15	38.86	2.81
1997–8	4.75	1.01	26.35	*−3.28*	1.20	5.01	*−9.41*	*−4.83*
1998–9	4.92	−0.14	*−10.83*	*−5.57*	1.90	5.40	5.54	1.61
1999–2000	10.71	0.57	*−21.67*	*−12.09*	3.32	4.64	*−221.9*	*−3.89*
2000–1	8.35	1.67	58.69	*−56.67*	3.94	8.02	46.69	9.23
2001–2	10.46	1.98	*−9.51*	*−8.84*	*−18.94*	2.30	5.30	1.13
2002–3	17.50	*−3.01*	25.56			4.93		

Notes: Negative figures (indicated in bold italics) refer to situations in which output increased but employment decreased. These can be viewed as a very large positive number. The boxed negative figures xxx refer to situations in which output decreased but employment increased, indicating that marginal labour productivity is very low.

Source: National Statistical Bureau of China, *China Statistical Yearbook*, various years.

suggest that China changes its economic development strategy by increasing the proportion of labour-intensive industries and labour-intensity in various production sectors so as to create more non-agricultural job opportunities for rural workers. Thus, those staying in the agricultural sector will have access to more land and capital, which may contribute to a decrease in the productivity gap between agricultural and non-agricultural sectors. This may be one of the few feasible approaches to eliminating poverty in China in the near future.

The second implication is that situations vary greatly between provinces and regions. The evidence cited above is not the same for all provinces. Because of the different pace at which changes in development strategy are implemented, there are different degrees to which poverty reduction has been achieved. According to China's official data, incidence rates of rural poverty vary greatly among different provinces (see Table 6.6). Tibet, Qinghai, Guizhou, Yunnan, Inner Mongolia, Jiangxi and Anhui have relatively higher rates of poverty, while these values were relatively low for the big cities and the coastal provinces. One study of Chinese urban poverty conducted by ADB (2003) shows that incidence rates of urban poverty also vary greatly across provinces (see Table 6.7). In 1998, Guangdong had the lowest urban poverty rate, at 0.68 per cent, while Ningxia had the highest, at 13.51 per cent.[18]

Hypothesis testing

In this section we use provincial panel data to test the effect of openness and development strategy on the incidence of rural poverty in China.

Proxies for openness and development strategy

In order to assess the impacts of globalization and development strategy on the incidence of rural poverty in each province in China, we need to have proxies for both openness and development strategy. For openness, we use the export and import dependent ratio (*EXIM*), defined as the sum of provincial imports (excluding imports from other provinces) and provincial exports (excluding exports to other provinces) divided by the provincial value-added each year.

Lin (2003) constructs a technological choice index (*TCI*) to measure the proxy for development strategy. Given the endowment structure of a province, the nature of its development strategy is characterized mainly by all the capital-intensity as well as the manufacturing industries of the province. When the province follows a CAF strategy, the optimum capital–labour ratio in manufacturing industries is determined endogenously by the province's capital–labour ratio. That is, the optimum capital–labour ratio in manufacturing industries is a function of the

Table 6.6   Rural poverty in the provinces of China, 1985–2002

Province	1985	1990	1995	2000	2002
Beijing	0.00	0.09	2.91	0.60	0.00
Tianjing	0.00	0.27	1.01	0.91	0.20
Hebei	4.90	12.23	4.10	1.93	2.90
Shanxi	4.10	15.52	9.80	6.74	5.00
Inner Mongolia	10.60	12.46	10.60	8.21	9.80
Liaoning	6.50	3.99	6.40	3.50	3.20
Jilin	10.30	7.92	8.60	4.10	2.60
Heilongjiang	14.10	12.98	8.21	5.59	3.40
Shanghai	0.00	0.09	0.00	0.00	0.00
Jiangsu	5.70	3.73	1.90	0.30	0.40
Zhejiang	4.50	3.27	1.60	0.20	0.40
Anhui	5.10	25.50	4.30	2.47	2.00
Fujian	6.30	1.30	1.30	0.33	0.40
Jiangxi	12.10	0.28	5.10	2.78	3.40
Shandong	2.30	3.75	2.90	0.70	0.70
Henan	24.90	20.02	7.60	2.97	1.70
Hubei	3.70	8.15	6.10	2.21	2.00
Hunan	12.60	2.82	7.61	2.29	1.90
Guangdong	1.10	0.28	1.00	0.11	0.00
Guangxi	22.20	6.42	10.50	5.00	2.70
Hainan	7.07	0.00	7.40	1.90	3.00
Sichuan	35.10	10.19	8.03	3.67	2.20
Guizhou	36.80	21.38	20.51	10.80	10.70
Yunnan	41.30	15.79	17.80	8.20	11.10
Xizang	4.00	10.67	23.58	19.80	15.60
Chongqing	35.10	0.00	11.24	4.24	3.00
Shaanxi	41.60	16.39	14.30	7.87	6.20
Gansu	43.90	26.49	18.10	9.70	9.20
Qinghai	5.00	16.32	16.10	18.60	16.10
Ningxia	53.00	20.53	18.96	14.50	8.90
Xinjiang	0.90	14.94	18.40	10.00	6.90

Source: National Statistical Bureau of China, *China Statistical Yearbook*, various years.

economy's capital–labour ratio, as shown in Equation (6.1):

$$\left(\frac{K_{i,t}}{L_{i,t}}\right)^{*} = f\left(\frac{\overline{K_{i,t}}}{\overline{L_{i,t}}}\right) \tag{6.1}$$

The left-hand side of Equation (6.1) refers to the optimum capital–labour ratio in the manufacturing industry of the ith province at time t; $\overline{K_{i,t}} / \overline{L_{i,t}}$ refers to the overall capital–labour ratio in the ith province at time t. In order to measure the deviation between the adopted development strategy and the CAF strategy in a province, a TCI is constructed. This is the quotient between

Table 6.7 Urban poverty in China, 1998

Province	Poverty line (yuan/person/per annum)	Total population with income below the poverty line (000s people)	Poverty rate (%)	Poverty rate (%) if poverty line increased by 15%
Beijing	3,118	54	0.73	1.45
Tianjing	2,993	360	6.77	10.71
Hebei	2,509	651	5.20	9.15
Shanxi	1,616	596	7.17	11.07
Inner Mongolia	1,824	510	6.40	10.03
Liaoning	2,203	1,150	6.13	11.63
Jilin	1,831	853	7.54	11.05
Heilongjiang	1,878	1,154	6.92	11.54
Shanghai	3,636	314	3.24	4.98
Jiangsu	2,228	244	1.20	3.09
Zhejiang	2,989	153	1.62	3.06
Anhui	2,138	348	2.89	6.57
Fujian	2,416	145	2.18	4.24
Jiangxi	1,809	310	3.42	7.49
Shandong	2,566	1,172	5.05	10.24
Henan	1,904	1,410	8.39	12.97
Hubei	2,283	934	5.67	10.37
Hunan	2,146	462	3.61	7.37
Guangdong	3,061	154	0.68	1.07
Guangxi	2,507	246	3.01	7.53
Hainan	2,465	150	7.94	14.15
Sichuan	2,004	711	4.72	6.75
Guizhou	2,137	260	5.00	8.08
Yunnan	2,359	225	3.69	6.44
Xizang	2,237	39	11.31	13.99
Chongqing	2,214	260	4.09	6.99
Shaanxi	2,014	932	11.95	17.66
Gansu	1,819	304	6.44	12.16
Qinghai	1,484	76	5.63	8.15
Ningxia	2,093	210	13.51	20.35
Xinjiang	1,772	383	6.16	7.04
National	**2,310**	**14,770**	**4.73**	**8.17**

Source: Asian Development Bank (2003).

the actual capital–labour ratio in the manufacturing industry[19] of a province and the endowed capital–labour ratio of the province, that is:

$$TCI_{i,t} = \frac{(K_{i,t}/L_{i,t})}{\overline{(K_{i,t}/L_{i,t})}} \tag{6.2}$$

Previous analysis shows that the provincial government's development strategy will affect the value of TCI in that province.

We then define the optimal technology choice index, $TCI_{i,t}^*$, for the *i*th province at time *t*. From the first-order Taylor expansion of Equation (6.1) at the origin and omitting the higher order terms, we obtain:

$$\left(\frac{K_{i,t}}{L_{i,t}}\right)^* = \omega \cdot \left(\frac{\overline{K_{i,t}}}{\overline{L_{i,t}}}\right) \tag{6.3}$$

where ω is a positive constant. The optimal technological choice index TCI^* is defined, accordingly, as follows:[20]

$$TCI_{i,t}^* = \frac{(K_{i,t}/L_{i,t})^*}{\overline{(K_{i,t}/L_{i,t})}} = \omega \tag{6.4}$$

The optimal K/L over industries is not a constant number. But it should be pointed out that the chapter measures development strategy at the province level rather than at industry level. What we assume to be a positive constant, ω, is a province's optimal technological choice index $TCI_{i,t}^*$, rather than the optimal capital–labour ratio of the province's manufacturing industry $(K_{i,t}/L_{i,t})^*$. Indeed, when capital is relatively abundant in a province, the optimum capital–labour ratio in the manufacturing industries of the province[21] will be higher than in a province where capital is relatively scarce. In other words, the higher the capital–labour ratio in a province's endowments (the denominator of $TCI_{i,t}^*$), the higher the optimum capital–labour ratio in its manufacturing industries (the numerator of $TCI_{i,t}^*$). To be more specific, what we assume to be a positive constant, ω, is $TCI_{i,t}^*$ rather than the numerate of $TCI_{i,t}^*$.

Given the definition of $TCI_{i,t}^*$, a deviation from the CAF strategy in the *i*th province at time *t* can then be measured indirectly, as follows:

$$DS_{i,t} = |TCI_{i,t} - TCI_{i,t}^*| = |TCI_{i,t} - \omega| \tag{6.5}$$

If a CAF strategy is adopted in the *i*th province at time *t*, $DS_{i,t} = 0$. When the actual $TCI_{i,t}$ is higher (lower) than optimal level, $DS_{i,t} > 0(< 0)$. The absolute value of $DS_{i,t}$ measures the deviation between the adopted strategy and the CAF strategy in the *i*th province at time *t*.

There are two types of CAD – that is, $DS_{i,t} > 0$ or $DS_{i,t} < 0$. Theoretically speaking, if taking only income distribution into account, a comparative advantage defying strategy, in either developing or developed countries, that encourages manufacturing industries that are much more labour intensive than the optimal level (that is, the case corresponding to $DS_{i,t} < 0$) could be even more effective in reducing poverty than a comparative advantage following strategy is. However, if taking the viability issue of such labour-intensive industries into account, it is obviously that the sustainability of both economic growth and employment opportunity growth will be jeopardized. In the long run, this approach is harmful to income equity.

According to our observations, all provincial governments in China have the intention of developing capital-intensive and technology-intensive projects inconsistent with the comparative advantages at their present stage of development, probably a result of the legacy of development concepts inherited from the old strategy before reform. The characteristic of development strategies in China's provinces is that of $DS_{i,t} > 0$. Given this fact, the deviation of adopted strategy from the CAF in the ith province at time t can be measured as: $DS_{i,t} = TCI_{i,t} - \omega$.

The specification of functional form[22]

In our empirical analysis, we hope to examine the effects of development strategies on openness and rural poverty. The econometric models are constructed as follows:

$$EXIM_{i,t} = \alpha_0 + \alpha_1 DS_{i,t} + \boldsymbol{\alpha}X + v \tag{6.6}$$

$$PI_{i,t} = \beta_0 + \beta_1 DS_{i,t} + \beta_2 EXIM_{i,t} + \boldsymbol{\beta}Y + \varepsilon \tag{6.7}$$

In the above equations, $EXIM_{i,t}$ refers to the trade dependent ratio of province i at time t, $PI_{i,t}$ refers to the incidence rate of rural poverty of province i at time t; α_0 and β_0 are constant; $DS_{i,t}$ is the outcome of (6.5), which represents the deviation from a CAF strategy in province i at time t. According to previous analysis, we expect that the larger the deviation, the lower the trade dependent ratio and the higher the rural poverty incidence rate. This means α_1 is negative and β_1 is positive. X and Y represent all other explanatory variables; $\boldsymbol{\alpha}$ and $\boldsymbol{\beta}$ are the coefficient vectors; v and ε are the error terms.

Since there is no observation for ω, $DS_{i,t}$ of Equation (6.5) cannot be calculated directly. However, since ω is assumed to be a positive constant, Equations (6.6) and (6.7) can be transformed into Equations (6.6') and (6.7'):

$$EXIM_{i,t} = \alpha_0' + \alpha_1 TCI_{i,t} + \boldsymbol{\alpha}X + v \tag{6.6'}$$

$$PI_{i,t} = \beta_0' + \beta_1 TCI_{i,t} + \beta_2 EXIM_{i,t} + \boldsymbol{\beta}Y + \varepsilon \tag{6.7'}$$

where $\alpha'_0 = \alpha_0 - \alpha_1 \omega$ and $\beta'_0 = \beta_0 - \beta_1 \omega$. The $TCI_{i,t}$ in Equations (6.6') and (6.7') is the quotient of the actual capital–labour ratio in the manufacturing industry and the endowed capital–labour ratio of province i in the year t.

Variables and data

Provincial rural poverty incidence rates have been obtained from the National Statistics Bureau (NSB). The TCI and other data used in the regression analyses are taken from Liu and Zhang (2005). $TCI_{i,t}$ is calculated using the following steps: (i) calculating the real capital ($K_{i,t}$) of the manufacturing industries of a province by devaluing the total value of fixed asset investments according to the fixed asset investment price index of that province; (ii) calculating the actual capital–labour ratio in the manufacturing industries; that is, $K_{i,t}/L_{i,t}$; (iii) based on the national accounting system for each province, calculating the capital stock($\overline{K}_{i,t}$) of all provinces using the perpetual-stock method; (iv) calculating the endowed capital–labour ratio; that is, $\overline{K}_{i,t} / \overline{L}_{i,t}$; (v) $TCI_{i,t}$ is that of the actual capital–labour ratio in the manufacturing industries divided by this province's one-year-legged endowed capital–labour ratio; that is, $(K_{i,t} / L_{i,t}) / (\overline{K}_{i,t-1} / \overline{L}_{i,t-1})$.[23] The dataset for $TCI_{i,t}$ is listed in the Appendix on page 164.

There are thirty-one provinces in mainland China, but as the data for Tibet and Hainan are incomplete, we have eliminated these two provinces from the regressions. Also, as Chongqing became a provincial-rank municipality only in 1997, we have combined the data for Chongqing and Sichuan after 1997 for comparability with past datasets. We therefore have data for twenty-eight provinces from 1985 to 2002.

Provincial rural poverty may also be affected by other variables. Other things being equal, the higher is agriculture productivity, the larger its contribution to the reduction of rural poverty will be. Therefore we introduced a variable for agriculture productivity (*AGR-PRO*) to control for its effect on rural poverty. The variable is defined as agricultural value-added according to current prices divided by total rural employment.[24] As the NSB revised its employment statistics from being based on local government reports to sampling surveys, there is considerable deviation in employment data before and after 1990. To ensure data comparability, we have restricted our use of employment data to post-1990, which decreases the sample size for regressions including agriculture productivity as an explanatory variable from 420 to 196.

Infrastructure, especially transportation, has a significant influence on rural poverty through labour mobility and the agricultural-products market. Thus indices of regional road density (*ROAD*) and railway density (*RAILWAY*) are also introduced.

The trade dependent ratio, *EXIM*, is endogenous to the development strategy of the government. In the estimation of its impact on rural poverty in Equation (6.7'), we need to use the fitted value *EXIM* in Equation (6.6') in the regression of Equation (6.7') in order to obtain consistent estimates of the coefficients in Equation (6.7′). The explanatory variables used in the regression of Equation (6.6′) include *TCI*, *AGR-PRO*, *ROAD*, *RAILWAY* and a *COAST* dummy to indicate whether the province is located in a coastal area. Coastal provinces are usually more open than inland provinces because of easier access to international markets. The dummy *COAST* is treated as an instrument variable in Equation (6.6′) in order to obtain the fitted value of *EXIM* for the second-stage estimation of Equation (6.7′).

Econometric results

We used the cross-sectional time-series FGLS regression in Stata v8.0 to conduct our estimation, under the assumption that the error structure across the panels is heteroscedastic but uncorrelated; and the form of auto-correlation is AR(1). The results for *EXIM* and *PI* are shown in Tables 6.8 and 6.9, respectively.

The estimation results in Table 6.8 show that *TCI* has a negative and highly significant effect on *EXIM*. That is, as the previous sections suggest, the greater a province's deviation from the CAF strategy, the less open that

Table 6.8 The effect of the development strategy on openness

Cons	13.62***
	1.32
TCI	−0.64***
	0.19
AGR_PRO	0.36
	1.92
ROAD	−17.51***
	3.58
RAILWAY	110.85***
	17.32
COAST	19.37***
	1.10
Number of obs	196
Log likelihood	−748.8619
Prob > Chi²	0.0000

Note: *** indicates significance at 0.1 per cent level; the numbers below each coefficient are standard errors.

Table 6.9   The effect of the development strategy on rural poverty

	I	II	III
Cons	0.0674***	0.0974***	0.1381***
	0.0080	0.0115	0.0119
TCI	0.0047***	0.0037*	0.0039*
	0.0014	0.0019	0.0021
EXIM1		−0.0023***	−0.0031***
		0.0003	0.0003
AGR-PRO			−0.0366***
			0.0097
ROAD			−0.0914***
			0.164
RAILWAY			0.3499***
			0.0540
Number of obs	364	196	196
Log likelihood	883.6	527.7	301.4
Prob > Chi^2	0.0011	0.0000	0.0000

Notes: *EXIM* is the fitted value from Equation (6.6). *, **, and *** indicate significance at 5%, 1% and 0.1% levels, respectively. The numbers below each coefficient are the standard errors.

province will be. The results also show that *AGR-PRO* does not have a significant effect on *EXIM*, whereas the other three explanatory variables are all highly significant. However, the negative sign for the *ROAD* value is unexpected.

Table 6.9 shows the results of fitting Equation (6.7′) with a two-stage approach where *EXIM* in the second stage is the fitted value from the first stage regression, as shown in Table 6.8. From the results, we can see that the development strategy followed in a province has a significant effect on rural poverty in that province. The greater the deviation from a CAF strategy in a province, the higher the incidence of rural poverty in that province.

The estimation results of *EXIM* are negative and highly significant. That is, the more open a province, the less rural poverty there will be in that province. The negative effect of openness on rural poverty is likely to arise from the fact that most exports from China are labour-intensive manufactured goods. The increase in exports will increase demand for the importing of intermediate inputs, while at the same time providing more job opportunities for rural migrants. As argued previously, the migration of the rural labour force from the countryside to non-agricultural production is one of the most important ways of reducing rural poverty.

The results also show that the increase in agricultural productivity (*AGR-PRO*) will reduce rural poverty significantly in that particular province and an increase in the road density will have an effect similar to that of an increase in agricultural productivity. However, the effect of railroad density

Table 6.10   Headcount index of Chinese poverty, 2000 (per cent)

	National poverty line		US$1 (PPP) a day
	Urban	**Rural**	
2000	< 2.0	3.5	16.1

Source: Asian Development Bank (2000).

on the appearance of poverty in a province (*RAILWAY*) is puzzling. In Model III, its coefficient is positive and highly significant. This question deserves further investigation.

Concluding remarks

Even though China has achieved great success in poverty reduction since reform began in 1978, there is still a long way to go before the country can claim victory in the war against poverty. First, if the international standard for poverty of US$1 a day using PPP is adopted instead of the domestic standard, the incidence of poverty in China, based on the estimations reported by the Asian Development Bank (ADB) for 2000, will increase dramatically from less than 2 per cent in urban areas and 3.5 per cent in rural areas to 16.1 per cent, as shown in Table 6.10. Moreover, the pattern of poverty will change over time. It is expected that the severity of urban poverty and poverty among migrants from rural areas will increase in the future with the progress of industrialization and urbanization.

A more serious challenge is, that while the Chinese economy is achieving dynamic growth, income disparities are also increasing. This means that the distribution of benefits from economic growth is becoming increasingly unequal. This will not only worsen the poverty problem but also slow down, or even block, the pace of removing extreme poverty. As we have pointed out above, the increasing productivity gap between the agricultural and non-agricultural sectors means that the dual nature of the Chinese economy is still a serious issue.

It is obvious from both the theoretical analysis and the empirical results that for poverty reduction in both urban and rural areas, an important and sustainable approach is to adopt a CAF development strategy and to promote the growth of labour-intensive industries during China's current stage of economic development. With this development strategy, the economy will grow dynamically, be open to international trade and be able to reduce poverty. This is an important experience that China can provide to other developing countries.

Appendix

Table 6.A1   Dataset for the technological choice index (TCI), 1984–99

Provinces	1984	1985	1986	1987	1988	1989	1990	1991	1992	1993	1994	1995	1996	1997	1998	1999
Beijing	2.9233	2.6197	2.2788	2.0686	1.8127	1.5738	1.4727	1.5499	1.6060	2.1215	1.5655	1.8659	1.6941	1.6602	1.8863	1.7084
Tianjin	2.0554	1.9007	1.7694	1.7218	1.7334	1.7251	1.6290	1.6482	1.6859	1.4929	1.6680	1.8908	1.7359	1.8082	2.4158	2.4957
Hebei	4.2771	3.3175	3.1557	3.1729	2.7331	3.1860	3.2930	3.6719	3.5402	3.3047	3.1246	2.8578	2.6911	2.5634	2.4950	2.4936
Shanxi	3.5230	3.7246	3.2928	2.8583	2.5605	2.4858	2.6892	2.6657	2.5396	4.0745	3.5068	3.9725	3.9904	4.0484	4.3705	4.0576
Inner Mongolia	6.0964	5.5199	4.7417	4.5526	4.2238	3.8756	4.1244	4.1717	3.8834	3.5234	3.5019	3.6616	3.5880	3.7228	4.6463	5.3463
Liaoning	4.1518	3.5660	3.2696	2.9316	2.6367	2.6696	2.5989	2.4596	2.4203	2.2379	2.1899	2.4587	2.6529	2.7347	3.5608	3.9971
Jilin	4.4789	4.0039	3.6249	3.6994	3.4045	3.0923	3.3966	3.7360	3.4757	3.6154	3.1261	3.3135	3.5348	3.6970	4.8241	5.0209
Heilongjiang	4.0382	3.5971	2.9867	2.7587	2.5513	2.3188	2.3646	2.2386	2.1431	2.0747	1.9359	2.0023	2.0333	2.2129	3.0246	2.8291
Shanghai	1.7720	1.5492	1.6088	1.4912	1.2952	1.1683	1.1510	1.2301	1.2642	1.2066	1.5825	1.3869	1.3041	1.3375	1.7169	1.7349
Jiangsu	3.0187	2.4365	2.3924	2.0957	1.8480	2.0721	2.1463	2.3183	2.1264	1.7823	1.7039	1.8747	1.8758	1.9378	2.1138	2.1915
Zhejiang	2.6047	2.6528	2.3732	2.1495	1.8273	1.9085	2.0444	2.0804	2.0453	1.8050	1.6543	1.7123	1.6197	1.6265	1.7505	1.7013
Anhui	8.9673	5.9713	5.2317	4.5488	3.7602	4.0962	4.3593	2.9422	2.6488	2.7690	3.1870	3.2917	3.4339	3.5320	3.7922	4.1014
Fujian	4.6001	3.7330	3.3514	2.9930	2.4262	2.4187	2.1877	2.0924	1.8812	1.9191	2.0757	2.4568	2.2745	2.2092	2.1183	2.0863
Jiangxi	5.5994	4.1956	4.7257	3.5288	2.5992	4.0119	3.8089	3.7576	3.7061	3.6693	3.9245	4.2954	4.2652	4.1597	4.6064	4.4884
Shandong	5.4818	3.6290	3.1805	2.9635	2.8114	2.9873	2.8166	2.6848	2.8155	3.2075	3.0970	3.1249	3.0136	3.5286	3.6292	3.4692
Henan	6.7153	4.5765	4.3598	3.7267	4.1520	4.2924	4.0632	4.2318	4.1502	3.7448	3.6115	3.7931	3.6199	3.4957	3.8693	3.9945
Hubei	6.5163	5.1297	4.5403	4.3889	3.9001	4.6918	4.1675	4.3696	4.1709	4.0572	3.6310	3.5334	3.4489	3.3062	3.8013	3.8084
Hunan	7.7157	7.6332	4.0008	6.0198	5.4578	5.7110	3.8479	3.6199	3.7137	3.4933	3.5170	3.8642	3.7057	3.9054	4.0319	4.1232
Guangdong	2.9197	2.4636	2.4504	2.4236	2.3076	2.5591	2.6282	3.3500	2.7349	2.8652	3.2138	2.9565	2.8298	2.8549	3.2599	3.0145
Guangxi	7.8751	7.0936	6.2782	5.6637	3.7559	4.7666	4.6499	4.5802	4.3286	6.8514	5.8289	7.4256	7.1732	6.9178	6.9291	7.0563
Guizhou	11.8961	9.2204	4.8355	5.5494	5.6977	5.1887	5.3582	5.2010	4.9324	5.1977	5.4170	5.4462	5.5529	5.4341	5.8933	6.0140
Yunnan	5.9259	5.0976	5.1607	5.5636	5.5440	5.6084	6.7829	6.4728	6.2375	5.5120	5.3752	6.0250	6.0494	6.0527	6.3665	6.4052
Shaanxi	6.6929	5.5195	5.9485	3.9648	3.9998	3.5117	3.1000	2.9693	3.2637	2.4638	2.5283	3.1672	3.1833	3.1534	3.7410	4.3313
Gansu	10.7659	10.0962	8.9586	8.6226	7.4697	7.2679	6.7679	6.6970	7.0460	8.0497	8.4045	10.0032	9.9807	11.0896	12.6249	11.8209
Qinghai	4.3398	3.5244	3.1782	4.2608	4.2425	5.2795	5.5843	4.5968	4.2157	4.4709	4.9769	5.5640	5.5155	7.0630	7.8109	10.3356
Ningxia	3.7827	3.6426	3.5156	3.1614	2.7374	2.4670	2.5486	2.6143	2.8955	3.2178	3.1264	3.3287	3.2440	3.5906	4.4157	4.6909
Xinjiang	4.9841	4.7845	4.1736	3.6316	3.3622	3.1868	4.1468	3.8556	3.6780	3.7459	3.1233	3.1453	3.4587	3.5053	4.0281	4.1671
Chongqing & Sichuan	5.7334	4.2287	3.9741	3.7920	3.0882	2.9308	2.9194	3.0369	3.2218	3.3174	3.0734	3.4390	3.2440	3.5333	3.8864	4.2215

Source: Liu and Zhang (2005).

Acknowledgements

The authors are grateful for the helpful comments by Machiko Nissanke, Erik Thorbecke, Willem Thorbecke and other members of JICA/UNU-WIDER meeting on The Impact of Globalization on the Poor in Asia. The authors also thank the three referees for comments.

Notes

1   China mentioned in this chapter refers only to the Chinese mainland, and does not include Hong Kong, Macao and Taiwan.
2   Annual growth rate here refers to annual compound growth rate.
3   Many people argue that share of tertiary industry is underestimated, but that of secondary industry is overestimated.
4   Life expectancy in 2000 as reported by NSB (2004) was 71.4 years, higher than reported in the World Bank's report. But, generally speaking, it is a fact that the life expectancy of the Chinese people has increased greatly.
5   The Chinese official poverty line is 300 yuan per person per year for rural areas based on 1990 prices; comparable poverty line for urban areas is not available.
6   Based on 2002 prices, the new poverty line is 850 yuan per person per year for rural areas and 1,200 yuan for urban areas. A consumption bundle at this poverty line can guarantee the people's daily needs of 2,100 calories.
7   Obviously, poverty problems exist not only in developing countries, but also in developed ones. But there is a big difference in the living conditions of those living in poverty in developing and developed countries. This chapter focuses on globalization and poverty problems in developing countries.
8   When applying just the income standard or consumption standard, the poverty rate was 4.6 per cent and 7.5 per cent, respectively.
9   The industries mentioned here refer to primary industry, secondary industry and tertiary industry.
10   There is a methodology issue here. Just as Solow (2001: 283) points out, when talking about cross-country regressions of economic convergence, 'the causality issue points to a deeper question: Do cross-country regressions define a meaningful surface along which countries can move back and forth at will?'
11   This section draws heavily on Lin (2003).
12   The concept of comparative advantage is most often used in trade theories. But the term we use here is not restricted to its conventional meaning. Even in a closed economy, an enterprise's cost-minimizing input structure will be determined by the economy's given factor endowment structure and market demand. If the relative intensity of the scarce resource used in the government's prioritized industry exceeds its optimal cost-minimizing level, then the government's development strategy is also a CAD strategy (Lin 2003).
13   There is a substantial literature concerning the relationship between international trade strategies such as import substitution and export promotion, and economic growth. Import substitution and export promotion are both special cases of CAD. However, even in a closed economy without international trade, developing countries should select their development strategies between CAD and CAF. It is one of the contributions of development strategy arguments to the development literature.

14 Development strategies have important effects on the income differences among all the sub-regions of a country. Lin and Liu (2008) argue that the CAD will lead to large income differences among the sub-regions of an economy while the CAF tends to lower the sub-regions' income differences. The empirical test of this chapter shows that the hypothesis is consistent with China's experience.

15 The long-term trend of labour productivity is consistent with that of the marginal productivity of labour.

16 It can be seen from Figure 6.7 that a large productivity gap exists not only between agriculture and other industries, but also among other non-agriculture industries. What needs to be mentioned specifically here is that relative productivity of the other tertiary industries is, in fact, underestimated, because the value-added of tertiary industry is underestimated.

17 The results in Table 6.5 are calculated with current prices.

18 Urban poverty lines are not the same in the various provinces. For example, in Guangdong province, the urban poverty line is 3,061 yuan per person per annum, while in Ningxia it is 2,093 yuan.

19 Actual capital–labour ratio in the manufacturing industry is equal to the ratio of the sum of actual capital input of all manufacturing industries in a province, to the sum of actual labour input of the province's manufacturing factors.

20 TCI^* is also affected by the level of economic development and the richness of natural resources in the economy. We shall not address these issues in this chapter.

21 The optimum capital–labour ratio in the manufacturing industries is equal to the ratio of the sum of optimum capital inputs of all manufacturing industries in a province, to the sum of optimum labour inputs of the province's manufacturing industries.

22 Development strategies do influence income distribution. We outlined the causality from development strategies to equity in an earlier paper and conducted econometric testing using national-level data (Lin and Liu 2003b). However, we have not conducted econometric analysis using the province-level data, and will test this kind of relationship in future research.

23 It is worthwhile to note that the capital endowment in each province is calculated from the fixed asset investments in each province's manufacturing industries. Therefore, the measurement has already captured the effects of FDI and the cross-province capital flow on each province's capital endowment. In addition, even though the movement of labour across provincial borders is easier today than in the past, there are still many hidden barriers. Therefore, we assume that the labour mobility does not change the labour endowment of each province significantly.

24 Of course, we can use agricultural productivity calculated by constant prices. But our econometric analysis shows that productivities calculated at current prices and constant price have similar behaviour in all the regressions. Another reason for us to use current prices is that productivity at current prices can reflect the impact of the price of agriculture products. The rural poverty incidence rate used as a dependent variable was also determined on the basis of poverty line adjusted by current price.

References

Anderson, K., Huang, J. and Ianchovichina, E. (2004) 'The Impacts of WTO Accession on Chinese Agriculture and Rural Poverty', in D. Bhattasali, S. Li and W. Martin (eds), *China and the WTO: Accession, Policy Reform, and Poverty Reduction Strategies* (New York: Oxford University Press for the World Bank).

Asian Development Bank (ADB) (2000) 'Poverty and Development Indicators'. Available at: www.adb.org/Statistics/pov_dev_indicators.asp/.

Asian Development Bank (ADB) (2003) 'Urban Poverty: New Challenges of China's Development', Technical Assistant Programme PRC33448 of the Asian Development Bank. (Beijing: Economic Science Publishing House).

Barro, R. J. and Sala-i-Martin, X. (1997) 'Technological Diffusion, Convergence, and Growth', *Journal of Economic Growth*, 2(1): 1–26.

Basu, S. and Weil, D. N. (1998) 'Appropriate Technology and Growth', *Quarterly Journal of Economics*, 113(4): 1025–54.

Chen, S. and Ravallion, M. (2004) 'Welfare Impacts of China's Accession to the WTO', in D. Bhattasali, S. Li and W. Martin (eds), *China and the WTO: Accession, Policy Reform, and Poverty Reduction Strategies* (New York: Oxford University Press for the World Bank).

Dollar, D. and Kraay, A. (2000) 'Growth Is Good for the Poor', Working Paper. World Bank, Washington, DC. Reprinted in A. Shorrocks and R. van der Hoeven (eds) (2004), *Growth, Inequality and Poverty: Prospects for Pro-poor Economic Development* (Oxford: Oxford University Press for UNU-WIDER).

Easterly, W. (2003) 'A Tale of Two Kuznets Curves: Inequality in the Old and New Globalizations', Paper presented at the NBER Pre-Conference on Globalization and Inequality, 24–25 October, Cambridge, Mass.

Harberger, A. C. (1985) *Economic Policy and Economic Growth* (San Francisco: International Center for Economic Growth, Institute for Contemporary Studies).

Harberger, A. C. (2003) 'Interview with Arnold Harberger: Sound Polices Can Free Up Natural Forces of Growth', *IMF Survey*, 14 July: 213–16.

Hertel, T., Zhai, F. and Wang, Z. (2004) 'Implications of WTO Accession for Poverty in China', in D. Bhattasali, S. Li and W. Martin (eds), *China and the WTO: Accession, Policy Reform, and Poverty Reduction Strategies* (New York: Oxford University Press for the World Bank).

Li, S. (2004) 'Deterioration of Urban Poverty in China and its Reasons in the Late 1990s', in S. Li and H. Sato (eds), *The Price of Transitional Economy – Empirical Analysis on Urban Unemployment, Poverty and Income Difference* (Tenghong: China Fiscal Economic Publishing House).

Li, S. and Knight, J. (2004) 'Three Urban Poverty Categorics in China', in S. Li and H. Sato (eds), *The Price of Transitional Economy – Empirical Analysis on Urban Unemployment, Poverty and Income Difference* (Tenghong: China Fiscal Economic Publishing House).

Lin, J. Y. (1992) 'Rural Reforms and Agricultural Growth in China', *American Economic Review*, 82(1): 34–51.

Lin, J. Y. (2003) 'Development Strategy, Viability, and Economic Convergence', *Economic Development and Cultural Change*, 51(3): 277–308.

Lin, J. Y. and Liu, P. (2003a) 'The Impact of Economic Development on Capital Accumulation per Capita and Technology Upgrade: Empirical Test on Chinese Experience', *China Social Science*, 4.

Lin, J. Y. and Liu, P. (2003b) 'Economic Development Strategy, Equity, and Efficiency', *China Economic Quarterly*, 2(2): 479–504.

Lin, J. Y. and Liu, P. (2008) 'Development Strategies and Regional Income Disparities in China', in G. Wan (ed.), *Inequality and Growth in Modern China* (Oxford: Oxford University Press for UNU-WIDER).

Lin, J. Y., Cai, F. and Li, Z. (1996) *The China Miracle: Development Strategy and Economics Reform* (Hong Kong: Chinese University Press).

Lin, J. Y. and Tan, G. (1999) 'Policy Burdens: Accountability and the Soft Budget Constraint', *American Economic Review: Papers and Proceedings*, 89(2): 426–31.

Liu, M. and Zhang, Q. (2005) 'China's Economic Growth Data: 1970–2002'. Available at: www.fed.org.cn/.

Milanovic, B. (2002) 'Can We Discern the Effect of Globalization on Income Distribution? Evidence for Household Budget Surveys', Policy Research Working Paper 2876, World Bank, Washington, DC.

National Statistical Bureau (NSB) of China (2004), *China Statistical Yearbook 2004* (Beijing: NSB).

Nissanke, M. and Thorbecke, E. (eds) (2007) 'Channels and Policy Debate in the Globalization–Inequality–Poverty Nexus', in *The Impact of Globalization on the World's Poor: Transmission Mechanisms* (Basingstoke: Palgrave Macmillan for UNU-WIDER).

Ravallion, M. and Chen, S. (2004) 'China's (Uneven) Progress Against Poverty'. Working Paper 3408, World Bank, Washington, DC.

Rodrik, D. (2004) 'Growth Strategies'. Available at: www.ksghome.harvard.edu/~drodrik/growthstrat10.pdf.

Solow, R. (2001) 'Applying Growth Theory Across Countries', *The World Bank Economic Review*, 15(2): 283–8.

World Bank (2002) *Transition: The First Ten Years – Analysis and Lessons for Eastern Europe and the Former Soviet Union* (Washington, DC: World Bank).

World Bank (2004) *World Development Indicators 2004* (Washington, DC: World Bank).

Xue, J. and Wei, Z. (2004) 'Urban Unemployment, Poverty and Income Difference', in D. Bhattasali, S. Li and W. Martin (eds), *China and the WTO: Accession, Policy Reform, and Poverty Reduction Strategies* (New York: Oxford University Press for the World Bank).

7

Vulnerability to Globalization in India: Relative Rankings of States Using Fuzzy Models

K. S. Kavi Kumar and Brinda Viswanathan

Introduction

Globalization is one of the important issues confronting developing countries. While globalization means different things to different people, this study interprets it as the component that arises from trade liberalization. Some argue that the inability of countries to integrate into the global economy because of a complex set of factors, including domestic policies, institutions and infrastructure, can cause economies to contract and poverty to rise, while others say that trade liberalization could help developing countries to address poverty issues more effectively. But, as Bardhan (2005) argues, the net impact of globalization on poor people is complex and context-dependent, making it an appropriate case for empirical analysis.

This study in the context of globalization attempts to develop state-level indices of vulnerability with respect to welfare loss[1] in India using a methodology based on fuzzy set theory. The contribution of the study is threefold: the conceptualization of vulnerability and linking it with formalization being attempted in other disciplines; the development of a methodology to measure vulnerability; and to apply the methodology to rank Indian states in terms of their relative vulnerability to globalization with respect to welfare loss. To capture the changing conditions across states, vulnerability assessment is attempted at two time points – one in the early and the other in late 1990s, representing 'pre' and 'post' economic reforms (initiated in 1991), respectively. It may be noted that economic reforms since the early 1990s saw the beginning of trade liberalization in India through the dismantling of inward-looking economic policies, in tune with the emerging WTO regime.

Trade liberalization and poverty in India

The jury is still out on the impact of trade liberalization on poverty, and in particular on rural poverty.[2] But two aspects on which there is widespread consensus are: (i) openness has had a long-run impact on growth, and countries with inward-looking trade policies fare worse in the aggregate and long-run development; and (ii) the reduction of poverty in countries that have liberalized in the recent past depends on a host of institutional, political and regional factors, leading to the understanding that trade liberalization, while it improves growth might not always be pro-poor.

Given wide spatial diversity in the level of development and sheer size of the country in terms of its area and population, India is an ideal case to use to analyse the impact of globalization. Given that India until very recently pursued an inward-looking trade policy, the issue of the impact of trade liberalization on the well-being of its people is debated widely within the country. In the wake of economic reforms that began in 1991, India has undergone several non-agriculture-related trade liberalizations, while agriculture-related ones are yet to become operational. However, under the WTO regime, greater importance is attached to trade than to pursuing flexible domestic policies that aim at food-grain self-sufficiency. Integration with world markets can bring huge price volatility and possibly affect the purchasing power of the net buyers of staple cereals. Further, there is serious apprehension about the impact of the WTO on the livelihood and maintenance of agriculture in developing countries, mainly because of the subsidy policies pursued by the developed countries. In an open market, the competitiveness of a country depends not only on exchange rate and domestic price policies but also on the policies of other exporting and importing countries. Gulati and Narayanan (2003) illustrate that, when the world price of rice fell, countries such as the USA (despite being less competitive in the world market) were able to stave it off through domestic subsidy policies, while countries such as Thailand, India and Vietnam not only accumulated massive domestic stocks but also exported at a loss during this period.

There are very few studies that have attempted to examine the impact of trade policy on the rural poor in India, mainly because the agriculture sector is not fully liberalized. Studies such as that by Misra and Rao (2003) highlight the indirect impact on the agricultural sector resulting from trade liberalization in the non-agricultural sector. The tariff reduction reduced the price of manufacturing, resulting in the terms of trade moving in favour of agriculture, thereby improving the aggregate crop output and real wages of the unskilled agricultural workers in the decade after 1991. This period also saw a decline in agricultural employment leading to a rise in the unemployment rate in rural areas; and a slowing-down of the agricultural growth rate, causing a slower rise in real wages. These two aspects would have countervailing effects on the rural poor, a point not addressed by Misra and Rao (2003). In earlier studies, Gulati and Kelley (1999) and Parikh *et al.* (1997) examined the implications of various trade liberalization scenarios for Indian agriculture and argued that globalization could have welfare-improving impacts. However, given the institutional rigidity and infrastructural shortcomings that exist in developing countries such as India, many suspect that the beneficial impacts of globalization may not materialize in these countries. In general, one could expect that winners and losers would emerge, as different crops, farmers and regions react differently to the changing incentive environment. Moreover, different regions would have a different exposure and adaptive capacity to absorb external shocks. Under these circumstances, the required approach to study the impact of macro-level policy changes would be a micro-level analysis focusing on smaller regions. This is important in the Indian context because there are wide regional variations in the growth in value-added from agriculture since the early 1990s, with a significant increase in the proportion of casual labourers in agriculture, constituting the dominant group among the rural poor. These are important concerns for policy-making, and more so because local governments are increasingly in charge of such policy formulation and at the same time have to compete for funds from the central government.

Thus a study of this kind enables us to focus on the regional effects of trade liberalization for an efficient allocation of funds, not only for enhancing the capabilities of the agricultural sector to participate in world trade but also designing intervention measures to reduce the impact of trade liberalization on those who are likely to be affected adversely. Since this involves assessing the impact of trade liberalization (risk) among not only those who are currently at low levels of well-being, but also those likely to suffer welfare loss in the future, the present study uses the concept of vulnerability as against conventional welfare criteria such as poverty.

Vulnerability assessment – developing a conceptual framework

Globalization brings with it winners and losers, and even among the losers varied experiences have emerged on who are the likely losers and the extent of loss in well-being (measured in various ways). Therefore, while formulating policies to alleviate the impact and making the poor more resilient to the shocks, it is very important to keep both the current and the future poor in mind. As it is, policy prescriptions are for future purposes and if one were to focus on the characteristic of the currently poor, then possibly a significant proportion of the population would be out of the welfare measures devised to meet their needs. Therefore, vulnerability assessment can be considered an appropriate concept while studying the impact of globalization on the welfare of people.

A brief review of vulnerability literature

The vulnerability concept is defined in a variety of ways in different disciplines, such as disaster management, food security and global climate change. The notion of risk is closely linked to the concept of vulnerability, and thus vulnerability depicts a *forward-looking* measure. What varies across these disciplines is the formalization of the linkage between risk and the future state of affairs, and therefore also its measurement. Consequently, this influences not only the constitution of the set 'who are vulnerable' but also the intervention policies designed for the vulnerable.

The commonly understood notion of vulnerability as susceptibility or defencelessness applies to the disaster management literature and deals essentially with vulnerability to a natural disaster (an event). The risk here is natural hazards, and individuals, or households or communities, are less or more vulnerable depending on their ability to 'anticipate, cope with, resist and recover' from the impact of a disaster. The assessment of vulnerability or its quantification is weakest in this strand, as what constitutes an outcome of a disaster is not clearly spelt out, and different studies focus on the impact on the poor, malnourished and so on, without identifying who in fact these vulnerable people are.

Social science literature has discussed vulnerability extensively via sociology and anthropology, but an attempt at quantification of vulnerability is distinctly visible only in economics. As Alwang *et al.* (2001) argue, the vulnerability literature across different disciplines can be classified broadly as either conceptually strong and empirically weak, or conceptually weak and empirically strong. Much of the literature on issues related to food security falls into the second category. The development of a conceptual basis for vulnerability followed empirical investigation in the food security literature, and Dercon (2001) suggests a causal chain of 'asset–income–outcome' to describe vulnerability. Since risks are likely to be experienced at each stage of this causal chain, the vulnerability in this literature stays away from risk specification and deals with 'vulnerability to outcome such as poverty' compared to the conventional notion of 'vulnerability to risk' (such as a disaster or global climate change) (Løvendal and Knowles 2006).

Thus the concept of vulnerability in economics looks mainly at outcome, which is usually poverty, arising from accumulated 'responses to risks' of a household (the usual unit of analysis in this literature). Vulnerability would be the propensity to fall below the (consumption) threshold, and its assessment therefore deals not only with those who are *currently* poor but also those who are *likely to be* poor in the future (Chaudhuri *et al.* 2002). More specifically, as Dercon (2001) argues, the focus of vulnerability assessment should be on at least four groups: (i) those who are currently poor and permanently poor (also referred as the chronic poor); (ii) those who are likely to become poor in the future because of some trend evolution; (iii) those who are likely to become poor through *predictable* events such as seasonality; and (iv) those who are likely to become poor because of risk and shocks. The outcome of interest is typically poverty in this literature, but other indicators such as health, education, crime and social exclusion have also been analysed separately. However, composite measures of vulnerability are few, because identification of a threshold for each outcome (as well as aggregation across different outcomes) is rather difficult.

Thus, the focus has usually been on consumption or income poverty, with some studies bringing in a time dimension more effectively and a few also highlighting the degree of shortfall from the threshold (Jalan and Ravallion 1998).

Further variations to this strand of assessing vulnerability deal with issues such as the role of assets in managing or coping with risk. The assets are invested to reap benefits in the future, and during periods of stress a household can draw on its assets, making it less vulnerable compared to households that do not have access to different assets. These two aspects are analysed in turn, based on 'extended entitlements' that include social and environmental assets as well as aspects like market structure and property rights, and how sensitivity and resilience[3] change over time. The empirical evidence is based mainly on case studies, as the emphasis is more on 'asset/livelihood' compared to 'outcome'.

Vulnerability in global change literature (the most recent among the three strands of literature mentioned above) is defined by the Intergovernmental Panel on Climate Change (Ahmad *et al.* 2001) as a function of the exposure, sensitivity and adaptive capacity of the entity, which in turn are defined as follows:

- *exposure* represents the magnitude and frequency of the stress experienced by the entity;
- *sensitivity* describes the impact of stress that may result in the reduction of well-being resulting from a cross-over of a threshold (below which the entity experiences lower well-being); and
- *adaptive capacity* represents the extent to which an entity can modify the impact of a stress to reduce its vulnerability.

Such a framework, when adopted for poverty issues, presents scope for assessing vulnerability from a broader perspective than the practice so far in the food security literature. Of course, such a framework also poses a challenge for empirical methodology, as focus is not on any specific outcome. Most studies in the global change literature attempting to measure vulnerability in this framework have adopted an indicator-based approach (Moss *et al.* 2001; Acosta-Michlik *et al.* 2004, 2006; Brenkert and Malone 2004; O'Brien *et al.* 2004); but there are also some studies that go beyond indicators[4] (Lures *et al.* 2003). Inherent vagueness associated with the use of linguistic statements in quantitative analysis is one of the limitations of the indicator-based approaches.

Following Ionescu *et al.* (2005), for any conceptualization of vulnerability to be meaningful, it must be able to capture the following three dimensions:

- *Who are vulnerable?* This is the entity under consideration. Examples include households, geographical regions and demographic groups.
- *Vulnerable to what?* This is the trigger or exogenous input that causes the entity under consideration to face the threat of undesirable outcomes.

> Examples include globalization, price fluctuations, weather extremes (for example, cyclones) and climate change.

- *Vulnerable with respect to what?* This is the outcome with regard to which certain preference criteria exist in societies. Non-attainment of outcome levels that correspond to a society's preference criterion means that the entity under consideration is vulnerable. Examples include break-even level of crop yield, or a poverty line based on consumption expenditure or other threshold levels.

Thus informative statements about vulnerability consider the vulnerability of an entity to an exogenous input, with respect to an undesirable outcome. The present study in the empirical analysis defines the above basic ingredients of vulnerability as follows: the geographical regions (namely, states) are considered to be the entities;[5] globalization, as represented by trade liberalization, is taken to be the exogenous input (or trigger) causing vulnerability; and welfare (proxied by consumption in various arguments) is used as the outcome of interest, with a well-defined preference order (namely, a higher consumption level is always preferred over a lower one).

Methodology

Quantifying vulnerability is difficult, for several reasons: (i) many factors may contribute towards vulnerability, and in complex ways; (ii) knowledge about the determinants of vulnerability is typically vague; (iii) the possibility of non-linear relationships between the determinants and vulnerability (for example, while a very high level of income inequality in the society can be associated with vulnerability, a small decline in this inequality may not lead to a corresponding decline in vulnerability); and (iv) lack of knowledge on weights to be attached to these determinants.

For these reasons, the methodology adopted in this chapter focuses on a range of determinants of vulnerability and makes use of linguistic models of vulnerability. The use of different factors for capturing vulnerability is not new, but identification and the use of different factors as per the conceptualization of vulnerability outlined in the previous section are not very common (see Acosta-Michlik *et al.* 2004; Brenkert and Malone 2004; O'Brien *et al.* 2004). Further, the application of fuzzy set theory to translate inexact linguistic statements into quantitative estimates is relatively limited in the vulnerability literature. Thus, a combination of the conceptualization of vulnerability to globalization (similar to global climate change literature) and the application of fuzzy set theory to make quantitative inference from linguistic statements makes the methodology of this chapter unique. The rest of this section describes the approach adopted for allocating various indicators chosen for analysis among the broad dimensions of exposure, sensitivity and adaptive capacity of the entity; and the tool used for quantitative analysis, namely the fuzzy inference system.

Indicators of vulnerability

Vulnerability of an entity is hypothesized to be a function of its exposure (to the external stressor causing the vulnerability), sensitivity of the entity's outcome to the external stressor, and its adaptive capacity in overcoming the adverse impact of the stressor on its outcome. While identifying the determinants of exposure could be relatively easy[6] (provided the cause of entity's vulnerability is identified unambiguously), categorizing the determinants of an entity's vulnerability among the sensitivity and adaptive capacity subgroups could be more daunting.

Since it is relatively easy to understand the notion of sensitivity and adaptive capacity with reference to natural systems, this subsection describes the same using a simple example and extends the concept to social systems. Considering the example of vulnerability of agricultural systems to rainfall fluctuations, the choice of a crop variety and seed commits the farmer to a certain impact on the farm yield caused by rainfall fluctuation (knowledge of which is not available to the farmer at the time of planting). This could be described as the sensitivity of the entity to rainfall fluctuation. More precisely, sensitivity of the entity is determined by intrinsic characteristics over which the entity has no direct control. The extent to which the entity could protect itself from the adverse impacts caused by external stressors can be described as its adaptation potential. The control the entity has over all the options that are helpful in ameliorating the adverse impacts caused by the external stressor defines its adaptive capacity. In the present example, once faced with the prospect of adverse yield change, the farmer could employ a range of options at his/her disposal – both before and after experiencing the yield loss – in order to protect himself/herself from the implications of the output change. Examples include the use of irrigation, subscribing to crop insurance and resorting to behavioural changes (say, reducing a component of current consumption because of a fall in income). Naturally, by definition, the entity has more control over the factors determining its adaptive capacity.

The insights from the above discussion could be translated into guiding principles for allocating various factors among sensitivity and adaptive capacity categories in social systems:

(i) both sensitivity and adaptive capacity are needed to deal with the outcome;

(ii) sensitivity is captured by indicators that represent the intrinsic features of the system that define the impact of the external stressor on the entity's output. The intrinsic features are those characteristics of the system that cannot be changed by the entity, at least in the short and medium term. Adaptive capacity, on the other hand, is captured by indicators that can be modified by the entity even in the short and medium term, and hence can influence the shortfall in outcome caused by the external stressor;

(iii) indicators capturing adaptive capacity can contribute either towards compensating adverse impacts caused by the external stressor, or strengthening the entity's capacity to absorb the adverse implications of output change; and

(iv) while sensitivity is represented by indicators that reflect the state of the system, adaptive capacity indicators are more like policy (or control) variables.

In the empirical analysis presented in the next section these guiding principles are used in allocating various indicators across the sensitivity and adaptive capacity categories.[7]

Fuzzy inference system

Fuzzy set theory is useful in translating linguistic statements such as 'high' or 'low' into numerical values. The use of fuzzy set theory in poverty analysis in economics is not new, and studies by Cerioli and Zani (1990) and Cheli and Lemmi (1995) provide fuzzy set theoretical measures of poverty. Qizilbash (2002) extends the application of fuzzy set theory to capture the notion of vulnerability to poverty. The use of fuzzy set theory in poverty is centred around the idea that an individual could be considered definitely poor if his/her income is below a lower threshold, and definitely non-poor if his/her income is above a higher threshold, with ambiguity associated with income lying between these two thresholds, as with such income the individual belongs to the set of poor people *to some degree*.[8] These studies essentially carry out what is described below as 'fuzzification' to translate a crisp value into a fuzzy number that falls in the interval [0,1]. Qizilbash (2002) interprets such fuzzy numbers as the individual's level of vulnerability to poverty; that is, to indicate how close one is to being labelled as definitely poor.[9]

The analysis presented in this study, on the other hand, uses the fuzzy inference system (FIS) – a popular methodology for implementing fuzzy logic in science and engineering disciplines. In economic analysis too, a few recent studies have proposed the use of FIS – Shapiro (2004), while reviewing applications of fuzzy logic in insurance industry document use of FIS in medical underwriting of life insurance applicants, and Martinetti (2006) suggests the use of FIS for assessing the multidimensional well-being of individuals. These studies, like the present study, involve aggregation over several variables to arrive at the outcome of interest while adhering to a set of parallel rules. The three main components of FIS – namely, fuzzification, fuzzy inference and defuzzification – are described here through an illustrative example.

Let human capability (HC) in a region be captured through two inputs – literacy rate (LR) and share of educational expenditure in total public expenditure (EE). Figure 7.1 shows the basic structure of the problem.

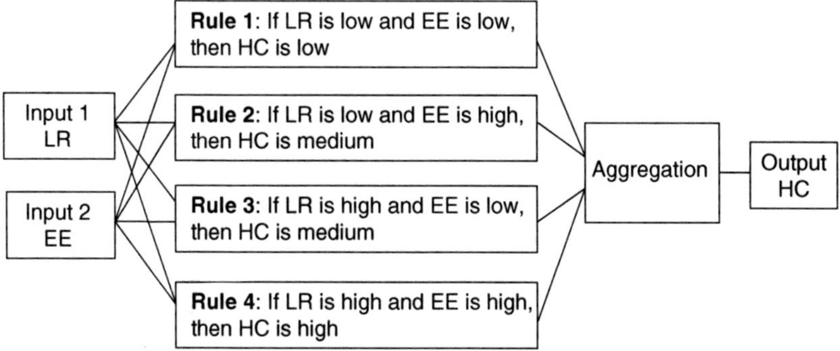

Figure 7.1   Structure of the problem using linguistic statements

Notes: LR, literacy rate; EE, share of education expenditure in public expenditure; HC, human capability.

Given the specific input for LR as 35 per cent and EE as 45 per cent, how to assess the human capability of the region? The three phases of FIS to answer this are discussed below.

Fuzzification

This involves the translation of propositions into quantitative values using membership functions. For example, consider the proposition: 'if the literacy rate is low, human capability is low'. In binary logic, levels such as 'high' and 'low' are assigned sharp boundaries, whereas in fuzzy logic it is possible to assign non-sharp (fuzzy) boundaries. The membership functions defined in a fuzzy model describe the 'degree of belief' of a particular value of a variable. In the present example, a literacy rate of 35 per cent need not be assigned either to the 'low' or 'high' literacy category, but can be a member of both categories, having a certain degree of membership in each category. For the sake of illustration, and for the analysis, two simple membership functions are used here – triangular and trapezoidal. Let the membership values of given LR of 35 per cent to the two membership functions 'low' and 'high' be mf_1 ('low') = 0.7 and mf_1 ('high') = 0.3. Similarly, let the membership values of EE = 45 per cent to its membership functions 'low' and 'high' be mf_2 ('low') = 0.4 and mf_2 ('high') = 0.6. It may be noted that while the choice of membership functions and construction of the functions is based on the nature of the problem and the judgement of the analyst; the membership values for a given input value can simply be read out once the membership functions are represented.

Fuzzy inference

Fuzzy inference evaluates each rule based on the fuzzy inputs and generates fuzzy output. For example, the first rule states that, if both LR and EE are low, then HC is also low. Figure 7.2 shows how the fuzzy inputs are combined using the fuzzy operator ('and' in this case) to generate the fuzzy output set.

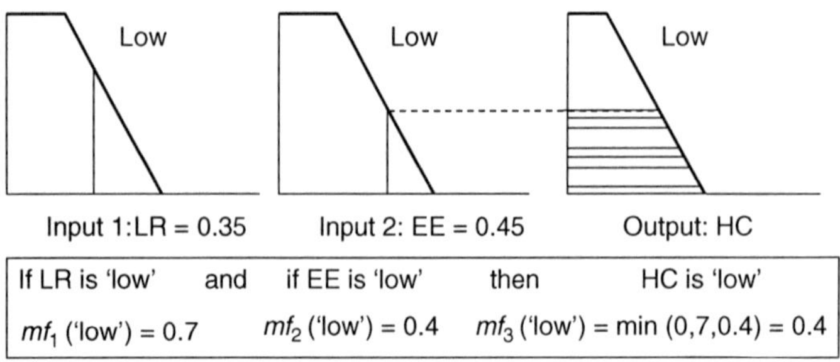

Figure 7.2   Fuzzy inference – illustration

The shaded area in Figure 7.2 shows the output fuzzy set that corresponds to 'low' membership function of the output (HC in this case). In a similar manner, other rules are also evaluated and the resulting output fuzzy set is shown in Figure 7.3. The four shaded areas correspond to the four rules specified in the problem. The degree of certainty attained by the output variable under the four rules can be readily verified as:

Rule 1: Human capability is low = min (0.7, 0.4) = 0.4
Rule 2: Human capability is medium = min (0.7, 0.6) = 0.6
Rule 3: Human capability is medium = min (0.3, 0.4) = 0.3
Rule 4: Human capability is high = min (0.4, 0.6) = 0.4.

Defuzzification

The results of each rule when combined give the aggregate fuzzy output set (the shaded area in Figure 7.3) that is useful in identifying the range of values the output can take. However, often one needs a single outcome that is the *best* estimate of the output within the aggregate fuzzy output set. The final step of defuzzification translates the aggregate fuzzy output set into a crisp number. Although there are several mathematical approaches for defuzzification, the most commonly used approach is the 'centre of gravity' method, which defines the crisp value of output to be the abscissa of the centre of gravity of the aggregate output set. In the present example, with LR = 35 per cent and EE = 45 per cent, the human capability index attains a value of 0.6 on a 0 to 1 scale.

In the empirical analysis presented in the next section, two or three indicators at several stages are grouped together to generate various indices. In terms of the procedure described here, this involves translating the input indicators into fuzzy numbers using fuzzification procedure, fuzzy inference is then applied to relate the input indicators and output index, and finally defuzzification is used to translate the fuzzy index into a crisp output.

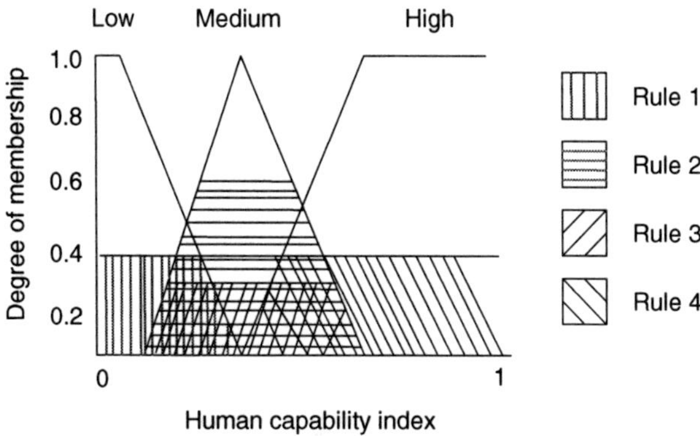

Figure 7.3   Rule strength and output fuzzy set – illustration

Vulnerability estimation: an application to Indian states

The units of analysis are sixteen large federal states of India – namely, Andhra Pradesh, Assam, Bihar, Gujarat, Haryana, Himachal Pradesh, Karnataka, Kerala, Maharashtra, Madhya Pradesh, Orissa, Punjab, Rajasthan, Tamil Nadu, Uttar Pradesh and West Bengal. While there has been a further subdivision of some of the states in 2000,[10] the analysis has been carried out for the sixteen undivided states mentioned above. The choice of these sixteen states is made keeping in mind (i) the availability of reliable data; (ii) large geographical coverage; and (iii) large population coverage.

As explained above, the framework for vulnerability estimation incorporates the notion of exposure, sensitivity and adaptive capacity, and indicators to represent each of these system characteristics are selected on the basis of (i) representativeness; (ii) data availability; and (iii) forward-looking nature. Figure 7.4 shows the overall framework of the analysis.

Vulnerability (to external shock) of a system is hypothesized to increase with exposure and sensitivity, but decline with adaptive capacity. Exposure is captured through two indicators: instability in cereal production; and share of investment in the manufacturing sector. Sensitivity is assessed through three broad indices: agricultural, demographic and health which, in turn, are assessed through six indicators, namely share of agricultural GDP, per capita calorie consumption, population density, population growth rate, percentage of malnourished children, and share of health expenditure in total expenditure. Adaptive capacity is measured through three broad indices: economic, human, and infrastructure which, in turn, are assessed through six indicators, namely per capita income, inequality measure, literacy rate, share of educational expenditure in total expenditure,

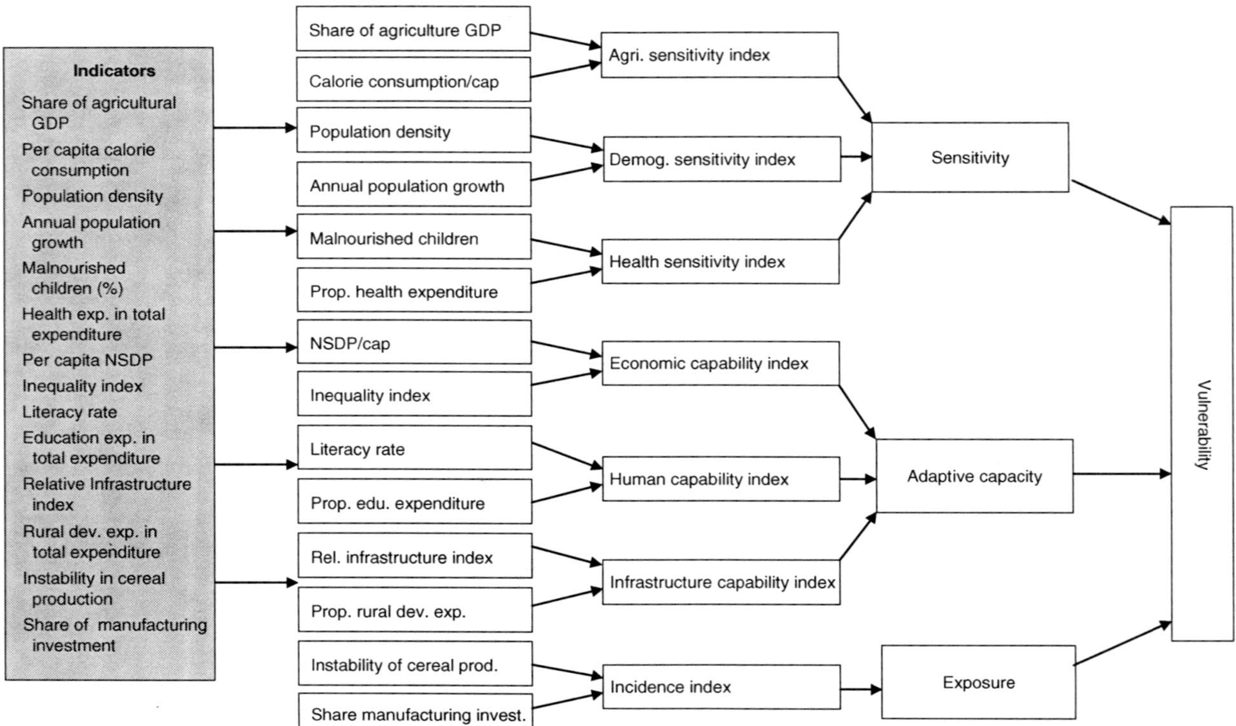

Figure 7.4　Framework for vulnerability analysis

infrastructure development index, and share of rural development expenditure in total expenditure.

Table 7.1 summarizes the rationale for the use of these indicators under each dimension of vulnerability by describing what each indicator represents and the expected functional relationship with the respective component. Even though the analysis does not define a specific outcome, the implicit impact of globalization on consumption (and hence poverty in that dimension) is used as the outcome of interest. Choice of sensitivity and adaptive capacity indicator reflect this aspect.

Agricultural sensitivity

Sensitivity of agriculture is considered to be important, given its role as the livelihood provider for a large section of the population. The extent of agricultural sensitivity is measured through the dependency of a region on agriculture (share of agricultural GDP in overall GDP of the region) and access to agricultural markets and public food distribution mechanisms (with the per capita calorie consumption of a region acting as a proxy). Both of these indicators reflect the state of the system, which cannot be changed in the short to medium term by the entity. It may be noted that per capita calorie consumption is determined, among other things, by the infrastructure and institutions in a region, and these cannot be modified by the individual in the short run. Overall vulnerability increases with an increase in the share of agricultural GDP, but decreases with an increase in per capita calorie consumption.

Demographic sensitivity

This sensitivity is included in the overall sensitivity measurement, given the varied population characteristics of Indian states. Population density is used as a proxy to represent access to resources as well as opportunities. The annual population growth rate is included to capture the ability of a region to allocate resources effectively over time. The higher population growth rate observed at present reflects the lower ability of the region to improve the resource allocation, and hence its higher sensitivity. Again, both these indicators reflect the state of the system and therefore could be viewed as sensitivity measures. Overall, vulnerability increases with an increase in both population density and the population growth rate.

Health sensitivity

The third sensitivity measure used in the analysis captures a dimension of social well-being – namely, health. The percentage of malnourished children among children below four years of age acts as a proxy for the life-cycle measure of health and human capital, because undernourishment leads to slow growth and a lower level of cognitive development. The proportion of health expenditure in total public expenditure reflects the concern for a

Table 7.1 Sensitivity, adaptive capacity and exposure – indicators and functional relationship

	Sector	Indicator	Represents	Functional relationship
Sensitivity	Agriculture	Share of agricultural GDP	Dependency on agriculture: the livelihood provider for majority population	Sensitivity increases as share of agricultural GDP increases
		Per capita calorie consumption	Access to agricultural markets and other food distribution mechanisms	Sensitivity decreases as per capita calorie consumption increases
	Demography	Population density	Access to resources and opportunities	Sensitivity increases as population density increases
		Annual population growth rate	Resource allocation over time	Sensitivity increases as population growth rate increases
	Health	Percentage of malnourished children	Life-cycle measure of health and human capital	Sensitivity increases as proportion of malnourished children increases
		Proportion of health expenditure in total expenditure	Concern for a healthy and productive society	Sensitivity decreases as health expenditure increases
Adaptive capacity	Economic	Per capita net state domestic product	Access to resources useful for adaptation	Adaptive capacity increases as per capita net state domestic product increases
		Gini coefficient	Degree of cohesiveness of society for adaptation	Adaptive capacity increases as inequity decreases
	Human	Literacy rate	Human capital and adaptability of labour force	Adaptive capacity increases as literacy increases
		Proportion of educational expenditure in total expenditure	Investment in human capital	Adaptive capacity increases as expenditure on education increases
	Infrastructure	Infrastructure development index	Physical resource capital for adaptation	Adaptive capacity increases with higher attainment of infrastructure development
		Proportion of rural development expenditure in total expenditure	Investment in rural sector: backward sector with larger proportion of population	Adaptive capacity increases as rural development expenditure increases
Exposure	Incidence	Instability in cereal production	Exogenous shock from market and physical (such as climatic) forces on agriculture	Exposure increases as instability in cereal production increases
		Percentage share of investment in manufacturing sector	Ability to make use of opportunities	Exposure decreases as share of investment in manufacturing sector increases

healthy and productive society, as such expenditure results in the improvement of human capital.[11] Vulnerability increases with an increase in the proportion of malnourished children but decreases with an increase in the share of health expenditure in total public expenditure.

Economic capacity

Economic capacity is an important determinant of adaptive capacity as it represents the availability of resources and scope for resource mobilization. The extent of economic capacity is measured through per capita income, which represents the ability to access resources that are useful for adaptation, and the inequality measure (Gini coefficient), which represents the degree of cohesiveness of society for adaptation. Both these indicators reflect the entity's control over influencing the outcome (or shortfall in outcome induced by the shock) and hence capture its adaptive capacity on the economic dimension. Overall, vulnerability decreases with an increase in per capita net state domestic product, but increases with an increase in inequality.

Human capacity

Human capacity is used as the second dimension of adaptive capacity, as it captures the inherent adaptive capacity of the vulnerable population. The degree of human capacity is assessed through the percentage of literate individuals in the society, which indicates the adaptability of the population to both adverse impacts caused by shocks and the opportunities created, and the proportion of expenditure on education in total public expenditure, which represents the investment in human capital. Again, both indicators reflect the extent of influence that an entity can exercise on its outcome and hence qualify as adaptive capacity indicators. An entity's vulnerability decreases with increase in both literacy levels and expenditure on education.

Infrastructure capacity

The third and final dimension of adaptive capacity is the infrastructure capacity, as it reflects the availability of physical resources that enable adaptation. The infrastructure capacity is measured through the infrastructure development index, which is developed on the basis of a range of physical resources and hence represents the accessibility of these to the vulnerable population. The proportion of expenditure on rural development in total public expenditure captures the investment into the relatively backward sector of the society (compared to the urban sector), which also provides livelihood for a large proportion of the population. Vulnerability decreases with an increase in both the infrastructure development index and rural development expenditure.

In sum, the three dimensions of sensitivity capture the influence of shock on outcomes through economic, demographic and social perspectives. The three adaptive capacity dimensions, on the other hand, reflect the entity's influence on outcomes (or a shortfall in an outcome caused by the shock) through the economic, human and physical resources at its disposal.

Exposure to external shock (namely, globalization) is difficult to capture because, contingent upon the stakeholder under consideration, it could be argued to contribute both positively or negatively to vulnerability. For example, if one looks at it from the perspective of agriculture, globalization leading to price fluctuations (along with natural factors such as climate variability) could cause instability in agricultural production. An increase in such an indicator of exposure could increase vulnerability. On the other hand, if one looks from the perspective of the manufacturing sector, globalization would provide opportunities for entry into new markets, and could provide scope for greater investment. The increase in such an indicator of exposure would decrease vulnerability, as higher exposure indicates the ability to make use of new opportunities. The exposure index constructed in the analysis captures these two conflicting aspects through instability in cereal production and the percentage share of investment in the manufacturing sector, respectively. The entity's vulnerability increases with an increase in instability in cereal production, but decreases with an increase in the share of investment in the manufacturing sector.

The data on all the indicators are collected for the sixteen Indian states for two specific time points: 1990–1 and 1999–2000.[12] The two points chosen belong to the pre- and post-reform periods, respectively, and a comparison of the results across these two periods is expected to provide an idea about the changing characteristics and conditions of the vulnerable entities. The sources of data include various Reserve Bank of India Bulletins, CMIE reports, Central Statistical Organization reports, and Census reports. The data on per capita calorie intake are collected from Ray and Lancaster (2005); per capita foreign direct investment (FDI) is from Singh and Srinivasan (2002); inequality index (Gini) is from GoI (2001) and Ozler *et al.* (1996); the relative infrastructure index is from Ahluwalia (2001); the percentage of malnourished children is from IIPS (1994, 2000); and share of manufacturing investment is from Thomas (2002).

Results

At the outset, the use of the word 'vulnerability' needs clarification. The index calculated is being interpreted as an individual's propensity to be low in welfare status when subjected to external stressors.

The analysis involves carrying out an aggregation of indicators, at three levels: (i) at the first level, seven pairs of indicators are aggregated separately to generate three sensitivity indices, three adaptive capacity indices and one incidence/exposure index; (ii) at the second level, three sensitivity indices are combined to form a sensitivity index, and three adaptive capacity indices are aggregated to form adaptive capacity index; and (iii) at the third and final level of sensitivity, adaptive capacity and incidence indices are combined to form an overall vulnerability index (see Figure 7.4).

At each level, FIS is used for aggregation and, among other things, this involves the choice of membership functions to translate the crisp inputs into fuzzy inputs, and the construction of a rule-base for implementing the inference procedure, as discussed previously. At the beginning of aggregation (that is, at the indicator level) all the variables are represented by three membership functions – low, medium and high. But the number of membership functions is gradually increased over the aggregation levels for accurate representation of finer gradation in the variables. Thus the output of the third and final level of aggregation, namely the vulnerability index, is represented by eight membership functions – lowest, very low, low, fair, medium, high, very high and highest. As mentioned above, while there are several types of membership functions available in the literature, the analysis here is restricted to two functional forms, for transparency and simplicity. Again for transparency, variables at all levels are represented through trapezoidal membership functions to capture the extremes, and a triangular membership function to capture the intermediate values. The number of rules at each level of aggregation is worked out to be exhaustive at that level. For example, at the first level of aggregation, where two inputs with three membership functions are considered, the total number of rules that capture adequately all possible combinations of input combinations is nine. Table 7.2 summarizes the total aggregations carried out at each level of aggregation as well as the information on membership functions and the number of rules used.

Figure 7.5 shows the performance of each state in terms of sensitivity, adaptive capacity and exposure indices for before and after the 'reform' periods. Table 7.3 shows the relative vulnerability rankings of Indian states before and after the 'reforms'. Table 7.3 also shows the state-wise rankings of sensitivity, adaptive capacity and exposure for the two time points of the analysis.

It may be noted that the analysis accounts for globalization and poverty only implicitly. Moreover, by no means it is implied that vulnerability is captured only through the selected set of indicators and the aggregation procedure followed. However, the proposed framework is believed to capture a forward-looking measure of well-being of the entity (states of India) subjected to stressors that could be attributed to the globalization phenomenon.

In the pre-reform period, Orissa, Bihar, Rajasthan, Karnataka, Himachal Pradesh, Haryana and Gujarat were the six most vulnerable states, whereas Kerala, Punjab, Maharastra, Andhra Pradesh, Tamil Nadu and West Bengal were the six least vulnerable states. Factors contributing towards vulnerability (or lack of it) are, however, different across different states. For example, Orissa and Bihar were both vulnerable because of poor performance on sensitivity, adaptive capacity and exposure, whereas, despite relatively lower

Table 7.2 Characteristics of different levels of aggregation

Aggregation level	No. of inputs in each aggregation	Membership functions		No. of rules
		Input	Output	
I: Seven aggregations to generate seven indices	2	3 – low, medium, high	4 – low, medium, high, very high	9 (for each index)
II: Two aggregations to generate two indices	3	4 – low, medium, high, very high	6 – very low, low, fair, medium, high, very high	64 (for each index)
III: One aggregation to generate one index	3	6 – very low, low, fair, medium, high, very high	8 – lowest, very low, low, fair, medium, high, very high, highest	144

Note: At the third level of aggregation, while two inputs (sensitivity and adaptive capacity) are characterized by six membership functions each, the third input (exposure) is represented by four membership functions, resulting in a total of 144 rules.

Table 7.3 Relative vulnerability ranking of Indian states

State	Vulnerability		Vulnerability		Sensitivity		Adaptive capacity		Exposure	
	Pre	Post	Pre	Post	Pre	Post	Pre	Post	Pre	Post
Andhra Pradesh	0.45	0.39	4	3	13	2	3	9	3	5
Assam	0.52	0.46	7	10	7	4	12	11	5	7
Bihar	0.68	0.65	15	14	15	16	16	15	10	14
Gujarat	0.55	0.44	10	8	3	11	5	3	12	13
Haryana	0.55	0.48	11	13	5	15	6	6	11	8
Himachal Pradesh	0.59	0.41	12	4	1	3	8	2	13	9
Karnata	0.62	0.38	13	2	12	5	9	8	14	2
Kerala	0.36	0.32	1	1	4	1	1	1	6	10
Maharastra	0.44	0.42	3	7	11	9	4	4	7	11
Madhya Pradesh	0.53	0.47	9	12	9	10	13	14	2	4
Orissa	0.70	0.68	16	16	10	12	14	16	16	15
Punjab	0.43	0.42	2	6	6	8	7	5	4	12
Rajasthan	0.67	0.66	14	15	2	7	15	13	15	16
Tamil Nadu	0.45	0.42	5	5	8	6	2	7	9	6
Uttar Pradesh	0.53	0.45	8	9	16	13	10	12	1	1
West Bengal	0.51	0.46	6	11	14	14	11	10	8	3

Notes: 'Pre' and 'post' represent the two time periods for which the vulnerability analysis is carried out. Low rank represents low vulnerability, low sensitivity, high adaptive capacity and low exposure.

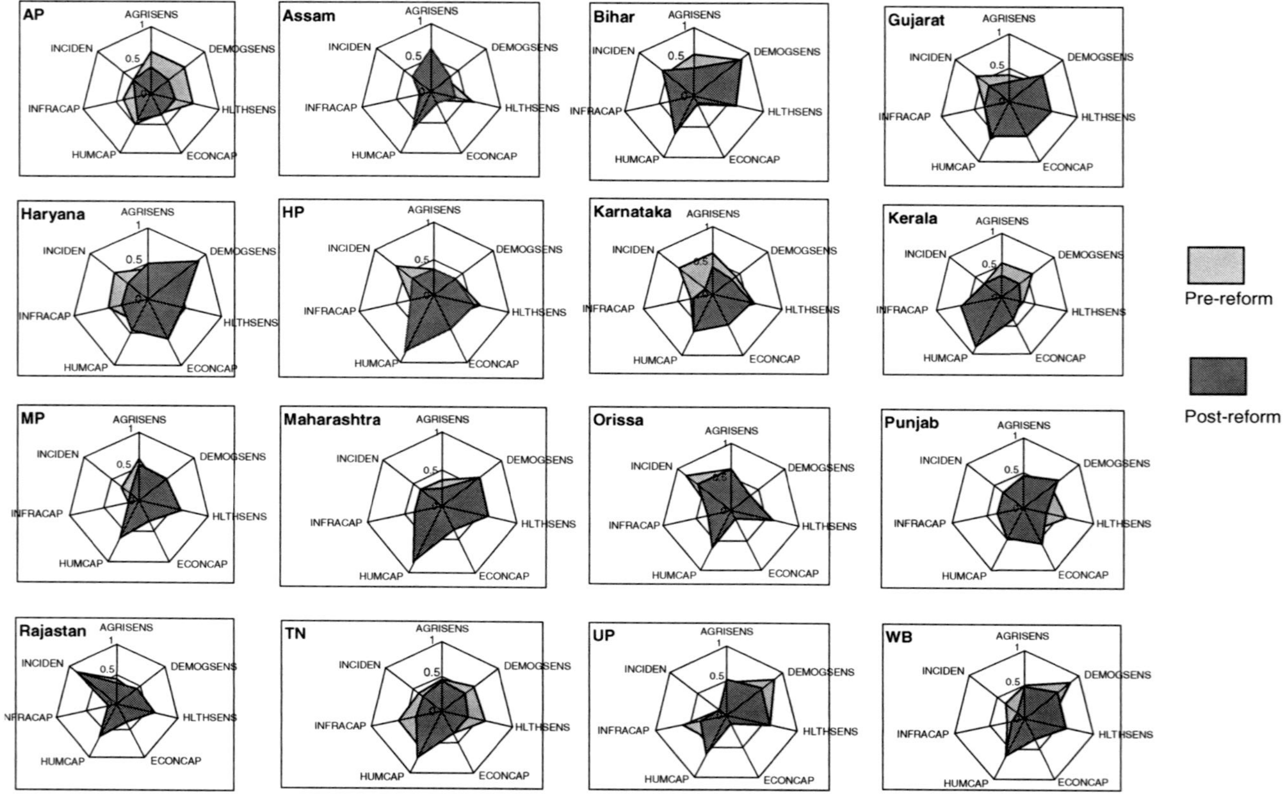

Figure 7.5 State-level performance on sensitivity, adaptive capacity and exposure indices

sensitivity and moderate adaptive capacity, high exposure makes Rajasthan the third most-vulnerable state. Similarly, Andhra Pradesh, despite having very high sensitivity, shows low vulnerability because of high adaptive capacity and low exposure. Factors contributing towards high sensitivity (and adaptive capacity) are also different across different states. Bihar and Orissa, while having similar levels of agricultural and health sensitivity, differ in terms of their demographic sensitivity, with Orissa faring relatively better on that front.

In the post-reform period, the six most vulnerable states were Orissa, Rajasthan, Bihar, Haryana, Madhya Pradesh and West Bengal, and the six least vulnerable states were Kerala, Karnataka, Andhra Pradesh, Himachal Pradesh, Tamil Nadu and Punjab.

Comparison of the vulnerability and relative rankings highlight the following:

- As expected, all states reduce their vulnerability in the 'post'-reform period compared with their vulnerability in the 'pre'-reform period. This could be attributed to a decline in exposure and sensitivity, along with improvement in adaptive capacity.
- Kerala remains the state with lowest vulnerability, whereas Orissa retains its rank as the state with the highest vulnerability among the sixteen states. Bihar and Rajasthan also remain among the top vulnerable states.
- Karnataka and Himachal Pradesh show a significant improvement in their ranking, but for different reasons. While Karnataka improved its ranking because of a sharp decline in exposure (which is also captured in lower agricultural sensitivity), Himachal Pradesh moves up the ladder as a result of lower exposure as well as high adaptive capacity. Maharashtra also improved its ranking through its lower sensitivity and higher adaptive capacity.
- The trade-off between sensitivity and exposure on the one hand and adaptive capacity on the other, which leaves the rank unaltered, is best illustrated in the case of Gujarat and Haryana, where higher sensitivity is compensated by higher adaptive capacity and lower exposure. Similarly, the rank of Tamil Nadu remains the same, even though its adaptive capacity deteriorates because of lower sensitivity and exposure.
- It may also be noted that the focus on relative rankings masks other significant changes. For example, the rank of Punjab deteriorates despite lower sensitivity and higher adaptive capacity. Similarly, the rank of West Bengal deteriorates despite a marked decline in exposure.

The rank correlations between different indices in the 'pre'- and 'post'-reform period indicate that adaptive capacity rankings remains significantly similar (with a correlation of about 0.82) across time, whereas the sensitivity rankings change widely (with a correlation of only about 0.4). The exposure rankings change moderately over time (with a correlation of about 0.52), to result in a reasonably robust overall vulnerability ranking between the two periods (with a correlation of about 0.6). However, the changing characteristics of a vulnerable entity is reflected in the changing ranks of states – with the exception of three states, all other states show rank changes between the two periods. This aspect of vulnerability measure is contrasted with other welfare indicators such as the human development index (HDI) in the following subsection.

Comparison of state rankings based on vulnerability and other indicators

One of the motivations for constructing the vulnerability index discussed here is to facilitate the transfer of funds from central government to state governments. Since several indices exist in the literature with presumably similar motivations, it would be useful to compare the state rankings based on vulnerability with those based on various other indices. Table 7.4 shows such a comparison across Indian states. The indicators used for comparison include other welfare indicators such the HDI and the share of 'below poverty line' (BPL) population, as well as performance indicators such as the flow of foreign direct investment (FDI) during the period 1991 to 2001, and an overall competitiveness index computed by the National Productivity Council (2004) that takes into account economic strength, business efficiency, governance quality, human resources and infrastructure.[13]

The state rankings remain almost constant between the two periods of time in the case of the welfare indicators HDI and the share of the BPL population (with a rank correlation of about 0.96 and 0.94, respectively), reflecting the static nature of such indicators. In contrast, the vulnerability rankings show considerable variation across the two periods of analysis. This is because of the comprehensive set of variables included in the vulnerability assessment that capture adequately the changing characteristics and conditions of the states.

FDI flows to a state indicate the investor's assessment of its lower vulnerability status. Thus higher FDI flows would always be to a low vulnerability region, while the reverse need not hold. This can be seen from the column on FDI flows in Table 7.4, where the FDI inflow into states such as Kerala and Punjab is significantly low despite their low vulnerability ranks, as estimated in this study. It may also be noted that the competitiveness index is fairly high for these states, reflecting their lower vulnerability status. This contrast is largely because of the nature of FDI flows, which are typically into the non-agricultural regions of developing countries.

Table 7.4 Comparison of state rankings: vulnerability versus other indicators

State	Vulnerability		HDI		Share of BPL population		Per capita FDI flow	Competitiveness index
	Pre	Post	1991	2001	1987–88	1999–2000	1991–2001	2004
Andhra Pradesh	4	3	10	11	7	8	7	7
Assam	7	10	11	15	13	10	n.a.	15
Bihar	15	14	16	16	2	2	14	13
Gujarat	10	8	7	7	11	12	3	3
Haryana	11	13	6	6	14	14	6	8
Himachal Pradesh	12	4	3	3	n.a.	n.a.	n.a.	n.a.
Karnata	13	2	8	8	8	9	2	4
Kerala	1	1	1	1	12	13	12	5
Maharastra	3	7	5	5	3	4	1	1
Madhya Pradesh	9	12	14	13	5	3	8	10
Orissa	16	16	13	12	9	6	5	11
Punjab	2	6	2	2	15	15	10	2
Rajasthan	14	15	12	10	10	11	11	12
Tamil Nadu	5	5	4	4	6	7	4	6
Uttar Pradesh	8	9	15	14	1	1	13	14
West Bengal	6	11	9	9	4	5	9	9

Notes: 'Pre' and 'Post' represent the two time periods for which the vulnerability analysis is carried out. FDI flow column shows the volume of per capita FDI flow during the period August 1991 to July 2001. Low rank represents low vulnerability, high HDI, high FDI flows, high share of BPL population; high competitiveness index.
Sources: Authors' own calculations for vulnerability rankings; Government of India (2001) for HDI rankings; Singh and Srinivasan (2002) for FDI flows; National Productivity Council (2004) for competitiveness index.

Conclusions

This study has proposed a framework for vulnerability assessment in the context of globalization and its impact on welfare. This framework was applied to study vulnerability with respect to welfare losses in sixteen major states of India. The vulnerability index is compared across two time periods – one corresponding to the pre-economic reform process initiated in 1991 in India, and another representing the situation a decade later.

The vulnerability of an entity is conceptualized (following the practice in global climate change literature) as a function of its exposure, sensitivity and adaptive capacity. Empirical analysis based on such conceptualization demands the use of an indicator-based approach, and the present study, while following an indicator-based approach, uses fuzzy methodology that captures adequately the vagueness inherent in such approaches. The results show that the vulnerability index estimated is comprehensive in the sense that it captures not only the intrinsic characteristics and ability to react, but also the exogenous conditions the entity faces. The fact that other welfare indicators such as HDI and the proportion of the population below the poverty line fail to capture such broad representation is clearly reflected in the significantly stable relative rankings of states based on those indices.

A few indicators used in the vulnerability assessment may need further refinement, such as the exposure index that captures globalization across states more appropriately. Some recent studies have attempted to construct such regional level indices, which may be helpful in developing the exposure index (see Marjit and Kar 2005). Similarly, other indicators for capturing exposure to globalization could be terms of trade, agricultural price volatility, and characteristics of the labour force in the informal sector in urban areas and the non-farm sector in rural areas.

Acknowledgements

We thank the participants of the JICA/UNU-WIDER project meeting for their feedback, and the project directors, Machiko Nissanke and Erik Thorbecke, for their encouragement. The authors gratefully acknowledge the detailed comments given by Takashi Kurosaki and those by four anonymous referees.

Notes

1 Though no specific indicator has been chosen to represent welfare, for much of the discussion, the level of consumption expenditure is used as a proxy to represent welfare.
2 Detailed discussions on the causality between trade liberalization and poverty can be seen in McCulloch *et al.* (2001); World Bank (2002); Bardhan (2005).
3 These concepts are elaborated further in the context of literature on vulnerability to global change.

4 This study attempts to develop a vulnerability metric that links wheat yield (outcome) to climate variability and change, and market fluctuations (stress) dynamically in the presence of varying degrees of adaptive capability.
5 While much of the vulnerability discussion in economic literature focuses on households as the entities, literature in other disciplines, especially geography, considers geographical regions as the fundamental unit of vulnerability analysis (Cutter 1996).
6 Which, incidentally, in this study proved to be very difficult as region-level data on trade liberalization were not readily available.
7 It is often difficult to identify explicitly whether a particular indicator represents sensitivity or the adaptive capacity of the entity. As many other studies have pointed out (see www://hero.geog.psu.edu), it is often a choice by the researcher between emphasizing present (current sensitivities) and past (historic adaptive strength or lack of it).
8 It is not necessary to define fuzzy set theoretic poverty measures on the income dimension alone, and the studies cited consider multiple dimensions of poverty.
9 Clarke and Hulme (2005) propose a unified framework that extends Qizilbash's approach to capture vagueness in depth, breadth and duration of poverty.
10 Bihar is divided into Bihar and Jharkhand; Madhya Pradesh is divided into Madhya Pradesh and Chattisgarh; and Uttar Pradesh is divided into Uttar Pradesh and Uttaranchal.
11 There is a case for this indicator to be labelled as an adaptive capacity indicator (see the discussion on other expenditure indicators). However, to capture health sensitivity effectively, this expenditure indicator is used as sensitivity indicator.
12 The data on certain indicators, such as population growth rate, instability of cereal production, and percentage share of investment in the manufacturing sector, correspond to the decades prior to 1990–1 and 1999–2000. Data on malnourished children correspond to 1993 and 1998–9. Data on the infrastructure development index correspond to 1990–1 and 1996–7.
13 The comparison is by no means the most appropriate; for example, HDI is assessed on the basis of only three indicators – namely, per capita income, infant mortality and life expectancy, as against fourteen indicators used in the construction of the vulnerability index reported in this study. This comparison is made only to reflect the comprehensive nature of vulnerability index.

References

Acosta-Michlik, L., Kavi Kumar, K. S., Klein, R. J. T. and Campe, S. (2004) 'Assessing State Susceptibility from a Socioeconomic Perspective for the Development and Application of Security Diagrams', EVA Working Paper 12, Potsdam Institute for Climate Impact Research.

Acosta-Michlik, L., Eierdanz, F., Alcamo, J., Kromker, D., Galli, F., Klein, R. J. T., Kavi Kumar, K. S., Campe, S., Carius, A. and Tanzler, D. (2006) 'An Empirical Application of the Security Diagram to Assess the Vulnerability of India to Climatic Stress', *Die Erde*, 137(3): 199–222.

Ahluwalia, M. S. (2001) 'State Level Performance under Economic Reforms in India', Working Paper 96, Center for Research on Economic Development and Policy Reform, Stanford University, Berkeley, Calif.

Ahmad, Q. K., Warrick, R. A., Downing, T. E., Nisioka, S., Parikh, K. S., Parmesan, C., Schneider, S. H., Toth, F. and Yohe, G. (2001) 'Methods and Tools', in J. McCarthy, O. F. Canziani, N. A. Leary, D. J. Dokken and K. S. White (eds), *Climate Change 2001: Impacts, Adaptation and Vulnerability* (Cambridge: Cambridge University Press).

Alwang, J., Siegel, P. B. and Jorgensen, S. L. (2001) 'Vulnerability: A View from Different Disciplines', Social Protection Discussion Paper, World Bank, Washington, DC.

Bardhan, P. (2005) 'Globalization and Rural Poverty', WIDER Research Paper 2005/30, UNU-WIDER, Helsinki. See also *World Development* (2006), 34(8): 1393–404.

Brenkert, A. L. and Malone, E. L. (2004) 'Modelling Vulnerability and Resilience to Climate Change: A Case Study of India and Indian States', *Climatic Change*, 72(1): 57–102.

Centre for Monitoring Indian Economy (CMIE) (various years) *Monthly Review of the Indian Economy: Public Finance in India* (Mumbai: CMIE).

Cerioli, A. and Zani, S. (1990) 'A Fuzzy Approach to the Measurement of Poverty', in C. Dagum and M. Zenga (eds), *Income and Wealth Distribution, Inequality and Poverty* (Berlin: Springer Verlag).

Cheli, B. and Lemmi, A. (1995) 'A "Totally" Fuzzy and Relative Approach to the Measurement of Poverty', *Economic Notes*, 24(1): 115–34.

Chaudhuri, S., Jalan, J. and Suryahadi, A. (2002) 'Assessing Household Vulnerability to Poverty: A Methodology and Estimates for Indonesia', Discussion Paper 0102–52, Columbia University, Department of Economics, New York.

Clarke, D. and Hulme, D. (2005) 'Towards a Unified Framework for Understanding the Depth, Breath, and Duration of Poverty', Paper presented at the conference Many Dimensions of Poverty, 29–31 August, Brasilia.

Cutter. S. L. (1996) 'Societal Vulnerability to Environmental Hazards', *International Social Science Journal*, 47(4): 525–36.

Dercon, S. (2001) 'Assessing Vulnerability to Poverty', Report prepared for DFID. Available at:www.economics.ox.ac.uk/members/stefan.dercon/assessing%20vulnerability.pdf

Government of India (GoI) (2001) *National Human Development Report* (New Delhi: Union Planning Commission, GoI).

Gulati, A. and Kelley, T. (1999) *Trade Liberalization and Indian Agriculture* (New Delhi: Oxford University Press).

Gulati, A. and Narayanan, S. (2003) 'Rice Trade Liberalization and Poverty', *Economic and Political Weekly*, 28 December: 5237–43.

International Institute for Population Sciences (IIPS) (1994) *National Family Health Survey 1992–93 (NFHS–1)* (Mumbai: IIPS).

International Institute for Population Sciences (IIPS) (2000) *National Family Health Survey 1998–99 (NFHS–2): India and Reports for Each State* (Mumbai: IIPS).

Ionescu, C., Klein, R. J. T., Hinkel, J., Kavi Kumar, K. S. and Klein, R. (2005) 'Towards a Formal Framework of Vulnerability to Climate Change', NeWater Working Paper 2 and FAVAIA Working Paper 1, Potsdam Institute for Climate Impact Research.

Jalan, J. and Ravallion, M. (1998) 'Transient Poverty in Post Reform China', *Journal of Comparative Economics*, 26: 338–57.

Løvendal, C. R., and Knowles, M. (2006) 'Tomorrow's Hunger: A Framework for Analysing Vulnerability to Food Insecurity', WIDER Research Paper 2006/119, UNU-WIDER, Helsinki. Reprinted in B. Guha-Khasnobis, S. S. Acharya and B. Davis (eds) (2007), *Food Security: Indicators, Measurement, and the Impact of Trade Openness* (Oxford: Oxford University Press for UNU-WIDER).

Lures, A., Lobell, D. B., Sklar, L. S., Addams, C. L. and Matson, P. A. (2003) 'A Method for Quantifying Vulnerability: Applied to the Agricultural System of the Yaqui Valley, Mexico', *Global Environmental Change*, 13(4): 255–67.

Marjit, S. and Kar, S. (2005) 'International Trade and Inter-regional Disparity in a Ricardian Framework with Application to India', ENRECA Project Report, Copenhagen.

Martinetti, E. C. (2006) 'Capability Approach and Fuzzy Set Theory: Description, Aggregation and Inference Issues', in A. Lemmi and G. Belli (eds), *Fuzzy Set Approach to Multidimensional Poverty Measurement* (New York: Springer-Verlag).

McCulloch, N., Winters, L. A. and Cirera, X. (2001) *Trade Liberalization and Poverty: A Handbook* (London: Centre for Economic Policy Research).

Misra, V. N. and Govinda Rao, M. (2003) 'Trade Policy, Agricultural Growth and Rural Poverty', *Economic and Political Weekly*, 25 October: 4588–603.

Moss, R. H., Brenkert, A. L. and Malone, E. L. (2001) *Vulnerability to Climate Change: A Quantitative Approach*, PNNL-SA-33642, Pacific Northwest National Laboratory, Washington, DC. Available at: http://www.globalchange.umd.edu/data/publications/Vulnerability_to_Climate_Change.pdf

National Productivity Council (NPL) (2004) *State Competitiveness Report, 2004* (New Delhi: Economic Services Group, National Productivity Council).

O'Brien, K. L., Leichenko, R. M., Kelkar, U., Venema, H., Aandahl, G., Tompkins, H., Javed, A., Bhadwal, S., Barg, S., Nygaard, L. and West, J. (2004) 'Mapping Vulnerability to Multiple Stressors: Climate Change and Globalization in India', *Global Environmental Change*, 14(4): 303–13.

Ozler, B., Datt, G. and Ravallion, M. (1996) *A Database on Poverty and Growth in India* (Washington, DC: World Bank).

Parikh, K. S., Narayana, N. S. S., Panda, M. and Ganesh Kumar, A. (1997) 'Agricultural Trade Liberalization: Growth, Welfare and Large Country Effects', *Agricultural Economics*, 17(1): 1–20.

Qizilbash, M. (2002) 'A Note on the Measurement of Poverty and Vulnerability in the South African Context', *Journal of International Development*, 14(6): 757–72.

Ray, R. and Lancaster, G. (2005) 'On Setting the Poverty Line Based on Estimated Nutrient Prices', *Economic and Political Weekly*, 1 January, 46–56.

Shapiro, A. F. (2004) 'Fuzzy Logic in Insurance', *Insurance: Mathematics and Economics*, 35(2): 399–424.

Singh, N. and Srinivasan, T. N. (2002) 'Indian Federalism, Economic Reform and Globalization', Working Paper 02–13, Santa Cruz Center for International Economics, Santa Cruz, Calif.

Thomas, J. J. (2002) 'A Review of Indian Manufacturing', in K. Parikh and R. Radhakrishna (eds), *India Development Report* (New Delhi: Oxford University Press).

World Bank (2002) *Global Economic Prospects and the Developing Countries: Making Trade Work for the World's Poor – 2002* (Washington, DC: World Bank).

8
Resource-Poor Farmers in South India: On the Margins or Frontiers of Globalization?

Rimjhim M. Aggarwal

Introduction

In this chapter we examine how globalization, while providing the potential for higher overall economic growth, may often fail to improve the wellbeing of the poor. Several recent econometric studies have examined the impact of globalization on poverty using data from a wide range of countries.[1] However, these studies have largely used reduced-form specifications that do not shed any light on the different pathways through which globalization affects the well-being of the poor. Thus it is not surprising that most of the current debate is focused on technical issues regarding whether, and to what extent, globalization has increased world poverty rather than on understanding how globalization affects the poor. The latter requires an analysis of the multiple pathways that different regions/countries have undertaken. The process of globalization integrates different regions, but there is a large diversity in the manner and the extent to which this integration takes place. Understanding this diversity is critical to the formulation of anti-poverty policies around the world.

Thus, for example, it is often argued that globalization leads to an increase in poverty through the process of marginalization of the poor (Murshed 2002). 'Marginalization of the poor' in this context implies that (i) the participation of the poor in growing markets is limited and is falling (in relative terms); and/or (ii) the opportunities for their growth are shrinking as the country opens up.[2] Marginalization may occur because the poor lack access to the resources (such as human capital, land, credit or other physical assets) that are needed in order to participate in the growing markets. The recent experience of many low-income countries – particularly in Africa and some in Latin America – is cited as strong evidence of globalization leading to the marginalization of the poor, and consequently to higher poverty.

Against this presumption of marginalization of the poor in the process of globalization, there are also numerous instances where the poor have increased their participation significantly in new export markets. However, the evidence regarding the effect of this increased participation on poverty levels is mixed.[3] In this chapter we are interested in understanding the processes by which increased market participation by the poor may lead, under certain conditions, to a further deterioration in their well-being. In order to do so, we examine the case of resource-poor farmers in the Telangana region in the north-western part of the state of Andhra Pradesh (AP) in India. We focus on AP because it is a stark representation of some of the paradoxes of globalization. When the World Bank started working directly with state governments in India, AP was its focus state. It was at the forefront of reforms initiated in the areas of fiscal discipline, decentralized governance and the encouragement of foreign direct investment.[4] The state was also a major recipient of funding from multilateral organizations as well as private investors. Since the mid-1990s, AP has witnessed higher growth rates than the average for the rest of the country. Its particularly impressive performance in the area of information technology brought it into the international limelight.

However, the greater market opportunities afforded by globalization did not translate automatically into greater welfare for the resource-poor farmers in this state. In the Telangana region, which accounts for roughly 40 per cent of the population in AP, real per capita expenditures for all farm size categories declined during the post-reform period from 1993–4 to 1990–2000 (Vamsi 2004). The decline was sharpest for small and marginal farmers as well as agricultural labourers, thus leading to an increase in rural inequality in the post-reform period. There have been several reports on widespread agrarian distress in other parts of the state as well (GoAP 2005). One disturbing symptom of this distress is the unprecedented and continued rise in the rate of farmer suicides in recent years (Vidyasagar and Chandra 2004). In this chapter, we argue that the reason why resource-poor farmers in AP have not benefited from globalization is *not* because they had become marginalized, as is generally believed. In fact, we find that these farmers increased their participation in export markets (in both absolute and relative terms) and have been highly receptive to international technology transfers. This is particularly true of poor farmers in the semi-arid Telangana region of the state, who did not benefit as much from the earlier green revolution technologies compared to the better-endowed coastal regions of the state. Trade liberalization provided them with the opportunity to expand their production of remunerative export crops, such as cotton, using modern technology in the form of hybrid seeds, fertilizers and pesticides. Thus it could be argued that these farmers, far from being left behind, were in the forefront of the globalization wave.

How did greater participation of the resource-poor farmers in the growing markets afforded by globalization lead to lower welfare? This is the central puzzle addressed in this chapter. A few explanations have been offered in the globalization literature to explain why this might happen. A common explanation is that the high volatility of international commodity markets leads to significant income shocks for poor farmers who lack adequate safety nets. This is true also for the cotton farmers in our study, but it is only part of the explanation. It explains temporary income shortfall, but not chronic poverty. An alternative explanation is that, in many developing countries (including India), trade liberalization occurred as part of the IMF/World Bank-initiated structural adjustment programmes that also included cutbacks in several pro-poor public investments and social programmes. These cutbacks in public spending may have contributed to the rise in poverty. However, it is also true – as proponents of these reforms are quick to argue – that such reforms give a powerful boost to private enterprise, which is arguably more efficient. In the Indian context, particularly, the growth of the private sector in the post-reform period has been spectacular. Ironically, our analysis reveals that it was the fast but largely unregulated growth of the private sector, even into areas traditionally reserved for the public sector (such as agricultural credit, research and extension) that explains a large part of the problem. Markets grew but their governance lagged far behind, and it was the poor who suffered disproportionately, as we shall show in this chapter.

Background

In this section we start with a brief overview of the macroeconomic scenario in the pre-reform and post-reform periods in India. We then discuss the long-term trends in the agricultural sector of Andhra Pradesh. The discussion in this section helps to view the later analysis on rural poverty and its underlying causes in a broader perspective.

Macroeconomic scenario: the pre-reform and post-reform periods

Since India became an independent nation in 1947 its policy regime has been characterized by extensive controls on domestic production, pricing, trade and a managed overvalued exchange rate. In the specific case of agriculture, the main thrust of policy since the mid-1960s had been on achieving food self-sufficiency. Domestic policy instruments used to attain this goal included input subsides on fertilizers, power and irrigation, minimum support prices for major crops (such as rice and wheat), and quantitative restrictions on agricultural exports and imports. While the industrial sector was heavily protected under the import substitution regime, agricultural production was in the aggregate actually 'dis-protected' (taxed) by as much as 20 per cent from 1970 to the mid-1990s (Gulati and Kelley 1999). This is because, while expenditure on price supports and input subsidies was large, this were more than offset by the relatively low domestic farm-gate prices that were sustained behind the border measures.

In 1991, faced with a balance of payments crisis, India embarked on an economic reform programme in line with the structural adjustment and stabilization policies initiated by the IMF and the World Bank. The reforms focused largely on trade liberalization, encouraging foreign direct investment, reforming capital markets, and deregulating domestic business. At the same time, the rupee was made convertible on the trade account, leading to a sharp depreciation of the exchange rate over the following several years. The reforms initiated the process of making Indian industry more competitive internationally, strengthening the balance of payments, and boosting economic growth. Since 1990, average annual growth has averaged 5.6 per cent and inflation has been relatively low (Gulati and Kelley 1999).

It is important to bear in mind that domestic and border policies directly affecting agriculture were not included in these early reform efforts. However, the reduced levels of industrial protection increased incentives in the agricultural sector through an improvement in the domestic terms of trade, as shown in Figure 8.1. The terms of trade between Indian agriculture and industry worked against agriculture through the mid-1980s but have begun to favour it since the early 1990s (Landes and Gulati 2003). In 1994, import restrictions on oilseeds, sugar and cotton were liberalized, but most agricultural products remained subject to import controls. As the reforms progressed and the foreign exchange situation became more comfortable, quantitative import restrictions on a whole range of agricultural commodities were phased out, beginning in 2001. The impetus for these changes came from the market access disciplines of the Uruguay Round Agreement on Agriculture (URAA). Another significant development in recent years has been the commercial introduction of

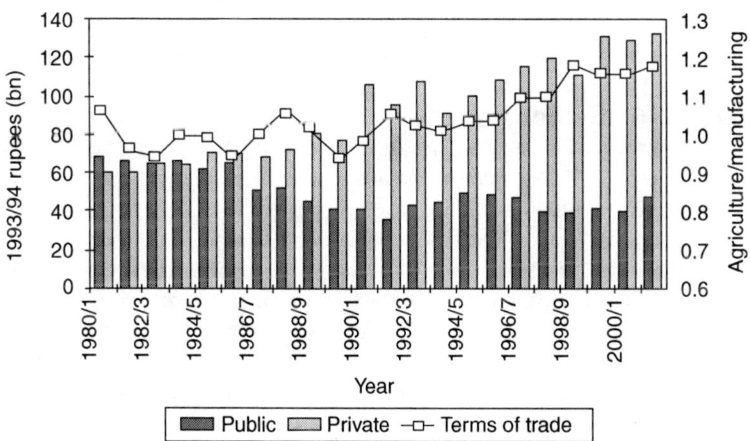

Figure 8.1   Terms of trade and gross agricultural capital formation in India
Source: Government of India (2004).

genetically modified cotton seed varieties in 2002 by the multinational corporation, Monsanto. In this chapter, however, we focus only on the effects of the limited agricultural trade liberalization that took place from the mid- to late 1990s. This is because poverty estimates (based on the latest round of the NSSO expenditure survey) are only available for this period.

It is interesting to note that, while the government pushed heavily for border policies, input subsidies on fertilizers, power and irrigation remained largely unaffected by the reforms.[5] Minimum support policy for major crops (such as wheat and rice) also remained virtually untouched because of the fear of political retaliation. The inability of the government to control the large outlays on subsidies for agricultural inputs and outputs, together with fiscal tightening, curtailed its ability to invest in rural infrastructure. Even in the pre-reform period from 1980–1 to 1990–1, gross capital formation by the public sector in agriculture had fallen by 32 per cent (at constant 1993–4 prices). Following the reforms in 1991, the downward trend continued, and by the year 2000–1 this statistic had fallen by a further 11 per cent from its 1990–1 level (see Figure 8.1). To some extent, this fall in the public sector's investment was compensated by the private sector, whose share in the total gross capital formation in agriculture increased from 49 per cent in 1980–1 to 78 per cent in 2000–1. However, the share of agriculture in the total gross capital formation in the economy fell from 15 per cent to 5 per cent during this period. In the case of AP, in particular, this falling trend in the share of agriculture has been even more pronounced. The share of agriculture and allied activity in state government expenditure under various plans declined from 11.8 per cent in 1980–1 to 1.8 per cent in 2001–2 (Rao and Suri 2006).

With the movement towards financial liberalization, greater pressure was put on nationalized banks to improve their performance.[6] Formal credit to agriculture was squeezed, as banks became even more averse to lending to agricultural borrowers (particularly smaller borrowers). The proportion of bank credit to small borrowers (below Rs 25,000) dropped from 18 per cent of total commercial scheduled bank credit in 1994 to 5 per cent by 2002 (Mahajan 2004). Priority-sector lending to the agricultural sector also suffered a significant blow, reducing from 16 per cent in 1990 to 11.6 per cent in 1999 (Singh and Sagar 2004). The relaxation of some of the earlier restrictions on the location of commercial banks further intensified the shift away from rural areas, as the cost of delivering credit in rural India is much higher than in urban India. The share of the rural sector in total credit fell from an already low level of 19 per cent in 1992–3 to 14 per cent in 1998–9. It is alarming to note that the share of rural areas, and in particular the agricultural sector, fell not only in relative but also in absolute terms. The number of bank accounts in rural areas fell by 8.41 million, and the number of borrowers from the agricultural sector decreased by 4.51 million during this period (Singh and Sagar 2004). In the next subsection we discuss the impact of this credit squeeze and other policy changes on agricultural development during the post-reform period in AP.

Long-term trends in agricultural sector in Andhra Pradesh

To set the discussion on the impact of reforms in perspective, it is useful to begin with a brief overview of the long-term trends in the agricultural sector in Andhra Pradesh. Located in the south-eastern part of the country, AP is the fifth-largest state in India. It is one of the major surplus producers of rice, accounting for about 13 per cent of the country's total production in 1998–9. The agricultural sector contributed 28 per cent of the state's gross domestic product (GDP) and employed about 70 per cent of the workforce in 1998–9. There has been a gradual deceleration in the growth rate of agricultural output in AP from 3.4 per cent per annum in the 1980s to 2.3 per cent per annum in the 1990s (GoAP 2005). The growth rate of the yield of rice, the state's principal irrigated crop, declined steeply from an annual rate of 3.1 per cent in the 1980s to 1.3 per cent in the 1990s. During the same period, the average annual growth rate of the yield of cotton also declined, from 3.4 per cent to 1.4 per cent.

An important structural change in the agricultural economy of AP has been the growing proportion of small and marginal holdings.[7] Around 66 per cent of operational holdings in AP were small or marginal in 1970–1. This proportion grew sharply over the years, and by 1995–6 it stood at around 80 per cent (see Table 8.1). The proportion of small and marginal holdings in the total cultivated area also grew sharply, from 19 per cent in 1970–1 to 43 per cent in 1995–6. The large proportion of marginal and small holdings in the agricultural economy of AP has important implications for the economic viability and sustainability of agriculture in the state, as we shall discuss later. In addition, after Punjab, AP also has the highest incidence of landlessness among rural households in India. Around 46 per cent of rural households in AP were landless in 1970–1, in contrast to 35 per cent

Table 8.1   Distribution of operational holdings in Andhra Pradesh, 1970–1 to 1995–6

Year	Marginal (<1 ha.)	Small (1–2 ha.)	Semi-medium (2–4 ha.)	Medium (4–10 ha.)	Large (>10 ha.)
Percentage of holdings					
1970–1	46.0	19.6	17.4	12.7	4.3
1995–6	59.4	21.3	13.2	5.3	0.8
Percentage of area					
1970–1	8.0	11.3	19.2	35.2	26.3
1995–6	20.2	22.5	26.0	22.5	8.9

Source: GoAP (2003).

at the all-India level. By 1999–2000, the proportion of the landless grew to 52 per cent in AP, compared to 41 per cent at the all-India level.[8]

Irrigation has been critical to the agricultural development of Andhra Pradesh in terms of increasing yields, facilitating multiple cropping, and providing insurance against the highly uncertain rainfall in the semi-arid regions of the state. The gross irrigated area in 1998–9 accounted for about 45 per cent of the total cultivated area in AP. While irrigation through publicly-funded sources (such as canals and tanks) has been historically very important in AP, the 1970s and 1980s witnessed rapid growth in the number of privately owned wells. As shown in Figure 8.2, net irrigated area under wells increased by 140 per cent between 1981–2 and 1998–9. In contrast, the area under canals and tanks declined in both absolute and relative terms in the 1990s because of a deceleration in public investment and public neglect of traditional water sources. Farmers from all ownership categories have invested heavily in private wells. However, since digging wells entails a large, fixed and highly risky investment, the probability of well ownership varies directly with land ownership (Aggarwal 2000). A World Bank-funded survey of irrigation technologies in AP in 1999–2000 finds that even though small and marginal farmers accounted for around 80 per cent of total holdings in the state, they owned only 48 per cent of the total number of electric-powered wells in the state (World Bank 2001).

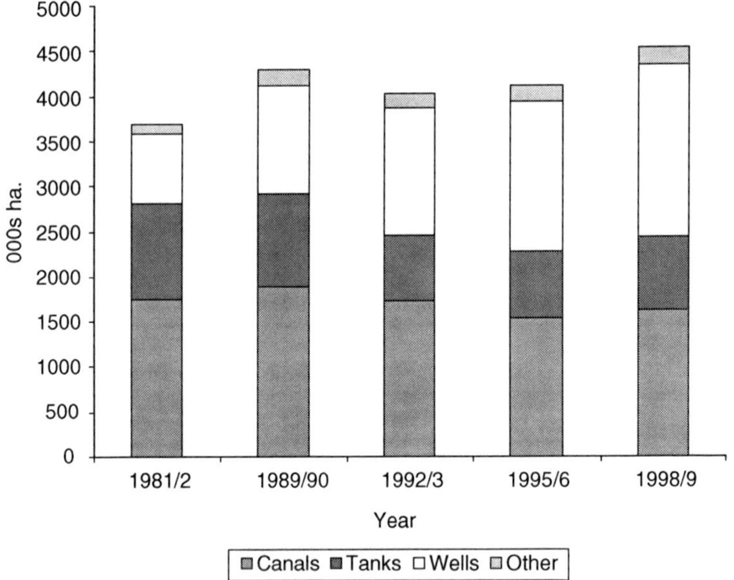

Figure 8.2   Net irrigated area by source in Andhra Pradesh (000s ha.)

Source: World Bank (2001).

The increase in groundwater irrigation during this period has been particularly sharp in the Telangana region, where it is now the major source of irrigation, compared to coastal AP, where canal irrigation is predominant. The Telangana region lies in the north-western part of the state and is generally considered to be the least developed.[9] It has a semi-arid climate and some of its subregions are highly drought-prone. The average rainfall is about 800mm per annum and varies considerably across the years. In the rest of this chapter, we shall focus largely on the Telangana region.

Trade liberalization and market participation of resource-poor farmers

In this section we begin by discussing the basic characteristics of resource-poor farmers in the Telangana region, and then examine why and to what extent these farmers increased their participation in export markets in the post-reform period.

Characterizing resource-poor farmers

In most rural poverty profiles, agricultural land ownership is used as an important (and often the sole) criterion to distinguish between poor and non-poor households. However, as argued earlier, irrigation is a critical input in agricultural production that effectively enhances the productive value of land, particularly in semi-arid regions. Thus, instead of distinguishing between farmers on the basis of their land ownership alone, we also take into account their access to different sources of irrigation, to reflect the fact that a farmer who owns a piece of land in a canal-irrigated area is much better-endowed than a farmer with an otherwise similar holding in a region with no access to public sources of irrigation. Moreover, since around 80 per cent of holdings in this region are classified as small or marginal, classification by land ownership alone is not very useful without information on whether these lie in rainfed or irrigated areas. Several studies report that poverty decreases as the availability of irrigation increases. For example, a recent study by Singh *et al.* (2002) found that poverty rates in 1993 among marginal farmers with no irrigation were 32 per cent, compared to a poverty rate of 22 per cent among their counterparts with more than 80 per cent of their land irrigated. In the semi-arid regions, this differential between irrigated and non-irrigated areas is likely to be larger. So, for the purposes of this study, we define resource-poor farmers as those small and marginal farmers who have no access to any assured source of irrigation.

Cropping patterns differ widely between farmers, depending on whether they have access to assured sources of irrigation. As shown in Table 8.2, for those who own wells with electric pumps or have access to canal irrigation, rice is the main crop grown in the *kharif* (rainy) and *rabi* (post-rainy) seasons. On the other hand, for those farmers who do not have an assured supply of

Table 8.2 Cropping patterns during different seasons in Andhra Pradesh across irrigation categories, 1999–2000 (percentage cultivated area under each crop)

Crop	Electric well-owners	Non-owners		
		Canal users	Water purchasers	Rainfed
Kharif (rainy) season				
Rice	49.48	60.30	54.15	17.10
Other cereals	4.99	3.19	0.99	13.89
Pulses	3.08	3.73	2.78	10.51
Cotton	8.17	14.19	6.71	17.04
Coconut	2.70	0.34	0.25	
Oil seed	5.14	2.76	3.83	21.90
Spices	6.24	6.46	4.50	6.57
Sugarcane	11.08	5.03	14.14	0.95
Tobacco	2.44	0.40	4.94	2.67
Fruits	4.08	0.23	2.34	
Vegetables	1.43	1.60	3.09	1.54
Other crops	1.17	1.17	2.28	7.83
Total	**100.00**	**100.00**	**100.00**	**100.00**
Rabi (post-rainy season) season				
Paddy	41.99	25.61	24.13	11.58
Pulses	14.66	9.81	13.81	24.65
Cotton	0.48	19.77	20.19	21.91
Coconut	2.90	0.42	0.41	
Fruits	4.88	0.29	3.86	
Oil seeds	7.08	18.58	12.61	28.84
Spices	0.64	7.97	6.91	7.28
Sugarcane	5.99	6.10		2.14
Vegetables	21.19	11.45	18.08	3.37
Other crops	0.19			0.23
Total	**100.00**	**100.00**	**100.00**	**100.00**

Source: World Bank (2001).

irrigation, coarse cereals, pulses, groundnuts, oil seeds and cotton are important. It is not difficult to see why rice is the preferred choice among farmers who have an assured source of irrigation. It is an important food crop that helps to meet the consumption needs of the farmer while also providing him with an assured market income, since rice is heavily protected through state intervention in the open market. Rice has also witnessed substantial yield increases in recent decades. Compared to yields in 1960–1, yields obtained in the early 1980s were 90 per cent higher (GoI 2004). The extension and research network for rice has also been much more extensive than for any other crop.

On the other hand, millet, maize, cotton, pulses, chillies and oil seeds have been the only viable alternatives for farmers with no assured sources of irrigation. These crops are less water-intensive and are grown under both rainfed and irrigated conditions. Expected net returns from the cultivation of these crops have been much lower than for the irrigated crops, while the risks are higher because of rainfall variability and price fluctuations (in the absence of effective price support polices). In particular, as shown in Figure 8.3, the price of cotton is associated with a much higher volatility than that of rice. In addition, cotton cultivation is also at risk of pest attacks. This factor, in particular, deterred many poor farmers from growing cotton in the pre-reform period.

Supply response of resource-poor farmers to cotton trade liberalization

Restrictions on the cotton trade were lifted in 1994 and as a consequence, cotton prices in the Telangana region rose from Rs1,339 per quintal in 1993–4 to Rs2,057 per quintal in 1994–5 (Centre for Environmental Studies 1998). This sharp increase in price suddenly made cotton a very attractive crop, particularly for farmers without access to irrigation. The total supply of cotton more than doubled, from 101,697 quintals in 1993–4 to 262,208 quintals in 1997–8, as farmers shifted to cotton cultivation even in regions where it had not traditionally been grown. This sharp supply response to rising prices is consistent with evidence from previous studies that also report a relatively high own-price elasticity of supply for cotton.[10] Most of the expansion in cotton cultivation was in the rain-fed areas, as farmers shifted

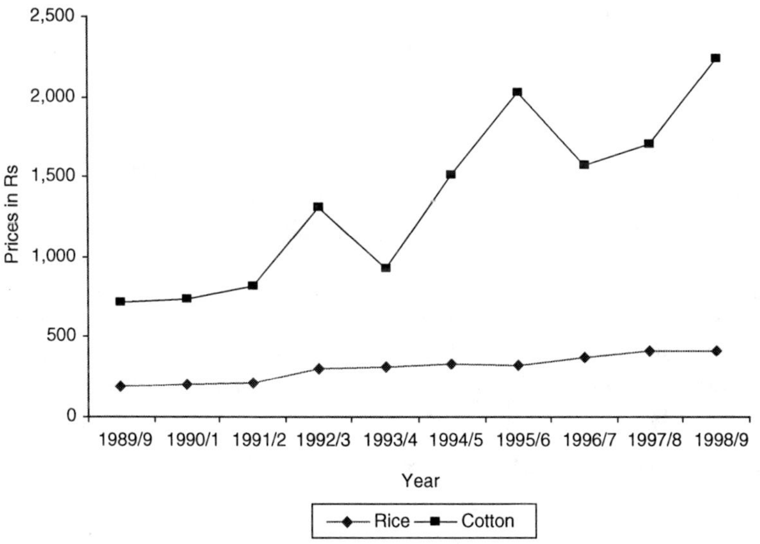

Figure 8.3   Rice and cotton prices in Telangana
Source: Centre for Environmental Studies (CES) /(1998).

away from millet and maize to cotton. As shown in Table 8.2, cotton accounted for more than 20 per cent of total acreage for rain-fed farmers in the 1999–2000 *rabi* season, while it accounted for less than 1 per cent of total acreage for well owners. In 1998–9, about 95 per cent of the rice and sugar cane areas were irrigated, 75 per cent of wheat, 34 per cent of maize, 20 per cent of groundnuts, but only 17 per cent of cotton.

India now has the largest area in the world under cotton cultivation (21 per cent of the total) but accounts for only 14 per cent of global production. Compared to global levels, the cotton yield in India is one of the lowest, mainly due to lack of irrigation, limited supplies of quality seeds, and poor management practices. Marketing of both cottonseed and lint is done by three major groups – the private traders, state-level co-operatives and the Cotton Corporation of India (CCI). Of the three groups, private traders handle more than 70 per cent of the cottonseed and lint, followed by the co-operatives and the CCI. The government establishes minimum support prices (MSPs) annually for various cotton varieties, on the basis of recommendations from the Commission for Agricultural Costs and Prices. The government-run CCI is entrusted with market intervention operations when the market price falls below the minimum support price.[11] However, as Rao and Suri (2006) argue, CCI's role in cotton markets in AP has been minimal, because the MSP for cotton has been set at a very low level and has consistently fallen far below the market price. In recent years, the government of AP has recommended higher MSPs for cotton because of the state's much higher costs of production relative to the all-India average (GoAP 2005). The union government, however, has not followed these recommendations and, according to several studies, the minimum support price is lower than the average cost of production (GoAP 2005; NCF 2006).

The path from increased market participation to debt trap

In this section we begin by discussing how the shift in the cropping pattern of resource-poor farmers from food crops (such as maize and millet) to cotton increased the need for working capital and exposed farmers to greater price and output risks. Then we examine the sources of credit (formal versus informal) for resource-poor farmers, and the emergence of private traders as an important source of credit. Finally, we take an in-depth look at the nature of contracts between private traders and farmers, and how these contributed to the rising levels of farmer indebtedness.

Greater working capital requirement for cotton

With the cropping pattern shifting away from millet and maize to cotton, agriculture in rainfed areas of AP became highly intensive in the use of purchased inputs, thus leading to a sharp increase in the working capital requirements of farmers. Cotton is the most pesticide-intensive crop grown in AP. Among all the states in India, AP now has the highest consumption of pesticides per unit of output and the second-highest consumption of fertilizers (GoAP 2005). At the all-India level, although cotton is grown in about 5 per cent of the cultivated area only, it accounts for nearly 50 per cent of pesticide consumption (Venugopal 2004). The per-hectare variable costs for unirrigated cotton cultivation in the Warangal district in the Telangana region in 1997–8 were almost four times that for maize and 2.5 times that for groundnut (see Table 8.3). Compared to irrigated crops (such as rice), the variable costs for irrigated cotton on a per-hectare basis are much higher (see Table 8.2).

This sharp escalation in working capital requirements is reflected, in part, in the data from the latest all-India survey of indebtedness among farm households carried out by the National Sample Survey Organisation (NSSO 2005b). The survey reports that 82 per cent of farm households in AP were indebted in 2001, compared to 49 per cent at the all-India level. The survey also finds that a growing proportion of outstanding loans among farm households in AP were used for meeting current agricultural expenditure, as opposed to capital expenditure. In 2001, current agricultural expenditure accounted for close to half of total outstanding loans in AP, while capital expenditure accounted for only about a quarter. In contrast to this, at the all-India level, only 35 per cent of outstanding loans were used for current expenditure and 37 per cent for capital expenditure. Even in agriculturally advanced states, such as Haryana and Punjab, a much lower proportion of outstanding loans were used for current expenditures (33 per cent and 43 per cent, respectively).

Exposure to greater risks

After the lifting of trade restrictions, the price of cotton increased by approximately 62 per cent in 1994–5, followed by a further 33 per cent increase in 1995–6 (see Figure 8.3). As discussed earlier, the resource-poor farmers saw this as an opportune moment to shift from traditional food crops to cotton cultivation. However, prices in the subsequent year fell 22 per cent from their peak level in 1995–6. Although prices in 1997–8 recovered somewhat (by around 8 per cent), that year's lack of rain produced very low yields. The reports of the Commission for Agricultural Costs and Prices (CACP) show that the net returns per hectare in current prices (after taking into account total costs) from cotton cultivation in AP were negative (a loss of Rs1,641) in 1996–7, and only Rs72 per hectare in 1997–8.[12] It is widely believed that the CACP underestimates many of the production cost elements in AP, thus it is possible that the actual situation was even worse (GoAP 2005).

This is particularly true in the more intensive cotton growing areas of the state, such as the Warangal district in the Telangana region. As shown in Table 8.3, in 1996–7 when cotton prices fell from their 1994–5 peak level of Rs2,057 per quintal to Rs1,685, farmers in Warangal were unable even to

Table 8.3 Per hectare costs and returns (in Rs.) for major crops in Warangal district in Telangana

	Cotton				Groundnut	Maize	Rice
	1996–7		1997–8		1997–8	1997–8	1997–8
	Irrigated	Unirrigated	Irrigated	Unirrigated	Unirrigated	Unirrigated	Irrigated
Human labour	14,844	8,719	15,788	9,053	4,076	1,778	4,248
Bullock labour	1,482	1,112	1,482	1,482	1,482	1,482	1,791
Seed	1,482	1,482	1,482	1,482	1,482	642	926
Manure	1,482	1,482	1,482	1,482	0	988	988
Fertilizer	4,619	4,199	5,088	4,594	371	2,100	2,099
Pesticides	5,558	4,199	7,287	5,706	494	1,544	642
Irrigation	2,470	494	2,470	494	741	0	3,705
Interest on working capital	3,816	2,601	2,470	494	618	363	835
Total variable costs	35,753	24,288	39,315	26,893	10,917	6,407	14,741
Total fixed costs	15,610	7,524	15,610	7,524	4,730	3,285	5,785
Total costs	51,364	3,181	54,925	34,397	15,647	9,692	20,526
Yield (quintal/hectare)	22.2	14.8	14.6	10.1	5.4	22.2	39.0
Price	1,685	1,685	1,960	1,960	1,100	440	440
Gross returns	34,726	23,208	27,071	19,007	5,977	8,892	18,673
Returns over paid costs	11,802	5,103	−1,707	−4,619	1,030	4,500	9,811
Returns over variable costs	−1,028	−1,079	−1,225	−7,867	−4,940	2,485	3,932
Returns over total costs	−16,638	−8,603	−27,879	−15,391	−9,670	−800	−1,880

Source: Centre for Environmental Studies (1998).

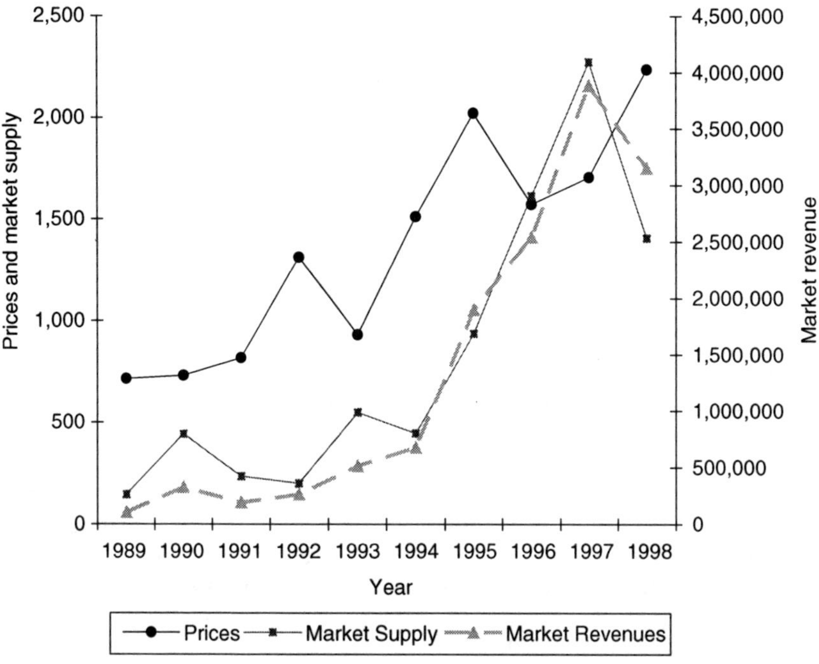

Figure 8.4   Price, market supply and market revenue of cotton in Warangal district in Telangana

Note: Price is in Rs per quintal, market supply is in metric tons and market revenue is in Rs '000. All of these variables were observed for the month of February (busy season).
Source: Author's calculations based on Centre for Environmental Studies (1998).

recover their variable costs. Prices over the next year recovered somewhat, to Rs1,960 (an increase of around 16 per cent), but this was not enough to compensate for the sharp (around 34 per cent) fall in yields caused by adverse weather conditions and pest attacks. It is estimated that in the early 1960s about 20 per cent of the cotton output was lost every year as a result of pest attacks (CICR 1998). By the late 1990s, as cotton cultivation intensified and the pest problem became more acute, an estimated half of the cotton output was lost because of insect pests (CICR 1998). Before the liberalization of the cotton trade, a shortfall in production from adverse weather conditions in a specific region would push prices up, therefore the fall in incomes would not be as drastic (see Figure 8.4). However, with the exposure to world markets, this link was broken and farmers were subjected to greater income volatility without any effective system of crop insurance.[13]

Formal versus non-formal sources of lending for resource-poor farmers

Several studies have noted that, in spite of the expansion of banking in the rural sector, a large section of the rural poor remains outside the fold of formal credit institutions. A recent survey of rural households' access to financial services, conducted in 2003, reports that only 24 per cent of rural households in AP accessed credit from formal sources (Basu and Srivastava 2005).[14] Of all the rural households, landless labourers, tenants and those with smallholdings face the worst situation. Thus, for instance, the RFAS 2003 survey observes that 87 per cent of marginal farmers had no access to formal credit sources and thus relied more heavily on non-formal sources of credit than other cultivating households. The situation is further aggravated by the fact that, in many parts of AP (particularly so in the Telangana region), the land registers are poorly maintained. As the *Report of the Commission on Farmers' Welfare* points out:

> [I]n many areas (especially Telangana region) the names of the current holders and actual cultivators are not recorded in the land registers, such cultivators are not eligible for institutional finance and a range of other public benefits such as compensation in the event of natural calamities, and so on. In addition, some regions (especially in more irrigated areas) have a high proportion of tenancy, which is typically unrecorded, and tenant farmers face similar difficulties in accessing bank loans and other benefits. They are therefore all driven to the informal credit market, which supplies loans at very high rates of interest, which in turn adds greatly to their cost of cultivation. In tribal areas there are even more difficult issues of land entitlement. (GoAP 2005: 26)

The interest rates on loans from non-formal sources, such as village money-lenders and traders, are significantly higher than those from formal sources. As shown in Table 8.4, the median interest rate on loans from the formal sector is around 12 per cent per annum. In sharp contrast to this, the dispersion of interest rates on non-formal sector loans is much larger, with the median interest rate on loans observed to be around 36 per cent per annum. Agricultural money-lenders have been important historically among the non-formal sources of credit. However, in recent years, private traders have emerged as important suppliers of credit, as we discuss next.

Extraction of surplus through interlinked contracts with private traders

To meet the farmers' growing credit needs, private traders in seeds, pesticides and output also began to supply credit. Such contracts between trader–lender and farmer–borrower are quite pervasive in India and in other parts of the world. In these contracts, the trader lends to the farmer in exchange for a promise to deliver the crop at a pre-agreed price discount, or at harvest time when market prices are at their lowest. Several formal and informal accounts suggest that the countryside in the Telangana region is flooded with pesticide dealers and their agents, with one recent report suggesting

Table 8.4 Source-wise interest charges on agricultural loans, selected villages of Andhra Pradesh

Rate of interest (%)	Institutional loans		Non-institutional loans		Total loans	
	No.	Percentage	No.	Percentage	No.	Percentage
<12	4	1.75	0	0	4	0.04
12	112	49.2	14	1.51	126	10.94
13–23	73	32.02	3	0.32	71	6.16
24	31	13.59	370	40.04	401	34.81
36	8	3.5	479	51.84	487	42.27
48	0	0	5	0.54	5	0.04
60	0	0	37	4	37	3.21
>60	0	0	16	1.73	16	1.39
Total	228 (19.79)	100	924 (80.21)	100	1152 (100)	100

Note: Totals may not exactly tally due to rounding. Numbers in parenthesis refer to percentage of total loans.
Source: GoAP (2005).

that there are as many as 13,000 dealers in the district of Warangal alone (Menon 2004). This would suggest that the pesticide market is quite competitive. However, as Venugopal (2004) argues, the market is differentiated by product (several different pesticide formulations are now available) and location (local village shop versus the market in the nearest town). Further, for the resource-poor farmers buying pesticides on credit, the market is limited to local traders who know them well. The personalized nature of such interlinking can act as a barrier to the entry of other parties, thus creating a fragmented market structure, with each trader commanding considerable monopolistic power. It is well known that, by operating in multiple markets (inputs and/or output and credit), a trader can extract a greater surplus than is possible through single markets (Basu 1997; Gangopadhyay and Sengupta 1987).[15]

An important factor contributing to the growing importance of the private traders in the post-reform period was the decline in public investment in agricultural extension services. Public expenditure on extension, which is borne by the state government, was only 0.02 per cent of the state's GDP during 1992–4 compared to the all-India average of 0.15 per cent (GoAP 2005). The *Report of the Commission on Farmers' Welfare* (GoAP 2005: 18) observes that 'with the virtual breakdown of the extension machinery and lack of access to institutional credit, small and marginal farmers became increasingly dependent upon the private traders for credit and extension services'. This is further corroborated by evidence from a recent NSSO survey on 'access to modern technology for farming' according to which only 9.4 per cent of the Andhra Pradesh farmers had access to information from extension workers in 2002 (NSSO 2005c). Private traders played a much larger role in AP, with around 30 per cent of farmers accessing information through them, compared with just 13 per cent at the all-India level.

This additional role of the trader as the provider of scientific information further enhanced the potential for strategic manipulation of contract terms and the extraction of gain. As mentioned earlier, cotton cultivation has a high risk of pest attack. This problem intensified as more and more farmers moved from other crops to cotton, thus creating cotton monocultures that are highly susceptible to pest attacks (Aggarwal 2005). Press reports and anecdotal evidence record several cases where pesticide dealers advised farmers to apply a greater amount of pesticide than was stipulated by the manufacturer.[16] For example, to calm the farmers' fears of attacks by pests, the pesticide dealers advised them to apply pesticides early, shortly after sowing. The advice in the scientific literature is to wait a few days before applying any pesticides. Early pesticide application, when not actually needed, often induces pests to acquire early resistance and therefore much stronger pesticides are required later in the growing period (Altieri 2002). As pests gradually acquired resistance and farmers started on the pesticide treadmill, the costs of cultivation increased sharply, leading to rising indebtedness.

In the literature on trader–lender interlinked contracts, an optimal interlinked contract is generally characterized by an interest rate discount, which is compensated by underpayment in the output market.[17] In our case, the interest rate discount is difficult to verify empirically because we have no direct information on what the interest rate would be in the absence of the interlinked contract. However, the interest rate discount, if present, is likely to encourage the farmer to borrow more than he/she would otherwise. Furthermore, given that the loan is fully collateralized against the value of the standing crop, the trader also has the incentive to overextend the loan. If this is so, then it is possible that this kind of interlinkage also leads to increased indebtedness for the farmer. Most models on interlinked contracts are based on one-period settings, and thus this possibility of growing indebtedness over time has not been formally analysed. In the next section we provide some empirical evidence on the indebtedness of cotton farmers.

The debt burden of cotton farmers versus other farmers: empirical evidence

It is important to bear in mind that the level of indebtedness (as measured by 'amount of loans outstanding') is not by itself a measure of a farmer's vulnerability. The critical question is regarding how the loan amount compares with the repayment capacity of the farmer (Panikar, 1963). Several measures have been proposed to assess 'safe' levels of debt. Among these, the two most commonly used measures are the 'debt to income' and 'debt to asset' ratios. For the purposes of our analysis, we are interested in testing empirically the hypothesis that the debt burden (as measured by either of these measures) was higher for cotton farmers relative to farmers growing other crops in the post-reform period.[18]

To test this hypothesis, we used household level data from a special survey conducted by the National Sample Survey Organisation (NSSO) entitled the *Situation Assessment Survey of Farmers*. This survey, conducted in the agricultural year 2002–3, collected information on various topics related to farming, including agricultural incomes and farmer indebtedness.[19] Using this data for the Telangana region, we estimated a multivariate regression model of farmer indebtedness. The dependent variable is the 'debt burden', measured as the 'ratio of current outstanding loans to net farm income'.[20]

The most important independent variable of interest is the dummy for cotton growers (equal to 1 if grows cotton, 0 otherwise) since our primary objective is to compare the debt burden of cotton growers with other farmers. However, this variable is likely to be endogenous and so we estimated a two-equation, full information maximum likelihood model in which the first equation is the treatment equation (with the dependent variable as the dummy for cotton growers) while the second equation is the outcome equation (with the dependent variable as the debt burden).[21] The independent variables used in this system of equations are listed in Table 8.5. These include household size, land owned, caste (= 1 if household does not belong to scheduled caste or tribe, 0 otherwise), primary occupation (= 1 if agriculture, 0 otherwise), education (= 1 if household head has at least completed primary education, 0 otherwise), sex of head of household (= 1 if female, 0 otherwise), actual rainfall in the previous year and percentage deviation of the actual rainfall from the normal, access to irrigation, and infrastructure variables (such as road density and banking infrastructure).[22]

The results of the treatment equation largely confirm the arguments made in the previous sections regarding characteristics of farmers who grow cotton (see Table 8.5). For example, the results show that the size of land ownership

Table 8.5   Results – farm household debt burden model (full information maximum likelihood estimates)

Variable	Treatment effect equation Dependent variable: Cotton grower		Outcome equation Dependent variable: Debt burden	
	Coefficient	Standard error	Coefficient	Standard error
Household size	−0.0060	0.0239	−245.389	336.077
Education	−0.0558	0.1151	4770.324*	1695.221
Female head	−0.7447**	0.2418	282.2513	2559.348
Primary occupation	−0.0558	0.1151	4770.324**	1695.221
Caste	−0.2823**	0.1070	4608.215**	1554.774
Land owned	0.4546**	0.0880	806.428	472.193
Land owned squared	−0.0003**	0.0001		
Actual rainfall	0.0017**	0.0006		
Deviation of actual rainfall from normal	−0.0618**	0.010		
Access to irrigation	−0.1990	0.1256		
Irrigation × land owned	−0.0001*	0.0001		
Road density	−0.0038**	0.0010	8.033	7.580
Banking infrastructure			307.175	649.191
Cotton grower			13943.19**	3605.358
Number of observations	1252			
Wald chi-square	60.18**			

Notes: ** significant at the 1% level; * significant at the 5% level.

has a significant quadratic effect on the probability of growing cotton, with the coefficient on the linear term being positive and that on the squared term being negative. This implies that the probability of growing cotton is very low for farmers with 'marginal' holdings, then, as landownership increases, the probability of growing cotton also increases, reaching a maximum for farmers characterized as 'small' farmers, and then declines again.[23] The interaction term of land owned with access to irrigation is found to be negative and significant, which suggests that access to irrigation further lowers the probability of growing cotton as landownership size increases. The results also show that cotton is less likely to be grown by households headed by females (probably because of the greater commercialization of cotton) and also less likely by households of a higher caste. Since cotton is largely grown under rainfed conditions, the rainfall variables also have a significant effect on the probability of growing cotton.

In the debt burden (outcome) equation, the coefficient on the dummy for cotton growers is found to be positive and highly significant. This supports the arguments made in the previous section that cotton growers have a significantly higher debt burden (as measured by the debt to farm-income ratio) than other farmers. The debt burden among cotton growers is estimated to be around Rs14,000 higher than that for other farmers. This is nearly 266 per cent higher than the average debt burden of Rs5,254 for other farmers. The results also show that farmers of higher caste, as well as those with at least a primary education, have a somewhat higher debt burden. The effect of land owned is also positive but significant only at the 10 per cent level. Interestingly, the effect of road density and banking infrastructure has not been found to be significant.

Summary and conclusions

It is generally believed that an important reason why globalization may lead to GDP growth but fail to reduce poverty is because the poor are unable to participate in the new market opportunities and are therefore marginalized. The implicit presumption of unresponsiveness of the poor to new market opportunities is not always justified. In this chapter we examined the experience of resource-poor farmers who participated aggressively in the new market opportunities opening up with trade reforms, but ironically failed to improve their well-being through this new opportunity. In fact, it led to higher input costs, rising indebtedness, environmental degradation, and chronic poverty.

In attempting to explore why this happened, we examined how policies in the pre-reform period – such as the provision of subsidized credit and other agricultural inputs, output price support, and the expansion of agricultural research and extension – had selectively favoured the better-endowed regions and farmers. The majority of small and marginal farmers without adequate access to irrigation or institutional finance became marginalized by the agricultural development that focused on a narrow range of irrigated crops rather than on the dry-land crops grown by these farmers. This pattern of agricultural development also led to falling groundwater tables, declining soil fertility, and a greater probability of pest attacks, all of which in turn gradually increased the long-term costs of agricultural production in the region.

Given this scenario, it is not surprising that when trade reform led to a sharp increase in the price of a crop such as cotton, which could be grown under rainfed conditions, resource-poor farmers seized the opportunity. However, cotton also requires much greater technical expertise, higher working capital, and a stronger marketing network than the traditional crops these farmers had grown previously. Interestingly, as state support declined, the network of private traders expanded at a fast pace to fulfil not only the marketing needs of the new crops but also to provide much-needed working capital and technical expertise. This expanded, and largely unregulated, operation of private traders in multiple markets also provided them with the opportunity to extract a greater surplus from the farmers through their inter-linked contracts. Thus, while increased participation in external markets exposed cotton growers to greater risks in terms of fluctuating prices and fraudulent dealings by the private traders, the shrinking role of the state reduced farmers' ability to cope with these risks, both *ex ante* and *ex post*. The result was greater vulnerability, particularly as reflected in the significantly higher debt burden among cotton growers.

To conclude, this study lends support to the argument that trade reform *alone* is not generally sufficient to reduce poverty, but this is *not* because the poor are unresponsive to new market opportunities. On the contrary, globalization may offer new opportunities for the poor in many developing countries who have been left behind during the decades of capital intensive development strategies. However, it needs to be recognized that integration into the global economy also poses new challenges and risks. Thus there is a need for complementary policies, such as those regarding the provision of institutional credit, targeted safety nets, technical expertise, marketing support and infrastructure that ensure that the poor are able to take full advantage of these opportunities. In countries such India and several other developing countries, where trade reforms have been part of structural adjustment programmes, state support has been cut back when and where it is needed the most. Thus it is not surprising that the impact of these reforms on poverty has been minimal.

Acknowledgements

An earlier version of this study was presented at the UNU-WIDER Project Meeting on The Impact of Globalization on the Poor in Asia, 25–26 April 2005 in Tokyo. I would like to thank Yujiro Hayami, K. L. Mehra, Machiko Nissanke, Silvia Pezzini and Erik Thorbecke for comments on an earlier version of this chapter. Jyoti Jain provided excellent research assistance.

Notes

1 See, for example, Chen and Ravallion (2000), Dollar and Kraay (2001), Bhagwati and Srinivasan (2002), and Winters *et al.* (2004).
2 Shorrocks (2002: xv) points out that marginalization means that the participation of the poor low-income countries 'in the increased trade that globalization brings is limited, and in many instances is declining in real terms. Their access to private international financial markets is practically non-existent, and their share of real inward investment is in many cases declining'. It should be noted that marginalization connotes a generalized tendency towards systematic and progressive fall in relative shares over the long run, and not just short-term variability.
3 See, for example, Harrison (2006) for a comprehensive survey of the evidence.
4 Under the leadership of reform-minded Chief Minister Naidu, Andhra Pradesh was widely hailed as 'the state that would reform India' (*The Economist*, 2000: 38).
5 Landes and Gulati (2003) point out that 'the budgetary outlays on the major input subsidies for inputs, have not been subject to discipline under the URAA. The subsidy outlays are below the de minimis levels permitted in the URAA and, at any rate, each of the major subsidies has been notified as a subsidy for low income and resource poor farmers and, hence, not subjected to discipline'.
6 For example, the Narasimhan Committee report in 1993 recommended that banks should focus on profitability and adopt prudential norms. This implied more stringent provisioning for non-performing loans than was the case earlier (Mahajan 2004).
7 These size categories are defined as follows: (i) marginal if land owned is less than 1ha; (ii) small if land owned is greater than 1ha but less than 2ha; (iii) medium if land owned is greater than 2ha but less than 5ha; and (iv) large if land owned is greater than 5ha.
8 These statistics are based on NSSO surveys.
9 Telangana consists of the districts of Adilabad, Karimnagar, Nizamabad, Medak, Ranga Reddy, Hyderabad, Mahbubnagar, Nalgonda, Warangal and Khammam.
10 For example, in a survey of several empirical studies from across India, Gulati and Kelley (1999) report price elasticity of the supply of cotton as ranging from 0.2 to 0.7, with a mean value of about 0.4. In contrast to this, the price elasticity of rice has been found to be somewhat lower, ranging from 0.16 to 0.47 (Gulati and Kelley 1999). As expected, supply elasticity for rice is highly significant with respect to the availability of irrigation.
11 An important exception is the state of Maharashtra, where there is state monopoly procurement. Cotton cultivators in this state are prohibited from selling seed cotton to any buyer other than Maharashtra State Co-operative Marketing Federation.
12 Cited in GoAP (2005).
13 The RFAS (2003) survey, cited earlier, reports that more than 82 per cent of households surveyed did not have any insurance, and almost none of the poorest households had insurance (Basu and Srivastava 2005).
14 Rural Financial Access Survey (RFAS 2003) conducted by the World Bank and the National Council of Applied Economic Research, New Delhi.

15 In the context of a Nash bargaining framework, Bell (1988) shows that the farmer may be worse-off with an interlinked set of transactions than with a separate set of bilateral bargains.
16 See, for example, Ghosh (2004) and the series of articles by Sainath on AP suicides in *The Hindu*. Available at www.hindu.com.
17 See, for example, Gangopadhyay and Sengupta (1987).
18 I am grateful to a referee for suggesting this.
19 Details on the sampling framework and the methodology can be found in NSSO (2005a, 2005b).
20 Complete information on the value of different assets currently owned by farm households was not collected in this survey, hence we could not use debt-to-asset ratios.
21 We used the *treatreg* procedure in the statistical software package STATA to estimate the model.
22 The data on these infrastructure variables is taken from http://www.apdes.ap.gov.in/AP%20admin%20Setup.htm.
23 Land ownership categories were defined in Note 7. The low probability of growing cotton among farmers with marginal holdings may be because of the high working capital requirement for cotton.

References

Aggarwal, R. M. (2000) 'Possibilities and Limitations to Cooperation in Small Groups: The Case of Group Owned Wells in India', *World Development*, 28(8): 1481–97.
Aggarwal, R. M. (2005) 'Globalization, Local Ecosystems, and the Rural Poor', WIDER Research Paper 2005/28, UNU-WIDER, Helsinki. See also *World Development* (2006), 34(8): 1405–18.
Altieri, M. A. (2002) 'Agroecology: The Science of Natural Resource Management for Poor Farmers in Marginal Environments', *Agriculture, Ecosystems and Environment*, 93: 1–24.
Basu, K. (1997) *Analytical Development Economics: The Less Developed Economy Revisited* (Cambridge, Mass.: MIT Press).
Basu, P. and Srivastava, P. (2005) 'Scaling-up Micro-Finance for India's Rural Poor', Policy Research Working Paper 3646, World Bank, Washington, DC.
Bell, C. (1988) 'Credit Markets and Interlinked Transactions', in H. B. Chenery and T. N. Srinivasan (eds), *Handbook of Development Economics* (Amsterdam: North-Holland).
Bhagwati, J. and Srinivasan, T. N. (2002) 'Trade and Poverty in the Poor Countries', *AEA Papers and Proceedings*, 92(2): 180–3.
Central Institute of Cotton Research (CICR) (1998) *Annual Report* (Nagpur: CICR).
Centre for Environmental Studies (CES) (1998) *Gathering Agrarian Crisis: Farmers' Suicides in Warangal District* (Warangal: Centre for Environmental Studies). Available at: www.artsci.wustl.edu/~stone/suicide.html.
Chen, S., and M. Ravallion (2000) 'How Did the World's Poorest Fare in the 1990s?', Development Research Group Working Paper 2409, World Bank, Washington, DC.
Dollar, D. and Kraay, A. (2001) 'Trade, Growth and Poverty', Development Research Group Working Paper 2615, World Bank, Washington, DC.
Economist, The (2000) 356 (8186) (2 September): 38.
Gangopadhyay, S. and Sengupta, K. (1987) 'Small Farmers, Moneylenders and Trading Activity', *Oxford Economic Papers*, 39(3): 333–42.

Ghosh, J. (2004) 'Detoxifying the Villages', *Macroscan*, 27 October. Available at: www.macroscan.com/the/food/oct04/fod271004Detoxifying_Villages.htm.

GoAP (Government of Andhra Pradesh) (2003) *Statistical Abstract of Andhra Pradesh* (Hyderabad: GoAP Directorate of Economics and Statistics).

GoAP (Government of Andhra Pradesh) (2005) *Report of the Commission on Farmers' Welfare* (Hyderabad: GoAP).

Government of India (GoI) (2004) *Agricultural Statistics at a Glance* (New Delhi: Department of Agriculture and Co-operation, GoI).

Gulati, A. and Kelley, T. (1999) *Trade Liberalization and Indian Agriculture* (New Delhi: Oxford University Press).

Harrison, A. (ed.) (2006) *Globalization and Poverty*, National Bureau of Economic Research Conference Report (Chicago: University of Chicago Press).

Landes, R. and Gulati, A. (2003) 'Policy Reform and Farm Sector Adjustment in India', Mimeo, International Food Policy Research Institute, Washington, DC. Available at: http://agadjust.aers.psu.edu/Workshop_files/Landes-Gulati.pdf.

Mahajan, V. (2004) 'Deregulating Rural Credit', *Seminar*, 541. Available at: www.india-seminar.com/2004/541.htm.

Menon, R. (2004) 'Putting Away the Toxic Spray', *India Together*, 4 June. Available at: www.indiatogether.org/2004/jun/env-warangal.htm.

Murshed, S. M. (2002) *Globalization, Marginalization and Development* (London: Routledge for UNU-WIDER).

National Commission on Farmers (NCF) (2006) *Jai Kisan: A Draft National Policy for Farmers: Fourth Report* (New Delhi: National Commission on Farmers). Available at: http://www.kisanayog.gov.in.

National Sample Survey Organisation (NSSO) (2005a) 'Some Aspects of Farming: Situation Assessment Survey of Farmers', 59th Round, Report 496. (New Delhi: Ministry of Statistics and Programme Implementation, GoI).

National Sample Survey Organisation (NSSO) (2005b) 'Indebtedness of Farmer Households: Situation Assessment Survey of Farmers', 59th Round, Report 498 (New Delhi: Ministry of Statistics and Programme Implementation, GoI).

National Sample Survey Organisation (NSSO) (2005c) 'Access to Modern Technology for Farming: Situation Assessment Survey of Farmers', 59th Round, Report 499 (New Delhi: Ministry of Statistics and Programme Implementation, GoI).

National Sample Survey Organisation (NSSO) (2005d) 'Household Assets and Liabilities in India, Situation Assessment Survey of Farmers', 59th Round, Report 500 (New Delhi: Ministry of Statistics and Programme Implementation, GoI).

Panikar, P. G. K. (1963) 'The Burden of Debt in Indian Agriculture', *Journal of Farm Economics*, 45(1): 195–204.

Rao, P. N. and Suri, K. C. (2006) 'Dimensions of Agrarian Distress in Andhra Pradesh', *Economic and Political Weekly*, 22 April: 1546–52.

Shorrocks, A. (2002) 'Foreword', in S. M. Murshed (ed.), *Globalization, Marginalization and Development* (London: Routledge for UNU-WIDER).

Singh, R. B, Kumar, P. and Woodhead, T. (2002) 'Smallholder Farmers in India: Food Security and Agricultural Policy', RAP publication 2002/2003 (Bangkok: FAO Regional Office for Asia and the Pacific).

Singh, S. and Sagar, V. (2004) 'Agricultural Credit in India', in Ministry of Agriculture, Government of India (ed.), *State of the Indian Farmer: A Millennium Study*, vol. 7 (New Delhi: Academic Foundation).

Vamsi, V. (2004) 'Immiserizing Growth and Anomalous Supply Response: A South Indian Economy under Globalization', Mimeo, University of Massachusetts, Amherst, Mass.

Venugopal, P. (2004) 'Input Management', in Ministry of Agriculture, Government of India (ed.), *State of the Indian Farmer: A Millennium Study*, 8 (New Delhi: Academic Foundation).
Vidyasagar, R. M. and Chandra, K. S. (2004) 'Debt Trap or Suicide Trap?', *Crosscurrents*, June. Available at: www.crosscurrents.org.
Winters, L. A., McCulloch, N. and McKay, A. (2004) 'Trade Liberalization and Poverty: the Evidence So Far', *Journal of Economic Literature*, XLII (March): 72–115.
World Bank (2001) 'Impact of Electric Power Sector Reforms on Agriculture in India', Mimeo, South Asia Energy Division, World Bank, Washington, DC.

9

Credit Constraints as a Barrier to Technology Adoption by the Poor: Lessons from South Indian Small-Scale Fisheries

Xavier Giné and Stefan Klonner

Introduction

Globalization has affected the livelihoods of fishing communities in South Asia in several ways since the late 1950s. In this chapter we study one facet of these developments – the adoption of beach-landing fibre-reinforced plastic (FRP) boats by fishing households in Tamil Nadu, India. The diffusion of this new technology, which replaces traditional wooden boats, is as much a product of ongoing globalizing trends as it is a response to distortions caused by previous waves of innovation triggered by globalization.

We shed light on this process by studying both the determinants of technology adoption as well as the resulting income and inequality dynamics over the process of technology diffusion within a fishing village. The data, collected by the authors in 2002 and 2004, cover sixty-five boat-owning households in a fishing village where the first fibre boats appeared in 2001. We found, first, that poorer households adopted the new boats later, while the ability to operate the new technology does not predict significantly the timing of adoption. Thus inequality and lack of wealth is responsible for a socially inefficient sequence of individual adoptions, whereby the richest and not the most able fishermen adopt first. Qualitative interviews with respondents suggest that lack of wealth delays technology adoption, mainly through credit constraints and, to a lesser extent, higher risk aversion among poorer households.

Second, we find that inequality during the process of technology diffusion follows Kuznets' well-known inverted U (1955). Initially, the technological innovation widens the gap between rich and poor, but after the entire community has completed the technological shift, inequality drops to a lower level than before, which implies that, in the long run, the innovation studied here benefits the poor more than proportionally. This pattern is also predicted by models of occupational choice such as Lloyd-Ellis and Bernhardt (2000) or its empirical estimation using data from the Thai economy from 1976 to 1997 by Giné and Townsend (2004). We conduct simulations to investigate how different counterfactual distributions of initial wealth across the sample affect adoption timings. Here we find that a redistributive policy favouring the poor results in accelerated economic growth and a shorter duration of sharpened inequality, albeit the quantitative impact of such a policy is small. When we simulate the adoption process for a sample of only rich households, in contrast, the process of adoption is completed ten times as fast as was observed in the actual data, implying that rich communities can enjoy the benefits of technological innovation, and thus grow considerably faster than poor ones. These findings provide a micro illustration of Nissanke and Thorbecke's (2006) point that the relationship between globalization and poverty is complex and may be non-linear. More generally, this chapter highlights two aspects of this complex relationship (see Nissanke and Thorbecke 2006). First, the reverse causality from poverty to globalization – that is, how poverty levels of fishermen determine the rate of adoption of FRP boats (globalization). Second, the distinction beween the short-run adverse impact and the long-run positive impact of globalization on poverty and inequality.

Among existing studies of technology adoption in low-income environments, the context studied here is of particular interest because we focus on a capital-intensive technology. In contrast, the bulk of the existing literature has focused on divisible, comparatively inexpensive technologies, such as high-yield variety seeds, the switch from food to cash crops, or the use of chemical fertilizers. As a consequence, the role of wealth and initial inequality among a group of entrepreneurs during the adoption process, as well as the resulting income and inequality dynamics, have received little attention.

The rest of this chapter is organized as follows. In the next section we provide some background on globalization and India's fishing sector. The third section introduces the context of this study and the data. The fourth section reviews relevant existing literature on technology adoption. The fifth section sketches a theoretical framework that illustrates how wealth affects the timing of technology adoption. The sixth section develops the empirical methodology and presents results, and in the seventh section we simulate the adoption process for alternative distributions of initial wealth. The final section evaluates the findings and draws conclusions.

Globalization and South India's fishing sector

To put the present study into the more general perspective of globalization and its impact on the poor, this section sketches important developments in South India's fisheries since the 1960s, with particular reference to the consequences of international development assistance and technology diffusion.

Until the 1950s, the prevailing vessel on the coasts of southern Kerala and Tamil Nadu was the kattumaram, a boat manufactured by hand, by tying together a few logs of wood shaped by traditional carpenters. Kattumaram literally means tied-log raft (*maram* is Tamil for log, while *kattu* means tied). The timber used for kattumarams is albizia, a light weight, fast-growing tropical tree found in forests throughout south India. Traditionally, kattumarams were equipped with a sail for propulsion.

South India's fisheries were hit by globalization as early as the late 1950s, when European donors implemented large comprehensive development projects. The case of the Indo-Norwegian project is particularly well documented (see, for example, Sandven 1959), which called for the mechanization of fishing boats, provision of repair facilities, introduction of new types of fishing gear, improvement of processing methods, building of ice plants, and supply of insulated vans and motor craft for transporting fresh fish. The most successful vessel introduced under the programme was a fully mechanized 32ft trawler with a powerful 84–90hp inboard engine. A new trawler cost around Rs.125,000 at 1978 prices (equal to about Rs.600,000 in 2004) and had a crew of fifteen to twenty members. The high cost of the gear and limited access to credit explains why the majority of trawler owners were businessmen and traders rather than original fishermen. Owners used to hire a captain and a crew to operate the vessel and provided incentives by entitling each of them to a share of the fish sales.

This and subsequent development projects led to a considerable change in the structure of asset ownership and labour relations in fishing communities. While family-sized, small-scale enterprises were previously the dominant mode, productive assets were now concentrated in the hands of a few businessmen and traders. Moreover, economies of scale made much of the labour previously employed in the fishing sector redundant, and many fishermen became wage labourers on trawlers as the traditional boats were not able to compete with the new technology. In consequence, while aggregate production soared, asset and income inequality also increased (Platteau 1984; Kurien 1994).

The introduction of mechanized vessels, moreover, has depleted the resource base on which small-scale as well as large-scale fishing was reliant, by harvesting shrimp in waters close to the coastline in large quantities. In this connection, it is estimated that Tamil Nadu currently has as many as twice the number of trawlers that could be sustained by the resource base in the long run (Vivekanandan 2002). Since the mid-1980s, these developments have increasingly threatened the livelihoods of small-scale fishermen along the coasts of south India. It should be noted that many places on the coast are not equipped with the harbour facilities required by a trawler.

The depletion of the resource base in waters adjacent to the shore, moreover, increased the pressure on small-scale fishermen to venture into deeper waters. These developments, in turn, created a rising demand for engine propulsion in the form of an outboard motor (OBM), which increases the radius of operations of a kattumaram considerably. At this point, globalization enters the picture once more, with India's federal government easing the previously heavily protective import policies, which led to a drop in cost of imported, internationally leading brands, such as Yamaha, Suzuki and Evinrude. It thus comes as no surprise that, since the mid-1980s, small OBMs of 8–9hp have spread rapidly throughout South India's coasts.[1] It became a common practice to mount such an engine on a kattumaram, which was previously only propelled by a sail and manpower (Kurien 1994).

Finally, in the mid-1990s, fibre-reinforced plastic (FRP) boats appeared. Several factors contributed simultaneously to this development. First, the technological hybrid of kattumaram and OBM proved to be problematic, as the vibrations of the engine strained and damaged the body of the vessel (Kurien 1995). Second, the material used for FRP production became cheaper relative to the timber used for kattumaram manufacture. On the one hand, through trade liberalization, fibre materials (which had been in use in the Western hemisphere in aerospace, automotive and marine industries since the 1950s) became less costly; and on the other, albizia became increasingly scarce and expensive because of successive deforestation and other demands. Finally, blueprints for appropriate shapes of FRP boats (capable of negotiating high surf and making a beach landing) became available. In 1995, a boatyard near Pondicherry began to manufacture a boat, the so-called Maruthi boat, resembling a vessel previously developed in Sri Lanka for similar coastal conditions to those encountered in southern Tamil Nadu (Kurien 1995). Moreover, supported by federal funds, the Tamil Nadu state government during the 1990s, sponsored the research and development of a new model particularly suited to the maritime conditions of India's south-eastern coasts. This went into production in 2000 (Pietersz 1993; *The Hindu* 2001). Both of these boat types are around 18ft long and are operated by a crew of three to four fishermen.

The combination of FRP boat and OBM facilitates a considerably wider radius of operation than the kattumaram, as well as greater carrying capacity and more convenience (*The Hindu* 2001). It is also worth noting that the emergence of the beach-landing FRP has left the labour-intensive character and fragmented ownership of the productive assets of kattumaram fisheries unchanged. In contrast to the great societal changes triggered by the earlier development programmes, FRPs thus appear to have the potential to improve individual livelihoods without turning the distribution of productive assets and the structure of labour markets upside down.

The study village

The village we studied is located in the southern part of the coast of the Gulf of Bengal, close to the pilgrim centre of Tiruchendur. With a population of 1,500, there were 75 boats operated by 67 households in late 2003. About 250 men worked on these boats, either as owner/captain, family crew or wage labourer. The village has neither a harbour nor a jetty, a fact that restricts operations to beach-landing boats. Vessels operating all year round have a crew of two to four men and are operated by local households. All these households belong to the exclusively Catholic boat-owning community of the village, which used to belong to a specific caste before converting collectively to Catholicism about 400 years ago.

On a typical day, boats leave the shore around 1 am and land at the village's market-place on the beach between 7 am and 11 am. There, local fish auctioneers market the catches to a group of buyers, comprising local traders as well as agents of fish-processing companies operating nationwide.

In our study village, the first FRPs were adopted in January 2001. By January 2004, 48 households were operating at least one FRP. The vast majority of FRPs are of the Maruthi type, 18ft long by 7ft wide, with two boats being slightly longer, measuring 21ft × 7ft. According to villagers, FRPs started to spread in 2001, but not earlier, as an FRP dealership opened in nearby Tiruchendur around that time, making such boats readily available. The cost of a vessel was around Rs.70,000. All the adopting households already owned a 7–9hp OBM, which sell at Rs.50,000–70,000. In comparison, a new kattumaram cost around Rs.20,000 at the time of our 2004 interviews.

According to the fishermen and our data, with the same number of crew, an FRP's landings are about 50 per cent bigger than those of a kattumaram. Given the yields of fibre-boat fishing, every owner of a kattumaram in the village we interviewed assured us that he wanted to switch to a fibre boat as soon as possible. Fishermen pointed out repeatedly, however, that fishing on an FRP requires a different set of skills from those needed to operate a kattumaram. For that reason it is common practice among the buyers of fibre boats in the village to hire migrant labourer-fishermen from Kerala as crew members, who are experienced with this technology.

Vessel financing and the marketing of fish catches are interlinked for almost all of the boat-owning households we interviewed. Although the focus of the present study is on the adoption of FRPs, it is instructive to start out with the credit-cum-marketing contract common for kattumarams. For the purchase of a craft, the auctioneer gives a loan of about Rs.15,000 to Rs.25,000. In return, the boat owner sells all daily catches through that auctioneer, who keeps 5 per cent of the value of the sales. The boat owner does not repay the principal. As a consequence, the commission comprises a compensation for the marketing services as well as an implicit interest payment on the amount owed. When a boat owner switches auctioneers, the new auctioneer settles the debt with the previous one. This switching of auctioneers does occur occasionally. The superiority of this interlinked share arrangement over separate debt and marketing contracts is probably a result of, first, the limited liability of the fisherman and, second, the costless monitoring of the fisherman's day-to-day progress by the auctioneer. It is interesting to note that this credit-cum-marketing arrangement is identical to the one reported by Platteau (1984) in fishing villages in Kerala twenty years earlier.

The contract for FRP financing is similar, albeit not identical. The auctioneer advances funds for the purchase of the vessel. However, in addition to a commission of 7 per cent, the auctioneer keeps another 10 per cent of daily sales, which he deducts from the principal owed by the boatowner. Unlike a kattumaram owner, whose level of debt remains constant, an FRP owner asks his auctioneer for additional funds from time to time. When such additional funds are granted, they bear no interest and are added to the fisherman's outstanding balance. The emergence of this feature of debt reduction and repeated renegotiation can be explained as follows. First, fibre-boat fishing consumes more working capital, such as nets. To cover these costs, the owner of an FRP has to incur expenses between Rs.5,000 and Rs.20,000 from time to time. Second, since the FRP is a new technology, each individual's ability to operate it is not known precisely at the start. Since the auctioneer's cash-flow depends directly on the fisherman's day-to-day success, however, the debt reduction component allows the auctioneer to drive down the debt level of an *ex post* unsuccessful fisherman to a level at which the auctioneer's opportunity cost of capital does not exceed his commission income.[2] Many fishermen interviewed stated that the funds extended by the auctioneer initially do not cover the entire cost of the technology switch. It was also stated that bank, and even money-lender, credit is generally unavailable for this purpose, as these lending sources do not accept a boat as collateral. Savings were therefore mentioned as the second most important source of funds to cover the cost of a fibre boat.

We shall discuss briefly the structure of labour contracts. On kattumarams, in Platteau's (1984) as well as our study village, typically at least two members (two brothers or father and son) of the family that owns the vessel sail on the boat, while the rest of the crew consists of labourer-fishermen. To ensure the daily availability of non-family labour, boat owners often tie labourers by advancing interest-free credit. On FRP boats, the common remuneration scheme for labourers is based on shares. Specifically, from the money that the boat owner receives from the auctioneer (that is, net of commission and debt reduction), the expenses for fuel (around Rs.200 a day on average) are deducted. The remainder is divided equally. One half goes to the boat owner and the other half is divided equally among all crew members who have sailed on the boat that day. If the boat owner himself sails, he also enjoys one of those shares.

Table 9.1 Descriptive statistics for the core sample

	Mean	Std dev.	Minimum	Maximum
Sample size	26			
Value of house (in Rs.000s)	75.38	97.74	20.00	500.00
Number of family members with other income source	2.00	1.01	1.00	5.00
Average monthly fish sales before adoption (Rs.)	22052.45	15860.84	5497.34	76017.63
Change in monthly sales from adoption (Rs.)[a]	8419.69	10550.01	−8750.07	48339.28
Household size	6.42	3.03	3.00	17.00
Literacy of household head[b]	0.38	0.49	0	1.00
Age of household head	38.46	12.12	21.00	65.00
Years as boat owner	10.57	5.06	3.00	20.00
Adopted FRP before January 2004	0.88	0.31	0	1
Adoption month[a]	Jan. 2002	8.88	Jan. 2001	Mar. 2003

Notes:

[a] for those households that had adopted before the interview, which took place in the 62nd month.

[b] equals one if head reports that s/he can read or write; zero otherwise.

FRP = fibre-reinforced plastic boat.

Our data, collected between 2002 and 2004, cover all 65 households that owned and sailed on either a kattumaram or an FRP by the end of 2003.[3] We collected information on the type of vessel operated and the time of adoption of an FRP if applicable. From auctioneers, we obtained data on monthly fish sales by household since 2000, and we conducted a household survey on household demographics and asset possession. Household-level data on fish sales with a kattumaram were the most difficult to collect, as auctioneers did not always have records on file dating back several years. For 26 of the 65 households, however, we were able to collect those data, and thus have a complete picture of sales before and after (if applicable) adoption, as well as household characteristics. This set of households will be referred to as the core sample. Descriptive statistics for these households are set out in Table 9.1.

Existing literature on technology adoption in low-income countries' primary sectors

Much of the literature that studies technology adoption in developing countries concludes that its pace has been rather slow. Feder *et al.* (1985), in their excellent review of the early literature, point to factors such as credit constraints, aversion to risk and limited access to information, to explain why adoption has not been faster. Most of the work they survey uses static models to explain adoption, while the dynamic properties of adoption are left to heuristic or comparative-static arguments at best. In particular, the role of savings, which may be crucial in contexts where credit or insurance markets are imperfect, especially if the technology is indivisible, does not receive much attention.

The literature distinguishes between divisible technologies – such as high-yield varieties (HYV) or new variable inputs; and indivisible technologies – such as tractors or the one we study here, FRP boats. If the technology is divisible, one can study the intensity of adoption of a given farmer as well as the aggregate intensity in a region. When the technology is indivisible, the decision at the individual level is necessarily a dichotomous variable and only the aggregate intensity is still continuous. In the case of technologies that are not capital-intensive, such as the adoption of high-yield variety (HYV) seeds, lack of credit is not seen as a major constraint. Instead, most of the more recent literature is concerned with the interaction between learning about a new technology and its diffusion. The first of these contributions is by Feder and O'Mara (1982), who show that aggregate adoption at each point in time can follow a sigmoid curve. They consider a scale-neutral risky innovation, with risk-neutral farmers holding prior beliefs about the mean yield of the new technology.

Besley and Case (1994) proceed in a similar fashion in their study of the diffusion of a new cotton variety in one of the South Indian ICRISAT villages. In their model, planting the new variety not only affects current profits but also generates public information on the profitability of the new versus the old varieties. Therefore, there is individual as well as social learning from planting the new crop. They find that adoption occurs with a delay because farmers initially underestimate the technology's profitability, and because they fail to learn from the positive informational externality created by other farmers when planting the new crop. Among other findings, they conclude that wealthier farmers tend to innovate first, because the informational externality is greatest for them. Poor farmers adopt later, as they benefit from the positive informational externality generated by rich farmers.

Foster and Rosenzweig (1995) take for granted that HYV of wheat and rice that became available during the Indian green revolution in the mid-1960s yield higher profits than traditional varieties. In their model, however, the profitability of HYVs is dictated by a target input model, whose optimal level has to be learnt. The issue is, again, individual versus social learning, in that each 'trial' with the a new variety generates additional information on the optimal level, and this information is conveyed not only to the farmer, but also to the entire village (at least to some extent). In contrast to Besley and Case (1994), however, planting the new crop comes at the cost of choosing an input level that is far from optimal, especially in earlier periods, when there is little knowledge about the optimal level. Farmers find themselves playing a dynamic, public-good game, where each farmer has an incentive to wait because information is generated costlessly by another farmer experimenting with the new crop. As a consequence, those farmers who expect the greatest benefits from experimentation adopt first. As in Besley and Case (1994), it is the relatively wealthy farmers those who adopt first, because by operating on a larger scale, they have the most to gain from learning about a new technology.

Bandiera and Rasul (2006) test for non-monotonicity of information spillovers among Mozambican farmers to whom a new sunflower variety was made available in 2000. They find an inverted U-shaped relationship between the amount of available information to a farmer and the probability that s/he adopts, suggesting that social effects on the individual adoption decision are positive when there are few adopters in the individual's information network, and negative when there are many. Differences in asset wealth are not found to have an impact on the adoption decision, which is not surprising, given that the NGO that provided the new variety covered all switching costs.

Munshi's (2004) study of the adoption of rice and wheat high-yield varieties during the Indian green revolution focuses on the effect of the sensitivity of farm-specific growing conditions on the extent of social learning. He finds that for rice HYVs – which are more sensitive to unobserved farm characteristics than wheat HYVs – individual adoption decisions are less responsive to the experience of neighbours. His analysis, however, does not take into account the effect of farmers' wealth on their adoption decisions.

To summarize, all these papers conclude that there is either a positive or no relationship between individual wealth and the decision to adopt a new technology. Wealth, however, is typically correlated with, or even indistinguishable from, other important individual characteristics, such as farm size, education, access to credit, availability of other inputs, and access to information. Thus, a positive relationship between wealth and early adoption can be a result of alternative factors, which are not disentangled by the existing empirical analysis. Policy recommendations, however, may well depend on the nature of the channel through which wealth affects adoption. In the papers focusing on learning, for example, it is generally argued that poor farmers adopt later because their valuation for information generated by initial 'trials' with the new technology is lower. Thus, an information campaign about the benefits would result in increased adoption. In general, however, it is not clarified whether alternative channels might also play a role. Other potential candidates are differential risk aversion (see Binswanger *et al.* 1980), access to capital, or availability of labour. For example, if the technological innovation is labour-intensive and wealthier households have better access to the labour market, a wealthier household may adopt earlier just because of labour market conditions. In the present study, we therefore make an attempt to identify thoroughly the channel through which wealth affects adoption decisions.

Individual wealth and technology adoption

Theory

In this section we sketch a simple model of the propensity to adopt a new, costly technology, and the role of initial wealth in this process. Given the discussion above, we assume that agents only have access to a savings technology to accumulate assets. Agents can produce with a traditional technology (kattumaram) that yields y_c or invest in a more profitable technology (fibre-boat) which yields y_F in expectation. The fibre-boat can be purchased at cost K. Since there is no possibility of borrowing, the investment of K must come from individuals' own resources. In line with the discussion in the third section above, we may think of K as the cost of the boat net of the loan from the auctioneer, and of y_t as income net of debt repayment and commission. Agents accumulate assets in the following manner:

$$a_{t+1} = y_t - c_t + \left(1 + r\right)a_t$$

where r is the interest rate on savings, a_t is the level of assets or liquid wealth in period t, and c_t denotes consumption in period t. We assume that agents start in the first period with an endowment of assets a_0.

To keep things simple, we assume that agents are risk neutral, live infinite periods and discount the future at rate $\dfrac{1}{1 + r}$. In each period, a household decides whether to purchase the fibre-boat and how much to save for the following period. More formally, a household's task is to choose the vector of next period's assets $\{a_{t+1}\}$ and the adoption date t^* to

$$\max_{\{a_{t+1}\},t^*} \sum_{t=0}^{\infty}\left(\frac{1}{1 + r}\right)^t c_t$$

s.t. $a_{t+1} = y_t - c_t + (1 + r)a_t - \iota\{t = t^*\}\,K,\ a_{t+1} \geq 0,\ a_0$ given

$$y_t = \begin{cases} y_C,\ t \leq t^* \\ y_F,\ t > t^* \end{cases} c_t \geq 0 \text{ for all } t$$

where $\iota\{\cdot\}$ denotes the indicator function.

The programme that solves this problem depends on the relative profitability of new versus old technology. In particular, if

$$y_F > y_C + rK \tag{9.1}$$

the optimal programme involves saving all income until $a_t \geq K$ and switching to the new technology in that same time period, which gives

$$t^* = \frac{\ln\left(\dfrac{rK + y_C}{ra_0 + y_C}\right)}{\ln(1 + r)}$$

where $c_t = 0\ \forall t < t^*, c_t = y_F, \forall t \geq t^*$.

When $y_F \leq y_C + rK$, on the other hand, the optimal programme involves dissaving instantly, $c_0 = y_C + a_0$, and consuming all income generated with the old technology concurrently, $c_t = y_t$ for all $t > 0$.

By differentiating the optimal adoption time t^* with respect to the different parameters of interest, it is easy to see that the higher the initial level of assets a_0, the higher the income from the kattumaram y_C, and the higher the interest rate r, the earlier the adoption time t^*. In this simple setup, t^* does not depend on y_F other than through Equation (9.1). When utility is concave, however, it can be shown that t^* is, moreover, decreasing in y_F. Finally, if several fishermen pool their savings (for example through a ROSCA), adoption can occur earlier, on average. It continues to hold, nevertheless, that a group of wealthier individuals can achieve an earlier adoption time, on average.

Estimation

In this section, we seek to identify empirically the determinants of the timing of technology adoption. As developed in the previous section, a risk-neutral fisherman seeks to adopt the new technology as quickly as possible when he expects the technology switch to increase his income. An important explanatory variable for the adoption decision is therefore the expected change in income resulting from the technology shift. If expectations are unbiased, the *ex post* change in observed income for fisherman i can be interpreted as the (most likely noisy) realization of i's expectations. We therefore first estimate the income change of each fisherman who adopted a fibre-boat before the interview date, and use these results in the subsequent analysis of the timing of adoption.

Estimating the income change from adoption

The goal of this section is to provide estimates of the average income that a fishing household earns with the old and new technology. With the share system that exists in the village for the compensation of labourers and the capital obtained from an auctioneer, household income is roughly proportional to monthly fish sales generated by that household. Since both catch quantities as well as daily fish prices are subject to substantial fluctuations, however, the following analysis aims at netting out the individual-specific component in how successfully each technology is operated by a given household. Moreover, we have to allow for the possibility of both individual and social learning when the new technology is used.

Learning by doing implies that individual catches trend upwards after adoption, as the individual concerned learns how to use the new technology more efficiently over time. Social learning (or learning from others), on the other hand, implies that an individual can use the expertise other individuals have acquired with the new technology to become more efficient himself. Quite generally, the latter implies that the 'learning curve' of an individual (his success as a function of time since adoption) depends on the amount of information available at the time he adopts. More specifically, the learning curve of a late adopter is flatter, because there is relatively more information available at the time of adoption.

With monthly sales data from 43 fishermen who switched to a fibre-boat before the date of our survey, a test for individual as well as social learning is thus facilitated by the regression specification:

$$\log(y_{sit}) = \mu_{si} + \delta_t + \iota\{t \geq t_i^*\}(\gamma_1\tau_i + \gamma_2\tau_{ii}^2 + \beta_1 t_i^*\tau_i + \beta_2 t_i^*\tau_i^2) + u_{sit} \quad (9.2)$$

where y_{sit} denotes monthly sales (in rupees) of fisherman i in month t who currently operates technology s, where $s = C$ for kattumaram and $s = F$ for a fibre-boat. Also consistent with the notation in the previous section, t_i^* denotes the time of adoption by individual i, and τ_i denotes time since adoption, so that $t = t_i^* + \tau_i$. μ_{si} is an individual-specific, technology-dependent fixed effect, while δ_t is a month-specific dummy that picks up aggregate fishing conditions and shocks. Finally, u_{sit} is an i.i.d. error term with $E\,[u_{sit}] = 0$.

This parametrization assumes that shocks affect sales generated through old and new technology identically in a proportional sense. This is strictly true as far as price fluctuations (per kg of fish) are concerned, as the price indices faced by kattumaram and fibre-boat fishermen are the same. Whether it is also an appropriate assumption for weather shocks remains an open question. It is to be expected, however, that at least the sign of the shock works in the same way for both technologies.

While the specification in Equation (9.2) does not allow for learning by fishermen who are operating the old technology that has been used over several decades, the term $\gamma_1\tau_i + \gamma_2\tau_i^2$ allows for learning-by-doing for fibre-boat owners. In that case, γ_1 is larger and γ_2 smaller than zero if learning-by-doing exhibits positive and decreasing marginal returns (Foster and Rosenzweig 1995). The term $\beta_1 t_i^*\tau_i + \beta_2 t_i^*\tau_i^2$ captures the possibility of learning from others by allowing for a different shape of the learning curve for later adopters. Here, time since adoption is interacted with a proxy for the amount of information available at the time of adoption by individual i, namely the time between the first adoption in the village and the adoption of individual i. With learning from others, the individual learning curve for a later adopter is flatter, as he starts out with more information in hand than any adopter before him (Foster and Rosenzweig 1995).

A test of the hypothesis of no learning-by-doing is thus:

$$H_L: \gamma_1 = \gamma_2 = 0$$

Analogously, a test of the hypothesis of no social learning is implemented by testing the composite hypothesis:

$$H_S: \beta_1 = \beta_2 = 0$$

The results of the estimation of Equation (9.2) together with F-test statistics for H_S and H_L are set out in Table 9.2. According to these results, the null hypotheses of no social and no individual learning are rejected, at least at the 10 per cent level. According to the point estimates of γ_1 and γ_2, the first adopters in the village experience an increase in sales for roughly the first ten months with the new technology.[4] The estimate of β_1, on the other hand, implies that the individual learning curve starts out flat for a fisherman who adopts a fibre-boat twelve months after the first adoption in the village (the absolute value of $\hat{\beta}_1$ equals roughly one-twelfth of $\hat{\gamma}_1$).

Table 9.2   Estimation results for Equation 9.2

	Parameter estimate	Standard error	T	p
τ_i	0.03852	0.01842	2.09	0.036
τ_i^2	−0.00187	0.00109	−1.72	0.086
$t_i^* \tau_i$	−0.00305	0.00131	−2.33	0.019
$t_i^* \tau_i^2$	0.00001	0.00004	0.14	0.885

	F	p
Test of H_L	2.48	0.0842
Test of H_S	4.34	0.0132
R^2	0.694	
No. of obs.	1471	

Notes: Coefficients for 60 monthly dummies and 30 individual-specific fixed effects for kattumaram-operating fishermen as well as 42 individual-specific fixed effects for fibre-boat-operating fishermen are not reproduced.

We use the insights from the previous estimation for deriving a more restrictive econometric specification, in which there is (positive) individual learning before some cut-off date, and none of it afterwards. More specifically, we estimate:

$$\log (y_{sit}) = \mu_{si} + \delta_t + \gamma_1 \iota\{t \geq t_i^*\} D_i(\kappa) + u_{sit} \tag{9.3}$$

where

$$D_i(\kappa) = \begin{cases} \tau_i & \text{if } t < t_0^* + \kappa \\ \max(0, t_0^* + \kappa - t_i^*) & \text{if } t \geq t_0^* + \kappa \end{cases}$$

Here, t_0 denotes the month of the first adoption in the village, while κ is a cut-off month (counted from the time of the first adoption in the village), after which no increase in individual sales occurs. The shape of the D_i function can be explained simply: for fishermen who adopted no later than κ months after the first adoption in the village, D_i equals a straight line with slope one before date $t_0^* + \kappa$. From $t_0 + \kappa$ onwards, it remains at the level attained in that period.

Estimation of Equation (9.3) by OLS yields a point estimate of $\kappa = 5$, which implies that learning-by-doing occurs during roughly the first six months of using the new technology.[5] This is not surprising, given that, in contrast to the duration of an agricultural cultivation cycle, fishing is a daily, and thus a high-frequency, activity.[6] The full estimation results for Equation (9.3) are set out in Table 9.3. The estimate of γ is positive and significantly so, suggesting an initial 11 per cent monthly increase in sales for early adopters. The results for the individual-specific fixed effects, μ_{si}, are depicted graphically in Figure 9.1 for the 25 households for which we have sales data for kattumaram as well as fibre-boat fishing. Each of the 25 data points has abscissa equal to $\hat{\mu}_{Ci}$ and ordinate $\hat{\mu}_{Fi}$. Notice that, for those fishermen who adopted before $t_0 + 5$, $\hat{\gamma}_1 D_i (5)$ has been added to $\hat{\mu}_{Fi}$. The diagram thus gives the long-run expected gains from technology adoption, which will also be used in the rest of this paper. The straight line depicts the 45° line. According to these results, three fishermen suffered a loss in sales of more than 1 per cent; two experienced virtually no change (less than 1 per cent change), while 20 enjoyed increases in average sales of between 3.5 per cent and

Table 9.3   Estimation results for Equation 9.3

	Parameter estimate	Standard error	T	p
κ	5			
$D_i(5)$	0.111	0.039	2.89	0.004
R^2	0.692			
No. of obs.	1471			

Notes: Coefficients for 60 monthly dummies and 30 individual-specific fixed effects for kattumaram-operating fishermen as well as 42 individual-specific fixed effects for fibre-boat-operating fishermen not reproduced.

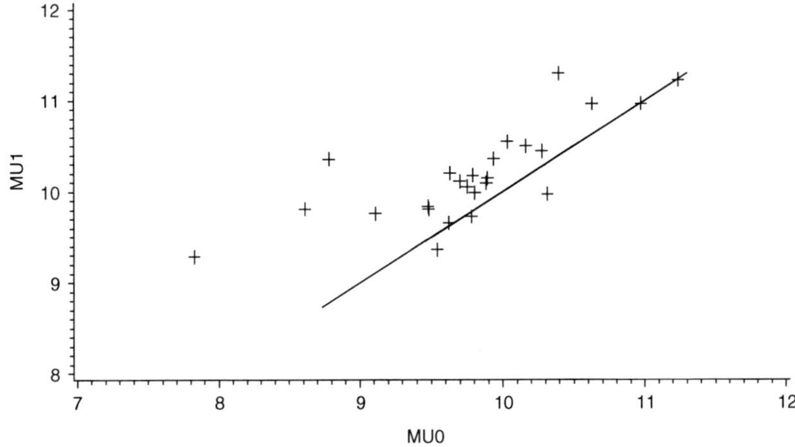

Figure 9.1 Individual average profitability with fibre-boat over individual average profitability with kattumaram, for 25 households*

Note: * For which sales data are available for both kattumaram and fibre-boat fishing.

158 per cent. The average change equalled 40.2 per cent, with a standard deviation of 46.8 per cent.

Determinants of the timing of technology adoption

When a technology is divisible, such as the adoption of new seeds in agriculture, a farmer with several plots can choose how many of them on which to try the new technology. In contrast, a fishing boat is by nature an indivisible productive asset for a household. Moreover, switching technologies is expensive, while with many technologies previously studied in agricultural contexts, a farmer can reverse the technology switch in subsequent growing cycles without incurring a cost from switching back. To summarize, in the context of adoption of new crop varieties in agriculture, the adoption decision is typically both divisible and reversible, while in the fishing situation, neither of these two properties holds.

Since adoption in the context of this study can be interpreted as a one-off transition from one state (kattumaram fishing) to another state (fibre-boat fishing) the timing of the individual adoption decision is modelled most suitably using methods from the statistical analysis of survival data. For the estimation, we adopt the common proportional hazard assumption. According to it, the hazard λ – that is, the probability that i adopts within the next period given, that he has not yet adopted – can be factored into a baseline hazard function, which is the same for all individuals in the population, and a function of individual characteristics, x_i. Specifically, it is assumed that

$$\lambda_i(t) = \lambda_0(t)(\mathbf{x}_i'\beta)$$

where β is a vector of parameters. From this structure of individual hazard, the likelihood of each observed adoption time can be derived as a function of the adoption time $t_i^*, \mathbf{x}_i$ and β. An expression for the likelihood can be obtained regardless of whether or not adoption occurred before the date of the interview. When the latter is true, the observation is treated as 'censored'. Using Cox's (1975) semi-parametric method of partial likelihood, maximum likelihood estimates of β can be obtained numerically without making any functional form assumptions about the shape of $\lambda_0(t)$.

An individual with characteristics $\mathbf{x}_i$ has a hazard higher than the sample average if he is more likely to adopt earlier than the average of the sample, because he faces a higher probability of switching at any time t' after date zero, conditional on not having switched already before t'. The sign of the relationship between an explanatory variable, x_{ik} say, and the outcome variable t_i^* thus goes the opposite way from an OLS model in which adoption time is regressed on $\mathbf{x}_i$: in the proportional hazard model, a positive value of β_k implies that an individual with a higher value of x_{ik} faces a higher probability of making the transition at any given point in time, and thus reduces the expected value of his adoption time, t_i^*. In the OLS model, in contrast, a positive value of β_k implies that an individual with a higher value of x_{ik} adopts later in expectation.

From the model of the previous section, one key explanatory variable of interest is the income gain that an individual expects from the transition. Recall that, in our simple model, an individual starts saving to finance the new technology as quickly as possible only if the expected net gain from adoption is positive. Unfortunately, the researcher does not observe individual *expected* net gain but only a measure of *realized* net gain, which can be retrieved from $\hat{\mu}_{Fi}$ and $\hat{\mu}_{Ci}$. We interpret realized net gain as a proxy for expected net gain. More specifically, when individual expectations are unbiased, realized net gain equals expected net gain plus a random error term which has an expectation of zero. Define

$$\Delta y_i = \exp(\mu_F) - \exp(\mu_C)$$

as the proxy for expected net gain in absolute terms. When Δy_i is included as a regressor in the vector $\mathbf{x}_i$, however, we potentially face the problem of a contaminated regressor, for at least two reasons. First, the applicable explanatory variable is an expected net gain while the variable used is a noisy realization of it. We are thus facing a problem analogous to the one of errors in variables in a linear regression model. The extent of the estimation bias induced by this problem depends, of course, on how accurate are individual expectations. If individuals can predict perfectly the actual income change, the use of Δy_i as explanatory variable is valid. The wider realized gains are distributed around expected gains, the more severe the bias introduced by using Δy_i.

Second, individual shocks may not be i.i.d. in each month, but may rather be correlated. For example, if a fisherman falls unexpectedly sick for an extended period of time right after purchasing a fibre-boat and this reduces his ability to go fishing, Δy_i underestimates his expected gains.

For both of these reasons, we shall experiment with two specifications in the empirical analysis: one where Δy_i is included in the $\mathbf{x}_i$ vector without modification; and one where, in the spirit of a two-stage least squares model, Δy_i is first regressed on a vector of instruments and its predicted values, $\hat{\Delta y}_i$, say, are used as explanatory variable in the subsequent regression of the timing of adoption. Indirect evidence for the 'noisiness' of Δy_i is provided by the fact that our estimates of Δy_i are negative for one-fifth of those households for which both kattumaram and fibre-boat sales data are available. For these households, individual rationality seems to be violated as they adopt, even though they expect smaller profits from the new technology.

To illustrate how income change and adoption time are related empirically, Figure 9.2 plots t_i^* over Δy_i. If Δy_i is an accurate measure of expected gains, unconstrained economic efficiency dictates that all households that realize a positive income change adopt immediately, while those with a negative Δy_i never adopt. When funds available to the fishing village are limited, constrained economic efficiency dictates that households that realize a positive

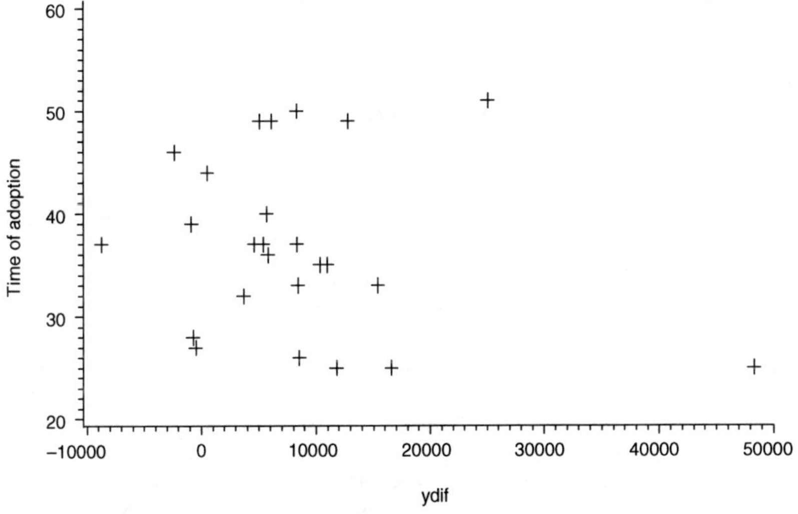

Figure 9.2   Adoption date over realized absolute income change, for 25 households*

Note: * For which sales data is available for both kattumaram and fibre-boat fishing. Time of adoption in number of months since first adoption in the village.

Source: Data come from 2004 round of boat owner survey collected by the authors, and the daily sales records kept by the auctioneers.

income change adopt in decreasing order of Δy_i. While there is some negative correlation between t_i^* and Δy_i (the correlation coefficient equals -0.04), this relationship is weak and statistically insignificant.

Another set of key explanatory variables refers to the capital market conditions a household faces. Here, we consider two categories: income and asset variables. Within the first, $y_{Ci} = \exp(\mu_{Ci})$, average sales generated with the old technology, proxies a household's income stream before adoption. If the technology switch requires own funds that are not present when the new technology becomes available, a household with higher y_{Ci} will be able to accumulate the required own funds faster. A significant negative relationship between y_{Ci} and t_i^* can thus be taken as evidence for a credit constraint faced by an income-poor household. Another income variable that will be used is the number of household members who earn an income.

The second variable – the value of the house at the time when the new technology became available – is an important component of the assets a household can collateralize to obtain credit. A significant negative relationship between a_{0i} and t_i^* can thus be taken as evidence for a credit constraint faced by an asset-poor household. Other variables that will be included initially are household size as well as the household head's literacy, age (both linear and squared), and years as a boat owner as a measure of experience.

Table 9.4 gives the results of the estimation of the determinants of adoption timing.[7] Column 1 gives coefficient estimates together with asymptotic p-values for the full set of regressors, including Δy_i not instrumented.[8] At conventional significance levels, only the value of the fisherman's house is a significant determinant of the timing of fibre-boat adoption. The positive sign of the coefficient means that a wealthier (in terms of assets) household is more likely to adopt the new technology earlier. Of the two variables that proxy for the income status of the household, y_{Ci} is significant at the 12 per cent level, while the number of family members who earn an income is insignificant. The same applies to household size and age. A Wald chi-square test of the hypothesis that both age coefficients are equal to zero fails to reject with a P-value of 0.58.

Column 2 gives coefficient estimates for a specification that uses predicted values of Δy_i, $\widehat{\Delta y_i}$, for the entire sample. As elaborated above, the concern addressed with this methodology is that there are reasons to believe that Δy_i is a noisy realization of the income change expected by an individual. The problem, however, is to find good instruments for Δy_i that do not affect the timing of adoption directly. The best one we could find in our data is the number of crew members employed by the head of household who belong to the extended family. It is, however, still a rather weak instrument. The only two noticeable changes with this estimation procedure are, first, that y_{Ci} is now substantially less significant; and, second, that our measure of experience, years as boat owner, becomes more significant. Finally, the Wald chi-square test of the hypothesis that both age coefficients are equal to zero fails to reject with a P-value of 0.92.

Table 9.4 Determinants of the timing of adoption (dependent variable: month of adoption)

	(1)	(2)	(3)	(4)
Value of house	0.00525	0.10697	0.00557	0.00528
	(0.070)	(0.064)	(0.022)	(0.026)
Family members with income	−0.17937	0.00521		
	(0.777)	(0.860)		
Average income before adoption	0.0000429	0.06286	0.0000414	0.0000287
	(0.122)	(0.439)	(0.057)	(0.158)
Income change from adoption	0.0000506	0.0000187	0.0000346	−0.0000074
	(0.151)	(0.786)	(0.161)	(0.912)
Household size	0.03444	−0.0000289		
	(0.868)	(0.760)		
Literacy of household head	−0.86901	−0.72087	−0.73734	−0.79233
	(0.156)	(0.246)	(0.173)	(0.138)
Age of household head	−0.22363	−0.02748		
	(0.311)	(0.919)		
Age squared	0.00273	0.0004796		
	(0.298)	(0.878)		
Years as boat owner	0.10930	0.12437	0.11890	0.14000
	(0.222)	(0.149)	(0.105)	(0.065)
Log-likelihood	−47.9	−48.9	−48.5	−49.3
Income change instrumented	No	Yes*	No	Yes*
Number of obs.	26	26	26	26
No. of obs. censored	3	3	3	3

Notes:
Asymptotic *p*-value in parentheses.
* Instruments: age, age squared, years as boat owner, number of crew members who belong to the extended family.

Guided by the findings of the specifications in Equations (9.1) and (9.2) and with regard to the fact that the sample underlying this estimation is small, we also estimate a more parsimonious version where the four least significant explanatory variables are omitted. According to column 3 of Table 9.4, both asset and income poverty significantly delay adoption. Households with a greater realized income gain are likely to adopt earlier, but this relationship is significant only at a level of 0.16. As before, greater experience in kattumaram fishing induces earlier adoption.

Column 4, where the income change is instrumented, confirms these findings. As in the full specification, instrumenting mainly affects the coefficient on y_{Ci}, which ceases to be significant at conventional levels in this specification. To summarize columns 1 to 4, we find compelling evidence that asset poverty delays adoption, and mixed evidence that income poverty does so as well. On the other hand, households that can expect a larger income change from adoption are not more likely to adopt earlier.

The role of wealth

We now discuss in some detail how asset wealth affects the timing of adoption. We start by considering the arguments of Besley and Case (1994) and Foster and Rosenzweig (1995), that asset wealth accelerates adoption because land-rich households enjoy higher intertemporal benefits from experimentation because of their larger scale of operation. In our sample, in contrast, each household operates exactly one boat before and after the switching of technologies, so we can safely discard the scale argument.

Another channel we can confidently rule out is that wealthy households adopt earlier because of better access to the labour market. In the situation studied here, the same amount of labour is employed to operate both old and new technology. Each household in our sample that adopts the new technology has previously operated the old technology and thus has already secured the amount of labour needed for the new technology.

What about better access of wealthier households to the new technology? Each household in the sample obtained its FRP from the nearby branch of a domestic FRP manufacturer, less than 4 kilometers away from the village and therefore no transaction costs for transportation are incurred in the purchase. Moreover, according to villagers, there has never been a supply constraint ever since the new technology became available in 2000. It can thus be ruled that wealth works through overcoming a supply constraint or having enhanced access to the new technology.

We next examine the relationship between initial wealth and risk-bearing attitudes. It is commonly believed that preferences for risk-bearing crucially depend on a household's wealth. In particular, under the plausible assumption of decreasing absolute risk aversion (DARA), households above a certain wealth level choose to incur a given lottery with a positive expected payoff, while households with wealth below that level choose to stay away from it, although they would accumulate assets to later choose the lottery.

Apparently, adoption of an FRP entails two forms of risk. First, the amount of fish catches fluctuates from day to day depending on weather and maritime conditions as well as individual luck. The question, however, is whether these fluctuations are more severe with an FRP than with a kattumaram. To obtain an answer, we run the regression:

$$\log(y_{sit}) = \mu_{si} + \delta_t + u_{sit}$$

separately for $s = C$ and $s = F$. The resulting root mean squared errors are 0.66 and 0.50, respectively. Thus, controlling for scale by considering the natural logarithm of sales, operating an FRP entails a smaller month-to-month risk than for a kattumaram. While it may be argued that daily catches may exhibit different volatility patterns across technologies than monthly ones, it is not likely that those are particularly relevant, as informal insurance arrangements seem to be prevalent in these villages. In this connection, boat owners report that they can easily obtain a short-term consumption loan from their auctioneer to compensate for a series of bad catches.

Second, as pointed out in the previous subsection, a kattumaram-operating boat owner may face uncertainty about the level of average gains (net of day-to-day fluctuations) from the technology shift. This, together with the DARA assumption, can explain later adoption by poorer but *ex post* equally successful households. This explanation competes with the remaining one of credit constraints. Since our quantitative data cannot provide a definite answer in favour of either one of the two, we shall use additional, perceptional data to get a sense of the relative importance of each of the two competing hypotheses. Our survey asked each boat owner the following question: 'Why did you wait (are you waiting) to switch to a FRP boat? Give the most important reason.' By far, the two most frequent answers were, first, 'It requires a lot of capital', and second, 'I was uncertain about the benefits'. Table 9.5 gives some statistics relating to the characteristics of the respondents by their answer to this question. The pattern we find is as follows. First, the capital requirement is mentioned roughly 50 per cent more often than benefit uncertainty. Second, wealth among those who cite benefit uncertainty as the main reason is on average more than 25 per cent higher than among those who mention the capital requirement first. This suggests that the capital constraint is more severe for poorer entrepreneurs, in fact to such an extent that it dominates the concern about benefit uncertainty, even though that latter concern is also of greater importance to poorer decision-makers when DARA is postulated. While the difference in asset wealth across answers is on the order of 30 per cent, this difference is not statistically significant. In the light of that, we do not have statistically significant, albeit economically important, evidence for the assertion that a lack of wealth affects the timing of adoption, mainly through limited access to capital.

Table 9.5   Wealth status by self-reported reason for delay of adoption, core sample

Answer	N	Mean	Std. dev.	Minimum	Maximum
Capital requirement	13	69.2	63.7	0	250
Benefit uncertainty	9	95.5	152.7	20	500
Other	4				

Simulation

The findings of the estimation suggest that asset poverty delays technology adoption. To be more precise, between two households that expect the same increase in average income from adoption, the wealthier one is more likely to adopt first. In this section, we address the policy-relevant question of how alternative distributions of wealth, as measured by house value, change the pattern of technology diffusion. We focus on the relationship between wealth distribution, which will be affected by the different economic policies considered, and the outcome variables of mean income (within the sample) and income inequality.

To conduct simulations, we first need to specify a baseline hazard function, $\lambda_0(t)$. We make the assumption of a constant baseline hazard:

$$\lambda_0(t) \equiv \lambda$$

given the small sample we have. Moreover, we consider a situation in which each household adopts exactly at the expected value of its adoption time:

$$\hat{t}_i^* = E[t_i^*|\mathbf{x}_i]$$

which is, of course, a function of $\hat{\beta}$. With a constant baseline hazard, we obtain:

$$\hat{t}_i^* = e^{-\mathbf{x}_i'\hat{\beta}}/\lambda$$

Finally, the parameter λ is calibrated as follows. In our sample, three households have not adopted before the interview date. We thus choose λ such that the date of the last adoption recorded before the date of the interview matches the fourth-to-last adoption date in the data simulated with the actual values of $\mathbf{x}_i$.

Figure 9.3 plots actual and simulated mean income. Notice that actual mean income uses all y_{si} for fixed t; that is, y_{Fi} (y_{Ci}) enters the average when household i has (not) adopted before date t. More formally, actual mean income is computed as

$$\frac{1}{n}\sum_{i=1}^{n}(\iota\{t<t_i^*\}y_{Ci} + \iota\{t\geq t_i^*\}y_{Fi})$$

The formula for predicted mean income is given by the same expression, except that t_i^* is replaced by $\hat{t}_i^*$. The predicted data is generated from the specification of Column 3 in Table 9.4. Without reproducing the results separately, we note that the shape of the predicted graph remains qualitatively unchanged when the instrumented version, Column 4 in Table 9.4, is used instead.

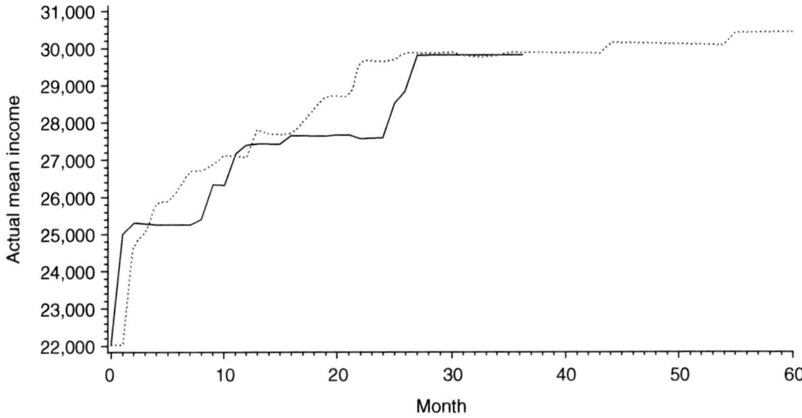

Figure 9.3   Mean income after the new technology became available, actual (solid line) and predicted by the model (dotted line)

Sources: Month (time of adoption) for 2004 round of boat owner survey collected by the authors; mean income, from daily sales whose records are kept by the auctioneers.

According to the solid line in Figure 9.3, there are three obvious 'waves' of adoption: at the beginning, then just before one year later, and finally a little more than two years later. Notice that the solid line ends at the 36th month, the last date for which we have data. Our simulation model appears to capture satisfactorily the main features of the data, though the predicted path is smoother than the stepwise pattern in the actual data. According to the simulation, the last household in the sample adopts 54 months after the technology has become available. At that time, predicted average income has increased by about 39 per cent.

Figure 9.4 depicts the Gini index of estimated actual incomes and the Gini as predicted by the simulation model. Notice that inequality during the adoption process exhibits the familiar inverted U-shape. This reflects first that, on average, adopters experience a substantial increase in income; and, second, that it is not the initially income-poor who adopt first, because in that case adoption would narrow the income gap between the initially income-rich and poor. In the data, we see an increase of the Gini from 0.34 to 0.38 during the first wave of adoptions. The second wave of adoptions a year later leaves inequality virtually unchanged, while the third wave results in a drop of the Gini of about 20 per cent to a level of 0.31, substantially lower than the value that prevailed before the new technology was known about. All in all, while the village experiences a substantial increase in inequality over a course of two years, the availability of the new technology can hardly be criticized for its long-term impact on the village economy since, at the same time, average income increases and inequality decreases substantially.

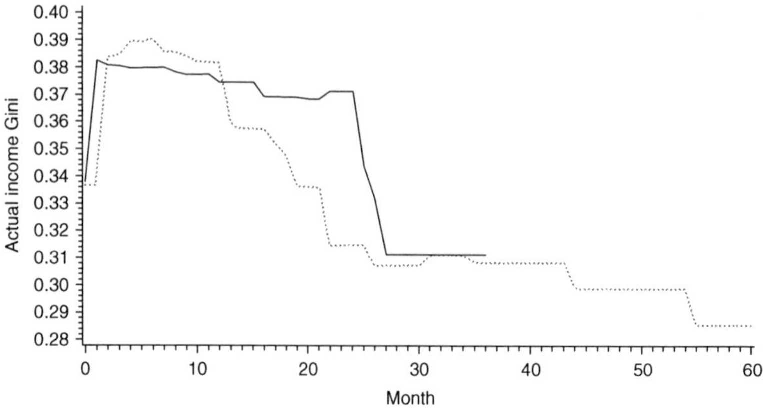

Figure 9.4   Income Gini after the new technology became available, actual (solid line) and predicted by the model (dotted line)
Sources: as per Figure 9.3; Gini calculated from daily sales records.

The predicted data captures satisfactorily the main features of the data. It correctly predicts the jump in inequality induced by the first wave of adoptions. The consequences of the second and third wave, however, are less clearly distinguishable in the simulated data, because, according to the dotted line, inequality gradually decreases from the eleventh month onwards. The last predicted adoption, in the 54th month, leads the village to a Gini of 0.285, 16 per cent lower than the one at date zero, where all households operate the old technology.

We now turn to the simulated policy counterfactuals. We first investigate the consequences of redistributive policies. Towards this, we assume that each household in the sample holds just the mean level of wealth observed in the data – that is, owns a house worth Rs.75,380. In such a scenario, the credit constraint is loosened for households whose wealth is below average, and tightened for the rest. If the relationship between wealth that can be collateralized and the extent to which a household is credit-constrained is concave, we expect adoption to occur more promptly on average with such a policy in place. The results for mean income and the Gini are plotted in Figures 9.5 and 9.6, respectively. According to Figure 9.5, equal redistribution does in fact result in a quicker adoption process. According to the simulation, the last adoption occurs a year earlier, in the 42nd instead of the 54th month, than with the actual wealth distribution. The effect on sales over the course of the adoption process, on the other hand, is rather small. With an equal asset distribution, simulated sales never exceed predicted actual ones by more than 7 per cent. Moreover, when we focus on differences between simulated and predicted actual sales of more than 3 per cent, simulated sales never lead predicted actual ones by more than five months.

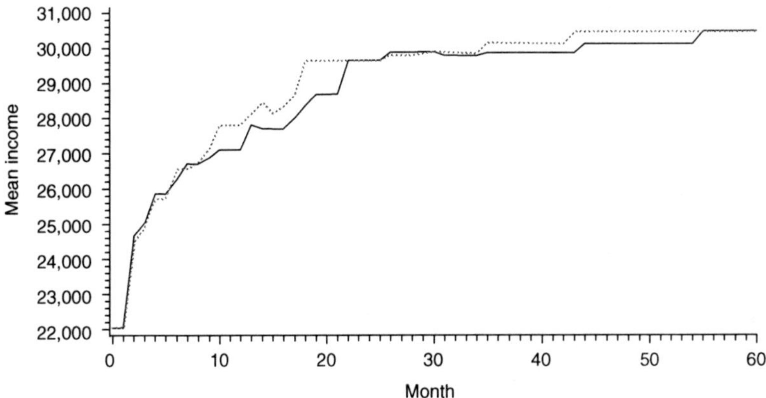

Figure 9.5   Predicted actual (solid line) and simulated (dotted line) mean income

Note: Simulation assumes perfectly equal distribution of wealth (measured by house value) over the sample. See Figure 9.2 for sources.

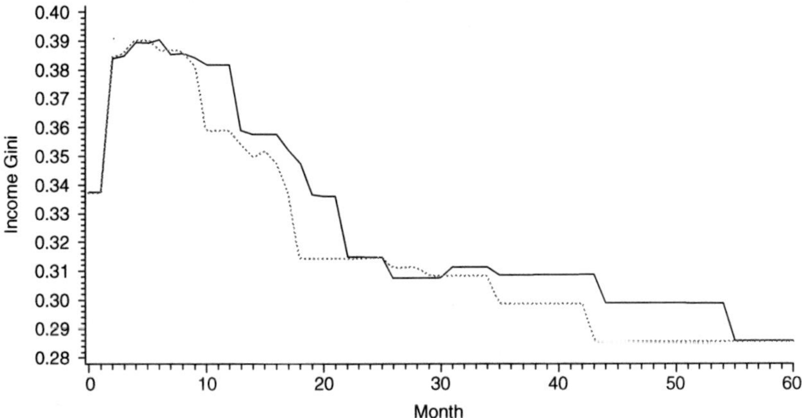

Figure 9.6   Predicted actual (solid line) and simulated (dotted line) Gini

Note: Simulation assumes perfectly equal distribution of wealth (measured by house value) over the sample. See Figure 9.4 for source.

According to Figure 9.6, a similar picture emerges for the dynamics of inequality. While the inverted U contracts by about 20 per cent towards the origin, the change in the general pattern of inequality as measured by the Gini can hardly be judged to be economically significant.

A second set of simulations investigates two extreme scenarios. The first assumes that each household in the sample holds only the smallest observed wealth; that is, each house is assumed to be worth Rs.20,000. The second, in contrast, assumes that each household in the sample holds the highest observed wealth; that is, each house is assumed to be worth Rs.500,000. The results for this set of simulations, together with the predicted actual values, are set out in Figures 9.7 and 9.8. We thus consider situations in which all households are either tightly credit-constrained or hardly face a credit constraint at all. The mean income and inequality paths for the first simulation follow very closely the respective paths generated from the actual asset data, which suggests that the observed income pattern accompanying the introduction of the new technology closely resembles a situation in which all households are substantially credit-constrained.

The results for the second simulation, where the credit constraint is released for the entire sample, are more striking. The dotted lines in Figures 9.7 and 9.8 suggest that, with a uniformly high level of asset wealth, the adoption process is completed in just five months. As a consequence, the village enjoys a substantially higher mean income for about two years, by which adoptions in the simulated data lead predicted actual ones. This result suggests that a community in which households face virtually no credit constraints is able to move up the technology ladder much faster than the one investigated by this study. Similarly, only a minor spike remains of the observed pronounced inverted U-shape of inequality.

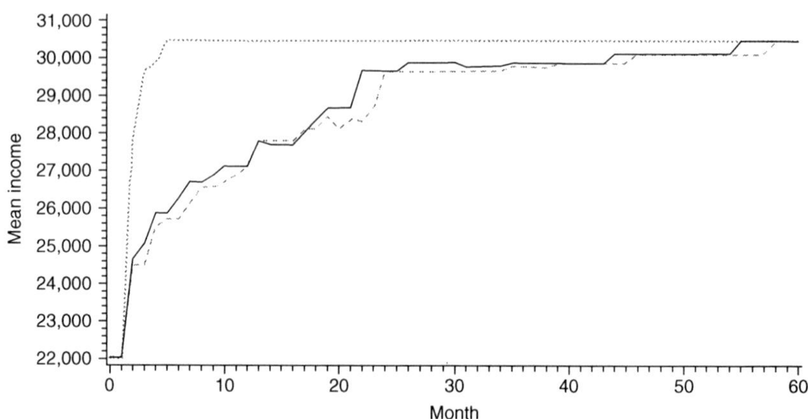

Figure 9.7   Predicted actual (solid line) and simulated mean income

Note: Simulation 1 (dashed) assumes the lowest observed wealth (house value equal to 20) for the entire sample; simulation 2 (dotted) assumes the highest observed wealth (house value equal to 500) for the entire sample. See Figure 9.2 for source details.

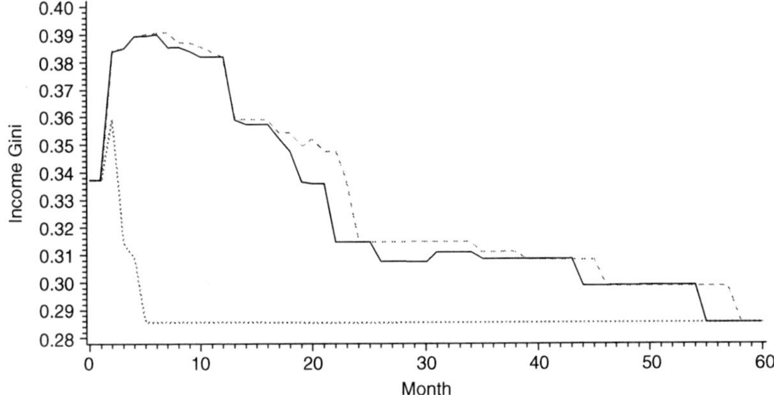

Figure 9.8   Predicted actual (solid) and simulated income Gini

Note: Simulation 1 (dashed) assumes the lowest observed wealth (house value equal to 20) for the entire sample; simulation 2 (dotted) assumes the highest observed wealth (house value equal to 500) for the entire sample. See Figure 9.4 for source details.

Conclusions

This chapter studied the diffusion of a new technology among South Indian fishermen, as much a product of ongoing globalizing trends as it is a response to distortions caused by previous waves of innovation triggered by globalization. We identified determinants of the timing of technology adoption as well as resulting income and inequality dynamics during this process. We find that lack of wealth is a key predictor for delayed adoption, and that the channel through which this mechanism is effective is a credit constraint. During the diffusion process, inequality follows Kuznets' well-known inverted U-shaped curve. Simulations suggest that a redistributive policy favouring the poor results in accelerated economic growth and a shorter duration of sharpened inequality, although the quantitative impact of such a policy is small.

One advantage of this chapter over other studies is that the context is well understood. Thus, the specific channels in which wealth matters for adoption, credit constraints as well as higher risk aversion are identified. We conclude, as did Platteau (1984), that overall our study village experienced a success story of globalization. According to our simulations, technology diffusion for the entire sample was completed in less than five years, and income gains for the initially poor are relatively larger than for the rich.

What remains unaddressed by this research are the long-run consequences for the resource base, and thus future generations of fishermen, resulting from increased efficiency in fishing. Future work will have to evaluate whether the short-term gains generated by the diffusion of fibre-reinforced plastic boats are both economically and environmentally sustainable. Previous instances of globalization and subsequent resource depletion in low-income countries warrant scepticism.

Notes

1   In contrast, previous attempts by leading international OBM manufacturers in the 1970s to target India's small-scale fishermen were largely unsuccessful (Pietersz 1993).
2   The debt dynamics in this context is analysed in Giné and Klonner, 2005.
3   Two households owned FRPs and hired a crew. In both cases, the primary occupation of the head of the household is not fishing, for which reason we excluded them from the sample.
4   This is obtained by calculating the maximum of the parabola implied by γ_1 and γ_2:

$$\frac{\hat{\gamma}_1}{2\hat{\gamma}_2}$$

5   Notice that the statistical properties of the point estimate of κ are non-standard, as minimization of the sum of squares over κ is a discrete problem. Therefore Table 9.3 only contains the point estimate of κ.
6   The estimate of κ can be reconciled with the estimates of Equation (9.2), which suggest that learning-by-doing lasts for twice as long. Notice that the quadratic function used there is downward-sloping for high values of τ_i and thus leads to an upward-biased estimate of the duration of learning if the learning curve is in fact flat for high values of τ_i.
7   Notice that Cox's method of partial likelihood does not identify an intercept term.
8   For the three censored observations in the sample used for this estimation we have to impute values of Δy_i. These are obtained by regressing Δy_i of the available 23 uncensored observations, for which we have both y_{Ci} and $y_{Fi} = \exp(\mu_{Fi})$ on house value, y_{Ci}, age, age squared, literacy and number of crew members who belong to the extended family, and using the estimated coefficients to generate predicted values of Δy_i.

References

Bandiera, O. and Rasul, I. (2006) 'Social Networks and Technology Adoption in Northern Mozambique', *Economic Journal*, 116: 869–902.
Besley, T. and Case, A. (1994) 'Diffusion as a Learning Process: Evidence from HYV Cotton', Working Paper 5/94, Princeton University Department of Economics, Princeton, NJ.
Binswanger, H., Dayantha, J., Balaranaia, T. and Sillers, D. (1980) 'The Impacts of Risk Aversion on Agricultural Decisions in Semi-Arid India', Working Paper, World Bank, Washington, DC.
Cox, D. R. (1975) 'Partial Likelihood', *Biometrika* 62, 269–76.
Feder, G., Just, R. E. and Zilberman, D. (1985) 'Adoption of Agricultural Innovations in Developing Countries: A Survey', *Economic Development and Cultural Change*, 33, 255–97.
Feder, G. and O'Mara, G. T. (1982) 'On Information and Innovation Diffusion: A Bayesian Approach', *American Journal of Agricultural Economics*, 64, 145–47.

Foster, A. and Rosenzweig, M. (1995) 'Learning by Doing and Learning from Others', *Journal of Political Economy*, 103, 1176–209.

Giné, X. and Klonner, S. (2005) 'Dynamic Lending with Limited Commitment and Uncertain Borrower Types: Theory and Evidence', Working Paper, Cornell University Department of Economics, Ithaca, NY.

Giné, X. and Townsend, R. (2004) 'Evaluation of Financial Liberalization: A General Equilibrium Model with Constrained Occupation Choice', *Journal of Development Economics*, 74, 269–307.

The Hindu (2001) 'Boon for Small-scale Fishermen', 22 March.

Kurien, J. (1994) 'Kerala's Marine Fisheries Development Experience', in B. A. Prakash, (ed.), *Kerala's Economy: Performance, Problems, Prospects* (New Delhi: Sage), 195–214.

Kurien, J. (1995) 'Plywood Boats in South India', *Appropriate Technology*, 22, 22–49.

Kuznets, S. (1955) 'Economic Growth and Income Inequality', *American Economic Review*, 45: 1–28.

Lloyd-Ellis, H. and Bernhardt, D. (2000) 'Enterprise, Inequality, and Economic Development', *Review of Economic Studies* 67(1), 147–68.

Munshi, K. (2004) 'Social Learning in a Heterogeneous Population. Technology Diffusion in the Indian Green Revolution', *Journal of Development Economics*, 73: 185–215.

Nissanke, M. and Thorbecke, E. (2006) 'Channels and Policy Debate in the Globalisation–Inequality–Poverty Nexus', *World Development*, 34, 1338–60.

Platteau, J. P. (1984) 'The Drive Towards Mechanization of a Small-Scale Fisheries in Kerala: A Study of the Transformation Process of Traditional Village Societies', *Development and Change*, 15, 65–103.

Pietersz, V. L. C. (1993) 'Developing and Introducing a Beachlanding Craft on the East Coast of India', Bay of Bengal Programme, Madras, India.

Sandven, P. (1959) 'The Indo-Norwegian Project in Kerala', Norwegian Foundation for Assistance to Underdeveloped Countries, Oslo.

Vivekanandan, V. (2002) 'The Introduction and Spread of Plywood Boats on the Lower South-West Coast of India', Technical Report, South Indian Federation of Fishermen Societies.

10
Trade Liberalization, Environment and Poverty: A Developing Country Perspective

Mahvash Saeed Qureshi

Introduction

The massive wave of trade liberalization that has continued for a decade has generated an interesting and contentious debate in terms of its impact on the environment. Environmental resources are an important input in all sorts of production.[1] A rapid expansion in the scale of economic activity is considered to have caused their overexploitation and misuse, the negative consequences of which are even more pronounced in the absence of appropriate environmental policies, because adverse externalities associated with production are not internalized. This is known as the *scale effect* of trade on the environment, which has the potential to encourage short-run growth at the cost of hampering long-run economic development through causing irreversible damage to the environment.

The fear of environmental degradation associated with trade is expressed in particular for developing and poor countries, most of which have weak regulatory infrastructure and lack environmental awareness. Environmentalists argue that, because of lax environmental regulations, these countries treat the environment as a relatively abundant factor of production and specialize in the production of pollution-intensive products as a result of free trade. This initiates a negative *composition effect* of trade that complements the scale effect, exacerbates natural resource degradation, and causes ecological poverty, which in turn accentuates economic poverty and gravely limits prospects for growth.[2]

The views of the environmentalists are challenged by the proponents of free trade, who assert that the lowering of barriers to trade and investment facilitates the movement of environmentally friendly technologies, management techniques and information across the countries. Thus, trade gives rise to a positive *technique effect*, which has the potential to outweigh the negative scale effect of increased production. Moreover, they argue that liberalization leads to a *positive* and not a *negative* composition effect via income growth. An increase in per capita income induced by greater openness enhances consumers' preference for environmentally friendly products, advances cleaner production techniques, and reduces the share of pollution-intensive products in total output.

The contradictory predictions of both schools of thought and the mixed empirical evidence suggest that, with reference to the environment, liberalization is a double-edged sword presenting both opportunities and threats. The manner in which resources are exploited as a result of free trade poses challenges for communities; none the less, opportunities are present through clean technology transfer and income growth. To maximize the gains from liberalization, governments must implement appropriate policies that promote both economic growth and environmental protection.

The determination and implementation of optimal policies, however, remain a difficult task for developing countries because of technical and financial constraints, and lack of political will. In general, these countries adopt the 'pollute now, clean up later' approach to fast-track growth and achieve economic development. Furthermore, earlier research on the issue, which has been confined largely to cross-country investigations that were sensitive to the choice of pollutants and the countries included in the sample, has been unhelpful in offering guidance and sound policy advice to the developing countries.[3]

In recent years, an increased emphasis is being placed on examining the experiences of individual countries so that policy frameworks are suggested according to their unique circumstances and resources. To date, however, few empirical assessments are available, especially for developing countries, because of a lack of data on environmental indicators. This chapter aims to fill this gap in the literature, and attempts to assess the environmental consequences of trade liberalization for a developing country, Pakistan, which makes an interesting case study for various reasons. First, like many other developing countries, Pakistan began a rapid liberalization from the early 1990s, and it is of interest to examine which types of industries, environmentally friendly or hazardous, have prospered under its liberalization policies. Second, Pakistan has experienced severe bio-diversity loss and a rise in pollution since the 1980s. It is therefore important to investigate whether increased trade activity has played a part in the deterioration of environmental quality. Finally, the environment is an area that has persistently been ignored in Pakistan, and environmental concerns have never been adequately addressed. This attitude may have non-trivial consequences because of the prevalence of a strong poverty–environment nexus in the country. As the costs associated with environmental degradation, such as reduced opportunities for earning livelihoods, and the health costs of being exposed to pollution, hit the poor hardest of all, it is critical to evaluate the environmental consequences of Pakistan's macroeconomic policies for devising appropriate poverty alleviation strategies.

Against this background, we address three key concerns pertinent to the trade–environment debate. First, we explore the environmental impacts of trade liberalization in terms of the industrial composition effect, and test the hypotheses that the exports of pollution-intensive products have increased, whereas the imports of pollution-intensive products have decreased after the reform process. Second, we examine the impact of environmental regulations in the importing countries on the exports of Pakistan's pollution-intensive products. Third, we review the implications of our findings for the poor, and suggest appropriate policy responses.

We use disaggregated manufacturing and bilateral trade data for our investigation. To our knowledge, this is the first study identifying compositional changes associated with liberalization using a bilateral trade flow framework. Also, unlike earlier literature, which assesses the pollution intensity of industries based on a single pollutant, we use a risk-weighted toxicity measure to classify industries as pollution-intensive. As industrial pollution intensities tend to vary across different types of pollutants, a risk-weighted toxicity index is a superior indicator of the overall hazardousness of a sector to individual intensities.

Economy and the environment in Pakistan

Corporate performance and trade liberalization: background and present scenario

Pakistan has recorded a mixed industrial performance since its establishment in 1947. Its transition from a high-tariff, import-substitution strategy in the 1960s and 1970s to an open economy began from the mid-1980s onwards, when liberalization reforms were undertaken including measures to reduce export controls, encourage imports of industrial raw material and machinery, and increase foreign investment (see Figure 10.1).

Overall, industrial performance was remarkable during the 1960s, when the manufacturing sector thrived and achieved high growth rates. Industrial growth, however, dampened during the 1970s because of the nationalization of the industrial and financial sectors in 1972 (see Table 10.1). The reason behind the slowdown was the great extent of protection provided to domestic firms without proper performance checks. Operating within a highly sheltered environment with no export obligation and no exposure to international competition, domestic industries had low productivity and remained technologically backward.

The 1980s witnessed a move away from the inward-looking import substitution policy to an outward-orientated strategy through the liberalization of trade and financial markets. In the early 1980s, exports were typically half or less than half of the import bill. By late the 1990s, however, processed commodities became more competitive internationally, and exports rose to around 90 per cent of imports (see Table 10.2). During 1985–91, tariffs were reduced on 1,134 items, approximately 700 items were removed from the

Figure 10.1 Pakistan's exports and imports of goods and services (constant US$)
Source: World Bank (2004).

Table 10.1 Annual average growth performance of various sectors (per cent)

Sector	1960s	1970s	1980s	1990s
GDP growth rate	6.8	4.8	6.5	4.6
Agriculture	5.1	2.4	5.4	4.2
Manufacturing	9.9	5.5	8.2	4.8
Services sector	6.7	6.3	6.7	4.6

Source: Government of Pakistan, *Economic Survey*, 2001, 2002.

Table 10.2 Pakistan's external trade

Year	Exports (US$ millions)	Imports (US$ millions)	Percentage share of GDP	
			Exports	Imports
1980–5	2,675	5,596	9.0	18.7
1985–90	4,167	6,275	11.3	17.1
1990–5	6,958	9,154	13.5	17.8
1995–2000	8,707	11,805	13.7	17.4
2000–1	9,202	10,729	15.7	18.4

Source: Government of Pakistan, *Economic Survey*, 2001, 2002.

negative list of imports, and the maximum tariff rate was decreased from 225 per cent to 100 per cent.[4]

The reform process, combined with political stability, paid off, and the economy recovered considerably in the 1980s. The manufacturing sector grew on average at 8 per cent per annum, and annual GDP at 6.5 per cent. Total exports in real terms increased by 9 per cent per annum, and the share of manufactured goods in total exports increased to 49 per cent in 1986, compared to 38 per cent in 1976 (see Table 10.3).[5]

The momentum of economic growth was lost again in the 1990s because of political instability caused by frequent changes of government and the deteriorating situation of law and order in major cities. Industrial and trade performance remained depressed, the average annual GDP growth rate fell to 4.6 per cent and that of the manufacturing sector to 4.8 per cent. The share of manufactured products in total exports, however, continued to rise, jumping from 45 per cent in 1980 to 62 per cent in 1995–6.

Liberalization efforts gained further momentum in the late 1990s with the introduction of wide-ranging structural reforms. Successive trade policies attempted to diversify the export base and to improve the export infrastructure to increase exports. On imports, almost all types of quantitative restriction (apart from customs duties) were removed. Customs duties themselves were lowered substantially, from 80 per cent in 1996 to 30 per cent in 2001, and to 25 per cent in 2002.[6] The average applied tariff rate fell from 42.7 per cent in 1996–7 to 20.4 per cent in 2001–2 (see Figure 10.2). Further, in 2002, only fifty seven items constituted the negative list of imports and 192 items remained on the restricted list, because of health and safety concerns. The accelerated pace of liberalization improved the trade balance significantly and Pakistan's trade deficit reduced from US$3.12 billion in 1995 to US$0.83 billion in 2003.

Table 10.3   Economic classification of exports and imports (percentage share)

Years	Exports			Imports		
	Primary	Semi-manufactured	Manufactured	Capital	Consumer	Industrial raw material
1975–6	44	18	38	35	21	34
1980–1	44	11	45	28	15	58
1985–6	35	16	49	37	18	45
1990–1	19	24	57	33	51	16
1995–6	16	22	62	35	14	51
2000–1	13	15	72	25	14	61

Source: Government of Pakistan, *Economic Survey*, various issues.

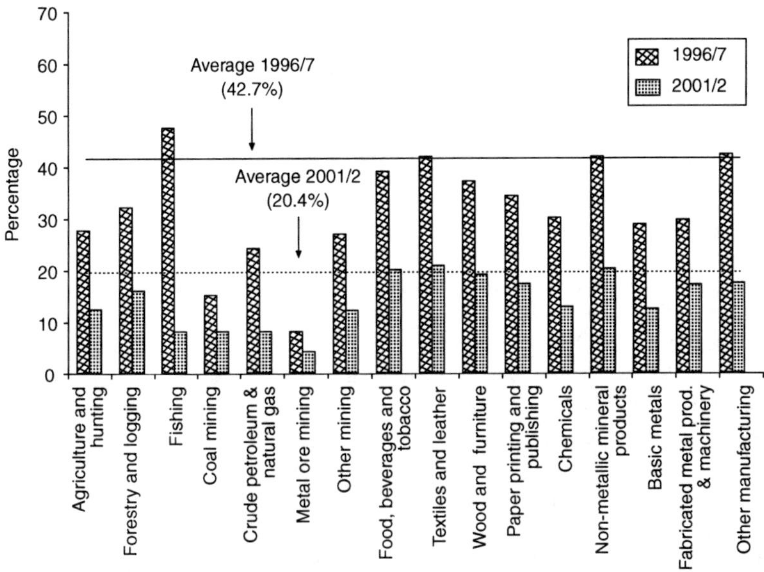

Figure 10.2   Applied tariff averages by 2-digit ISIC category, 1996–7 and 2001–2
Source: WTO (2001).

Environmental profile

A population size of approximately 145 million, coupled with a population growth rate of 3 per cent per annum, an average GDP growth rate of 4.5 per cent per annum, and rapid urbanization has put immense pressure on Pakistan's natural resource base and environmental absorptive capacity. Pakistan's main environmental problems include industrial and vehicular emissions, domestic waste-water pollution, deforestation, rangeland degradation and water-logging and salinity. No comprehensive database on environmental degradation exists, however. According to World Bank estimates, environmental damage exceeds 5 per cent of GDP at 1992 values (Brandon and Ramankutty 1993).

Although data on industrial pollution are fragmentary and cannot be compared over time, the industrial sector is considered to be a major contributor to overall pollution. Almost 80 per cent of industrial growth in Pakistan has occurred in major urban areas, where firms release carcinogens and manufacturing waste matter indiscriminately into the water and the air. Most industrial clusters have been established without planning permission, and a majority of firms do not have end-of-pipe treatment facilities. Untreated waste-water is disposed of in drains, canals, rivers and on agricultural fields, which has brought existing water resources under severe threat.[7]

In Karachi, the largest city of Pakistan, with a population size of 10 million, more than 6,000 industrial units have been established along the coastal belt. With the exception of a handful of these, most discharge untreated effluent containing heavy metals, detergents, lubricating oils, chlorine and various organic and inorganic toxic compounds into the sewers or rivers and adjacent creeks leading to the Arabian Sea, which is having an adverse effect on the fishing and shrimp industry.

The situation is no different in other parts of the country. According to Punjab Environmental Protection Department estimates, approximately 9,000 million gallons of waste-water with 20,000 tons of biological oxygen demand (BOD) are discharged daily into water bodies by firms in the main industrial cities of the Punjab province. The water available in most of these areas is unfit for human consumption and it is therefore hardly surprising that approximately 40–50 per cent of total deaths in Pakistan are the result of water-borne diseases (GoP-IUNC 1992).[8]

The deterioration of air quality is another serious issue. Recently, a joint study done by the Environment Protection Agency and the Japan International Co-operation Agency revealed that the average suspended particulate matter (SPM) in the ambient air of Lahore, Islamabad and Rawalpindi is 6.4 times higher than the World Health Organization's guidelines, and 3.8 times higher than Japanese standards. From 1963 to 1990, it is estimated that the levels of six types of industrial pollutants – toxics, heavy metals, BOD, suspended-solid water pollutants, SPM, and sulphur dioxide (SO_2) – increased by six to ten times, whereas the average GDP growth rate was only 3 per cent (ADB 1998). Table 10.4 shows that the average increase in SO_2 was twenty-three-fold, and in carbon dioxide (CO_2) emissions fourfold from 1977–8 to 1997–8. The major contributors to this increase are the manufacturing and power-generating sectors (see Figure 10.3).

Figure 10.4 shows that total primary energy consumption and CO_2 emissions have been increasing exponentially over time, whereas the damage

Table 10.4 Estimated air pollutants from various economic sectors (000s tonnes)

Sector	1977–8		1987–8		1997–8	
	CO_2	SO_2	CO_2	SO_2	CO_2	SO_2
Industry	12,546	19	27,234	431	54,468	1,002
Transport	7,242	53	10,506	58	19,380	107
Power	3,672	4	11,424	97	54,162	1,016
Domestic	16,932	5	24,582	16	40,800	41
Agriculture	867	5	4,590	29	6,528	41
Commercial	1,734	11	2,652	13	4,386	26
Total	**42,993**	**98**	**80,988**	**645**	**179,724**	**2,232**

Source: Government of Pakistan, *Economic Survey*, 2000, 2001.

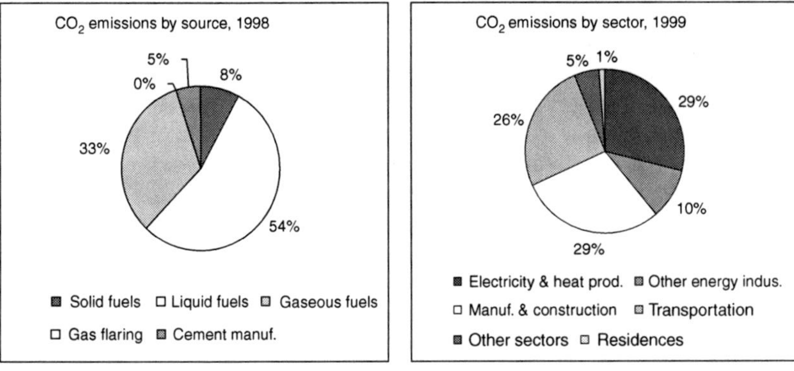

Figure 10.3 CO_2 emissions by source and sector in Pakistan

Source: Government of Pakistan, *Economic Survey*, 2000, 2001.

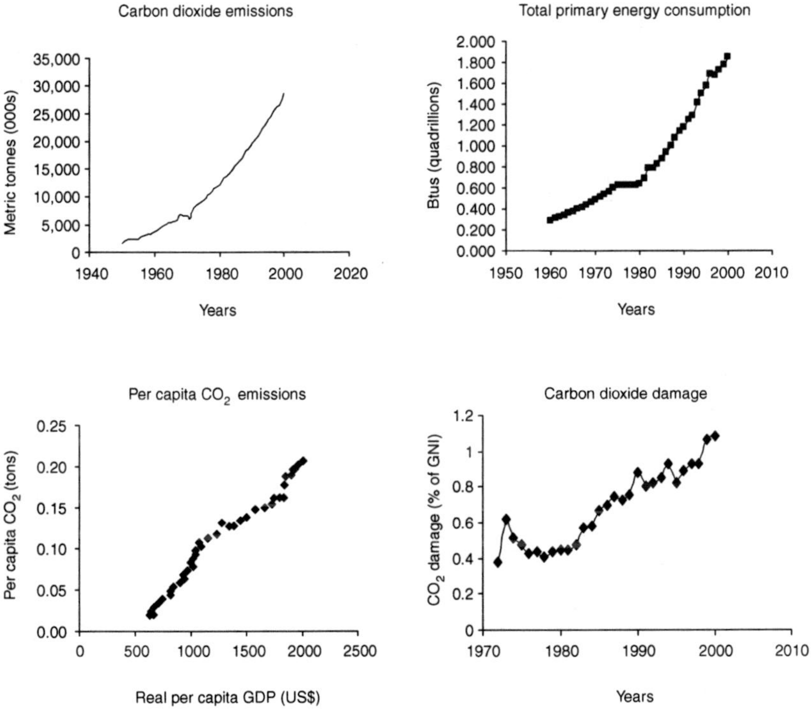

Figure 10.4   Indicators of environmental quality

Source: World Bank (2004).

incurred by CO_2 emissions as a percentage of gross national income exhibits a positive linear trend. Table 10.5 presents the performance of Pakistan *vis-à-vis* the rest of the world. The most striking observation is the rapid increase in CO_2 emissions – whereas the percentage increase in world emissions during 1990–8 was 8 per cent, it was 43 per cent in Pakistan. Another noticeable feature is its high emission intensity (emissions per unit of output), which is almost double the average world intensity.

The Environmental Sustainability Index (ESI) compiled by the Yale Centre for Environmental Law and Policy, and the Centre for International Earth Science Information Network, ranked Pakistan as 137 out of 146 countries in 2005. The highest-ranking country was Finland, almost doubling Pakistan's score. Pakistan recorded poor environmental performance compared to its neighbouring countries as well as to its counterparts in the low-income group (Figure 10.5).

Environmental regulation in Pakistan

The response to environmental pollution in Pakistan began in the early 1990s. In 1992, as part of its preparations for participating in the Rio Earth Summit, the government of Pakistan prepared the National Conservation Strategy (NCS), which outlined an environmental agenda for the country and set out goals for natural resource conservation. In 1993, environmental concerns were brought to the fore, and National Environmental Quality

Table 10.5 CO_2 emissions in Pakistan

Carbon dioxide (CO_2) emissions	Pakistan	World
Total emissions in 000s metric tons, 1998	97,109	24,215,376
Percentage change in total emissions since 1990	43	8
Emissions as percentage of global CO_2 production	0.4	
Per capita CO_2 emissions in 000s metric tons, 1998	1	4
Percentage change in per capita emissions since 1990	12	−2
CO_2 emissions (metric tons) per million dollars GDP, 1998	1,445	773
Percentage change in CO_2 intensity since 1990	3	−10
Cumulative CO_2 emissions, 1900–99 (billions metric tons)	1,771	933,686

Source: World Resources Institute (2003).

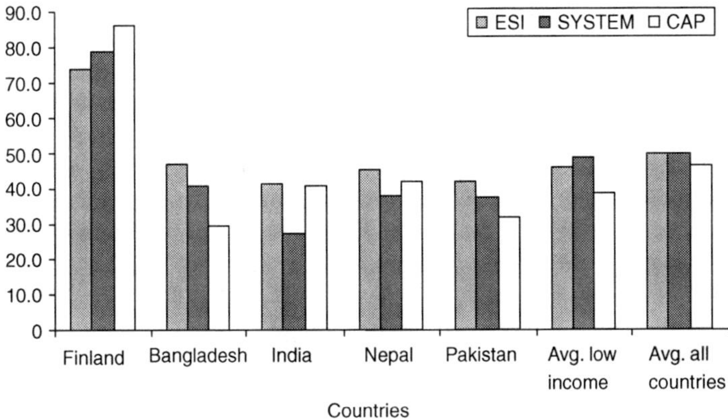

Figure 10.5   ESI comparision – Pakistan and other countries, 2002

Source: ESI database.

Standards (NEQS) were approved to set limits on major industrial and vehicular emissions, municipal effluents and noise. The NEQS were, however, rejected by the industrial sector and deemed to be unrealistic. They were revised in 1996 and made compatible with the standards of other developing countries with a similar industrial base.

After several years of deliberations, the Pakistan Environmental Protection Act (PEPA) was enacted in 1997. This led to the establishment of four provincial environment protection agencies (EPAs) to facilitate the monitoring of compliance in the provinces.[9] In 2001, the government approved a National Environment Action Plan (NEAP) to initiate activities to protect the environment, safeguard public health and promote sustainable livelihoods. However, despite the progress made on the institutional and policy fronts, there is no political will to ensure the enforcement of NEQS. The environmental regulatory authorities face numerous financial, technical and human resource constraints, and remain extremely weak enforcement bodies.[10] This issue was realized in the mid-term review of the NCS in 2000, which pointed out that the NCS has led to institution building but not to actual improvements in natural resource and environmental management (GoP 2005a).

Recently, a National Environment Policy (NEP) has been drafted by the government for 2005–15 to address aggravating environmental concerns. The policy highlights key environmental issues at the national level and provides an overarching framework for protecting, conserving and restoring the country's environment (GoP 2005a, 2005b). It remains to be seen, however, whether the EPAs are given adequate enforcement powers, and the policy objectives of NEP are realized.

Conceptual framework

The impact of trade liberalization on the environment has been the subject of many theoretical and empirical investigations. The trade–environment literature is closely linked to growth–environment studies which, following the pioneering contribution of Grossman and Krueger (1993), examine the effect of economic growth on the environment by decomposing emissions into *scale, composition* and *technique effects*. The decomposition of the total emissions released during the production of a commodity X is expressed as:[11]

$$Z = eX = e\xi S \tag{10.1}$$

where Z is the total emissions released, e is the pollution intensity of X, ξ is the share of output X in total output of the economy, and S is the scale of total output. Taking logs and totally differentiating, we obtain:

$$\hat{Z} = \hat{S} + \hat{\xi} + \hat{e} \tag{10.2}$$

where $^\wedge$ denotes a percentage change. The first term on the right-hand side is the *scale effect*, which implies that, everything else remaining constant, an expansion of economic activity increases environmental damage because more emissions are created as a by-product. The second term is the *composition effect*, which refers to any changes in emissions solely as a result of structural changes in the economy; that is, *ceteris paribus*, a move towards pollution-intensive production would generate more pollution, and vice versa. Finally, the last term in Equation (10.2) represents the *technological effect*, which indicates changes in pollution as a result of changes in the production processes while holding the scale and composition of economic activity constant.

In the context of trade liberalization, the scale, composition and technological effects reflect the environmental consequences of the increase in production as a result of increased market access opportunities, the changes in the industrial structure brought about by changes in the relative prices of goods, and technological progress as a result of technology transfer, respectively. In general, the scale and technique effects are considered to be negative and positive, respectively, but the direction of the composition effect is the most controversial. The latter has therefore been a subject of much discussion and research in recent years, which has given rise to two competing points of view on the issue: the *factor endowment hypothesis* and the *pollution haven hypothesis* (PHH).

The *factor endowment hypothesis* predicts that factor endowments rather than environmental policy are the prime determinants of trade patterns. In this view, developed countries that have a comparative advantage in capital-intensive products are more likely to specialize in capital-intensive and, hence, more pollution-intensive products regardless of the environmental regulations in place. Among others, the findings of Tobey (1990), Grossman and Krueger (1993), Jaffe *et al.* (1995), and Mani and Wheeler (1999) lend support to this argument, and they report no relationship between environmental regulations and trade patterns.

The PHH, however, asserts that environmental policy plays an important part in determining the comparative advantage of a country. Firms in countries with weak (or no) environmental regulations consider the environment to be a relatively abundant factor of production, and pollute freely. The production and export of environmentally hazardous products therefore increase under trade in these countries. A number of studies find evidence in support of this argument, for example, Low and Yeats (1992); Lucas *et al.* (1992); Heil and Selden (2001); Jha and Gamper-Rabindran (2004); Mani and Jha (2005).

In order to investigate the PHH, two approaches have traditionally been used: the factor content of trade approach; and the trade-in-goods approach. The factor content approach studies the effect of trade on the environment indirectly by tracking changes in the pattern of environmental factor services embodied in traded commodities, in the form of pollution emitted domestically (Walter 1973; Robison 1988; Xu and Song 2000). If environmental regulations differ across countries, then countries with low (high) environmental standards are expected to export (import) goods with relatively higher embodied environmental services and import (export) goods with relatively lower embodied environmental services. In contrast, the trade-in-goods approach examines the changes in trade patterns directly in a bilateral or multilateral framework (Grossman and Krueger 1993; Cole and Elliott 2003; Ederington *et al.* 2003). We assess the changes in Pakistan's trade pattern pre- and post-liberalization in a comprehensive manner by employing both approaches in this chapter.

Factor content of trade

We study the embodied environmental factor content of Pakistan's trade by building our framework on the standard multifactor, multicommodity and multicountry Heckscher–Ohlin–Vanek (HOV) model of trade-in-factor services, developed by Vanek (1968). The HOV model, an extension of the traditional two-good, two-factor Heckscher–Ohlin (HO) model, interprets trade in goods as an international exchange of factor services embodied in the traded goods and shows that, under balanced trade, countries will have an embodied net export and net import of relatively abundant and scarce factors, respectively.

Following Coase (1960), and treating environment as a factor of production, we use the HOV model to estimate environmental services embodied in trade.[12] Thus, if f countries produce j types of goods with i factors of production then, under the standard HOV model, assumptions of identical and constant returns to scale technologies across countries, homothetic consumer preferences, different cross-country factor endowments, international mobility of goods and immobility of factors, no possibility of joint production and no factor intensity reversals, the vector of net exports for country f is given by:

$$T^f = X^f - M^f \tag{10.3}$$

where X^f and M^f denote the vectors of exported and imported goods, respectively.

If $A = [a_{ij}]$ denotes the input–output coefficient matrix for country f, where a_{ij} represents the per-unit input requirement, then the factors embodied in X^f are given by V^X, such as:

$$V^{X^f} = AX^f \tag{10.4}$$

Similarly, the factors embodied in M^f are given by:

$$V^{M^f} = A^* M^f \tag{10.5}$$

where A^* denotes the input–output coefficient matrix of the foreign country from where the imports of country f originate.[13] Thus the net factor content of trade, as specified by Deardorff (1982), is expressed as:

$$V^{T^f} = V^{X^f} - V^{M^f} = AX^f - A^* M^f \tag{10.6}$$

where V^T is the vector of net factor trade. With identical technologies across countries and factor price equalization, we have $A = A^*$ and Equation (10.6) may be simplified.

Equation (10.6) is a straightforward and convenient tool for comparing the factor content of exports and imports over time and across countries. A positive (negative) value of an element in V^T indicates that the factor is net exported (imported). When considering only one factor of production, Equation (10.6) can be written as:

$$V_i^{T^f} = \sum_j a_{ij} X_j^f - \sum_j a_{ij} M_j^f = \sum_j X_j^f \sum_j \left[\frac{a_{ij} X_j^f}{\sum_j X_j^f} \right] - \sum_j M_j^f \sum_j \left[\frac{a_{ij} M_j^f}{\sum_j M_j^f} \right] \tag{10.7}$$

where V_i^T is the net export of the ith factor; and X_j and M_j are the exports and imports of the jth good, respectively.

The trade-in-goods approach

The trade-in-goods approach followed here differs from earlier studies, since we analyse bilateral trade flows by employing the gravity model to examine the effect of trade liberalization on the composition of exports and imports. In a discussion paper, van Beers and van den Bergh (2000) argue that useful information is lost in a multilateral framework because of aggregation; hence, a bilateral approach is preferable to a multilateral analysis. Further, previous studies (for example, Ederington and Minier 2003; Ederington *et al.* 2003; Jha and Gamper-Rabindran 2004) follow Grossman and Krueger's (1993) HOV framework and express net exports of each sector as a function of the labour, capital and pollution intensity of that sector. For Pakistan, however, the available industrial statistics are limited and unreliable, which makes it difficult to adopt the HOV model for regression analysis.

The gravity model, which follows the law of universal gravitation from physics, is a popular tool for predicting trade flows. It models trade as being proportional to the economic size and proximity of trading partners, and inversely proportional to distance and other obstacles to trade. Although specified simply, gravity models have performed extremely well empirically, and have therefore been used extensively for both inter- and intra-national trade flow analysis. In recent years, the models have been augmented to examine determinants of trade other than distance and size, and, most commonly, dummy variables are included to capture the influence of various political, cultural and historical factors on trade flows.

In its most general form, a gravity model is specified as:

$$F = X\beta + D\lambda + \varepsilon, \quad \varepsilon \sim N(0,\sigma^2) \tag{10.8}$$

where F is a vector of (logs of) bilateral trade flows, X is a matrix of (logs of) explanatory variables, D is a matrix representing the dummy variables, and ε is the vector of normally distributed error terms.

To test the hypothesis that trade liberalization is associated with an increase in the export of dirty products relative to clean products in Pakistan, we introduce an interaction term of sectoral pollution intensities with a measure for trade liberalization, T, alongside the traditional variables of gravity model. Hence Equation (10.8) may be expressed as:

$$\begin{aligned}
\ln(F_{ijkt}) = {} & b_0 + b_1 \ln(I_{it}Y_{jt}) + b_2 \ln(POP_{it}\,POP_{jt}) + b_3 \ln(Area_{it}\,Area_{jt}) \\
& + b_4 \ln(DIST_{ij}) + b_5 P_k T + b_6 D_{LANDLOCK} + b_7 D_{COL} \\
& + b_8 D_{LANG} + \mu_{ijk} + \lambda_t + \varepsilon_{ijkt}
\end{aligned} \tag{10.9}$$

where F_{ijkt} denotes the export or import of a four-digit SITC industry k from country i to country j in time period t.[14] Y_i and Y_j denote real per capita income, POP_i and POP_j represent total population and $Area_i$ and $Area_j$ are the geographical land areas for countries i and j, respectively. $DIST$ is the distance between the trading partners, and $D_{LANDLOCK}$, D_{COL} and D_{LANG} are dummy variables that equal one if the importing country is landlocked, if the trading partners share colonial ties, and if the two countries have a similar language, respectively; and are equal to zero otherwise.[15]

The variable of interest in Equation (10.9) is the interaction term between the pollution intensity (P) of sector k and the trade liberalization measure (T). We use a dummy variable as a measure of trade liberalization, such that T is equal to one for the post-liberalization period, and zero otherwise.[16] For the exports equation, a positive b_5 indicates that the exports of more pollution-intensive products have increased after trade liberalization, whereas, for the imports equation, b_5 is expected to be negative if liberalization has reduced imports of pollution-intensive products into the country.

Anderson and van Wincoop (2001) show that, in equilibrium, bilateral trade depends on the relative prices of the exporting and importing countries, which themselves depend on the existence of trade barriers or 'multilateral resistance' from other countries. Omitting relative prices could, therefore, bias the estimates. To control for this source of bias, we introduce importing country-industry effects, μ_{ijk}, obtained by interacting importing country fixed effects with the industry dummies.[17] Further, to take into account any effects that remain the same for all industries across all country pairs but change over time, we introduce time-specific effects, λ_t, in Equation (10.9). Finally, ε_{ijkt} is the idiosyncratic error term, which is assumed to be independently and normally distributed ($\varepsilon_{ij} \sim N(0,\sigma)$).

Data issues and empirical results

Like most other developing countries, no comprehensive database on environmental indicators and industrial pollution exists in Pakistan, because of a lack of plant-level monitoring. Past efforts at collecting data at the industrial level have been fragmentary, resulting in the compilation of incomplete and unreliable information that cannot be used for in depth analysis and time series comparisons.

To overcome the data constraints, we use the toxic pollution intensity index known as the Linear Acute Human Toxicity Index (LAHTI) developed by the Industrial Pollution Projection System (IPPS) of the World Bank specifically for the purpose of estimating pollution loads in developing countries (Hettige *et al.* 1994). IPPS combines the industrial activity data of 200,000 factories in the USA with their pollution emissions data to calculate pollution intensity factors – the level of pollution emissions per unit of industrial activity – for different types of air and water pollutants. The pollution intensity coefficients are combined with toxicity estimates of the pollutants to create LAHTI for different sectors, a weighted average of various effluents, with weights measuring the risk the pollutants pose to human health.

LAHTI is a useful tool, since it takes into account the different types of pollutants released by a sector and gives an overall assessment of the environmental and health risks associated with that sector. It is preferable to using individual pollutant intensities, because sectoral pollution intensity correlations for the various types of pollutants have a diverse pattern – they are higher for pollutants in the same category, but tend to be lower across categories (Hettige *et al.* 1994). For example, an industry might have high pollution intensities for SO_2 and NO_x that are both air pollutants, but a lower intensity for BOD, which is a water pollutant. Taking into account the pollution intensity for only one or a few pollutants therefore might not depict accurately the total toxicity associated with an industrial sector.[18]

The IPPS pollution intensity coefficients and indices have been used widely to estimate pollution loads and to study the environmental footprint of industrial development in countries with insufficient information on industrial pollution (Cole *et al.* 1997; Laplante and Smits 1998; Jha and Gamper-Rabindran 2004). The main advantage of estimating pollution loads with IPPS is its relatively modest data requirement, which has made it a convenient and viable option for research purposes. The estimates might not be conclusive in terms of magnitude, but they indicate the overall trend in the industrial pollution of a country.

It is likely that pollution coefficients and indices constructed with US data understate the pollution generated by Pakistani industries.[19] However, we prefer to use LAHTI, for two main reasons: first, the ranking of industries on the basis of LAHTI is very similar to the assessment made by the Environmental Protection Agency of Pakistan (EPA).[20] This confirms the observation of earlier studies, that the highest-polluting sectors are similar across countries, though their pollution intensities may vary from one country to another. Second, the purpose of this chapter is to identify the compositional changes that have occurred in Pakistan's economy, and not to provide estimates of industrial pollution loads per se. Thus LAHTI provides an appropriate approximation for our analysis.[21]

Data sources

The data on bilateral trade flows from 1975 to 2003 are obtained from the United Nations Commodity Trade Statistics Database (COMTRADE). These data are grouped according to the United Nations Standard International Trade Classification (SITC) system, which differs from the International Standard Industrial Classification (ISIC) codes that are used for representing industrial statistics. Hence, we first map the SITC categories to ISIC codes, and calculate the value of exports and imports for manufacturing industries in Pakistan according to four-digit ISIC codes. The industrial production data are taken from various issues of the *Census of Manufacturing Industries* (CMI), available from 1975–6 to 1995–6 only. Data on real income per capita, population and land area are obtained from World Bank's *World Development Indicators 2004*, whereas information on all other variables is taken from Centre d'Études Prospectives et d'Informations Internationales (www.cepii.fr) and Rose (2004), respectively.

Identifying compositional changes

We begin our analysis by estimating the environmental consequences of the compositional changes in Pakistan's manufacturing sector. To do so, we follow the approach of Cole and Neumayer (2004) and calculate the sectoral shares during 1975–6, then multiply these shares with the aggregate industrial output of 1995–6 to obtain estimates of sectoral output if industrial composition in 1995–6 had remained the same as in 1975–6.[22] Both the actual and counterfactual sectoral production of 1995–6 is then multiplied with the IPPS sectoral pollution intensities for nitrogen oxide (NO_x), sulphur dioxide (SO_2), and carbon monoxide (CO), and for the overall toxicity index, LAHTI. The counterfactual statistics indicate the level of emissions if industrial composition had remained the same as in 1975–6, and the sign of the difference between the counterfactual and actual emissions indicates whether the compositional effect alone has been benign or harmful for environmental quality in Pakistan.

The direction of the composition effect and the approximate percentage changes in emissions of the four types of pollutant are presented in Table 10.6.[23] The percentage changes may be considered as the lower bounds of actual changes, since the pollution intensities used here are for the USA. The calculations reveal a negative compositional effect in terms of LAHTI as well as for the three air pollutants. This indicates that the emissions from industrial manufacturing in 1995–6 were much higher than if the composition of production had remained the same as in 1975–6.

Table 10.7 presents the shares of different types of industries classified into 'highly pollution intensive', 'moderately pollution intensive' and 'less pollution intensive', based on LAHTI. In 1975, the share of highly pollution intensive industries in total manufacturing output was 48.2 per cent, which increased to 55.9 per cent in 1996. However, the shares of moderately and less polluting sectors in total industrial output have been decreasing over time. Figure 10.6 presents the percentage contribution of various pollution-intensive

Table 10.6   Compositional changes, pre- and post-liberalization

LAHTI	Environmental effect	Negative
	Percentage change	16.2
NO_x	Environmental effect	Negative
	Percentage change	23.2
SO_2	Environmental effect	Negative
	Percentage change	21.17
CO	Environmental effect	Negative
	Percentage change	10.78

Table 10.7 Sectoral shares in total manufacturing output (per cent)

ISIC codes		1976	1986	1996
Highly polluting industries				
321	Textiles	24.99	18.97	30.21
323	Leather & products	1.78	2.39	1.47
341	Paper & products	1.61	1.22	1.57
342	Printing & publishing	0.89	1.05	1.05
351	Industrial chemicals	4.26	6.41	6.09
352	Other chemical products	5.26	6.37	6.63
355	Manufacture of rubber products	1.63	1.45	0.78
369	Non-metallic mineral products	3.13	4.52	4.09
371	Iron & steel basic industries	4.65	6.43	4.07
372	Non-ferrous metals	0.07	0.02	0.04
	Sub-total	**48.27**	**48.83**	**56.00**
Moderately polluting industries				
311	Food	22.63	22.18	18.59
313	Beverages	1.08	1.53	1.08
314	Tobacco	4.35	4.76	2.44
331	Wood & products	0.20	0.30	0.22
362	Glass & products	0.20	0.50	0.24
381	Fabricated metal products	1.65	0.82	0.72
383	Electrical machinery	3.01	3.48	4.68
384	Transport equipment	5.40	4.24	4.51
	Sub-total	**38.52**	**37.81**	**32.48**
Less polluting industries				
322	Wearing apparel	0.30	1.42	1.53
324	Footwear(except rubber/plastic)	0.17	0.24	0.59
332	Furniture & fixtures	0.11	0.08	0.05
356	Plastic products	0.16	0.66	0.59
361	Pottery/china/earthenware	0.09	0.20	0.13
382	Non-electrical goods	2.89	3.32	1.90
385	Professional & scientific equipment	0.35	0.26	0.34
390	Others	9.14	7.18	6.39
	Sub-total	**13.21**	**13.36**	**11.52**
	Total	**100.00**	**100.00**	**100.00**

Source: Government of Pakistan, *Census of Manufacturing Industries*, various issues.

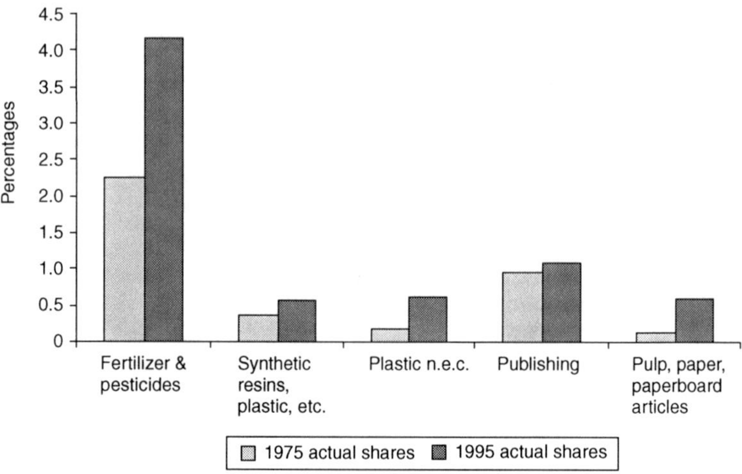

Figure 10.6   Shares of pollution-intensive industries (percentages)

industries to total manufacturing in 1975–6 and 1995–6, and shows that their respective shares have increased over time.

Empirical results

Factor content of trade

We investigate changes in the pattern of embodied environmental factor services (EEFS) in Pakistan's traded goods by examining bilateral trade data between Pakistan and the Organisation for Economic Co-operation and Development (OECD) countries from 1975 to 2000. The OECD countries – Pakistan's principal trading partners – are considered to have the most stringent environmental regulations in the world.[24] If PHH holds true for Pakistan, then we would expect a rise in the *net* exports of EEFS to the OECD countries in the post-liberalization period.[25]

The average EEFS in tradable commodities is measured using LAHTI. Since time-series industrial pollution data are unavailable for most countries, we assume that LAHTI is applicable to all countries in our sample. This assumption is justifiable, considering that the most pollution-intensive industries tend to be the same globally. Another important measurement issue pertains to the indirect input requirements as measured by Leontief's inverse matrix. Under the assumption of identical technology across countries, the input–output coefficients are the same for both exports and imports. If this assumption is violated, then per-unit input requirements might be different across countries, and the factor content of trade must be measured using producers' technology (Deardorff 1982). However, because of the difficulty in obtaining sufficiently disaggregated input–output tables for countries, we could either calculate the direct input requirements instead of total input requirements, or apply the same input–output table to the exporting and importing countries. We apply both methods, but do not gain much from this, since the curve obtained from the latter method is simply shifted upwards.[26] We therefore present and discuss the results of the direct factor input requirement methodology only.

Our findings are presented in Table 10.8, where the successive columns indicate the average net exports of EEFS during each period. Following Xu and Song (2000), we facilitate comparison across the years by taking 1975–9 as our base year, and normalizing the average net exports in that period to unity. The normalization yields a negative unity for Pakistan, which indicates that the effluent content of Pakistan's imports was higher than the effluent content of its exports to the OECD countries in 1975–9. Over time, however, the trend has reversed, and the embodied effluent content of Pakistan's exports has increased, whereas the embodied effluent content of its imports has decreased (Figure 10.7).

The increase in the net exports of EEFS was the greatest during 1990s, coinciding with the time that liberalization efforts were increasing in the country. Table 10.8 also reveals interesting trends in terms of trading partners. For Canada and the USA, we observe significant structural changes in the pollution content of trade as the sign of the net exports of EEFS changes

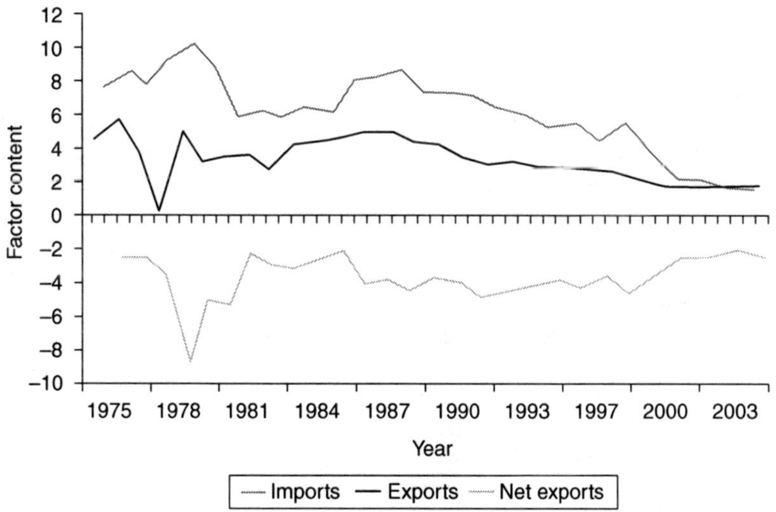

Figure 10.7 Net exports of embodied environmental factor services to OECD economies

Table 10.8 Net exports of embodied environmental factor services to OECD economies

Year	1975–9	1980–4	1984–9	1990–4	1995–9	2000–3
All OECD countries	−1.590	−0.994	−0.910	−0.966	−0.651	0.015
Australia	−0.953	0.5365	1.477	1.095	1.343	−1.238
Canada	−0.732	−0.002	0.076	0.128	0.127	0.097
Europe*	−5.839	−3.574	−2.507	−3.745	−2.385	−0.358
Japan	−0.568	−0.236	−0.094	−0.184	−0.245	−0.150
USA	−2.498	−3.150	−3.870	−3.413	−2.161	0.742

Note: * Includes European OECD member countries only.

from negative in 1975 to positive in 2003. For Europe and Japan, Pakistan remains a net importer of EEFS, but its exports to the two regions have also increased substantially over time. Australia was a net importer of EEFS during the 1980s and 1990s, but became a net exporter during 2000–3.

Trade in goods

The gravity model as specified in Equation (10.9) is estimated using Pakistan's bilateral trade data (at the four-digit ISIC level) with the OECD countries between 1975 and 2003. The measure of pollution intensity is the ranking of sectors according to LAHTI, where the most pollution-intensive sector has the highest score (= 63) and the least polluting sector has the lowest (= 1).[27]

The first five columns of Table 10.9 report the regression results for the exports equation, where the gravity model is estimated with and without fixed effects. The results obtained are satisfactory and correspond to the theoretical predictions of the model. The traditional variables of the gravity model, income and population, have statistically significant and positive coefficients in all estimations. The geographical distance between the trading partners, the size of the land area, and the landlockedness of countries have a negative influence on exports in the estimation without fixed effects. Historical colonial ties and common language positively affect exports, though the effect is insignificant for the latter.

When the country–industry fixed effects are controlled for, all time-invariant variables drop from the model (columns (2)–(5)).[28] In all specifications, we find evidence to support the share of exports growing in the dirty, pollution-intensive sectors as liberalization gained momentum. This is because the coefficient on the interaction term ($P_k \times T$) is positive and highly significant, indicating that, with increased liberalization, exports from pollution-intensive sectors have risen.

Table 10.9 Liberalization and pollution intensity of exports

Variable	OLS			Fixed effects			Tobin model	
	(1)	(2)	(3)	(4)	(5)		(6)	(7)
$\text{Log}(Y_iY_j)$	0.439	0.257***	0.305***	0.257***	0.305***		0.821***	2.109***
	(33.85)***	(5.29)	(4.52)	(6.31)	(5.46)		(4.81)	(7.75)
$\text{Log}(N_iN_j)$	−0.078***	0.104	0.283*	0.104	0.283**		0.830**	1.935***
	(5.86)	(0.88)	(1.93)	(1.04)	(2.27)		(2.03)	(3.97)
$\text{Log}(A_iA_j)$	−0.055***							
	(8.06)							
$\text{Log}(DIST)$	−0.108***							
	(2.96)							
$P_k \times T$	0.001	0.004***	0.007***	0.004***	0.007***		0.013***	0.027***
	(0.91)	(10.49)	(12.31)	(13.02)	(14.88)		(10.01)	(14.63)
LANDLOCK	−0.323***							
	(11.98)							
D_{COL}	1.003***							
	(17.28)							
D_{LANG}	0.026							
	(1.10)							
Time effects	No	No	Yes	No	Yes		No	Yes
Industry-country	No	Yes	Yes	Yes	Yes		Yes	Yes
N	85652	85652	85652	85652	85652	N	85652	85652
F-stat	767.04	830.60	711.81	1243.68	137.23	*LR* chi^2	64859.24	65276.93
Prob. $> F$	0.00	0.00	0.00	0.00	0.00	Prob. $>$ chi^2	0.00	0.00
R^2 overall	0.07	0.65	0.65	0.78	0.78	Pseudo-R^2	0.32	0.32

Note: The independent variable is the log of exports; values in parentheses are the robust *t*-statistics; a constant is included in all regressions; * indicates significance at 10% level; ** indicates significance at 5% level; *** indicates significance at 1% level.

In general, disaggregated bilateral trade datasets have a significant number of zero observations. This represents the case when either no exchange between countries took place, or it was very small and remained unrecorded. For data configuration it is well known that OLS estimators are inconsistent and biased downwards. Further, if the zero observations are excluded and the model is estimated with the positive value of exports only, then there is no guarantee that $E(\varepsilon_{ijkt})$ will be zero, and most probably the coefficient estimates would be inconsistent and biased upwards.

For these types of datasets, it is suggested that all observations should be retained in the sample, and a limited dependent variable estimation technique, such as the Tobit model, should be applied (McDonald and Moffitt 1980). Hence, we re-estimate Equation (10.9) using the maximum likelihood Tobit procedure. The result is reported in the last two columns of Table 10.9. The signs and significance of all coefficients are similar to those obtained earlier but, as expected, the magnitude of the coefficients is larger.

The above analysis is repeated for imports into Pakistan from the OECD countries (see Table 10.10(a)). In this case, we obtain a statistically negative coefficient for the interaction term, suggesting that imports of pollution-intensive commodities have decreased after trade liberalization. For imports, we also estimate an alternative specification where the sectoral tariff rates are used as a proxy for trade liberalization. This estimation, however, is conducted for a smaller sample, since disaggregated tariffs data are available only from 1995 onwards. The positive coefficient of b_5 reported in Table 10.10(b) confirms the earlier findings that a reduction in tariffs may have been accompanied by a decrease in the import of pollution-intensive products from OECD countries. Interestingly, the tariff rate has a negative and statistically significant coefficient, which suggests that tariff reductions have had a positive effect on imports from OECD countries.

Do environmental regulations matter to trade?

Next, we analyse the PHH from a slightly different perspective, and investigate if the differences in environmental regulations across Pakistan's trading partners have any effect on its exports of dirty products. Our study differs from previous studies in two notable ways. First, we use bilateral trade flow data between Pakistan and its trading partners disaggregated at the sectoral level. Earlier studies have used either single-country and multilateral trade flow data (Tobey 1990; Low and Yeats 1992) or data for multiple countries and bilateral trade flows (van Beers and van den Bergh 1997; Cole and Elliott 2003).

Second, we differ in our measure for the strictness of domestic environmental regulations. A majority of studies use 'input-orientated' measures of environmental stringency, such as industrial or firm-level pollution abatement costs (Ederington and Minier 2003; Levinson and Taylor 2004).[29] In

Table 10.10(a) Liberalization and pollution intensity of imports ($N = 85652$)

Variable	OLS			Fixed effects			Tobin model	
	(1)	(2)	(3)	(4)	(5)		(6)	(7)
$Log(Y_iY_j)$	0.809***	−0.256***	0.257***	−0.257***	0.257***		−0.955***	0.717***
	(51.25)	(3.93)	(2.68)	(5.21)	(3.71)		(7.84)	(3.65)
$Log(N_iN_j)$	0.144	1.332***	2.271***	1.332***	2.271***		3.963***	5.893***
	(8.87)***	(8.43)	(12.02)	(10.97)	(14.96)		(13.43)	(16.79)
$Log(A_iA_j)$	−0.226***							
	(27.69)							
$Log(DIST)$	−0.547***							
	(13.02)							
$P_k \times T$	−0.009***	−0.002***	−0.001*	−0.002***	−0.001***		−0.004***	−0.004***
	(18.64)	(3.09)	(1.92)	(4.27)	(2.64)		(4.42)	(2.92)
LANDLOCK	−0.038							
	(1.06)							
D_{COL}	1.893***							
	(33.78)							
D_{LANG}	−0.267							
	(9.92)							
Time effects	No	No	Yes	No	Yes		No	Yes
Industry-country	No	Yes	Yes	Yes	Yes		Yes	Yes
N	85652	85652	85652	85652	85652	N	85652	85652
F-stat	3412.87	830.60	1149.38	376.83	50.06	LR chi^2	81619.78	81968.88
Prob. $> F$	0.00	0.00	0.00	0.00	0.00	Prob. $>$ chi^2	0.00	0.00
R^2 overall	0.23	0.65	0.61	0.80	0.79	Pseudo-R^2	0.25	0.25

Note: The independent variable is the log of imports; values in parentheses are the robust *t*-statistics a constant is included in all regressions; * indicates significance at 10% level; ** indicates significance at 5% level; *** indicates significance at 1% level.

Table 10.10(b) Liberalization and pollution intensity of imports ($N = 15180$)

Variable	OLS			Fixed effects		Tobin model		
	(1)	(2)	(3)	(4)	(5)		(6)	(7)
$Log(Y_iY_j)$	0.827***	−0.272	−0.103	−0.272	−0.103		−0.185	0.065
	(18.71)	(0.63)	(0.63)	(0.86)	(0.33)		(0.27)	(0.09)
$Log(N_iN_j)$	0.181***	1.277	3.649***	1.277*	3.649***		2.12	6.139**
	(4.15)	(1.38)	(2.41)	(1.91)	(3.20)		(1.51)	(2.84)
$Log(A_iA_j)$	−0.237***							
	(12.02)							
$Log(DIST)$	0.104							
	(1.02)							
$P_k \times Tariff$	0.001***	0.000	0.000	0.001**	0.001**		0.001	0.001*
	(15.48)	(1.55)	(1.50)	(2.26)	(2.21)		(1.25)	(1.85)
$Tariff$	−0.012***	−0.002	−0.003	−0.002	−0.003		−0.002	−0.005
	(8.91)	(0.63)	(1.15)	(0.92)	(1.72)*		(0.42)	(1.03)
$LANDLOCK$	−0.082							
	(0.96)							
D_{COL}	1.337***							
	(10.28)							
D_{LANG}	−0.083							
	(1.27)							
Time effects	No	No	Yes	No	Yes		No	Yes
Industry-country	No	Yes	Yes	Yes	Yes		Yes	Yes
N	15180	15180	15180	15180	15180	N	15180	15180
F-stat	586.39	290.71	285.43	5.53	26.46	LR chi^2	16100.03	16179.52
Prob. $> F$	0.00	0.00	0.00	0.00	0.00	Prob. $>$ chi^2	0.00	0.00
R^2-overall	0.22	0.64	0.65	0.87	0.87	Pseudo-R^2	0.26	0.26

Note: The independent variable is the log of imports, values in parentheses are the robust *t*-statistics; a constant is included in all regressions; * indicates significance at 10% level; ** indicates significance at 5% level; *** indicates significance at 1% level.

their paper, van Beers and van den Bergh (1997) argue that input-orientated measures might not reflect the state of environmental stringency accurately in a country if governments compensate the pollution-intensive industries by providing them with financial assistance in the form of subsidies, export rebates and so on. They therefore propose to use 'output-orientated' measures that capture the ultimate outcome of environmental regulations and use a regulatory indicator developed by the UNCTAD, which relies on self-reporting by national governments, as a proxy for environmental governance.

In this analysis, we apply both input- and output-orientated measures of environmental stringency by using two components of the Environment Sustainability Index (ESI) – the Social and Institutional Capacity (*CAP*) and Environmental System (*SYSTEM*) – which to our knowledge have not been applied to this type of empirical exercise before. *SYSTEM* captures the state of natural and managed environmental systems, such as cultivated systems, air and water quality, water quantity, forests or biodiversity, and therefore appears to be an appropriate indicator for regulatory outcome. In contrast, *CAP* includes indicators for environmental governance, the use of environmentally friendly production methods, and private-sector responsiveness to environmental problems. It is a broader measure than the traditionally used input-orientated regulatory stringency measures, since it includes sources of formal regulation (for example, legislation, government effectiveness) as well as sources of informal regulations (for example, social pressure, market-orientated incentives).

Once again, we use the gravity model for our analysis, specified as:

$$\ln(X_{ijk}) = \log\beta_0 + \beta_1 \log(Y_i Y_j) + \beta_2 \log(N_i N_j) + \beta_3 \log(A_i A_j)$$
$$+ \log \beta_4 \log(DIST)_{ij} + \beta_5 \log(ENV)_j + \beta_6 LAND + \beta_7 LANG$$
$$+ \beta_8 BORDER + \beta_9 COL + u_{ijk} \qquad (10.10)$$

where X_{ijk} represents the exports of industry k from country i to country j; ENV_j denotes the strictness of environmental regime in the importing country j; and the definitions of the remaining variables are the same as in Equation (10.9). The *SYSTEM* and *CAP* variables are used as measures of environmental strictness, where a higher score represents better performance and vice versa.[30] Equation (10.10) is estimated for the ten most pollution-intensive sectors as identified by LAHTI, using data for the year 2002. The sectors include: fertilizers and pesticides; industrial chemicals; tanneries and leather finishing; synthetic resins, plastic materials and manmade fibres; paper and paperboard containers; other plastic products; textiles; printing and publishing; non-ferrous metals; and iron and steel.

The results from the Tobit estimation of Equation (10.10) are reported in Table 10.11. The estimated coefficients show theoretically expected signs. The effect of income per capita and population is significantly positive on exports, whereas distance between trading partners and being landlocked

Table 10.11 Tobit estimation results of sector-specific 'dirty' export flows

Variable	Pooled[a]	Pooled[a]	Industrial chemicals	Industrial chemicals	Leather tanneries	Leather tanneries	Plastic	Plastic	Plastic n.e.c.	Plastic n.e.c.
$Log(Y_i Y_j)$	0.407***	0.316***	0.393**	0.192*	0.316**	0.239*	0.383*	0.288*	0.528***	0.414
	(0.057)	(0.057)	(0.189)	(0.169)	(0.137)	(0.135)	(0.237)	(0.235)	(0.168)	(0.159)***
$Log(N_i N_j)$	3.038***	2.507***	5.555***	4.326***	3.569***	2.863**	5.143***	4.367***	3.518***	2.876
	(0.364)	(0.326)	(1.352)	(1.048)	(0.777)	(0.704)	(1.643)	(1.473)	(1.100)	(0.944)***
$Log(A_i A_j)$	−0.315	0.217	−1.744*	−0.425	−0.329	−0.496	−0.126	0.676	−0.289	−0.383
	(0.278)	(0.260)	(1.022)	(0.874)	(0.609)	(0.576)	(1.182)	(1.136)	(0.831)	(0.768)
$Log(DIST)$	−3.576***	−4.498***	−7.264***	−9.33***	−2.519*	−3.091***	−7.988***	−9.310***	−3.873**	−5.257
	(0.647)	(0.875)	(2.373)	(2.311)	(1.389)	(1.363)	(2.891)	(3.012)	(1.906)	(1.915)**
$Log(SYSTEM)$	9.391***		16.874***		19.366***		11.377		10.214	
	(2.127)		(7.392)		(4.806)		(9.216)		(6.331)	
$Log(CAP)$		8.073***		15.615***		10.360**		9.348**		10.030
		(0.988)		(3.297)		(2.218)		(4.251)		(2.907)***
LAND	−5.288***	−5.586***	−12.077***	−12.16***	−3.525*	−3.693**	−7.408*	−7.746**	−3.488	−3.937
	(0.907)	(0.875)	(3.592)	(3.155)	(1.871)	(1.796)	(3.951)	(3.846)	(2.577)	(2.437)
LANG	3.778***	2.504***	4.985*	2.262	0.844	−1.168	5.927**	4.471	6.711	5.177
	(0.713)	(0.688)	(2.399)	(2.105)	(1.649)	(1.610)	(2.961)	(2.880)	(2.083)*	(1.956)***
BORDER	−3.661*	−3.605*	−5.597	−5.871	−4.042	−4.227	−9.105	−9.375	−0.399	−0.484
	(1.974)	(1.904)	(6.401)	(5.597)	(4.77)	(4.601)	(7.856)	(7.676)	(5.732)	(5.405)
COL	4.296**	4.002**	−0.796	−1.167	0.846	0.786	4.005	3.816	4.918	4.404
	(2.071)	(1.982)	(6.837)	(5.858)	(5.259)	(5.068)	(8.269)	(8.007)	(6.188)	(5.788)
Observations	1170	1170	117	117	117	117	117	117	117	117
Log-likelihood	−1799.47	−1775.37	−180.61	−170.91	−285.58	−283.26	−174.53	−172.81	−198.74	−193.76
LR-chi^2	736.00	784.20	65.61	85.02	56.11	60.74	50.52	53.97	55.03	64.99
Prob. >M chi^2	0.00	0.00	0.00	0.00	0.00	0.00	0.00	0.00	0.00	0.00
Pseudo-R^2	0.17	0.18	0.15	0.20	0.09	0.10	0.12	0.14	0.12	0.14

Variable	Printing	Printing	Textiles	Textiles	Iron & Steel	Iron & Steel	Non-ferrous Metals	Non-ferrous Metals
$\text{Log}(Y_i\,Y_j)$	0.479	0.358	0.028	0.003	0.849	0.797	0.704	0.548
	(0.164)***	(0.152)**	(0.061)	(0.061)	(0.306)***	(0.309)**	(0.297)**	(0.287)*
$\text{Log}(N_i\,N_j)$	2.934	1.904	1.450	1.378	7.929	8.013	5.483	4.003
	(1.099)**	(1.908)**	(0.330)***	(0.308)***	(2.528)***	(2.456)***	(2.386)**	(2.013)**
$\text{Log}(A_i\,A_j)$	−0.378	0.555	−0.110	−0.020	−4.421	−4.508	−1.630	−0.377
	(0.824)	(0.735)	(0.258)	(0.243)	(1.953)**	(1.901)**	(1.679)	(1.509)
$\text{Log}(DIST)$	−7.736	−9.325	0.038	−0.182	1.522	0.595	−3.674	−5.431
	(2.109)***	(2.172)***	(0.582)	(0.580)	(3.707)	(3.739)	(3.805)	(3.983)
$\text{Log}(SYSTEM)$	16.633		1.869		−5.888		20.789	
	(6.492)***		(1.995)		(11.806)		(12.718)*	
$\text{Log}(CAP)$		11.970		2.128		3.117		14.128
		(2.913)***		(0.958)**		(5.384)		(6.108)**
$LAND$	−4.039	−4.436	−2.628	−2.737	−10.098	−11.325	−3.087	−3.462
	(2.582)*	(2.379)*	(0.785)***	(0.773)***	(6.653)*	(6.613)*	(5.141)	(4.912)
$LANG$	8.288	6.519	0.258	−0.027	−2.805	−2.256	7.147	4.991
	(2.153)***	(1.955)***	(0.707)	(0.694)	(4.222)	(4.014)	(4.030)*	(3.747)
$BORDER$	−3.313	−3.567	−2.448	−2.413	−3.508	−2.853	−9.090	−9.180
	(5.531)	(5.089)	(2.147)	(2.108)	(9.764)	(9.797)	(11.612)	(11.374)
COL	3.534	3.193	0.886	0.692	8.872	7.998	−0.641	0.771
	(5.923)	(5.398)	(2.388)	(2.345)	(9.773)	(9.665)	(10.434)	(9.555)
Observations	117	117	117	117	117	117	117	117
Log-likelihood	−172.342	−166.61	−297.58	−295.60	−119.72	−119.67	−94.27	−92.504
LR-chi^2	58.13	69.59	50.54	54.49	37.58	37.67	22.94	26.47
Prob. $>$ chi^2	0.00	0.00	0.00	0.00	0.00	0.00	0.00	0.00
Pseudo-R^2	0.14	0.17	0.08	0.08	0.14	0.14	0.11	0.13

Notes: [a] Industry-specific fixed effects included; Industrial chemicals includes fertilizers and pesticides; * indicates significant at 10% level; ** indicates significant at 5% level; *** indicates significant at 1% level; values in parentheses are standard errors; all regressions include a constant term not reported here.

have negative effects. Common language and colonial ties are significant and positive in a few specifications only. The negative sign of *BORDER* may seem counterintuitive, as adjacent countries are expected to trade more. However, considering the fact that Pakistan's trade relations with most of its neighbouring countries are restrained because of historical and political factors, a negative and largely insignificant effect that sharing a border has on Pakistan's exports is not surprising.

The estimates of the coefficient of *SYSTEM* and *CAP* are significant and positive in all estimations apart from the iron and steel and textile sectors. The estimated elasticity of exports with respect to environmental stringency in the remaining specifications is relatively large, ranging from 9.0 to 20.0. This suggests that the environmental regulations of the importing countries play an important part in determining Pakistan's exports from the dirty sectors, and countries with relatively stronger governance import more of these products.

Industrial pollution in Pakistan: implications for poverty

The objectives of Pakistan's trade and industrial policies have been to spur the manufacturing sector and promote economic growth. The main reason behind the lax implementation of environmental regulations and the 'pollute first, clean up later' path that Pakistan is currently following is the popular belief that the domestic industry is not yet prepared to factor environmental considerations into its production methods and bear the additional costs. The lack of an active environmental policy framework might not have had such important implications for the country if industrial emissions were growing from very low levels.[31] However, this is clearly not the case, and the existing emission levels are already high, with a significant economic and human health impact, especially on the poor.

Pakistan has one of the highest poverty rates in the world. Over 75 per cent of its total population lives on less than US$2 a day, more than half of them living in suburban and rural areas. This population depends directly on natural resources and ecological services for their sustenance and livelihood. At the same time, industrial pollution is worst in these poor areas, as heavily pollution-emitting factories are usually located in suburban regions close to farmland and villages, where the income of the residents is well below the national average.

The poor bear the brunt of factory pollution directly as well as indirectly. Direct effects include the high health costs imposed on the poor, who are also more vulnerable to pollution because of their low nutritional intake, crowded living and poor hygienic conditions. According to estimates, over 40 per cent of a poor household's income is spent on medical expenditures in Pakistan, most of the poor being health caused by environment-related hazards (IUCN 2002).

In addition, pollution limits the livelihood, food and nutritional security of the poor by destroying natural resources. According to surveys conducted by national and international agencies, air pollution has severely damaged the production of wheat and rice in many areas of Pakistan (Moss 2001). Furthermore, industrial effluents and waste water released on agricultural lands have contaminated the groundwater, destroyed the fertility of the soil and affected the nutritional quality of food produce. Contamination of the coastal marine environment of Karachi and Gawadar and adjoining creeks has substantially reduced fisheries production, adversely affecting the livelihoods of thousands of poor fishermen (GoP 2005b). However, because of a lack of awareness and appropriate resources, the poor are unable to take remedial action. Also, in many cases, the factories are a source of employment and income for many of the local poor, therefore they are hesitant to voice their concerns.

Indirectly, pollution affects poverty by having a negative influence on economic growth. The economic contribution of sectors that are heavily dependent on environmental goods – for example, agriculture, livestock, fisheries, forestry and natural-resource-related manufacturing – is over 50 per cent to national income and employment, and 75 per cent to foreign exchange earnings in Pakistan. Damage to the natural resource base reduces output and employment, hampering poverty alleviation efforts and socio-economic development. It also limits the capacity of the poor to engage in alternative livelihoods and diversify their livelihood strategies, increasing their vulnerability to external shocks and aggravating poverty.

Dixon and Perry (1986) observe that most of the effects of environmental mismanagement in Pakistan are rooted in environmental literacy and lack of awareness. Knudsen (1999), however, argues that even where people know they have a stake in environmental protection, the problem resides in the structures and institutions that prevent them from playing any meaningful role in environmental management.

Quantifying the direct and indirect effects of industrial emissions is important, to assess the seriousness of the situation, set a strategic pro-poor growth plan, and monitor the improvement in environmental management over time. However, no relevant statistics are available, with the result that no serious research has been conducted on the issue. The government appears to be slowly becoming aware of the importance of pollution monitoring and control in poverty reduction and pro-poor growth. For example, the interim poverty reduction strategy paper (I-PRSP) prepared in 2001 had eight policy objectives initially. These included the banking and financial services sector, civil service, and gender-related reforms; social development; health and nutrition; family planning; water supply and sanitation; and targeted social assistance. Environmental management was a glaring omission from the list; however, this oversight was remedied by mainstreaming environment in Pakistan's poverty reduction strategy. The government is also developing a framework to measure and compile various poverty–environment indicators at federal, provincial and district levels, to facilitate the evaluation of environmental outcomes. In addition, clean production initiatives have been undertaken in some industrial clusters; for example, in Kasur, Sialkot and Korangi, with the financial and technical assistance of donor organizations.

Concerted efforts and a serious commitment are required by both the public and private sectors to prevent further environmental damage, protect the most vulnerable segments of the society, and break the vicious circle of economic and ecological poverty in Pakistan. Industrial development provides opportunities to reduce poverty through employment and income creation. However, gains from industrial development and trade liberalization can only be maximized if an integrated and holistic approach is adopted that both improves environmental governance and promotes economic growth. This is because, even if the composition effect is held constant, the scale effect induced by growth implies an increase in output and an increase in total industrial pollution. To keep the scale effect in check, the pollution intensity of industrial activity must be decreased. This is possible through the transfer of cleaner technology if sectoral pollution is a function of the vintage of technology and through the enforcement of environmental regulation where pollution depends on end-of-pipe treatment, as in the paper, leather and textiles industries (Gallagher 2000).

Overall, industrial pollution loads are high in Pakistan because of the inefficient management of resources, obsolete technology and the employment of environmentally unfriendly production methods. Raising awareness and building capacity to improve in-house management may assist Pakistan's industrial sector in reducing its environmental footprint as well as its production costs.[32]

Conclusion

One of the most hotly contended issues in the globalization debate is the impact of increased openness on the environment of developing countries. It is argued that asymmetries between the environmental regulations of developed and developing economies create a competitive advantage for the latter to specialize in the production of pollution-intensive products, which entails significant environmental, economic and social repercussions. The purpose of this study was to revisit this issue in the context of Pakistan.

Using a combined toxicity index of manufacturing industries, we examined the composition of Pakistan's exports and found evidence to support the claim that exports have grown in the pollution-intensive sectors relative to cleaner ones after liberalization efforts gained momentum. Despite data limitations, we made a modest empirical assessment using the IPPS database developed by the World Bank. Although US pollution intensities are not a substitute for actual data, a comparison of the ranking of industries according to their pollution intensities in Pakistan and the USA reveals a very high correlation, indicating that the most pollution-intensive sectors are similar across both countries.

Our results suggest that earlier estimates of a negligible impact of laxity of environmental regulations on trade flows based on cross-country regressions should be viewed with scepticism. While identifying the compositional changes that might have occurred in Pakistan's economy, we find evidence that the manufacturing sector has switched to more pollution-intensive production over time. Applying the sectoral shares in output for 1975–6 to the manufacturing data for 1995–6, we found that total air emissions would have been significantly lower if industrial composition had remained as in 1975–6.

The results of the factor content approach reveal that the total net exports of embodied environmental services to the OECD economies have increased between 1975 and 2003. The trade-in-goods approach supports these findings and shows that liberalization has been accompanied by an increase in exports and a decrease in imports of pollution-intensive products to and from OECD countries, respectively. Further, the environmental policy–trade analysis confirms that the stringency of environmental regulations in the importing countries is an important determinant of Pakistan's exports of dirty products.

Our findings therefore point to a change in the composition of output and exports towards more pollution-intensive manufacturing that parallels the opening of the economy. This suggests that Pakistan's transition from a closed to an open economy may have had non-trivial consequences in terms of industrial pollution, since policies to internalize adverse externalities were not strengthened simultaneously. Considering the various channels through which pollution affects the poor, the gaps in environmental policy must be filled to protect natural assets, public health and the poor, and to secure sustainable pro-poor growth. The analysis also highlights the importance of undertaking systematic empirical investigations of this nature for developing countries that are contemplating further trade liberalization – but lack statistics on environmental quality – to draw broad inferences regarding changes in pollution levels because of shifts in industrial activity and assess the implications of their reforms.

Appendix

Table 10.A1 Ranking comparison of most pollution-intensive industries

LAHTI ranking	EPA ranking
Fertilizers and pesticides	Fertilizers and pesticides
Industrial chemicals	Industrial chemicals
Tanning and leather finishing	Pulp and paper
Synthetic resins, plastic materials and man-made fibres	Tanning and leather finishing
Paper and paperboard	Textile processing
Plastic products	Rubber products
Textiles	Paints, varnishes and lacquers
Printing and publishing	Printing
Non-ferrous metals	Steel industry
Iron and steel	Petroleum refining

Source: Compiled by the author with data from Government of Sindh (1999) and Hettige *et al.* (1994).

Table 10.A2 Pakistan's direction of trade statistics

Year Organization	1991/2	1992/3	1993/4	1994/5	1995/6	1996/7	1997/8
	Percentage share in total imports						
OECD	62.2	58.6	52.6	49.3	49.9	48.7	46.5
OIC	16.5	16.9	20.9	21.3	22.4	26.0	23.3
ASEAN	7.3	8.5	9.5	12.6	11.2	9.0	12.6
SAARC	1.5	1.5	1.6	1.4	1.5	2.4	2.3
Other	12.5	14.5	15.4	15.4	15	13.9	15.3
	Percentage share in total exports						
OECD	54.9	56.7	60.0	58.6	55.3	59.7	59.5
OIC	14.6	16.0	13.7	12.9	12.9	11.8	12.5
ASEAN	5.6	5.2	3.7	4.0	5.3	2.5	3.2
SAARC	4.7	3.8	3.1	3.4	2.7	2.5	3.5
Other	20.2	18.3	19.5	21.1	23.8	23.5	21.3

Notes: OIC is the Organization of the Islamic Conference; SAARC is the South Asian Association for Regional Co-operation.
Source: Government of Pakistan, Statistical Supplement to *Economic Survey*, 1997–8.

Acknowledgements

I am grateful to Ajit Singh, Terry Barker, Arik Levinson, and participants of the UNU-WIDER project meeting on Globalization and the Poor in Asia, 25–26 April 2005 in Tokyo, for their helpful comments and suggestions. Any errors are my responsibility.

Notes

1   Environmental resources are factors of production, not created by effort – for example, air, water, soil, timber, minerals, oil, and so on.
2   Ecological poverty refers to the lack of a healthy natural resource base to safeguard public health and local economies (Aggarwal 2001).
3   See Vincent (1997) and Stern *et al.* (1997) for a critique of cross-country investigations of economic growth–pollution relationships.
4   Negative list consists of items that are not allowed on the grounds of public health, environmental concerns, morality or national security.
5   Khan (1999) shows that the emergence of the manufacturing sector as Pakistan's primary export is a consequence of trade liberalization reforms.
6   This excludes certain types of automobiles and alcoholic beverages.
7   A study by Punjab Environmental Protection Department estimates biological oxygen demand in Pakistan's main river, Ravi, to be as high as 300 mg/l as compared to the acceptable WHO limit of 9 mg/l.
8   Cases of waterborne diseases caused by industrial pollution in Pakistan have gained international attention. Two notable examples are the industrial fluoride poisoning case, when hundreds of villagers in eastern Punjab were diagnosed as suffering from bone deformities caused by bone fluorosis, and the Kasur tannery case, where thousands of people in Kasur – the hub of leather industry – suffered from cancer, eye disorders and skin diseases due to soil and water pollution caused by the tanneries.
9   The provincial EPAs were in addition to the Federal EPA established in 1984.
10   The government is now encouraging self-monitoring and reporting of effluents and emissions, but this initiative has received a lukewarm response from the industry so far.
11   This approach concentrates on industrial emissions and does not take into account pollution caused by the transportation of products as a result of trade liberalization (Jenkins 1998).
12   The factor content of the trade approach is commonly applied to test the validity of the HOV model for labour and capital (Leontief 1953; Deardorff 1982; Leamer 1984). When environment is taken as an input, variations in national environmental regulations imply that the endowment of environment differs across countries, and therefore the pattern of environmental service flows may also vary among them.
13   Deardorff (1982) suggests that the input–output matrix A should measure the total factor demand; that is, direct plus indirect use of input factors when the model has more goods than factors. The total factor demand may be expressed as $A = F(I - B)^{-1}$, where F is the direct factor input requirement matrix and $(I - B)^{-1}$ is the Leontief inverse matrix, which represents the amount of output required as an intermediary.
14   To include the zero observations in our sample, we follow Eichengreen and Irwin (1998) and Chen (2004), and express $\ln(X_{ij}) \approx \ln(1+X_{ij})$.

15 The common border dummy is not included because of the nature of the dataset.
16 We consider 1990 onwards to be the post-liberalization period, since liberalization efforts gained rapid momentum through the structural adjustment programme.
17 b_3, b_4, b_6, b_7 and b_8 are not identified if u_{ijk} is included and Equation (10.9) is estimated as a fixed-effects model.
18 For example, the leather industry is highly toxic and a major source of water pollution. However, it is a moderately polluting industry in terms of air pollution.
19 Studies that estimate pollution loads for developing countries, such as Brazil, China and Mexico, confirm that they have higher pollution intensities in general than do their US counterparts (Gallagher 2000). This is because of weaker environmental regulations, low productivity, old technology and the adoption of cost-saving, highly pollution-intensive production methods in these countries.
20 See Appendix Table 10.A1.
21 Recently, data on pollution intensities have been compiled for a few developing countries – for example, China and Mexico. These datasets are, however, limited in scope, since they are highly aggregated and do not classify industries according to their overall hazardousness.
22 Data for 1995–6 are used because this is the most recent year for which industrial statistics are available.
23 These estimates are constructed using the statistics from CMI, which covers only registered firms (firms with at least ten employees) and does not take into account production by small-scale, unregistered firms. Consistent time-series data for small-scale and household manufacturing industries (SSHMI) are unavailable. Prior to 1988–9, ad hoc surveys were conducted, with different geographical coverage. Information gathered by the relatively recent census of SSHMI is therefore not comparable to the previous surveys (GoP 1989).
24 See Appendix Table 10.A2 for the direction of trade statistics.
25 A notable exception to this is Mexico, which is therefore not included in our sample.
26 This is because we used the same input–output table for the entire period. More accurate results might be obtained if annual tables were to be used, but this is not possible in our case because of the unavailability of data.
27 The model was estimated with the actual values of LAHTI, and the results obtained were almost identical. However, we prefer to use the ranking of sectors as it coincides with the ranking made available by EPA Pakistan.
28 To confirm that the fixed-effects approach is the appropriate estimation technique, the Hausman test is undertaken. We obtain a significant Hausman statistic for the exports equation (chi2 = 10.72) and a significant statistic for the imports equation (chi2 = 68.29), which indicate the presence of fixed effects in both cases.
29 These studies tend to focus on the USA because consistent time-series data on pollution abatement costs are most easily available for the USA.
30 The correlation between *SYSTEM* and *CAP* is 0.23, which validates the need to use both the indicators as proxies for environmental strictness.
31 The findings of Cole and Neumayer (2004) suggest that provided the environmental Kuznets curve holds, it would take Asian developing countries (excluding India and China) at least another 60–80 years to reach the per capita income levels where enough social and political pressure is generated for most of the air pollutants to start exhibiting a declining trend. Considering the existing environmental quality in most of these countries, such a timeframe may be too late to prevent irreversible ecological damage.

32 For example, according to estimates, the industrial sector could save approximately 22 per cent of its total energy consumption without any loss of output if it utilizes the inputs more efficiently (GoP, *Economic Survey 2000–01*). This would not only reduce air emissions but also substantially decrease the energy costs faced by firms.

References

Aggarwal, A. (2001) 'The Value of Natural Capital', *Development Outreach*, Winter Issue (Washington, DC: World Bank).

Anderson, J. E. and van Wincoop, E. (2001) 'Gravity with Gravitas: A Solution to the Border Puzzle', NBER Working Paper 8079, National Bureau of Economic Research, Cambridge, Mass.

Asian Development Bank (ADB) (1998) *Asia Least-cost Greenhouse Gas Abatement Strategy: Pakistan Country Report* (Manila: Asian Development Bank).

Brandon, C. and Ramankutty, R. (1993) 'Toward an Environmental Strategy for Asia', Discussion Paper 224, World Bank, Washington, DC.

Chen, N. (2004) 'Intra-national versus International Trade in the European Union: Why Do National Borders Matter?', *Journal of International Economics*, 63(1): 93–118.

Coase, R. H. (1960) 'The Problem of Social Cost', *Journal of Law and Economics*, 3: 1–44.

Cole, M. A. and Elliott, R. J. R. (2003) 'Do Environmental Regulations Influence Trade Patterns? Testing Old and New Trade Theories', *The World Economy*, 26(8): 1163–86.

Cole, M. A. and Neumayer, E. (2004) 'Environmental Policy and the Environmental Kuznets Curve: Can Developing Countries Escape the Detrimental Consequences of Economic Growth?', in P. Dauvergne (ed.), *International Handbook of Environmental Politics* (Aldershot: Edward Elgar).

Cole, M. A., Rayner, A. J. and Bates, J. M. (1997) 'Trade Liberalization and the Environment: The Case of the Uruguay Round', *The World Economy*, 21(3): 337–47.

Deardorff, A. V. (1982) 'The General Validity of the Heckscher–Ohlin Theorem', *American Economic Review*, 72(4): 683–94.

Dixon, R. K. and Perry, J. A. (1986) 'Natural Resource Management in Rural Areas of Northern Pakistan', *Ambio*, 15: 301–5.

Ederington, J., Levinson, A. and Minier, J. (2003) 'Footloose and Pollution-free', NBER Working Paper W9718, National Bureau of Economic Research, Cambridge, Mass.

Ederington, J. and Minier, J. (2003) 'Is Environmental Policy a Secondary Trade Barrier? An Empirical Analysis', *Canadian Journal of Economics*, 36(1): 137–54.

Eichengreen, B. and Irwin, D. (1998) 'The Role of History in Bilateral Trade Flows', in J. Frankel (ed.), *The Regionalization of the World Economy* (Chicago: University of Chicago Press).

Gallagher, K. (2000) 'Trade Liberalization and Industrial Pollution in Mexico: Lessons for the FTAA', GDAE Working Paper 00–07, Global Development and Environment Institute, Tufts University, Medford, Mass.

GoP (Government of Pakistan) (various issues) *Census of Manufacturing Industries* (Islamabad: Federal Bureau of Statistics).

GoP (Government of Pakistan) (various issues) *Economic Survey* (Islamabad: Ministry of Finance).

GoP (Government of Pakistan) (1989) *Census of Small and Household Manufacturing Industries 1988–89* (Islamabad: Federal Bureau of Statistics).

GoP (Government of Pakistan) (1998) *Compendium on Environmental Statistics* (Islamabad: Federal Bureau of Statistics).

GoP (Government of Pakistan) (2005a) *National Environment Policy of Pakistan* (Islamabad: Ministry of the Environment).

GoP (Government of Pakistan) (2005b) *State of the Environment Report 2005* (Islamabad: Ministry of the Environment).

GoP/IUCN (Government of Pakistan/International Union for the Conservation of Nature and Natural Resources) (1992) *Pakistan National Conservation Strategy* (Islamabad: GoP–IUCN).

Government of Sindh (1999) *Report on Industrial Monitoring of Various Sectors (118 Industries) Monitored by EPA Sindh* (Sindh: Environmental Protection Agency).

Grossman, G. M. and Krueger, A. B. (1993) 'Environmental Impacts of a North American Free Trade Agreement', in P. M. Garber (ed.), *The Mexico–US Free Trade Agreement* (Cambridge, Mass.: MIT Press).

Heil, M. T. and Selden, T. M. (2001) 'International Trade Intensity and Carbon Emissions: A Cross-Country Econometric Analysis', *Journal of Environment and Development*, 10(1): 35–49.

Hettige, H., Mani, M. and Wheeler, D. (1997) 'Industrial Pollution in Economic Development: Kuznets Revisited', Policy Research Working Paper 1876, World Bank, Washington, DC.

Hettige, H., Martin, P., Singh, M. and Wheeler, D. (1994) 'The Industrial Pollution Projection System', Policy Research Working Paper 1431, World Bank, Washington, DC.

International Union for the Conservation of Nature and Natural Resources (IUCN) (2002) 'Why Is Sustainable Environment and Natural Resources Management Necessary for Poverty Alleviation in Pakistan?', Paper prepared for Pakistan Human Development Forum, 24–26 April, Islamabad.

Jaffe, A. B., Peterson, S. R., Portney, P. R. and Stavins, R. N. (1995) 'Environmental Regulation and the Competitiveness of US Manufacturing: What Does the Evidence Tell Us?', *Journal of Economic Literature*, 33(1): 132–63.

Jenkins, R. (1998) 'Industrialization, Trade Pollution in Latin America: A Review of the Issues', Paper presented at the meeting of the Latin American Studies Association, 24–26 September, Chicago, Illinois.

Jha, S. and Gamper-Rabindran, S. (2004) 'Environmental Impact of India's Trade Liberalization', Paper presented at the Cornell University International Colloquium on '75 Years of Development Research', 7–9 May, Ithaca, NY.

Khan, S. R. (1999) *Do World Bank and IMF Policies Work?* (London: Macmillan).

Knudsen, A. J. (1999) 'Deforestation and Entrepreneurship in the North-Western Frontier Province, Pakistan', in S. Toft Madsen (ed.), *State, Society and the Environment in South Asia* (Richmond, Surrey: Curzon).

Laplante, B. and Smits, K. (1998) 'Estimating Industrial Pollution in Latvia', Policy Research Working Paper, World Bank, Washington, DC.

Leamer, E. E. (1984) *Sources of International Comparative Advantage: Theory and Evidence* (Cambridge, Mass.: MIT Press).

Leontief, W. W. (1953) 'Domestic Production and Foreign Trade: The American Capital Position Re-examined', *Proceedings of the American Philosophical Society*, 97(4): 332–49.

Levinson, A. and Taylor, S. (2004) 'Unmasking the Pollution Haven Hypothesis', NBER Working Paper 10629 National Bureau of Economic Research, Cambridge, Mass.

Low, P., and Yeats, A. (1992) 'Do "Dirty" Industries Migrate?', in P. Low (ed.), *International Trade and the Environment*, Discussion Paper 159, World Bank, Washington, DC.

Lucas, R. E. B., Wheeler, D. and Hettige, H. (1992) 'Economic Development, Environmental Regulation and the International Migration of Toxic Industrial Pollution:

1960–88', in P. Low (ed.), *International Trade and the Environment*. Discussion Paper 159, World Bank, Washington, DC.

Mani, M. and Jha, S. (2005) 'Trade Liberalization and the Environment in Vietnam', Mimeo, World Bank, Washington, DC.

Mani, M. and Wheeler, D. (1999) 'In Search of Pollution Havens? Dirty Industry in the World Economy 1960–95', in P. Fredriksson (ed.), *Trade, Global Policy and the Environment*, Discussion Paper 402, World Bank, Washington, DC.

McDonald, J. and Moffitt, R. (1980) 'The Uses of Tobit Analysis', *Review of Economics and Statistics*, 62(2): 318–21.

Moss, J. (2001) 'Pollution and Crops', Agricultural Report. Washington, DC: Voice of America. Available at: www.manythings.org/voa/01/010529ar_t.htm.

Pilot Environmental Sustainability Index (ESI). Dataset compiled by World Economic Forum (WEF), Yale Center for Environmental Law and Policy (YCELP), Center for International Earth Science Information Network (CIESIN). Available at: http://sedac.ciesin.columbia.edu/es.esi.

Robison, H. D. (1988) 'Industrial Pollution Abatement: The Impact on Balance of Trade', *Canadian Journal of Economics*, 21(1): 187–99.

Rose, A. K. (2004) 'Do We Really Know that the WTO Increases Trade?', *American Economic Review*, 94(1): 98–114.

Selden, T. M. and Song, D. (1994) 'Environmental Quality and Development: Is There a Kuznets Curve for Air Pollution Emissions?', *Journal of Environmental Economics and Management*, 27(2): 147–62.

Stern, D. I., Common, M. S. and Barbier, E. B. (1997) 'Economic Growth and Environmental Degradation: The Environmental Kuznet Curve and Sustainable Development', *World Development*, 24(7): 1151–60.

Tobey, J. (1990) 'The Effects of Domestic Environmental Policies and Patterns of World Trade: An Empirical Test', *Kyklos*, 43: 191–209.

van Beers, C. and van den Bergh, J. (1997) 'An Empirical Multi-Country Analysis of the Impact of Environmental Regulations on Foreign Trade Flows', *Kyklos*, 50(1): 29–46.

van Beers, C. and van den Bergh, J. (2000) 'The Impact of Environmental Policy on Foreign Trade: Tobey Revisited with a Bilateral Flow Model', Tinbergen Institute Discussion Paper 2000–069/3, Tinbergen Institute, Amsterdam.

Vanek, J. (1968) 'The Factor-Proportions Theory: The N-Factor Case', *Kyklos*, 21(4): 749–56.

Vincent, J. (1997) 'Testing for Environmental Kuznets Curves within a Developing Country', *Environment and Development Economics*, 2(4): 417–31.

Walter, I. (1973) 'The Pollution Content of American Trade', *Western Economic Journal*, 11(1): 61–70.

World Bank (2004) *The World Development Indicators* (Washington, DC: World Bank).

World Resources Institute (2003) 'Climate and Atmosphere: Country Profile Pakistan'. Available at: http://earthtrends.wri.org.

World Trade Organization (WTO) (2001) *Trade Policy Review: Report by the Government*. WT/TPR/G/95 (Geneva: WTO).

Xu, X. and Song, L. (2000) 'Regional Cooperation and the Environment: Do "Dirty" Industries Migrate?', *Weltwirtschaftliches Archiv*, 136(1): 137–57.

Yale Center for Environmental Law and Policy (YCELP) (2005) *Environmental Sustainability Index: Benchmarking National Environmental Stewardship* (New Haven, Conn: YCELP).

Index

Key: **bold** = extended discussion; f = figure; n = endnote/footnote; t = table.

9 780230 201880